FEMINIST PSYCHOTHERAPIES: INTEGRATION OF THERAPEUTIC AND FEMINIST SYSTEMS

Developments in Clinical Psychology

Glenn R. Caddy, series editor
Nova University

MMPI-168 Codebook, by Ken R. Vincent, Iliana Castillo, Robert I. Hauser, H. James Stuart, Javier A. Zapata, Cal K. Cohn, and Gregory O'Shanick, 1984

Integrated Clinical and Fiscal Management in Mental Health: A Guidebook, by Fred Newman and James Sorensen, 1986

The Professional Practice of Psychology, edited by Georgiana Shick Tryon, 1986

Clinical Applications of Hypnosis, edited by Frank A. DePiano and Herman C. Salzberg, 1986

Full Battery Codebook, by Ken R. Vincent, 1987

Developments in the Assessment and Treatment of Addictive Behaviors, edited by Ted D. Nirenberg, 1987

The Behavioral Management of the Cardiac Patient, by D. G. Byrne, 1987

Feminist Psychotherapies, edited by Mary Ann Dutton-Douglas and Lenore E. A. Walker, 1988

In Preparation:

Language and Psychopathology, by Stephen Schwartz

Child Multimodal Therapy, by Donald B. Keat II

Behavioral Medicine: International Perspectives Vols. 1–2, edited by D. G. Byrne and Glenn R. Caddy

Feminist Psychotherapies: Integration of Therapeutic and Feminist Systems

Edited by

Mary Ann Dutton-Douglas and Lenore E. A. Walker

ABLEX PUBLISHING CORPORATION

NORWOOD, NEW JERSEY

Library of Congress Cataloging-in-Publication Data

Feminist psychotherapies.

  (Developments in clinical psychology)
  Bibliography: p.
  Includes index.
  1. Feminist therapy. I. Dutton Douglas, Mary Ann,
1949– . II. Walker, Lenore E. A. III. Series.
RC489.F45F45 1988   616.89'14   88–16705
ISBN 0–89391–387–1

Ablex Publishing Corporation
355 Chestnut St.
Norwood, NJ 07648

Contents

PART I

Theoretical Integration of Feminist and Psychotherapy Systems

CHAPTER 1

Introduction to Feminist Therapies

Mary Ann Dutton Douglas
Lenore E. A. Walker

This book represents the shift from feminist therapy as a philosophy to a pluralistic view of feminist therapies which itself documents the influence that feminist philosophy has had on the major psychotherapy systems. Feminist therapy is defined by its analysis of power differences between women and men and how that differential impacts on both men's and women's behavior (cf. Rawlings & Carter, 1977). Initially, feminist philosophy called for a thorough scrutiny of environmental factors which oppress women. Therapists could then use this philosophical overlay in addition to whatever therapy theory guided their work. Generally feminist theory called for active roles for both therapist and client. The belief that the personal is political, that psychological effects result from the social oppression and victimization of women and that political action to overcome oppression is therapeutic fundamentally differentiates nonsexist from feminist therapy theory.

Over a decade of feminist theory impacting the major therapy systems has led to a new generation of feminist therapies. This book outlines that impact to demonstrate that there is no one feminist therapy at this time, but rather a variety of feminist therapies. Each has grown from the integration of feminist principles with multiple therapy theories. We present several products of this integration as models in this book. However, given the explosion of the knowledge base generated from feminist theory, it is already clear to us that the future direction will be toward fully developed feminist theories of human behavior which themselves will form the basis of feminist therapies. In the last chapter, we attempt to outline the path by which a feminist therapy theory may begin to take shape. But, it was the excitement of the

3

integration between feminist and therapeutic systems that spurred us to compile this book.

The purpose of psychotherapy has evolved over the years, first beginning as a means of fostering adjustment to the mainstream life-style following a medical model of mental illness to cure aberrant behavior. Later, in the 1960s, the adjustment model expanded to include facilitating personal growth. Feminist therapy is less interested in the psychotherapy client's conformity to the mainstream than in helping to identify and overcome rampant oppressive social pressures for both women and men. Thus, the ultimate goal of the feminist psychotherapy is primarily the elimination of the patriarchal power structure so as to facilitate both women's and men's personal growth. In feminist therapy with individual clients, this goal necessarily takes the form of helping the client to overcome the effects of oppression in her (or his) own life circumstances, recognizing the external social and environmental factors which render this task impossible to accomplish fully.

INTEGRATION OF FEMINIST THEORY WITH PSYCHOTHERAPY SYSTEMS

Early feminist therapy has provided a philosophical framework to guide the analysis of external and internal factors causing emotional distress and psychotherapeutic intervention to facilitate women clients' growth toward positive mental health. However, at the time this book is being written, feminist therapy has not been based on any particular theory of human or personality development, of psychopathology or psycho-therapy intervention. In practice, although not in theory, feminist therapy exists as a pluralistic concept defined by the parameters of the therapist's feminist philosophical tenets and of the psychological theory or theories of human behavior to which she ascribes. Yet, there has been little formal effort to integrate the philosophical principles of feminist therapy with theoretical principles of psychological theory. This book is an effort to do that.

By going beyond a definition of feminist therapy to a multiplicity of feminist therapies, several goals are accomplished. First, since all psychotherapy systems affect women (and men), it is imperative to examine how each can and cannot be integrated with principles of feminist therapy in order that potentially all psychotherapy systems be held accountable for their effects on women's and men's lives. Second, the growing body of knowledge in the field of psychology of women needs to be applied to women's lives. One avenue for doing so is in the arena of psychotherapy. Research, theory, and application of feminist therapies can mutually inform each other.

Influence of Science of Psychology

There are some who believe that science is objective, neutral, and free from bias that impacts other systems of knowing. In fact, science, which is only an ordering of facts into a set of truths, has been riddled with sex role bias that influences the selection of whose truth it is. Critics of empiricism, which emphasizes observable facts, suggest that women's way of knowing defines truth differently; it places facts within a context rather than isolating them from the rest of knowledge (Dobash & Dobash, 1981). Psychology has grown out of the empirical philosophy of logical positives. It follows the scientific methodology which is based on experimentation and mathematics that come out of physics. The separation between theoretical context and measurable observations places an inordinate amount of reliance on the experimental method to build a knowledge base.

The myth that the experimental method alone can discover pure truth has come under sharp scrutiny by feminist scholars (cf. Wardell, Gillespie, & Leffler, 1983). Psychological researchers have also been sharply critical of how the values which guide the choice of questions to be asked and human behavior to be studied are not scrutinized for gender bias, precisely because of the faulty belief that science is value-neutral (cf. McHugh, Koeske, & Frieze, 1986). It is this knowledge base gained by the science of psychology which has guided its application into clinical areas. Even though few psychotherapy theories, except behaviorism, have adhered to vigorous scientific methodology in their formation, all theories are riddled with biases. So, the gender stratification gets multiplied until it becomes reified in the therapeutic systems. Feminism has taken an active role in challenging the misogynous aspects of these therapeutic systems.

Feminist influence on research. Feminist challenges to androcentric bias in psychological research have been voiced clearly (cf. Wallston 1981). The issues have included the nature of the experimental questions selected for study, the experimental methodology used, including subject selection, and distinctions between qualitative and quantitative methods, and the interpretation of results. Even the education process, which guides the training of mental health professionals, has been examined for the influence of perception of gender, including social interactions guided by such sexist expectations perpetuated by those in power (cf. Tittle, 1986).

The classic and widely cited Broverman, Broverman, Clarkson, Rosenkrantz, and Vogel, (1970) study demonstrated the presence of sex role bias in mental health professionals' evaluation of healthy psychological functioning in women, men, and adults. This finding was supported by the APA Task Force on Sex Bias and Sex Role Stereotyping in Psychotherapeutic Practice (APA, 1975). More recently, Rosenburg and Broverman (1985) found that those other behaviors associated with the healthy male also facilitated positive mental health in women. Research on sex roles and mental health demonstrate that either androgynous (Kelly, O'Brien, & Hosford, 1981) or masculine sex role (Jones, Chernovetz, & Hansen, 1978), but not feminine sex role, is related to positive mental health in women. These data suggest a maladaptive function of the stereotypical sex role for women. An alternative interpretation would take into account the social context and suggest that it is the patriarchial structure within which stereotypical sex role behavior is not functional.

Research on gender influences on psychotherapy outcome, although tentative, have suggested that women therapists may demonstrate greater client benefit and satisfaction than, especially inexperienced, male therapists (Beutler, Crago, & Arizmendi, 1986; Orlinsky & Howard, 1980). Differences in male and female capacity for relational bonding in the therapeutic interaction may be highlighted by these data (Caplan, 1985). This explanation may be used to account for why experience for male, but apparently less so for female, therapists is related to therapy outcome (Orlinsky & Howard, 1979). Beutler, et al. (1986) suggest that perhaps the therapist's flexibility in sex role attitudes is more important than gender itself in determining influence on psychotherapy.

Research on marriage and mental health is another area where feminist influence on empirical research has been demonstrated. Marriage appears to exert more negative mental health effects on women than men (Guttentag, 1980; Radloff, 1975). The greater negative economic impact of separation and divorce on women compared with men (Collier, 1982) places women in double jeopardy.

A major area where feminist influence on research has been felt has been with victims of sexual and physical abuse, including battered women (Browne, 1987; Douglas, 1984; Walker, 1984, 1988), incest (Herman, 1981; Walker, 1988), marital rape (Russell, 1982), rape (Burgess, 1983), and sexual exploitation of clients by therapists (Bouhoustos, 1984; Holyrod & Brodsky, 1977). The cumulative contribution of these efforts has been to define certain types of mental health dysfunction as a typical response to victimization, rather than as pathology based on internal causes. When symptoms are viewed either as intrapsychic in origin or simply unrelated to victimization, they can be erroneously viewed as an explanation of the victimization itself.

In summary, feminist influence on research has led to the investigation of many questions which otherwise may never have been considered important to examine. The accumulation of a feminist body of knowledge about women's lives can only further the development of feminist psychotherapy with both women and men.

Feminist influence on psychological theory. Feminist theory has influenced the development of psychotherapy from as early as 1941 with the work of Clara Thompson. Feminist challenges to psychoanalytical theory and practice have continued since then, including work by Horney, Chesler, Dinnerstein, Chodorow, Eichenbaum and Orbach, and more recently, Lerman as well as Daugherty and Lees (this volume). Beyond providing feminist challenges to existing theory has been the more proactive development of psychological theory which addresses women's psychological development directly, rather than as a variation of male psychological development.

There is a direct challenge to psychoanalysis by feminist women psychoanalysts, many of whom have formed their own organizations to have greater voice with the more orthodox establishment. The Association for Women in Psychiatry is one such group with influence given to revisionists such as Teresa Bernardez (1984), Marjory Braude (1987), Jean Baker Miller (1976) and Alexandra Symonds (1979). Psychoanalytical psychologists are impacting the training programs (Block, 1986; Shapiro, 1986), literature (Alpert, 1986; Cantor & Bernay, 1985; Claster & Dilling, 1985; Kaplan and Surrey, 1984), and politics. If it is possible to rewrite psychoanalytical theory eliminating the sex role stereotypes currently contained within it, it will be done by these women as well as others, some cited in Daugherty and Lees's chapter.

Miller's (1976) work is important in redefining as strengths those characteristics which have been referred to as weaknesses in women. More recently, Kaplan and Surrey (1984) at the Stone Center have begun to challenge the concepts of enmeshment and separation-individuation as they have been applied to female personality development. The notion of female personality development in the context of self-in-relationship challenges the view that psychological development invariably progresses in the direction of greater autonomy, at least for women. In fact, the relational qualities referred to as enmeshment may represent normative female relationship functioning. At issue is the labeling of it as dysfunctional or pathological, simply because it may not represent normative relational characteristics for males. A focus on separation-individuation as central to personality development may place emphasis on the wrong issue for women for whom connectedness may be more essential. Behaviorism does not escape criticism by feminist theorists either. Early behavior therapy, with an almost exclusive focus on behavior, excluded key elements of women's lives in particular the emotional and cognitive arenas. The application of cognitive-behavioral and social learning theories has increased the relevance and usefulness of behaviorally oriented therapies to women. A critical sociopolitical analysis of the social and family systems within which women and girls live is essential for adequate assessment and effective intervention. A recognition of the differences in social, economic, and political power between women and men, boys, and girls, is central to the analyses guided by social learning and cognitive-behavioral theories.

Historically, family therapy, heavily dominated by androcentric theory and application, has not served women well. More recently, family therapy theory has come under challenge by feminist analysis (Bograd, 1984, 1986; Hare–Mustin, 1980). Challenges from within traditional family therapy groups are beginning to occur, for example from the Women's Project in Family Therapy founded by Betty Carter, Olga Silverstein, Peggy Papp, and Marianne Walters.

Developmental theory sets the norm for what is considered to be appropriate child and adult development. Recent theoretical advances have expanded our thinking about female development. For example, Gilligan's (1982) work on the development of moral reasoning and views of rights and responsibilities involved with justice provides a framework to understand women's cognitive thinking as inclusive, nonlinear, circular, and setting fact within context. Redefining normative cognitive processes for female development as unique from that of males in some areas provides an opportunity to understand the problems women encounter from a more appropriate theoretical framework. Hence, psychotherapy informed by feminist psychological theory of development has tremendous potential for impact on the lives of women and girls. For example, measuring creativity and giftedness from a female-based orientation focuses the issue away from an androcentric notion of eminence. Feminist developmental theory places the roles of mother and father in child rearing in perspectives very different from earlier views.

OVERVIEW OF BOOK

The book is organized into two major sections—Theoretical Integration of Feminist and Psychotherapy Systems, and Application of Feminist Therapies. We have chosen these particular psychotherapy systems because of their major influence in training programs for mental health practitioners, although we recognize that these are not exhaustive. The theory section begins with a chapter on feminist frameworks of psychotherapy (Cammaert & Larson), which traces the influence of feminism on the development of feminist therapy, discusses a variety of professional issues (e.g., consumer rights, traditional techniques, business practices) and the goals of feminist therapy. Next is a chapter which discusses developmental issues: Feminine Development Through the Life Cycle (Conarton & Silverman). Here the authors present an exciting new theory of stages of development for women. Following this chapter begins a series of chapters which examine the interface between feminist and psychotherapy systems. These chapters focus on psychodynamic (Feminist Psychodynamic Therapies, Daugherty & Lees), cognitive behavioral (Cognitive Behavior Therapy: Evaluation of Theory and Practice for Addressing Women's Issues, Fodor), and family systems theories (Power, Gender, and the Family: Feminist Perspectives on Family Systems Theory, Bograd).

The second major section, Application of Feminist Therapies includes chapters on feminist therapies with women (Feminist Therapies with Women, Rosewater), single female parents (Feminist Therapy With Divorced, Single, Female Parents, Rawlings & Graham), men (Feminist Therapy with Male Clients, Ganley), lesbians and gays (Feminist Therapy With Lesbians and Gay Men, Brown), ethnic minorities (Feminist Therapy With Ethnic Minority Populations: A Closer Look at Blacks and Hispanics, Mays & Comas–Diaz), and the elderly (Feminist Therapies with the Elderly, Midlarsky). Each chapter addresses the particular issues which arise when applying feminist therapy to the particular client population in question. Inherent in the organization of this section is the idea that feminist therapy is not limited in its application to feminist women, nor to women generally, but is useful in working with men as well as children. The application of feminist therapy to these populations heretofore has been largely ignored.

The last chapter, Future Directions: Development, Application, and Training of Feminist Therapies (Walker & Douglas) is an effort to set a course for feminist therapy, one that moves feminist therapy to the mainstream, involves dissemination of feminist therapy knowledge base, and addresses feminist therapy ethics.

REFERENCES

Alpert, J. (Ed.). (1986). *Psychoanalysis and women*. Hillsdale, NJ: Analytic Press.

American Psychological Association. (1974). Report of the task force on sex bias and sex role stereotyping in psychotherapeutic practice. *American Psychologist, 30* (1), 1169–1175.

Bernardez, T. (1984). Prevalent disorders of women: Attempts toward a different understanding and treatment. *Women & Therapy, 3* (3–4), 17–27.

Beutler, L. E., Crago, M., & Arizmendi, T. G. (1986). Therapist variables in psychotherapy process and outcome. In S. L. Garfield & A. E. Bergin (Eds.), *Handbook of psychotherapy and behavior change, 3rd edition.* New York: Wiley.

Block, H. L. (1986). Feminist scholarship and the training of psychoanalytic psychologists. Presented at Clark Conference on Training in Psychoanalytic Psychology. Worchester, M.A. October, 1986.

Bograd, M. (1984). Family systems approach to wife battering: A feminist critique. *American Journal of Orthopsychiatry, 54,* 558–568.

Bograd, M. (1986). A feminist examination of family therapy: What is women's place? *Women and Therapy.*

Bouhoustos, J. C. (1984). Sexual intimacy between psychotherapists and clients: Policy implications for the future. In L. E. A. Walker (Ed.), *Women and mental health policy* (pp. 207–227). Beverly Hills: Sage.

Braude, M. (Ed.). (1987). *Women, power, and therapy.* New York: Hayworth Press.

Broverman, I., Broverman, D. M., Clarkson, F. E., Rosencrantz, P. S., & Vogel, S. R. (1970). Sex role stereotypes and clinical judgements of mental health. *Journal of Clinical and Consulting Psychology, 34* (1), 1–7.

Browne, A. (1987). *When battered women kill.* New York: The Free Press-MacMillian.

Burgess, A. (1983). Rape trauma syndrome. *Behavioral Sciences & the Law, 1* (3), 97–113.

Cantor, D., & Bernay, T. (Eds.). (1986). *Psychology of today's woman: New psychoanalytic vision.* Hillsdale, NJ: Analytic Press.

Caplan, P. J. (1985). *The myth of women's masochism.* NY: Dutton.

Collier, H. V. (1982). *Counseling women: A guide for therapists.* New York: Free Press.

Dilling, C., & Claster, B. (Eds.). (1985). *Female psychology: A partially annotated bibliography.* New York: Coalition for Women's Mental Health.

Dobash, R. E., & Dobash, R. P. (1983). The context specific approach to theoretical and methodological issues in researching violence against wives. In D. Finkelhor, R. Gelles, G. Hotaling, & M. Straus (Eds.), *The dark side of families* (pp. 261–276). Beverly Hills: Sage.

Douglas, M. A. (1984 August). Mental health risks: A study of battered women and abusive men. Paper presented at the Second National Conference for Family Violence Researchers. Durham, N.H.

Gilligan, C. (1982). *In a different voice: Psychological theory and women's development.* Cambridge, MA: Harvard University Press.

Guttentag, M. (1983). *Too many women.* Beverly Hills: Sage.

Hare-Mustin, R. (1980). Family therapy may be dangerous for your health. *Professional Psychology, 11,* 11–24.

Herman, J. (1981). *Father-daughter incest.* Cambridge, MA: Harvard University Press.

Jones, W. H., Chernovetz, M. E., & Hansen, R. O. (1978). The enigma of androgyny: Differential implications for males and females. *Journal of Consulting and Clinical Psychology, 46* (2), 298–313.

Kaplan, A. G., & Surrey, J. L. (1984). The relational self in women: Developmental theory and public policy. In L. E. A. Walker (Ed.), *Women and mental health policy* (pp. 79–94). Beverly Hills: Sage.

Kelly, J. A., O'Brien, G. G., & Hosford, R. (1981). Sex roles and social skills: Considerations for interpersonal adjustment. *Psychology of Women Quarterly, 5* (5), 758–766.

McHugh, M. C., Koeske, R. D., & Frieze, I. H. (1986). Issues to consider in conducting non-sexist psychological research. *American Psychologist, 41* (8), 879–890.

Miller, J. B. (1976). *Toward a new psychology of women.* Boston: Beacon Press.

Orlinsky, D. E., & Howard, K. I. (1980). Gender and psychotherapeutic outcome. In A. Brodsky & R. Hare-Mustin (Eds.), *Women and psychotherapy: Theory, research and practice.* New York: Guilford Press.

Radloff, L., & Cox, S. (1981). Sex differences in depression in relation to learned susceptibility. In S. Cox (Ed.), *Female psychology: The emerging self.* New York: St. Martin's Press.

Rawlings, E. I., & Carter, D. K. (Eds.). (1977). *Psychotherapy for women: Treatment toward equality.* Springfield, IL: Charles C. Thomas.

Rosencrantz, P. S., DeLorey, C., & Broverman, I. (1985). One half a generation later: Sex role stereotypes revisited. Paper presented at the Annual Convention of the APA, Los Angeles, CA, August.

Russell, D. E. H. (1982). *Rape in Marriage.* New York: MacMillan.

Symonds, A. (1979). Violence against women: The myth of masochism. *American Journal of Psychotherapy, 33* (2), 161–173.

Tittle, C. K. (1986). Gender research and education. *American Psychologist, 41* (10), 1161–1168.

Walker, L. E. (1979). *The battered woman.* New York: Harper & Row.

Walker, L. E. A. (1984). *The battered woman syndrome.* New York: Springer.

Walker, L. E. A. (Ed.). (1988). *Handbook on sexual abuse of children: Assessment and treatment issues.* New York: Springer.

Wallston, B. S. (1981). What are the questions in psychology of women? A feminist approach to research. *Psychology of Women Quarterly, 5,* 597–617.

Wardell, L., Gillespie, D. C., & Leffler, A. (1983). Science and violence against wives. In D. Finkelhor, R. Gelles, G. Hotaling, & M. Straus (Eds.), *The dark side of families.* Beverly Hills: Sage.

CHAPTER 2

Feminist Frameworks of Psychotherapy

Lorna P. Cammaert
Carolyn C. Larsen

BACKGROUND

The recent women's movement, the beginning of which is usually cited as the publication in 1963 of Betty Friedan's *The Feminine Mystique,* has provided the milieu and impetus for the development of feminist therapy. The focus of the movement has been to eliminate the social and cultural barriers that prevent women's full and equal participation in our society. A feminist believes in and advocates political, economic, and social equality for women. As Gilbert (1980) notes, "the basic assumption underlying feminist therapy is that ideology, social structure and behavior are inextricably interwoven" (p. 247). The contradiction that women experience between the stated ideology of equalitarianism in our society and the social reality of the patriarchal system provides an understanding of and explanation for many of women's problems (Wilson–Schaef, 1981).

The harmful effects of sex role stereotyping on women has been elaborated in numerous psychologists' writings, such as that of Franks and Rothblum (1983). While acknowledging improvement in the status of women, these authors find that women continue to be overrepresented in certain mental health clinical problem areas, e.g., depression, agoraphobia. They present a cogent argument which attributes this phenomenon to the traditional sex role socialization of women. Traditional psychotherapists have encouraged women to remain in or return to sex roles which are constricting and maladaptive for many women. One needs only to peruse the self-help bookshelf to see how pervasive is this view. Feminist therapists exert a different influence both through therapy with women and by educating other therapists to view and treat women with increased knowledge, realistic attitudes and effective skills. Only recently have feminist self-help books begun to compete (e.g., Cammaert & Larsen, *A Woman's Choice,* 1979; Orbach & Eichenbaum, *Fat is a Feminist Issue* 1979).

Bardwick (1979) describes three types of feminists: conservative, mainstream and radical, a continuum that can be used for feminist therapists as well. Conservative feminists are those who agree with the tenet of equal pay for work of equal value, have worked toward role responsibility changes in their personal relationships and are aware of some ways their lives have been affected by sexism but do not work to change the status quo. Mainstream feminists are proactive, working to change laws, policies, and practices which are sexist and to implement affirmative action programs. These feminists, who are the most visible group and whom most people identify as feminists, are seeking change through reform. Radical feminists, on the other end of the continuum, have more extreme objectives which require basic changes to society. They include political marxists and others who believe change can only take place with revolution. Many radical feminists, (e.g., Hogie Wyckoff, 1977), do not support therapy for women as they believe it only placates or silences the anger needed for revolution. The knowledge, experience, attitudes and activity of feminist therapists determine where their position is on this continuum.

Sturdivant (1980) lists six factors out of which feminist therapy has grown. Some of these factors are referred to elsewhere in this chapter, but they are summarized here for purposes of clarity:

1. The re-emergence of American feminism.
2. The development of consciousness-raising groups with the recognition that "the personal is political."
3. "The feminist critique of Freudian and analytic theory as legitimizing sex-role stereotypes by embedding them in a 'scientific' theory of human behavior that has been used against women in psychoanalytic treatment" (p. 72).
4. The feminist criticism of the male-dominated profession of psychotherapy as having a double standard of mental health for men and women, which encourages women to adjust to existing sex roles, thus continuing their oppression.
5. "The emergence of a 'grassroots' feminist therapy movement in response to the call by feminists for a new kind of therapy for women" (p. 72).

6. An increasing awareness by professionals of sex bias inherent in the theory and practice of psychotherapy which has led to seeking ways to correct the bias and meet women's needs.

There are many points on which feminist therapists agree and which help define feminist therapy. One is the feminist critique of society, which rejects the traditional view of biological determinism and espouses the view that men and women are equal and that the different roles they take have resulted from socialization processes and institutionalized sex roles. The second issue on which there is agreement follows from the first. It is that women are economically and politically oppressed in our society. While traditional sex roles oppress both men and women, women are seen to suffer most as they have few opportunities to self-actualize and are viewed as second-class citizens. Just as various groups in the women's movement seek to change the policies, attitudes, and behaviors that keep women "in their place," feminist therapists seek to help women by changing at least one of the institutions, psychotherapy, which has contributed to their oppression.

We see two basic approaches to considering feminist frameworks of psychotherapy. Until recently, most feminist therapists have been trained in conventional psychology programs. They have not experienced many women teachers as role models. Their feminist ideas and practices have been incorporated into the traditional theoretical backgrounds they have acquired. Initially feminist therapy was considered an addition of theory to already established therapy approaches (Lerman, 1976). But feminist criticisms and modifications contributed to the development of these other approaches and provided impetus for change (e.g., Douglas, 1984, cognitive behavioral theory; Eichenbaum & Orbach, 1983, psychoanalytic theory). As feminist therapy has become an increasingly integrated treatment approach in its own right, therapists have utilized aspects of traditional approaches but feminist theory and practice more and more have provided the primary thrust. Today, it is accurate to assert that feminist therapy is a free-standing, established therapy. One of the outcomes of the latter approach has been the development of feminist therapy training within and outside the conventional programs and a blending of traditional and feminist approaches (Rothberg & Ubell, 1985).

THERAPIST VARIABLES AND BEHAVIOR

The basic core concept of feminism is that the therapist respects the woman and honors her perceptions of her world. The way that a woman is viewed by a therapist, individually and as a class, significantly affects the therapy which she will receive. As Rosewater (1984) states, "feminist therapy involves a redefining of therapy. It demands new and innovative approaches . . . feminist therapists need to learn to look and see differently" (p. 271). This premise guides much of the therapist's knowledge, attitudes, and skills in counseling women. Sturdivant (1980) outlines four traits that are utilized as criteria for feminist therapists. They are: "(1) the therapist must be a woman, (2) she must be aware of her own values and be willing to make these values explicit for her clients, (3) she should be involved in social action for women, and (4) she should be working toward optimal functioning in her own life" (1980, p. 150). These issues and others related to feminist therapist will be discussed within a tripartite organization of values, knowledge, and skills.

FEMINIST VALUES

There are a number of values that form the foundation for feminist therapy. As feminist therapy has evolved more from a philosophical system than a prescription of technique (Brown, 1985b), it is essential to make that philosophy explicit. Some of these values are well established, other are evolving, and some are controversial. These values and concepts are interrelated, each building on and reinforcing the others. A number of them have been modified as feminist therapy matures, and it has become apparent that some of these ideals are difficult, if not impossible, to attain in reality. For the sake of understanding, these values are listed and elaborated briefly below.

The Personal is Political

Each woman's personal experience and situation is a reflection of the position of women generally in our society. Feminist therapists help clients see that their problems have social as well as personal causes. Similarly, therapists' personal experiences, including their work as therapists, reflect women's position in society, and can lead to social action on behalf of clients. As well, clients may take social action on their own behalf, which needs to be respected for its political statement. In contrast, traditional therapists might view such action in light of the consequences, e.g., if a protester is jailed it could be labeled self-defeating behavior. Consciousness raising has been a powerful technique to help women become aware of their restrictive place in society, to bond with other women, validate female experience, and consider change. Women are relieved of the blame of being totally responsible for their problems, learning that the cause is not only intrapsychic but also rooted in society. This feminist interpretation does not relieve women of the responsibility for engaging in efforts toward their own change, but helps them develop an awareness of the communality of women's problems. As a result, women's groups for both political and therapeutic change have become powerful influences.

By sharing their knowledge and skills in a consultative model, feminist therapists empower their women clients to become their own change agents.

Choice

Women have had limited life choices as a result of their economic and social oppression and the internalized beliefs which stem from that oppression. Goals of feminist therapy are to help women be aware of their options and self-actualize by developing psychological and economic autonomy (Rawlings & Carter, 1977). Sturdivant (1980) summarizes feminist therapy as a "highly positive belief in the ultimate capacity of each woman for self-actualization based not on sex-role stereotypes but on her own self-knowledge and human potential." A key goal is self-defined, optimal functioning (Sturdivant, 1980, p. 162), which involves a therapist's fostering self-determination and increased autonomy of a client.

The assumption is that women will exercise a variety of options in their lives if they are aware of the opportunities and believe they have a choice. It is essential today for women to be, or have the skills to be, economically independent. Most women are supporting or will have to support themselves and dependents at some time during their lives. Williams (1976) states that one of her definitions of a healthy woman is one who "is able to support herself in work that is fun for her and gives her a sense of competence" (p. 23). There is much research that clearly supports the idea that enhancing autonomy and self-confidence is important to successful therapeutic outcome (Lorr, 1965; Martin & Sterne, 1976; Orlinsky & Howard, 1978; Saltzman, Luetgert, Roth, Creaser, & Howard, 1976).

One implication of women's ability to support themselves economically is that it changes the nature of their dependence on men. Psychological autonomy of women seems less realistic and less desirable as a goal than psychological interdependence (Kaplan & Surrey, 1984) whether that be with men and/or with other women. Exploring the autonomy–dependence conflict is a frequent theme in therapy with women. Choice involves women becoming personally independent, knowing what it means to be a woman and her own identity as a woman. Becoming more self-determining is an important goal.

Some of the ways to encourage choice are: seeing clients as consumers, encouraging them to be active in selecting a therapist, setting their own goals in therapy, and evaluating therapy. In these ways, women clients practice new decision-making skills in the therapy relationship by taking control of their own treatment. Feminist therapists may not always agree with the choices their clients make but respect and encourage their choices.

Choice, control, and power are closely linked. A client becoming aware of her own power within the therapy relationship can facilitate choices. As Lerman (1976) has so aptly stated, "you don't make people change, you help them become aware of emotional costs and alternatives" (p. 384) and attempt to empower the client to become autonomous and as economically independent as possible. Seidler–Feller (1976) presents some strategies by which the client shares the therapist's power, for example, fee negotiation, contracts, and client feedback on the therapist's effectiveness.

Equalization of Power

Feminists believe that power between people in various positions should be equal. While individuals possess different characteristics, knowledge or skills, each deserves respect and the right to have equal personal power in relationships. As most therapists are men and most clients are women, (Russo, 1984), there are inherent gender power differentials in the therapy relationship in addition to the expert power attributed to the therapist. The power relationship between therapist and client has been a focus of feminist therapy and achieving a more equalitarian therapist–client relationship has been a goal of feminist therapy.

Having women therapists working with women clients removes the male–female gender effect, though not the power-of-the-expert effect (Douglas, 1985; Speare, 1984). Seeing the client as her own best expert is one way of enhancing the client's power in the therapy relationship. A feminist therapist values the client as a person, respects her perception of her world, and credits her knowledge about herself and possible solutions to her problem. Power is further equalized by keeping the client's needs as primary in the relationship.

Feminist therapists have become aware that an equalitarian relationship with clients is more an ideal than a reality. Brown (1985a) suggests feminist therapists be aware of the power differences inherent in the therapy setting and "share our power and privilege consciously and actively" (p. 300). She warns that if a feminist therapist is not actively working to share her power, then there is a high probability that she will assume the power of her position and/or be given it in large measure by others (Brown, 1985a). The first step in sharing or changing the power structure is to acknowledge the power you have (Douglas, 1985).

She suggests two principles to guide the balance of power in feminist therapy. The first is to "define the therapeutic relationship as one of temporary inequality with the goal one of terminating it and/or re-defining it as equalitarian" (p. 246). The second principle is "to make the inequality as least disparate as possible" (p. 246). We continue to strive for equalitarian relationships within therapy and the struggle heightens awareness of power differentials. This struggle may help the client develop skills to manage other person relationships outside the therapy relationship. It is important for the feminist therapist to use that power responsibly and perhaps conceptualize it as the capacity for impact (Smith & Siegel, 1985).

Therapist as a Role Model

Throughout the process of feminist therapy, the therapist presents herself as a role model who believes that a complex life is possible. She presents herself as a woman and as a therapist. As Williams (1976) aptly states, the feminist therapist is "living proof that a woman can be supportive and helpful, involved with the growth and development of others and yet at the same time involved with her own intellectual and professional growth, with political issues, and with her economic self-interest" (p. 21). This is not an easy task, as Gluckstern (1977) points out, "I had to face my own tendency toward passivity and the ambivalence I felt about taking action. It meant becoming a role model, and learning to take risks and assume leadership" (p. 444). The effort appears to be well worth it, as research indicates that clients who viewed their therapists as more equalitarian than authoritarian had significantly better outcomes than did other clients (Lorr, 1965). There is little research available on the effects of the therapist's operating as a role model, although what is available is supportive (Johnson, 1976; Sapolsky, 1965). Appropriate self-disclosure assists in developing the potential bond that arises out of the communality of women's experiences in our society and facilitates the positive aspects of modeling by the therapist. Research indicates that effective therapists are spontaneous and self-disclosing (Brody, 1984a).

Early feminist writing urged the therapist to disclose immediately her feminist values with her client. The purpose of this was to identify the therapist's values explicitly, which would allow the client to know them, rather than be subtly coerced by them. Thus, the client could screen the therapist's interpretations through these expressed values. At times it appeared to have the opposite effect: Clients did not feel more free and powerful, but more intimidated or coerced by the therapist's values. As the field has matured, feminist therapists are reporting that they have more understanding of their clients and do not use the privilege of their position to proselytize. Rather, they respect the client's position and start therapy where she is instead of where they would like her to be (Speare, 1984).

Androgyny

An early and persistent objective of feminist therapy has been to help women develop their fullest potential. The feminist critique of society sees women (and men) as limited by their sex roles. The real differences in characteristics and skills between men and women have developed artificially and are perpetuated by the socialization process. An androgynous person can possess an effective combination of male and female characteristics which break the bonds to traditional sex roles. Put simply, for women this has meant adopting behaviors that are more instrumental, assertive, and rational, and for men it has meant to become aware and more expressive of their emotions.

Psychologists are beginning to understand female development, characteristics and behavior as different but not less than that of males (Gilligan, 1982). Some of this has occurred because woman identified characteristics have consistently been devalued by the mental health community (e.g., Broverman, Broverman, Clarkson, Rosenkrantz, & Vogel, 1970). While feminist therapists have always considered women's experience as valid, promoting women's characteristics and behaviors as well as encouraging women to value and take pride in their femaleness has become a more prominent therapeutic goal than seeking androgyny.

Social Action

It has been a value in feminist therapy that to be effective the therapist should be involved in social action for women. This follows from the feminist belief that women's problems are based in society as well as in the person and therefore, a feminist therapist should work to change the system to benefit the client and other women. An expected outcome of therapy has been that the client will engage in social action to bring about change in areas that contribute to her problems. This goal of therapy has been tempered with experience, with social action now being seen as appropriate for some clients, but not expected of all. As well, the kinds of social action can vary and may involve public and/or nonpublic expressions. In her survey of feminist therapists, Thomas (1975) found that all those she interviewed clearly placed a higher priority on meeting the client's needs and on reaching therapeutic goals, than on politicizing the client to become involved in social action.

Lerman (1976) perhaps exemplifies this best when she says that "the goal is to help them become the best person they can be, within the limits of their personal circumstances and the patterns of society in general" (p. 383). She goes on to say that "sometimes they make choices you yourself would not make. Sometimes the past influence of society and prior choices already made limit the real possibilities in the present" (p. 384). Brody (1984a) reiterates the same sentiment but in a different manner when she says, "I hope to encourage women to strike out and dare to be different—but I also must have empathy with those for whom the struggle is still too great" (p. 19).

Ethics

Because of its philosophical base, ethical issues occupy a primary role in feminist therapy and are woven into the fabric of that therapy. The ethical codes of professions, e.g., APA Ethical Principles of Psychologists (1974), in which feminist therapists have been trained traditionally, often describe ethics that are inconsistent with a feminist reality (Berman, 1985; Brown, 1985b).

As well, the need for special guidelines for working with women became apparent as the evidence of sex bias and stereotyping in therapy with women mounted. Blatant sexual exploitation of clients by therapists did not become officially unethical until 1978. The American Psychological Association Task Force Report on Sex Bias and Sex Role Stereotyping in Psychotherapeutic Practice (1975) presented four categories of therapist behaviors which are considered sexist: (1) fostering traditional sex roles, (2) bias in expectations and devaluation of women, (3) sexist use of psychoanalytic concepts, and (4) responding to women as sex objects, including seduction of female clients. Thirteen "Guidelines for Therapy with Women" (American Psychological Association . . . , 1978) developed from these categories provide direction for "ethical and effective psychotherapy with women" (p. 1122), and provide a basis for training therapists.

Division 17, Counseling Psychology, of the American Psychological Association adopted 13 "Principles Concerning the Counseling and Therapy with Women" in 1978. The principles focused on the need for therapists with women clients to have specialized knowledge, attitudes and skills. As well, 10 "Guidelines for Therapy and Counselling with Women" were developed by a subcommittee of the Canadian Psychological Association Status of Women Committee (Canadian Psychological Association, 1980), which illustrate the application of the principles.

Guidelines for feminist therapy have also been emerging. As many feminist therapists are not credentialed in orthodox programs, they may not have access to professional organizations and their ethical codes. Many feminist therapists, eligible or not, refuse on principle to be members of organizations they consider patriarchal and exclusionary. While it is important and helpful for guidelines or codes of ethics to develop out of and be approved by traditional professional associations, it is also essential for feminist groups to develop their own ethics.

As a feminist therapist, one must be aware of not adding to the oppression of women through one's actions. The feminist therapist must be responsive and act responsibly in using her power. Ethics in feminist therapy not only prohibit abuse of the therapist's power and privilege, but demand that the therapist actively use her power and privilege in social activism (Brown, 1985b; Rosewater, 1985a).

One set of eight guidelines for feminist therapy was developed by the Feminist Therapy Collective, Inc., of Philadelphia (Fondi, Hay, Kincaid, and O'Connell, 1977) and, on the basis of her own experience, were presented and elaborated by Butler (1985). The guidelines were originally used to screen feminist therapists who wanted to be on a referral list.

The Advanced Feminist Therapy Institute has developed a feminist code of ethics. This group, whose members have been practicing feminist therapy for a minimum of 5 years, has met annually since 1980. Papers on ethics have been presented and discussed each year, culminating with the 1985 institute's theme of "Feminist Ethics." A Feminist Therapist Code of Ethics (Rave & Larsen, 1985) provided a focus for struggling with personal and professional issues. This development of feminist-ethics is evolutionary, unique, and will be ongoing.

Two major ethical issues for feminist therapists are the necessity of a cognitive framework for therapy which is current and acknowledgment of overlapping roles. Because of the various theoretical bases, styles, and techniques used in feminist therapy, it is extremely important for a feminist therapist to be very clear on her cognitive framework for therapeutic intervention. Utilizing this cognitive framework, a feminist therapist is ethically obligated to be aware of new information and knowledge about the psychology of women.

Second, while most traditional ethical codes contend that the therapist should not allow overlapping roles, because of the contiguity of the feminist community even in large centers, it is most probable that feminist therapists will have to deal with dual roles or overlapping roles (Berman, 1985). A feminist therapist must be very aware of the ethical issues involved in dual roles and must ethically discuss them with her client(s), must be aware of situations in which she may abuse her power and privilege, and is especially obligated to maintain confidentiality and not to become sexually involved with a client. Feminist therapists must be wary of the obvious and more subtle forms of enmeshment that can occur between therapists and clients to ensure that they are not damaging their clients because of an abuse of their power. In all cases which involve role overlap, the therapist must put the needs of the client in a primary position. To avoid harm to the client and any potential abuse of power, a feminist therapist must be cognizant of the overlap of roles and must develop strategies to prevent any abuse of her power and privilege.

In addition, consciousness raising is a continuous process to which the feminist therapist is open. She provides information, knowledge, and skills to her clients but also learns much from each therapeutic encounter.

KNOWLEDGE

The existence of a growing body of knowledge about girls and women of which psychologists need to be aware before offering services to them was brought to psychologists' attention by the American Psychological Association Division 17 Counseling Psychology Principles Concerning the Counselling and Therapy of Women (1979). Feminist therapy has emphasized the need for a female model of development which reflects women's unique development and is not simply a male model warmed over or redone (Klein, 1976; Miller, 1976). Such a model is beginning to evolve with the work of various individuals and groups: the idea of sex role development of women as put forward by Frieze, Parson, Johnson, Ruble, and Zellman (1978); and the work at the Stone Center, utilizing a model of interrelatedness or self-in-relation, which is original and exciting (Kaplan & Surrey, 1984). These theorists allege that women develop their sense of self in relation to others, not as autonomously as the male-identified models of personality development state. Thus, a woman's interpersonal relationships are of paramount importance in the development of positive mental health.

Another aspect stressed in feminist therapy is that there are distinct women's issues which reflect all the psychological experiences that are unique to women. According to Lerman (1976), these experiences are ignored by men and are not mentioned by women while in the company of men. One major women's issue is the area of sexuality where it is imperative that women redefine female sexuality from the viewpoint of their own experiences and desires (Cammaert, 1984; Seidler–Feller, 1985). The issue of sexuality includes menstruation, pregnancy, childbirth, sexual satisfaction, and sexual preference, as well as sexual harassment, assault, and rape. Other issues that have been highlighted in feminist therapy are those of women who are battered (Walker, 1979, 1984), girls and women who were victims of childhood sexual abuse (Herman, 1981), women and work (Hansen & Rapoza, 1978; Sales & Frieze, 1984) and working more sensitively with lesbian women (Siegel, 1985). As well as focusing on specific issues, feminists are beginning to draw common threads from many areas so that books on topics which are not usually related are emerging, e.g., *Sexual Exploitation: Rape, Child Sexual Abuse, and Workplace Harassment* by Diana Russell (1984).

Some areas of concern have not held the focus yet and feminist therapy has been accused of not considering class values and characteristics as valid, significant elements of reality and thus "unintentionally perpetrating much the same sort of ignorance on women in poverty as that that traditional psychotherapy imposes on all women" (Faunce, 1985b). This criticism can also be leveled at feminist therapy concerning women of color. Until now feminist therapy has, as has its mother feminism and its father psychology, reflected its white, middle-class origins (Maracek, Kravetz, & Finn, 1979) but its philosophical underpinnings demand that it be broader in its knowledge and orientation. This process has begun with the emergence of a few articles (e.g., Belle 1984, Brody, 1984b; Larsen & Cammaert, 1985; Trotman, 1984).

From this specific knowledge of women and the realization that many problems which women present in therapy are system rather than individually caused, most feminists have adopted a psychoeducational model of therapy. The emphasis becomes growth rather than adjustment or remediation, development rather than blame or illness. Clients are seen as learners, rather than patients with emphasis on their strengths. Weaknesses are de-emphasized and behaviors that have been typically viewed as negative are cognitively restructured into valued strengths, e.g., survival skills for battered women described by Walker (1979).

The lives and work of women are valued and celebrated by feminist therapists and this formulates a basic attitude that permeates feminist therapy. Several studies have found that female therapists and especially feminist therapists, in contrast to male therapists, perceived female clients as stronger and healthier, and also saw them generally in more positive terms (Bosma, 1975; Brodsky & Hare–Mustin, 1980; Jones & Zoppel, 1982).

Collier (1982) sees this therapeutic-educational process as occurring through: (a) counteracting the negative consequences of socialization by sharing information about options, teaching skills, and developing "functional models of thinking, feeling and behaving" (p. 15); (b) providing whatever the client is unlikely to get from her own environment, such as awareness of resources and emotional support; and (c) working openly with any problem women bring to therapy.

The feminist therapist uses a variety of skills to assist in this educational process. Therapists model behaviors and attitudes which help clients to see alternatives for themselves. Through appropriate self-disclosure, therapists reveal their own struggles for development, their strengths and humanness. Self-disclosure also establishes a communality of experience between client and therapist. Demystification of the therapy process and techniques occurs by explanation, and engaging with the client in the mutual search for understanding. The client experiences her own power as she is able to take increasing responsibility for the direction of her life.

Feminist therapists utilize a wide variety of theoretical backgrounds, some of which are explicitly dealt with in other chapters within this book, and this is considered a strength of the approach. A feminist therapist must carefully examine her choice of theoretical base or system for its inevitable sexist assumptions and bias before utilizing it in her work with clients. No matter what theoretical basis is used, the emphasis is on the client's being an active participant in the change process and on an equalization of power in the relationship. Adoption of these basic principles makes it incompatible for the feminist therapist to use power-seeking therapy techniques where outcome is stressed over process, although it may be possible to blend some aspects of these techniques into the framework of a power-equal setting (Brown, 1982).

In addition to utilizing new theories and information on women, feminist therapists use traditional psychological knowledge for women's benefit. An excellent example of this is in the area of psychological testing. Some feminist writing has strongly stated that diagnostic testing and labels are never or seldom used in feminist therapy (Levine, 1984;

Rawlings & Carter, 1977). However, feminists have discovered that utilization of such tests with a feminist interpretation can be a means of effective advocacy for change on the woman's behalf (Rosewater, 1985b).

Although feminist therapists must have a coherent system for understanding the problems which clients experience, they do not normally use standard diagnostic terminology. Feminist therapists tend to be descriptive rather than increasing the mystification of therapy with labels reminiscent of medical jargon. Feminists have spoken against the new DSM–III diagnostic categories as being inaccurate, sexist, and demeaning (Brown, 1985a; Kaplan, 1983), and will work to change this system of the patriarchy. Nevertheless, the DSM–III diagnostic labels are considered essential by health insurance companies for coverage, which has led some feminists to use them when it was necessary for the client to have the cost of therapy covered by insurance. In these cases, Brown (1985a) recommends that the therapist discuss the situation with her client, including the consequences of having a psychiatric diagnosis on her record. If it is mutually agreed, the therapist will utilize the least pejorative label possible, e.g., Adjustment Disorder, since it is disordering to live in the patriarchy and continually try to adjust oneself to it or Post Traumatic Stress Syndrome for rape victims since the situation of trauma creates the distress. As Brown points out, this is an excellent example of the tightrope that must be walked between a feminist's value system and the patriarchy in which she operates.

Another aspect to be considered by feminist therapists is the knowledge and acknowledgment of the many aspects of privilege in our society. Privilege may result from race, gender, education, class, age, able-bodiedness, affectional/sexual preferences, and/or financial resources (Brown, 1985a). A therapist needs to be aware not only of privileges held by her clients but which she does not share, but also of the effect of her own privileges when they are not shared by her clients.

Feminist therapists have led the profession in becoming advocates for consumer rights in psychotherapy, resulting in consumer guides for choosing therapists, etc. (e.g., NOW's "A Consumer's Guide to Nonsexist Therapy," 1978; "Women and Psychotherapy: A Consumer Handbook," 1985.) This attitude towards consumer rights is pervasive throughout the therapy process. During the initial interview a feminist therapist usually provides her client with information about how she practices. In later interviews, she may inform the client when options regarding intervention techniques are appropriate and, throughout the therapy, encourages questions or feedback regarding the therapist's orientation or techniques (Brown, 1985a; Seidler–Feller, 1976). Also, the client actively participates in evaluating the treatment outcome (Sturdivant, 1980). In addition to ensuring consumer rights within her own therapy, the feminist therapist is normally active in community education efforts about consumer rights and supports the creation of systems of redress for clients who have been abused by therapists (Brown, 1984).

It is obvious that the values of a feminist pervade both the process and content of psychotherapy, including her business practices. The structure of fees expresses a feminist ethic and reflects the therapist's value of her own work in balance with the realization that many women cannot afford the usual rates for psychological services (Lasky, 1985). Feminist therapists have evolved different resolutions. Three popular methods currently used are negotiating fees, having a sliding fee scale, and bartering. Barter arrangements are arrived at in a feminist manner, where the decision is made cooperatively between the client and therapist. Brown (1985a) cautions, bartering be undertaken only if the recipient is getting something she values and the giver is providing goods or services "that she feels a sense of personal worth for doing or creating" (p. 302). Of course, rates for barter are set at fair market prices.

Another aspect of business practice, which is consistent with the therapist's feminist values, is that the office location and environment is safe, accessible by local transportation, and comfortable for the clientele. Furniture is arranged in a conversational manner rather than in the traditional power arrangement often found in other situations (Brown, 1985a). For many feminist therapists these considerations may not be a problem, since they have found it more comfortable, feasible, and, at times, profitable to be in private practice where the surroundings are within their control. If the feminist therapist has chosen to work in an institution, e.g., hospital or university, she attempts to influence the setting as much as possible toward these objectives. Improvising by placing the desk chair in front of the desk closer to the client's chair rather than behind the desk is an obvious example.

Strengths of a client are emphasized throughout the therapy. Usually the feminist therapist adopts a holistic approach, knowing that emotional stress can have physical and spiritual effects (Faunce, 1985a; Feminist Therapy Support Group, 1982). To foster independence from the therapist and to acknowledge the value of other relationships, the client is encouraged to utilize other community resources, to enhance her friendship relationships, and to participate in group counseling. The feminist view of women, with its emphasis on the key concepts of choice and empowerment, gives rise first to a validation of women's experience, and second to the focal point on change or growth through a problem-solving approach.

The process of feminist therapy has been described as having three distinct stages (Smith & Siegel, 1985). The first stage facilitates change by providing resocialization where values of society and the client are explicitly examined in order for the client to understand personally what is meant by "the personal is political." In essence, "we help the woman client to differentiate between what she has been taught and has accepted as socially appropriate and what may actually be appropriate for her" (Lerman, 1976). This combination of looking outward, as well as the more traditional looking inward, helps the client realize what aspects are being imposed on her by society or other people. Through this process the client can enhance her sense of personal power and, most importantly, learn that she is not crazy but rather that society is unjust (Kaplan, 1983; Lerman, 1976). In feminist therapy, symptoms are often viewed as "adaptive solutions to societal oppression rather than as individual expressions of pathology" (Porter, 1985). These "adaptive solutions" have costs associated with them, often of a very large order e.g., the woman's mental health.

One technique used in this stage is sex role analysis as developed by Brodsky (described in Rawlings & Carter, 1977, p. 64), where the therapist, while providing emotional support, brings to the client's attention relevant but unconscious sex role expectations. As women become aware, and remedy sex role constrictions in their behavior, they discover strengths within themselves. Sex role analysis helps women understand the "personal is political" statement in a personal way and conveys to the client she is not at fault that she is in a particular situation, yet that she is responsible for changing her situation.

Cognitive templating (Pyke, 1979) is another feminist technique for helping a client examine her past socialization and her possible attributions. Through this examination it is possible to discern powerful self-statements that hinder the client's development, and to restructure such statements cognitively so that they lose their negative power and become more positive, constructive statements which encourage the client's further growth.

At this stage, it is most important for the feminist therapist to validate the feelings felt by the client and to help her overcome the well-learned self-doubt, which impedes her sense of power and self-definition. One feeling that emerges through this process is anger, a feeling which must be validated by the therapist. The woman's anger is viewed as a legitimate response, but the power of the anger felt by the woman may scare and offend her and, of course, others if she expresses it outside the therapy situation. Although society teaches that women should not be angry (and most people experience a great deal of discomfort when anger is expressed, especially by women), the anger felt by the client is real, rational, and often appropriate. Through therapy, she can become aware of the anger, realize that it is appropriate, and learn how to work with it constructively rather than repressing, denying, or venting it inappropriately. There is some research support for the importance of facilitating the client's expression of anger (Crowder, 1972; Mintz, Luborsky, & Auerbach, 1971; Nichols, 1974).

A technique that has been developed to aid the client in expressing emotions such as anger, sadness, and joy is feminist body psychotherapy (Moss, 1985). This technique integrates verbal exploration with "gentle movements, soft energetic touch, natural breathing, and voice work" (Moss, 1985, p. 84), which increases the woman's awareness of chronic tension, repressed feelings, and habitual posture patterns. Through feminist body psychotherapy, the woman's body frees itself of restrictions without excessive pain, force, or stress.

The second stage in the process of feminist therapy involves two parts: the woman is introduced to her strengths and the therapeutic relationship becomes a model of an equalitarian relationship. Strengths which are traditionally labeled weaknesses may be revealed during the exploratory first stage. In the second stage, these strengths are more fully explored and the client is encouraged to develop them further. One example of this is that a client is encouraged to develop her self-nurturing skills. Women have been well taught in our society to nurture others, but this is often at the expense of their own nurturance. In therapy, the client is encouraged to use her excellent nurturing skills for herself; she is given permission to take time and resources for herself because she deserves it and is worth it. This technique is inevitably tied to enhancing the woman's self-esteem.

Although the therapeutic relationship usually starts with unequal distribution of power, as the client begins to know and understand her strengths she gradually expands her own skills until both she and her therapist achieve an equalitarian relationship. As previously mentioned in the section on values, the feminist therapist has been aware of her power and has actively worked toward the goal of sharing her power through demystification of therapy and appropriate self-disclosure. In the second stage, this begins to come to fruition as the therapeutic relationship becomes more equalitarian. With this model of an equal relationship, the client may find it possible to generalize the situation to other relationships in her life. Some would label this process as transference, but it has a broader meaning when used by feminists. It includes healthy situations as well as the client's own projections shaped by the therapist's values.

The third stage of feminist therapy provides opportunities for the woman to learn and practice new, more effective behaviors in her personal and work environments. Communication in a direct and honest manner has been identified as a major area for skill development in feminist therapy (Rawlings & Carter, 1977).

One of the most popular feminist therapy programs to help women develop effective communication skills and thus enhance their personal powerfulness and self-esteem has been assertiveness training (Jakubowski–Spector, 1973). With assertiveness skills, it was felt that the woman would be able to "negotiate her traditional roles more effectively as well as to consider, choose, and function in new roles" (Williams, 1976, p. 213). Although helpful in some situations, the consequences of being more assertive can be negative for women in our society (Lineham & Egan, 1979; Solomon & Rothblum, 1984). This has led Fodor (1985) to question the whole issue of women's assertiveness skills, especially whether women are even deficit in assertiveness, and whether there is a model of effective assertiveness for women. She suggests that much more work is required in this area, using a four-pronged approach of developing more effective models of female assertiveness, more research on the consequences of assertive responding, addressing societal misconceptions and mislabeling of female assertiveness, and educating the wider community e.g., supervisors, corporate executives, and media, so that a more receptive environment is developed for the assertive woman.

GOALS OF THERAPY

The goals of feminist therapy have been expressed in a variety of ways, some of which have been quite absolute. With its coming of age, feminists appear to have tempered some of the extremely idealistic goals and have emerged with goals that better reflect the values and philosophy of feminism. Klein (1976) discussed seven major goals for treatment outcome of feminist therapy: symptom removal, increased self-esteem, improved quality of interpersonal relationships, competence in role performance, resolution of target problems through problem solving, increased comfort with body image and sensuality, and encouragement of political awareness and social action. She suggests that evaluation of the therapy is a cooperative process in which the client and therapist engage throughout therapy. To assist in the evaluative process, she lists a series of nine sets of questions.

CONCLUSION

Sturdivant (1980) concluded that, "feminist therapy forges a conceptualization of therapy-as-process" (p. 179). As authors of this chapter, we have become very aware that feminist therapy is therapy-in-process as well, and, in fact, we see the two as complimentary. Values, knowledge, and skills about women and feminist therapy are constantly expanding and changing because feminist therapy has focused on the social context for the client, both outside and within the therapeutic situation. The focus of the process highlights the major progress made in feminist therapy, but also delineates areas where more information and research are needed.

Since a central assumption of feminist therapy is that cultural factors contribute to the psychological distress of women, Sturdivant (1980, p. 182) points out that this is a crucial area for research. It is important to determine how much of women's psychological distress is due to cultural programming, what the interaction is between the cultural and intrapsychic factors, how resocialization can be best accomplished, and to evaluate successful resocialization as a treatment outcome. Gilbert (1980) concludes that future research efforts should concentrate on what happens in feminist therapy, what client and therapist variables are important to what happens within feminist therapy, and what positive and enduring outcome effects result from feminist therapy. Once these are known it will be possible to determine if feminist therapy does that which it purports to do—a basic question for any therapy.

In order to conduct this research, there is a need for innovations in research methodology. "Investigation of the client–therapist interaction requires collaboration and trust between the therapist and the researcher" (Gilbert, 1980, p. 261) and research on feminist therapy must include the client as well. At this point in time, it seems necessary that feminist therapy be studied by feminist researchers despite the inherent problems many of which are addressed by Johnson and Auerbach (1985). In addition to innovations in research methodology, new tools and instrumentation may be necessary to measure new constructs or old constructs from a new viewpoint. Although the traditional psychological methodology may be appropriate for researching some aspects of feminist therapy, researchers also are exploring the wealth of material that is emerging through sociological and anthropological methodology. Many researchers contend that these methodologies may be more appropriate and fruitful in examining the content, process, and outcome of feminist therapy (Sturdivant, 1980, p. 184).

The review of feminist therapy in process raises questions other than those which can be addressed by research. As mentioned earlier, the question of feminist ethics is still being discussed and evolved. Lerman (1985) raises a different question which is more philosophical and perhaps more basic: "Is doing feminist therapy the best use of our resources and is it feminist?" (p. 5). She contends that feminist therapists are helping clients to live in a "crazy and non-affirming world"; "we help people ease their pain in living, we help them live in a world which they are less motivated to try to change" (p. 5). Thus in the last analysis, the work of feminist therapists may be contrary to the stated overall goal of changing society, and feminist therapists implicitly may be helping the system to perpetuate itself. Such questions need to be discussed as the process progresses.

These and other questions will continue to be raised and answered, because feminist therapy is in process, and is a process. As this review has pointed out, conceptualizations will be used as long as they are useful, will be modified through practice, and may be discarded in time because they have become outmoded. This process can be frustrating for those who desire a complete but static package. Since feminist therapists are critical of other therapy systems, they sometimes feel it is imperative that feminist therapy should be conceptually sound, well grounded in research, and be functionally complete as more traditional therapies claim to be. Although these are valid goals, the strength of feminist therapy is in its active process and its questioning nature, which may not allow the finished conclusion some desire. This chapter has attempted to capture the current state of the art, and the authors are hopeful it will be but a step in the exciting process of discovery on which feminist therapists have embarked.

REFERENCES

American Psychological Association. (1974). *Ethical principles of psychologists.* Washington, DC: Author.

American Psychological Association Report on the Task Force on Sex Bias and Sex Role Stereotyping in Psychotherapeutic Practice. (1975). *American Psychologist, 30*(1), 1169–1175.

American Psychological Association Task Force on Sex Bias and Sex-Role Stereotyping in Psychotherapeutic Practice. (1978). *American Psychologist, 13,* 1122–1123.

American Psychological Association Division 17 Counseling Psychology (1979). Principles concerning the counseling and therapy of women. *Counseling Psychologist, 8*(1), 21.

Bardwick, J. M. (1979). *In transition: How feminism, sexual liberation and the search for self-fulfillment have altered America.* New York: Holt, Rinehart, & Winston.

Belle, D. (1984). Inequality and mental health: Low income and minority women. In L. E. Walker (Ed.), *Women and mental health policy* (pp. 135–150). Beverly Hills, CA: Sage.

Berman, J. R. S. (1985). Ethical feminist perspectives on dual relationships with clients. In L. B. Rosewater & L. E. A. Walker (Eds.), *Handbook of feminist therapy: Women's issues in psychotherapy* (pp. 287–296). New York: Springer.

Bosma, B. J. (1975). Attitudes of women therapists toward women clients, or a comparative study of feminist therapy. *Smith College Studies in Social Work, 46,* 53–54.

Brodsky, A. M., & Hare–Mustin, R. (Eds.). (1980). *Women and psychotherapy.* New York: Guilford Press.

Brody, C. M. (1984a). Authenticity in feminist therapy. In C. M. Brody (Ed.), *Women therapists working with women: New theory and process of feminist therapy* (pp. 11–21). New York: Springer.

Brody, C. M. (1984b). Feminist therapy with minority clients. In C. M. Brody (Ed.), *Women therapists working with women: New theory and process of feminist therapy* (pp. 109–118). New York: Springer.

Broverman, I. K., Broverman, D. M., Clarkson, R., Rosenkrantz, P., & Vogel, S. (1970). Sex role stereotypes and clinical judgments of mental health. *Journal of Consulting and Clinical Psychology, 34*(1), 1–7.

Brown, L. (1982). *Ethical issues in feminist therapy: What is a feminist ethic?* Presented at the Advanced Feminist Therapy Institute, Washington, DC.

Brown, L. (1984). *Power and responsibility: Developing ethical guidelines for feminist therapists.* Presented at the Advanced Feminist Therapy Institute, Oakland, CA.

Brown, L. (1985a). Business practice in feminist therapy. In L. B. Rosewater & L. E. A. Walker (Eds.), *Handbook of feminist therapy: Women's issues in psychotherapy* (pp. 297–304). New York: Springer.

Brown, L. (1985b). *Ethical and conceptual issues in theory-building for feminist therapists: Some introductory thoughts.* Paper presented at the Advanced Feminist Therapy Institute, Bal Harbor, FL.

Butler, M. (1985). Guidelines for feminist therapy. In L. B. Rosewater & L. E. A. Walker (Eds.), *Handbook of feminist therapy: Women's issues in psychotherapy* (pp. 32–38).

Cammaert, L. P. (1984). New sex therapies: Policy and practice. In L. E. Walker (Ed.), *Women and mental health policy* (pp. 247–266). Beverly Hills, CA: Sage.

Cammaert, L. P., & Larsen, C. C. (1979). *A woman's choice: A guide to decision-making.* Champaign, IL: Research Press.

Canadian Psychological Association. (1980). *Guidelines for therapy and counselling with women.* Ottawa: Author.

Collier, H. V. (1982). *Counseling women: A guide for therapists.* New York: Free Press.

Crowder, J. E. (1972). Relationship between therapist and client interpersonal behaviors and psychotherapy outcome. *Journal of Counseling Psychology, 19,* 68–75.

Douglas, M. A. (1984). *Feminist cognitive behavior therapy: A critique and reformulation.* Paper presented at the Advanced Feminist Therapy Institute, Oakland, CA.

Douglas, M. A. (1985). The role of power in feminist therapy: A reformulation. In L. B. Rosewater & L. E. A. Walker (Eds.), *Handbook of feminist therapy: Women's issues in psychotherapy* (pp. 241–249). New York: Springer.

Eichenbaum, L., & Orbach, S. (1983). *Understanding women: A feminist psychoanalytic approach.* New York: Basic Books.

Faunce, P. S. (1985a). Teaching feminist therapies: Integrating feminist therapy, pedagogy and scholarship. In L. B. Rosewater & L. E. A. Walker (Eds.), *Handbook of feminist therapy: Women's issues in psychotherapy* (pp. 309–320). New York: Springer.

Faunce, P. S. (1985b). *Women and poverty: A challenge to the intellectual and therapeutic integrity of feminist therapy.* Paper presented at the Advanced Feminist Therapy Institute, Bal Harbor, FL.

Feminist Therapy Support Group. (1982). Feminist therapy. *Healthsharing,* Winter, 12–18.

Fodor, I. G. (1985). Assertiveness training for the eighties: Moving beyond the personal. In L. B. Rosewater & L. E. A. Walker (Eds.), *Handbook of feminist therapy: Women's issues in psychotherapy* (pp. 257–265). New York: Springer.

Fondi, M., Hay, J., Kincaid, M. B., & O'Connell, K. (1977). *Feminist therapy: A working definition.* Unpublished manuscript, University of Pennsylvania.

Franks, V., & Rothblum, E. D. (Eds.). (1983). *The stereotyping of women: Its effects on mental health.* New York: Springer.

Frieze, I. H., Parson, J. E., Johnson, P. B., Ruble, D. N., & Zellman, C. L. (1978). *Women and sex roles.* New York: W. W. Norton.

Gilbert, L. A. (1980). Feminist therapy. In A. M. Brodsky & R. T. Hare–Mustin (Eds.), *Women and psychotherapy* (pp. 245–266). New York: Guilford Press.

Gilligan, C. (1982). *In a different voice: Psychological theory and women's development.* Cambridge, MA: Harvard University Press.

Gluckstern, N. B. (1977). Beyond therapy: Personal and institutional change. In E. I. Rawlings & D. K. Carter (Eds.), *Psychotherapy for women: Treatment toward equality* (pp. 429–444). Springfield, IL: Charles C. Thomas.

Hansen, S., & Rapoza, R. S. (1978). *Career development and counselling of women.* Springfield, IL: Charles C. Thomas.

Herman, J. L. (1981). *Father–daughter incest.* Boston: Harvard University Press.

Jakubowski–Spector, P. (1973). Facilitating the growth of women through assertive training. *Counseling Psychologist, 4,* 75–86.

Johnson, M. (1976). An approach to feminist therapy. *Psychotherapy: Theory, Research, & Practice, 13,* 72–76.

Johnson, M., & Auerbach, A. H. (1985). Women and psychotherapy research. In L. E. Walker (Ed.), *Women and mental health policy* (pp. 59–77). Beverly Hills, CA: Sage.

Jones, E., & Zoppel, C. (1982). Client and therapist gender and psychotherapy. *Journal of Consulting & Clinical Psychology, 50,* 259–272.

Kaplan, A. G., & Surrey, J. L. (1984). The relational self in women: Developmental theory and public policy. In L. E. Walker (Ed.), *Women and mental health policy* (pp. 79–94). Beverly Hills, CA: Sage.

Kaplan, M. (1983). A women's view of DSM III. *American Psychologist, 38*(7), 786–792.

Klein, M. (1976). Feminist concepts of therapy outcome. *Psychotherapy: Theory, Research, & Practice, 13*(1), 89–95.

Larsen, C. C., & Cammaert, L. P. (1985). Feminism at the grassroots. In L. B. Rosewater & L. E. A. Walker (Eds.), *Handbook of feminist therapy: Women's issues in psychotherapy* (pp. 110–118). New York: Springer.

Lasky, E. (1985). Psychotherapists' ambivalence about fees. In L. B. Rosewater & L. E. A. Walker (Eds.), *Handbook of feminist therapy: Women's issues in psychotherapy* (pp. 250–256). New York: Springer.

Lerman, H. (1976). What happens in feminist therapy. In S. Cox (Ed.), *Female psychology: The emerging self* (378–384). Chicago: SRA.

Lerman, H. (1985). *The ethical case against psychotherapy in a non-feminist world.* Paper presented at the meeting of the Advanced Feminist Therapy Institute, Bal Harbor, FL.

Levine, H. (1984). Feminist counselling: Approach or technique? In J. Turner & L. Emery (Eds.), *Perspectives on women in the 1980s* (pp. 74–87). Winnipeg, University of Manitoba Press.

Lineham, M., & Egan, K. (1979). *Assertion training for women: Square peg in a round hole.* Paper presented at the annual meeting of the Association for Advanced Behavior Therapy, San Francisco.

Lorr, M. (1965). Client perspectives of therapists: A study of the therapeutic relation. *Journal of Consulting Psychology, 29,* 146–149.

Maracek, J., Kravetz, D., & Finn, S. (1979). Comparison of women who enter feminist therapy and women who enter traditional therapy. *Journal of Consulting & Clinical Psychology, 47,* 734–742.

Martin, R. J., & Sterne, A. L. (1976). Post hospital adjustment as related to therapists' in-therapy behavior. *Psychotherapy: Theory, Research, & Practice, 13,* 267–273.

Miller, J. B. (1976). *Toward a new psychology of women.* Boston: Beacon Press.

Mintz, J., Luborsky, L., & Auerbach, A. (1971). Dimensions of psychotherapy: A factor-analytic study of ratings of psychotherapy sessions. *Journal of Consulting & Clinical Psychology, 39,* 106–120.

Moss, L. E. (1985). Feminist body psychotherapy. In L. B. Rosewater & L. E. A. Walker (Eds.), *Handbook of feminist therapy: Women's issues in psychotherapy* (pp. 80–90). New York: Springer.

National Coalition for Women's Mental Health. (1985). *Women and psychotherapy: A consumer handbook.* Tempe, AZ.: Author.

National Organization for Women. (1978). *A consumer's guide to nonsexist therapy.* New York: Author.

Nichols, M. P. (1974). Outcome of brief cathartic psychotherapy. *Journal of Consulting & Clinical Psychology, 42,* 403–410.

Orbach, S., (1979). *Fat is a feminist issue.* New York: Wyden Books.

Orlinsky, D. E., & Howard, K. I. (1978). The relation of process to outcome in psychotherapy. In S. L. Garfield & A. E. Bergin (Eds.), *Handbook of psychotherapy and behavior change.* New York: Wiley.

Porter, N. (1985). New perspectives on therapy supervision. In L. B. Rosewater & L. E. Walker (Eds.), *A handbook of feminist therapy: Women's issues in psychotherapy* (pp. 332–343). New York: Springer.

Pyke, S. (1979). Cognitive templating: A technique for feminist (and other) counselors. *Personnel & Guidance Journal, 57*(6), 315–318.

Rave, E., & Larsen, C. C. (1985). *Feminist therapy code of ethics.* Unpublished manuscript presented at Advanced Feminist Therapy Institute, Bal Harbor, FL.

Rawlings, E. I., & Carter, D. K. (Eds.). (1977). *Psychotherapy for women: Treatment toward equality.* Springfield, IL: Charles C. Thomas.

Rosewater, L. B. (1984). Feminist therapy: Implications for practitioners. In L. E. Walker (Ed.), *Women and mental health policy* (pp. 267–280). Beverly Hills, CA: Sage.

Rosewater, L. B. (1985a). *Feminist ethics: Proactive, not reactive.* Paper presented at the Advanced Feminist Therapy Institute, Bal Harbor, FL.

Rosewater, L. B. (1985b). Feminist interpretation of traditional testing. In L. B. Rosewater & L. E. A. Walker (Eds.), *Handbook of feminist therapy: Women's issues in psychotherapy* (pp. 266–273). New York: Springer.

Rothberg, B., & Ubell, V. (1985). The co-existence of system theory and feminism in working with heterosexual and lesbian couples. *Women & Therapy, 4*(1), 19–36.

Russell, D. E. H. (1984). *Sexual exploitation: Rape, child sexual abuse, and workplace harassment.* Beverly Hills, CA: Sage.

Russo, N. F. (1984). Women in the mental health delivery system: Implications for research and public policy. In L. E. A. Walker (Ed.), *Women and mental health policy* (pp. 21–41). Beverly Hills, CA: Sage.

Sales, E., & Frieze, I. H. (1984). Women and work: Implications for mental health. In L. E. Walker (Ed.), *Women and mental health policy* (pp. 229–247). Beverly Hills, CA: Sage.

Saltzman, C., Luetgert, M. J., Roth, C. H., Creaser, J., & Howard, L. (1976). Formation of a therapeutic relationship: Experiences during the initial phase of psychotherapy as predictors of treatment duration and outcome. *Journal of Consulting & Clinical Psychology, 44,* 546–555.

Sapolsky, A. (1965). Relationship between patient–doctor compatibility, mutual perceptions, and outcome of treatment. *Journal of Abnormal Psychology, 70,* 70–76.

Seidler–Feller, D. (1976). Process and power in couples psychotherapy: A feminist view. *Voices, 12,* 67–71.

Seidler–Feller, D. (1985). A feminist critique of sex therapy. In L. B. Rosewater & L. E. A. Walker (Eds.), *Handbook of Feminist therapy: Women's issues in psychotherapy* (pp. 119–130). New York: Springer.

Siegel, R. J. (1985). Beyond homophobia: Learning to work with lesbian clients. In L. B. Rosewater & L. E. A. Walker (Eds.), *Handbook of feminist therapy: Women's issues in psychotherapy* (pp. 183–190). New York: Springer.

Smith, A. J., & Siegel, R. F. (1985). Feminist therapy: Redefining power for the powerless. In L. B. Rosewater & L. E. A. Walker (Eds.), *Handbook of feminist therapy: Women's issues in psychotherapy* (pp. 13–21). New York: Springer.

Solomon, L. J., & Rothblum, E. D. (1984). Social skills problems experienced by women. In L. L. Abate & M. A. Milan (Eds.), *Handbook of social skills training in research.* New York: Wiley.

Speare, K. H. (1984). *Fine lines: The paradoxes of power in feminist therapy.* Paper presented at the Advanced Feminist Therapy Institute, Oakland, CA.

Sturdivant, S. (1980). *Therapy with women: A feminist philosophy of treatment.* New York: Springer.

Thomas, S. A. (1975). *Moving into integration: A study of theory and practice in feminist therapy.* Portland, OR: Portland State University.

Trotman, F. K. (1984). Psychotherapy with black women and the dual effects of racism and sexism. In C. M. Brody (Ed.), *Women therapists working with women: New theory and process of feminist therapy* (pp. 96–108). New York: Springer.

Walker, L. E. (1979). *The battered woman.* New York: Harper.

Walker, L. E. (1984). *The battered woman syndrome.* New York: Springer.

Williams, E. F. (1976). *Notes of a feminist therapist.* New York: Dell.

Wilson–Schaef, A. (1981). *Women's reality.* Minneapolis: Winston Press.

Wyckoff, H. (1977). Radical psychiatry for women. In E. I. Rawlings & D. K. Carter (Eds.), *Psychotherapy for women: Treatment toward equality* (pp. 370–391). Springfield, IL: Charles C. Thomas.

CHAPTER 3

Feminine Development
Through the Life Cycle

Sharon Conarton
Linda Kreger Silverman

INTRODUCTION

Feminist psychotherapy developed in response to the oppression of women perpetrated by traditional therapeutic approaches. Traditional therapy models are grounded in psychological theories based on the experiences of men (Brickman, 1984; Sturdivant, 1980), and only tangentially related to those of women. Reaction against inappropriate values, methods, and therapeutic goals for women has given rise to guidelines and principles for conducting nonsexist therapy (American Psychological Association . . . , 1978) but has not yet produced a comprehensive theoretical basis for the therapeutic process. Feminist therapists have had to incorporate feminist values and approaches into existing frameworks, and this volume demonstrates the scope of possible applications.

What is still lacking is a comprehensive theory of women's development to inform and direct therapeutic practice. Steps in this direction are beginning to be taken, most notably in the work of Gilligan (1979, 1982) and the Stone Center (Kaplan & Surrey, 1984). The tapestry of women's developmental process is complex and intricate, and it will require the combined insights of many women to construct the entire design. In this chapter, we will briefly critique existing developmental theories, outline a cycle of developmental phases that are unique to women, and describe how an understanding of these phases can guide the practice of feminist therapy. This effort represents another section of the tapestry that is gradually being woven.

The developmental phases as we envision them are:

Phase 1: Bonding
Phase 2: Orientation toward others
Phase 3: Cultural adaptation
Phase 4: Awakening and separation
Phase 5: The development of the feminine
Phase 6: Empowerment
Phase 7: Spiritual development
Phase 8: Integration

The phases are listed in the order in which they are first experienced. We initially thought of them as "stages" of development, then realized that stages imply a linear progression. In contrast, we find that women re-experience these phases at deeper and deeper levels throughout their lives. At this point, we see the eight phases comprising a cycle of development, with each repetition of the cycle bringing women to a new level of awareness, capability, and integration. Our discussion of these phases will incorporate concepts from existing theories, pertinent research, metaphor, and clinical experience.

Throughout this chapter, we will emphasize the development of the gifted woman, since her experience amplifies the phenomena we are attempting to describe. Although giftedness is an asset in males, it is often a liability in females, isolating them from peers and drawing derision from society rather than support.

Most gifted women are unaware of their giftedness; they are only aware of their pain—the pain of being different from the way women are supposed to be. They try in vain to see the emperor's new clothes, but fail to ingest the collective image. They never feel as though they fit in. Striving to understand what separates them from others, they often become involved in therapy, either as clients or as therapists or both. Feminist therapy is particularly attractive to them, since they have a natural tendency to question the roles that society has fashioned for them, and to envision other potentials for themselves. Therefore, unrecognized gifted women comprise a substantial portion of the clients and therapists exploring feminist therapy today.

DEVELOPMENTAL THEORIES
AND FEMINIST THERAPY

The original purpose of psychotherapy was to cure mental illness; therefore, all internal conflicts were perceived as evidence of "dis-ease," rather than as natural concomitants of growth. Even when these conflicts were the result of obvious external factors, such as assault, rape, loss of a loved one, or war, the person's pain was described as "emotional disturbance" or "mental imbalance." The medical model of viewing psychological processes is still very much alive today, as is readily observed by perusing the third edition of the *Diagnostic and Statistical Manual of Mental Disorders* (American Psychiatric Association, 1980).

A developmental perspective, with its emphasis on stages and cycles, seems more consonant with women's experience. However, early developmental theories only addressed the development of children. The study of adult development is still in its infancy; only recently have we begun to acknowledge that women's development is different from men's (Gilligan, 1982). The stage is now set for a comprehensive theory of the development of women throughout the life cycle.

A developmental view fits well with the tenets of feminist therapy. Human nature is seen as essentially healthy, evolving toward higher levels of actualization of potential. Internal conflicts are portrayed as desirable propellants toward higher levels of development (Dabrowski, 1964). These concepts undergird the therapist's affirmation of the client's feelings and potential for growth and change. Since the therapist is involved in her own growth process, she acts as more of a guide and facilitator of her client's developmental process, than as a remediator of the client's deficiencies. This equalizes the relationship between therapist and client (Rawlings & Carter, 1977).

Although a developmental framework has the potential to be highly relevant for women, the major developmental theories have been oriented toward males, and prove unenlightening when applied to females. Developmental theorists have sought to construct a set of "universal principles" of development that would apply to the entire species. When females fail to conform to these universal principles, their development is seen as aberrant (Gilligan, 1982). To acknowledge that women might develop along different paths has been unthinkable, since it would suggest that the basic premise of universality is flawed.

A CRITIQUE OF THEORIES OF DEVELOPMENT

A review of traditional theories of development reveals the extent to which women's experiences have been either ignored or misinterpreted. The first theory of development in recorded history was given to us by Aristotle (384–322 B.C.), who described three epochs of childhood, each of 7 years duration: infancy, boyhood, and young manhood (Muus, 1975). It is unclear whether females were thought by Aristotle to develop along similar lines, or whether their development was simply deemed unworthy of consideration.

The foundation for modern theories of development was laid by Jean Jacques Rousseau (1712–1778), who described four stages of development in his famous book *Emile* (Rousseau, 1780/1911). In Rousseau's theory, children progress from the "animal stage" of infancy (ages 4–5), through the "savage stage" (5–12), through the age of reason (12–15), and eventually to adolescence (15–20), at which time they transform selfishness into social consideration. It comes as no great shock that Rousseau confined his observations to male children. The progression from concern for self to concern for others becomes a common theme in later developmental theories.

Although Charles Darwin (1809–1882) never proposed a stage theory, his theory of biological evolution (Darwin, 1859) exerted a profound influence on developmental theories. His declaration that we evolved from lower animals, and his doctrine of the survival of the fittest, supported the "natural order" of male dominance as an elevated form of development. From his research, Darwin concluded that the male members of all species were more advanced on the evolutionary scale than the females, due to greater variability of secondary sex characteristics. It was clear to him that women were inferior to men intellectually since so few women had attained eminence.

> The chief distinction in the intellectual powers of the two sexes is shown by man's attaining to a higher eminence, in whatever he takes up, than can woman—whether requiring deep thought, reason, or imagination, or merely the use of the senses and hands. (Darwin, 1871, p. 564)

The work of Rousseau and Darwin captured the imaginations of theorists early in this century. G. Stanley Hall (1916), echoing both of his predecessors, formulated a psychological theory of recapitulation, which presumed that the developmental stages of childhood retraced the evolutionary stages of "mankind." Children were thought to progress from animal-like primitivism through a period of savagery, eventually becoming civilized. For example, ages 4 to 8 were supposed to correspond to the cave period, when hunting and fishing were the main activities of "man." This was thought to explain why children of these ages were found to build caves, play hide-and-seek and cowboys and Indians, and use toy weapons. Again, these examples illustrate that the children observed were male.

Freud (1925) also proposed a recapitulation theory of development, maintaining that the stages of psychosexual development are a re-enactment of earlier experiences of the race. The stages in Freud's theory—oral, anal, phallic, latent, and genital—re-create an ancient drama revolving around incest taboos, in which the male child falls in love with his mother, learns to repress these feelings through rituals which enable him to identify with his father, and eventually finds a more suitable love object. These stages were thought to be genetically determined. The Oedipal conflict—rivalry between the father and the son for the mother's love—is rooted in the survival of the fittest. For the "Oedipal complex" to be perceived as a universal phase of development, it was necessary for Freud to construct corollary experiences for women, such as "penis envy." In such ways, the male developmental process was superimposed upon female development. Much more could be said of Freud, but ample critiques can be found elsewhere (Firestone, 1970; Friedan, 1963; Greenspan, 1983; Millett, 1970; Sturdivant, 1980).

Piaget (1932, 1950), strongly influenced by Rousseau and Darwin, proposed a universal theory of cognitive development. In Piaget's theory, children progress through an invariant sequence of discontinuous stages—sensorimotor, intuitive, preoperational, concrete operational, and formal operational—culminating their development somewhere around the age of 12. In the first three stages, the child's thinking is considered egocentric. Formal operational thought, the pinnacle of development, is marked by the capacity to think logically, deductively, and rationally. These higher abilities are demonstrated through the mastery of Piagetian tasks, such as solving problems involving proportions, isolating variables in a chemical experiment, and applying principles of physics. Needless to say, males do appreciably better on such tasks than females (Dulit, 1972).

Piaget (1932) theorized that moral development grows out of an ever-expanding conception of rules that children learn through playing games. He noted that girls seem less concerned with rules and more willing to make exceptions to the rules; he surmised that this impeded them in developing a legal sense.

Kohlberg (1964), elaborating upon Piaget's theory of moral development, developed a six-stage hierarchy of ethical judgment. The stages, each of which is qualitatively different from and more advanced than the previous stage, progress from self-centeredness to an impartial concern for the rights of others. At Stage 1, individuals are motivated by fear of punishment; at Stage 2, by self-aggrandizement; at Stage 3, by desire for approval; at Stage 4, by a reverence for maintaining law and order; at Stage 5, by a democratic concern for the protection of individual rights; and at Stage 6, by universal principles of justice. While Piaget (1972) thought all members of the species eventually progress through all of the stages, Kohlberg thought individuals could terminate their development at any stage in the hierarchy. He found more women apparently operating at Stage 3, while more men appeared to be functioning at Stage 4 (Kohlberg & Kramer, 1969).

Gilligan (1979) challenged Kohlberg's findings, asserting that the values of mercy and attachment reflected in Stage 3 development had been relegated to an inferior position within Kohlberg's masculine framework. In her book, *In a Different Voice* (1982), Gilligan described her own theory of women's moral development, based on an ethic of responsibility and caring. In Gilligan's theory, women progress from a lack of responsibility for self and others, through a stage of selfless responsibility for others, and eventually to a stage in which they can care for both themselves and others. This effort represents a promising step toward the creation of a comprehensive theory of women's development.

Gilligan (1982) points out how most of the major developmental theories were based upon the study of male samples and then extrapolated to women. Erikson's (1968) "stages of man" is another case in point. Building on Freud's psychosexual theory, Erikson focuses more on social forces, and embraces the entire life cycle rather than birth through adolescence. Erikson's first five stages correspond to Freud's, each stage presenting a developmental task that must be resolved. The stages are as follows: (1) trust vs. mistrust; (2) autonomy vs. shame and doubt; (3) initiative vs. guilt; (4) industry vs. inferiority; (5) identity vs. identity confusion; (6) intimacy vs. isolation; (7) generativity vs. stagnation; and, finally, (8) integrity vs. despair. Identity precedes intimacy in this hierarchy, and the focus is on separateness. Erikson (1968) acknowledges that the sequence is somewhat different for women, but his theory remains unchanged.

Erikson was not the only theorist who thought that adults continue to develop. Although Jung (1923) did not formulate a comprehensive stage theory, he did describe principles of adult development, some of which are particularly applicable to women. He recognized that male and female development are different and he constructed concepts and terms to describe these differences. He believed that actualization of one's potential ("individuation") could only occur through the development of the "contrasexual"—the masculine aspect of women ("animus") and feminine aspect of men ("anima"). The attributes of the masculine and feminine are archetypal, meaning they are psychic imprints, inborn patterns of experiencing. The feminine principle has to do with relatedness, the interior, feeling, intuition, cooperation, nurturing. The masculine principle is associated with aggression, cognition, rationality, focusing, structure, competition, and hierarchy.

Jung provided a starting point for an understanding of women, but he did not go far enough. Ulanov (1971) explains:

If we seek from Jung a precise definition of the feminine, we will seek in vain. His presentation is limited in quantity and uneven in quality. Jung glances over profound truths, repeats the obvious ones, loses threads of arguments, and is often inaccurate in his observations. At the same time, however, a mere passing comment will reveal a new depth; a chance remark will inspire a whole field of research, and for all his disjointed, unsystematic method, Jung fundamentally pays serious attention to the feminine as an original psychic mode of being rather than as a deficient masculinity. The positive result is not so much what Jung accomplishes as what he has inspired others to do. (p. 154)

Another theorist concerned with adult development, whose work is not well known in America, is Kazimierz Dabrowski. Dabrowski (1964) offered a "theory of positive disintegration," which stressed the importance of inner conflict and crises in the developmental process. The theory postulates five distinct levels of development, from total egocentricity to complete altruism. According to Dabrowski, emotional sensitivity is essential to higher level development: Those at lower levels have very restricted emotional responses.

At the first level, the individual experiences no internal conflict, no self-evaluation, and no empathy. One uses others to help gain what one wants in the world, which is usually power. Dabrowski thought most world leaders function at this level. At Level 2, the person begins to experience a great deal of anxiety, due to the pushes and pulls of the environment. This level is marked by personal insecurity, confusion, and extreme vulnerability to social forces.

At Level 3, the individual becomes aware of a higher set of values, and begins to strive toward a life imbued with those values. The initial attempts are not usually successful, so this period is marked by intense inner conflict, feelings of shame and doubt, and often lack of adjustment in the world. There is also a deepening of one's own convictions and of one's relationships with others.

Level 4 is similar to Maslow's (1962) level of self-actualization. It is at this level that the person feels capable of contributing and living a life of integrity. But beyond this, there is a fifth level, one in which the individual has compassion for all. Mother Teresa of Calcutta is an example of one who has attained this highest level of human functioning.

Dabrowski's theory has many feminine aspects, particularly its emphasis on emotional development. But it too suffers from a masculine hierarchization from egocentricity to autonomy and eventually to compassion. The reverberation of this theme throughout the theories reflects the masculine pattern of development; there is serious question as to whether the pattern applies equally well to feminine development. While males move from a separated, egocentric state to a level of greater intimacy and social concern in adult life, females develop social responsibility much earlier in the developmental sequence, and need more assistance in achieving autonomy.

Some of the concepts outlined in the above theories can be applied to a fuller understanding of women's development, but the structure must be different. In the following section, we will describe the sequence of women's development as we currently understand it, synthesizing some basic principles of development with our own clinical experiences. We will discuss the eight phases of women's development in order, from early childhood to maturity. These eight phases are: bonding, orientation to others, cultural adaptation, awakening and separation, the development of the feminine, empowerment, spiritual development, and integration.

BONDING

In the normal separation sequence as described by object relations theory (Mahler, Pine, & Bergman, 1975), during the period from 0 to 3 months, the child is at one with the mother, feels as the mother does, and does not differentiate from the mother. During the symbiotic stage, from 3 to 18 months, there is an interdependent relationship, in which the combined energies of both partners is necessary for the existence of each. Apart from each other, each member appears to perish. The mother mediates every perception, every action, every insight, and every bit of knowledge. She functions as an auxiliary ego for the child, controls frustration tolerances, sets limits, protects, perceives reality, and is a buffer against inner and outer stimuli. She gradually organizes these stimuli for the infant and orients him or her to the inner vs. the outer world in boundary formation and sensory perception.

From 18 to 36 months, the child enters the separation/individuation stage, which parallels the physical ability to move away from the mother. The child's sense of individual identity develops. An intrapsychic separation begins when the child perceives his or her own image as being entirely separate from the mother. This is the period in which abandonment feelings of separation are established.

Object relations theory, based upon male norms, stresses separation and individuation as primary goals of children's identity formation (Mahler et al., 1975). Until recently, it was assumed that all infants go through these stages of the separation process in the same manner and at the same time in their development. However, Chodorow (1978) called attention to the differences in maternal relationships with sons and daughters. Since then, other feminist writers have recognized the uniqueness of the mother–daughter relationship and the role this plays in feminine development (Eichenbaum & Orbach, 1983; Kaplan & Surrey, 1984; Rubin, 1983).

While separation and individuation are fundamental goals in the psychological development of all individuals, there are marked differences perceived in these processes for males and females. Males appear to begin the separation process in early infancy, but females usually do not begin the major part of this process until midlife, and the manner in which it occurs is barely recognizable.

Differences in the separation processes of boys and girls appear to account for many of the differences found in the behavior of adult males and females. A boy child is different from a girl child. He is "the other," and from early on, the mother knows that he is the other. The girl child is not perceived as "the other"; she is perceived as being the same as the mother. Manifesting more of the archetypal feminine characteristics than the boy, the girl is more certainly identified with the mother; both mother and daughter operate with more open emotional connection and boundary flexibility. The sense of being the same as mother necessitates her taking on the feelings of mother. If mother is angry, she is angry; if mother is guilty, she is guilty. Without the basic preliminary separation, the intrapsychic bond between mother and daughter becomes stronger and stronger.

> This emotional sensitivity develops into cognitive and affective interactions that we later identify as empathy. The connectedness and the capacity for identification is the basis for the later feeling that to understand and to be understood are crucial for self acceptance and are fundamental to the feeling of existing as a part of a unit or a network larger than the individual. (Kaplan & Surrey, 1984, p. 86)

Bright children in particular have high degrees of emotional sensitivity, and are likely to show compassion for others even as toddlers (Silverman, 1983). According to Alice Miller (1979), gifted children have an amazing ability to perceive and respond intuitively to the mother's needs. This ability is then extended and perfected until they become responsible for their siblings, and mothers to their own mothers. The special sensitivity they develop to the unconscious signals of the needs of others often leads them to become psychotherapists. "Who else, without this previous history, would muster sufficient interest to spend the whole day trying to discover what is happening in the other person's unconscious?" (p. 9). However, although the deep level of attachment and empathy of gifted girls is a positive developmental sign, there is also a danger of the child's ego being absorbed by the mother's.

The depth of the bonding process for females must be taken into account in the therapeutic process. Traditional theories, which stress the importance of separation and individuation, may lead to inappropriate therapeutic goals for women. Separation and individuation processes take place at a later point in women's developmental cycle than in men's, and for entirely different reasons. Within traditional therapies, feminine attachment is seen as pathological dependence—something to be fixed (Eichenbaum & Orbach, 1983). It is important for the therapist to realize that bonding, empathy, and attachment are the basis of feminine development. This understanding will guide her in supporting these healthy aspects of her clients' development.

ORIENTATION TO OTHERS

The developmental cycle of women must be viewed with the awareness that women's primary striving is for relatedness and connection. Since women's ego development is influenced by this relational concept, a different theory of ego formation is needed for males and females. "The basic feminine sense of self is connected to the world; the basic masculine sense of self is separate" (Chodorow, 1978, p. 169).

Ego formation is different for a male because he is more aware of his boundaries. The boundaries of the feminine ego are very thin. After experiencing herself as an extension of the mother, it is hard for the girl child to know where she stops and the other begins. As the girl child continues her strong intrapsychic connection with the mother, she is not as readily able to discern what she wants for herself from what the mother's ego wants from her or for her. This is a critical point. Without establishing a strong sense of her own ego, the girl may transfer her own ego attachment from the mother to her friends, and eventually to her lover, husband, or someone else in the world. Even as an adult, a woman may have very keen perceptions of everyone else's feelings, needs, and desires, but very little awareness of her own.

A girl child's sincere desire to please, to nurture, to be needed, and to be part of someone else are all reinforced in the world. These are endearing traits in daughters: They are highly valued by others and by the daughter herself, because they enable her to be empathic toward the needs and wants of others. But by sacrificing her own wants and serving others, she develops an unconscious expectation that she will be loved and cared for in the same manner she cares for others. In fact, she usually does not receive this reward, or, if she does, she finds she may indeed have to be who others want her to be.

The senses of separateness of the male and connectedness of the female present the basis for relationship problems between men and women. The boy child, being cut off from the mother's feelings to a greater extent, experiences his own wants and needs and seeks his own independence as he continues to expect and receive nurturance from the mother. This expectation becomes prototypical of his desires as an adult male. While women are naturally attuned to other people's needs and socially conditioned to meet them, men expect to pursue their own goals while being nurtured by women.

A man's fear of experiencing the preseparation symbiotic engulfment of mother results in a fear of closeness or intimacy; at the same time, the feminine partner is seeking the continued bonding, understanding, and connection so familiar to her (Rubin, 1983). She does not realize that males do not share her other-orientation, her ability to be aware of the wants, feelings, and needs of others. If she keeps seeking this in men, she is continually frustrated and disappointed (Eichenbaum & Orbach, 1982). Relationships with women, whether friends or lovers, can be rewarding in that they allow her to experience another who shares these qualities, but they may also present boundary identification and merger difficulties (Burch, 1985).

The gifted female usually excels at taking care of others. Her antennae may be so attuned to the needs of others that people come to expect more and more from her. She will have a tendency to overextend her energies as she has less awareness of her own needs and little appreciation of her limitations. It is deeply satisfying to feel needed, and it may take a long time before a woman realizes that her relationships are unbalanced. She does all the giving, while the others in her world are doing all the receiving. Therapy could involve examining the extent to which she might be fostering unnecessary dependency in others, helping her develop mutually satisfying relationships, and teaching her how to care for herself—how to be self-nurturing.

There are many positive aspects of the feminine orientation to others. A woman's intensified awareness of others and her deep sense of connectedness enhance the quality of life for everyone. Giving comes easily. It is this trait that supports relationships, creates new life, and nourishes the lives of everyone around her. The major markers in a woman's life are most often the birth and death of relationships. The psychic reality of "self-in-relation" is the fundamental factor in woman's core sense of self (Kaplan & Surrey, 1984). Her whole sense of purpose is tied to this capacity to care (Gilligan, 1982). Recognition of the value of this orientation is essential to the therapeutic process.

The feminist therapist must be aware that this sense of orientation to others is appropriate, not symptomatic of inadequate ego development. One of the basic precepts of feminist therapy is that the therapist acknowledges and validates the client's reality. It is easier for a female therapist, who shares this other-orientation, to value sincerely the central role of relationships in the client's life. The client may very easily transfer her attachment to the therapist, which is actually helpful during early parts of the therapy. However, the therapist must be cautious to reinforce the client's own sense of self, and help her to develop more equal, mutual relationships.

CULTURAL ADAPTATION

It is not enough to become a woman in our society; in addition, a woman has to become a pseudo-man. Men usually write the television scripts and the textbooks; they hire and fire; they decide what will be published. From the time girls enter school, they learn that there is another reality beyond their own, one that is more acceptable, and they adapt. If they are clever, they learn new ways of thinking, talking, and writing, and develop another layer to their personalities.

The other-orientation in females leads to a form of hyperadaptability. After they learn to adapt to the feminine role at home, they are thrust into a coeducational school environment that supposedly sets up similar expectations for them and for boys. Their entrance into the male world is gradual. In preschool, their teachers are women, the main goal is social awareness, and the emphasis is on process, not product. Elementary school is more achievement-oriented, but, again, the main role models are women, and the mastery of factual information comes easily. Girls excel at the school game.

Then junior high school begins, and these confident, young girls seem to "plateau," while their less successful male counterparts suddenly experience a "growth spurt" which thrusts them into the lead in academic achievements. And this lead is maintained throughout the rest of their school years and in their achievements in adult life. Girls, even very bright girls, lose something in junior high school that is never quite regained: their confidence in their abilities (Silverman, 1986).

The difference in achievement of adult males and females was once thought to constitute absolute "proof" that females are inferior to males in intelligence (Darwin, 1871; Galton, 1869; Thorndike, 1910). Today, such claims would not be made publicly in educated circles, but they remain an ingrained prejudice in the majority of the population. Ironically, from the time the first IQ test for children was developed in this country, researchers found that girls' IQ scores were slightly higher than boys' scores from the ages of 2½ to 14 (Terman, 1916).

What happens to girls when they reach junior high school age? Why do they suddenly lose their edge? Gilligan (in Van Gelder, 1984) observes that an 11-year-old will hold out for her point of view, whereas a 15-year-old will yield. She surmises that the problem is rooted in the shift from factual knowledge to interpretive knowledge in the junior high school curriculum. Girls do not trust their interpretive powers, because their own interpretations differ widely from the masculine perspectives presented in the textbooks. Gilligan contends that the interpretive level of any discipline is oriented toward a masculine viewpoint, one that excludes the experiences of females. As girls see their own experience disappear from supposedly authoritative representations of human experience, their confidence in their own perceptions becomes eroded, leaving them feeling that their only chance at success is through imitation of males.

The imitation process intensifies as girls proceed through higher levels of education. At each level in the educational hierarchy, females face more male teachers, more masculine models of reality, and more requirements to reason, write, and perform like men. Most contemporary successful women have attained a masculine-oriented education, learned to operate in a male system, adopted male values, and lived by male norms. These women begin to feel an alienation from their own selves. Something is missing. Through the process of cultural accommodation, they have subtly absorbed the male value of denigrating and devaluing feminine knowledge and feminine ways of performing. Intuition and feeling are repressed, empathy is less rewarded than competition, and personal experience is denied in favor of deference to authority.

By the time they complete graduate school, women have learned how to put three references after every idea of their own in order to be believed. In their work experience, they have learned how to "dress for success," adhere to rigid rules and regulations, adopt an obsessive work ethic, be a good team player (which means not questioning the boss), and hide their personal lives, feelings, and experiences.

Robbed of their intuitive, feeling, experiential world, women become alienated from themselves in a masculine environment. They feel like "imposters" (Clance, 1985) when they try to be simulated men, and are continuously plagued with self-doubt. Although men also suffer from the imposter phenomenon, Clance (1985) found far more women who experience these feelings. If their behavior stems from imitation rather than a grounding in their own feminine knowledge, such feelings would be anticipated.

Gifted women are especially good candidates for imposter experiences. Bright females receive so many mixed messages about their abilities from early childhood that they do not feel safe demonstrating their talents. The following letter written by the mother of a kindergarten-aged child is illustrative:

> I have a daughter who is in public school in kindergarten. . . . At the first parent/teacher conference I was informed that she was working at or below grade level. She was in a low pre-reading group and a low math group. (She has been reading since three years old and has done basic addition and math since four.)
>
> I urged them to please look more closely. At another conference at semester end the teacher informed me of something strange which she had discovered. When my daughter worked with her best friend she worked below grade level (as did her friend—she is below grade level). In fact their work was almost identical. With more advanced children she worked at their level. The quality of her work seemed to depend almost entirely on her association.
>
> When asked about this, she thought about it for awhile and then told me she wanted the other kids to like her. I am unable to convince her that she doesn't have to do this to be liked. To her, being friends is to be just like each other. She is extremely adaptable.
>
> The school is becoming aware, but is not willing to help very much. At least they admit now she can read. They gave her a Silveral Reading Test two weeks ago and she reads fourth grade level. They are unprepared to do anything. She continues in a pre-reading group. (Perry, personal communication, February 7, 1986)

It is no wonder that through the cultural adaptation process, gifted girls learn how not to be gifted, and eventually lose all recognition of their own abilities. Even after these abilities have been demonstrated, the school refuses to acknowledge them or nurture them. Differential treatment of bright boys and girls by their teachers has been well documented (Cherry, 1975; Dweck & Bush, 1976; Dweck, Davidson, Nelson, & Enna, 1978; Frey, 1979; Sears & Feldman, 1966). Giftedness in childhood is correlated with "success" in adult life—for males; no such correlation exists for females (Terman & Oden, 1959). Some gifted girls do become productive adults, but they often have to sacrifice friendships to get there.

Achieving women very often attempt to be "superwomen"; that is, they try to become excellent males and excellent females simultaneously.

These two roles combined are physically and mentally exhausting. When these women are pulled in too many directions, stress mounts—sometimes to the breaking point. They often try to fulfill their various responsibilities at the expense of sleep, which eventually erodes their health.

When "superwomen" seek therapy, the therapist can help them to reorganize their priorities, learn to delegate, and make a commitment to take time for themselves before they fall apart. Most important, the therapist can acknowledge these women's talents, and help them to see that they don't have to work twice as hard to prove themselves in a man's world. There are other options; together they can find them.

Unfortunately, more often than not "superwomen" do not seek therapy. They are too busy. Instead they drive themselves into physical illness, and the illness provides the opportunity to stop, get off the merry-go-round, and really examine their lives (Taube, in preparation). At this point, they begin the deeper journey into self. If physical illness does not provide an escape, symptoms of high anxiety often begin to appear, heralding the next phase in women's developmental cycle. These symptoms are also prevalent in women who have devoted their lives to homemaking, for even in the home the masculine reality has led them to deny their feminine knowledge. Their emotional sensitivity is seen as "irrational," their intuitive judgment is ridiculed, and their value as human beings is questioned, since they have no achievements in the world to demonstrate their worth.

AWAKENING AND SEPARATION

The other-oriented, selfless, culturally adapted woman who fits the stereotypical pattern of a patriarchical society has been an endangered species for some time. Recognition of this fact has been slow. Previously, women were forced into a conspiracy of silence for survival. The women who spoke or wrote about the evolutionary process of women faced severe societal rebuke, even from other women. Kate Chopin's attempt is a case in point.

In her novel, *The Awakening,* Chopin (1899/1972) tells of a woman who is waking up and discovering her own self. Edna is married to a benevolent autocrat. She is encouraged to be a child with her children. Her husband is kind, well adjusted for his era, and provides well for his family. Edna becomes infatuated with a young man during a summer vacation, and begins to experience herself as more than wife and mother. In the succeeding months, she discovers her own artistic talents, and decides that she wants to paint and earn some of her own money.

This idiosyncratic behavior is tolerated by her permissive husband until she decides to move out of the family home into a carriage house of her own.

Soon Edna starts to look at child rearing differently; she decides not to be the kind of wife or mother society prescribes. She makes the statement that she would die for her children, but that she would not give up her life for them. The story centers on Edna's turmoil, her bouts with depression, and her growing courage to be her own person. But her desire for autonomy is perceived as mental illness.

> It sometimes entered Mr. Pontellier's mind to wonder if his wife were not growing a little unbalanced mentally. He could see plainly that she was not herself. That is, he could not see that she was becoming herself and daily casting aside that fictitious self which we assume like a garment with which to appear before the world. (Chopin, 1899, p. 96)

In the end, realizing that she would always be "owned" by someone— her father, her husband, her lover, or her children—Edna chooses the only form of freedom available to her, she takes her life. The heroine in the book necessarily had to die, even if it was only to conform with moral values of the day.

The author chose to focus on Edna's inner struggle to attain freedom, rather than on the wrath and rejection she might have incurred from her husband and friends, but Edna's behavior did not go unpunished. Edna's death was not enough to appease Chopin's critics; they were morally offended that Edna had "lived" at all, and chastised the author severely for creating her. Chopin, by then a famous author, was refused membership in the St. Louis Fine Arts Club because of the novel, and her book was banned in St. Louis. The critics stoned her with their literary commentary, and she died 4 years after this important work (Culley, 1976). Society was not ready to accept women forming individual identities.

Although this book was written almost a hundred years ago, it profoundly relates to lives of women today. Edna's despair in trying to own her own life mirrors the feelings of contemporary women who embark on the emotionally painful journey toward autonomy. Chopin's novel describes what we call women's separation process. However, in many psychiatric circles, Edna's journey into self is often regarded as a classic case study of "borderline syndrome."

Borderline syndrome, so aptly described by Masterson (1976) and Kernberg (1975), is an excellent example of how women's development is perceived in traditional masculine-oriented psychotherapy. *The Diagnostic and Statistical Manual of Mental Disorders* (DSM—III; 1980), the practical authority on the subject, describes the Borderline Personality Disorder:

> The essential feature is a Personality Disorder in which there is instability in a variety of areas, including interpersonal behavior, mood, and self-image. No single feature is invariably present. Interpersonal relations are often intense and unstable, with marked shifts of attitude over time. Frequently there is impulsive and unpredictable behavior that is potentially physically self-damaging. Mood is often unstable, with marked shifts from a normal mood to a dysphoric mood or with inappropriate, intense anger or lack of control of anger. A profound identity disturbance may be manifested by uncertainty about several issues related to identity, such as self-image, gender identity, or long-term goals or values. There may be problems tolerating being alone, and chronic feelings of emptiness or boredom. (p. 321)

The etiology of the borderline syndrome varies according to the clinician describing his particular bias. In *New Perspectives of Psychotherapy of the Borderline Adult,* Masterson (1978) theorized separation-individuation failure; Kernberg (1978) stressed developmental arrest or ego fixation; Searles (1978) depicted the situation as one where the patient's sense of inner and outer reality is flawed; externalization as a defense mechanism was elaborated by Giovacchini (1978).

Edna may be said to have manifested most, if not all, of the behaviors characteristic of the borderline personality. Yet, these characteristics are typical for a woman going through a separation-individuation process. "Many women diagnosed as borderline may actually be functioning in a normal way for a woman, even though their behavior may make male-identified therapists anxious" (Walker, 1984, p. 15).

The borderline syndrome is a relatively new disease entity coinciding with the changes in contemporary women's lives. The definition and clinical picture is as "complex and shifting" (Masterson, 1976, p. x) as are the changes in women's consciousness. Previously, women did not separate and become autonomous. They were their mother's daughter, their husband's wife, or their children's mother. This is, of course, changing. Women are now developing their own egos and identities, and as more women begin the separation process, the more this process will be recognized as a normal phase of women's development.

The pain of this developmental period is intensified if a woman seeks traditional therapy and is perceived by the therapist to be psychologically ill. A woman experiencing separation does exhibit many of the characteristics of the so-called "borderline syndrome" (as does a man with a strongly developed feminine side); however, the fact that she is considered sick and ostracized by society severely complicates this process.

Another example of the way in which women's normal emotional development and behavior are classified as pathological is in the current propositions that "premenstrual dysphoric disorder" (premenstrual syndrome) and "self-defeating personality"—characterized by masochistic and self-destructive behavior (e.g., being beaten by one's spouse) be added as categories of "personality disorder" in the 1987 revision of the DSM–III (Holden, 1986).

At the present time, it is still not acceptable for a woman to think of her own self or personal wants and goals before the needs of others— loved ones, children, or friends. The unconscious mandate is to be unselfish and to serve the ones they love. To many women, to be selfless is the highest order of love. However, when individuals continually do what others want them to do at the expense of their own desires, they become resentful. This resentment turns into unconscious manipulation of others, as in the caricature of the "Jewish mother," but even she consciously values selflessness.

It is no wonder that a woman striving to develop a sense of her "self" in the individuation process exhibits symptoms of separation anxiety: depression, anger and rage, fear of abandonment, guilt, passivity, helplessness, and emptiness. She is in a severe triple bind. She wants to be there for others, her culture demands that she be there for others, and at the same time she wants to be there for herself. No matter what action she takes at this point she is betraying some internal or external mandate. If she does not do what she wants to do she betrays herself. If she does put herself first, she betrays the internal lifelong mandate to be unselfish as well as the expectations of all the people around her who are accustomed to her putting their needs above her own.

Because she deeply values connectedness, a woman fears that her self-development will sever her most precious ties with others. These fears are usually justified. Her selfless attention to the needs of others has become a given to her loved ones. When she begins to be aware of her own needs and to act on her awareness, those intimately involved with her feel she is taking something away from them. They feel cheated and become angry with her, often going away, just as she feared. The culture punishes her for not playing her role.

The mood swings, self-disparagement, and problems in interpersonal relations which typify this phase of development are viewed as positive indications of higher-level development, rather than as symptoms of illness, in Dabrowski's theory of positive disintegration (1964). According to the theory, these behaviors signal the dissolution of a rudimentary level of development, which is necessary before a more conscious, evolved psychic milieu can be formed.

Symptoms of Dabrowski's third level of development include guilt, shame, dissatisfaction with oneself, "positive maladjustment," and the beginning of an inner hierarchy of values. Individuals in this third level are often seen as "maladjusted," but Dabrowski calls this "positive maladjustment" since their development is progressing beyond the weaker, external values of the peer group into deeper, inner-directed values. People in this stage are often seen as a threat to society since they are less tractable than less-evolved individuals. It is interesting to note that current research on the theory has found more women than men entering this level of development (Lysy & Piechowski, 1983; Silverman & Ellsworth, 1980).

Dabrowski's theory has its most significant application in the development of gifted and creative individuals (Piechowski, 1975). The gifted are more likely to question the values of their peer group and to strive for deeper levels of integrity. Gifted women are sensitive to the discrepancies between illusion and reality, and may reach the breaking point—the break with societal values—earlier in their developmental cycle. Not all women have a period of "awakening"; some remain in an unconscious state of development throughout life. But the gifted woman is more likely to find herself in a developmental crisis that precipitates the deeper phases of her growth and development.

For the woman who is experiencing separation anxiety, support for her own reality is of utmost importance. She is probably alone and in conflict with herself and those around her. Her world and all her illusions are changing. She may have been treated by a male-identified therapist who indeed has seen her as sick. She may even have been given tranquilizing drugs to allay her anxiety, which is actually her body's alarm system letting her know she must pay attention to her own feelings.

The impact of this transition in a woman's life is shattering. Individual therapy is indicated, as well as group therapy—particularly if she does not have a support group. She needs other women to identify with so that she knows she is not alone in her view of the world. She needs women's support to be able to tolerate the pain and punishment that result from seeing and speaking her truth. She cannot grasp why others do not understand and support her growth and change the way she would support theirs. Since relationship is so important to her, her relationship with her therapist becomes central to her life during this phase of development.

THE DEVELOPMENT OF THE FEMININE

There are no clear guidelines to illuminate the journey into self. The deeper phases of women's development are better suited to symbolic representation than to objective description. Women need subjective realities with which to identify; an abstract theory or an idea is not sufficiently real to assist them in gaining insight and bringing about change. One way of teaching women about the deeper layers of the feminine is through myth or metaphor, laden with imagery.

Christine Downing (1981), in *The Goddess,* states:

> We need images and myths through which we can see who we are and what we might become. As our dreams make evident, the psyche's own language is that of image, and not idea. The psyche needs images to nurture its own growth; for images provide a knowledge that we can interiorize rather than "apply," can take to that place in ourselves where there is water and where reeds and grasses grow. Irene Claremont de Castillejo speaks of discovering the inadequacy of all *theories* about the female psyche, including the Jungian framework into which she had for so long tried to fit her own experience and that of her female patients. For now, she suggests, we need simply to attend lovingly and precisely to the images spontaneously brought forward in our dreams and fantasies. (p. 2)

Women have been asleep for a long time. The journey toward consciousness involves re-examining the self; trusting one's intuitive knowledge to sort through the myriad of demands and determine what is really important to oneself; mobilizing the will to implement the necessary changes; developing spiritual awareness; and integrating these aspects of self. Through Jung's theory, these various tasks can be seen as having masculine and feminine components.

Particularly applicable to the woman seeking to integrate her inner feminine and masculine sides is the tale of Psyche and Eros (von Franz, 1980). There are similar tales from all cultures. Essentially, the story deals with a woman who loses her masculine partner, Eros, through disobedience and must perform a series of tasks to regain him. Here, Eros represents both the outer man and the inner masculine of a woman. In our interpretation of the myth, the integration of Psyche's inner masculine with her inner feminine brings her deeper feminine truths into consciousness.

We will begin in the middle of the story, and examine the tasks Psyche must perform. The first task that the goddess Venus has assigned Psyche is to sort out a huge pile of seeds—corn, beans, etc. This must be done by morning or she will die. She becomes overwhelmed and collapses. As she sits and waits, ants come to sort out the seeds, and the job is done by morning.

Contemporary women are presented with a myriad of overwhelming choices (seeds). They must attend to their families, community, household tasks, daily maintenance, career, education, spiritual and intellectual development, as well as the bombardment of everyone else's needs and expectations. They feel a responsibility to everything and everyone. They even apologize if it rains at a picnic. How will they organize? What do they want? Which must they choose first?

The sitting and waiting Psyche must do, waiting for the ants (symbolic of her instincts), is analogous to women getting in touch with their own feelings and intuition. For women who have externalized their lives it may take a long time to know what they want, to know their own path, and take the action to realize it.

The following dream of a gifted, young, woman physician illustrates this waiting process:

> There is a wooden sailing vessel floating in a vast expanse of turbulent sea. I am steering the boat; there are ten crew members. We approach a dark, threatening storm which tosses the boat about. We are afraid. I call the crew together for a meeting and announce to everyone that we are in danger and need to figure out what to do. I suggest that each of us offer ideas on what to do. My idea is that we get out all our maps and compasses and figure out a route to follow to land. The second crew member suggests we take cyanide tablets. The third suggests we take down the sail. The other crew members in turn offer their suggestions. Just as we are ready to make our final decision, a large figure emerges from below deck. He is a handsome captain. He approaches the huddled crew and says, "We won't act on any of your plans. WE WILL DO NOTHING."

The dream occurred in an overwhelmingly turbulent time for this woman. It was time for her to stop trying to figure everything out in her masculine way. The message of the dream, symbolized by the captain (a positive masculine figure), was for her to quiet her mind, to go inside and make contact with her feminine feeling and intuition, to experience her own self.

Women in this stage of their development must be taught how to sit with themselves and their feelings. When women have been experiencing others' feelings, the task of feeling their own is frightening at first, and they find all kinds of busy-ness to attend to rather than experiencing their own selves. They feel selfish, bad, guilty, and extremely anxious.

Only by bringing their repressed, ignored feelings up to consciousness can women know who they are and what they want for themselves. When they do this, they may be surprised to learn that they want something different from what their parents or the culture convinced them they wanted. They will also find that they are uniquely different from the cultural role model: They may not be the "good girls" they were supposed to be and thought themselves to be.

The sorting process is not an act of will; it is an internal, instinctual, feeling process. Every living organism has a drive to be whole. It is this striving toward wholeness that we call "instinctual." The feminine process is a teleological movement toward wholeness.

EMPOWERMENT

Psyche's second task is to get the golden fleece from wild aggressive solar rams. Again she is overwhelmed and despairing, ready to throw herself into the river. This depression takes her into a descent to the unconscious, virtually a pit. As she comes up the other side she brings with her a piece of knowledge that will enable her to take the next step. This time Psyche is helped by whispering reeds that tell her the rams are unapproachable at midday and that she must wait until evening when their ferocious temperament calms. If she approaches them too early, they will tear her to bits.

This task represents woman exerting her will in a male-dominated world which is threatening and dangerous. If she meets the rams head on, with only masculine aggressiveness, she will be attacked and over-powered. The reeds (her intuition) teach Psyche to utilize more indirect methods of dealing with the male world. Her own feminine ways are more circular and cunning, rather than linear and confrontational. If she uses a male attitude it will drown out the activity of the intuitive, feeling part of herself. She must follow the advice of the reeds, and gather pieces of fleece from the brambles in the evening, when the rams are unaware—to wait for the right moment to move.

This is the phase of empowerment. Women have been taught to emulate the external power of men. Masculine power is power over others. It is such a strong, motivating force in the masculine world that it often rules men's lives. Women usually do not strive to have power over other individuals; their motivation for empowerment derives from a desire to have control over their own lives—to keep from being disempowered by others.

When women are left to their own methods they will use their power for cooperation, consensus, and mediation. Their skills have been devalued by negative connotations, such as "women's wiles" and "manipulation." Women, too, have been taught to be ashamed of their indirect, influencing abilities by this constant derision. But the ability to exert one's will gently, without the need for credit or glory, comes from a place of strength, not weakness. It is the subtle, yielding power heralded in Aikido and some of the other Oriental arts.

At the present time, women are not acknowledged for having their own ways of dealing with masculine tasks. For example, whereas men often work on a singular task, undistracted until they reach completion, women find it easier to work in cycles, rotating their energies among several tasks, in a natural, feminine manner. Rarely having had the luxury of experiencing uninterrupted time of their own, women have learned to work around distractions. These breaks serve a creative function; they provide frequent opportunities for incubation and re-organization, and allow women to tap deeper layers of their intuitive knowledge. Unfortunately, this work style is viewed as "scattered" and "unfocused," even by the very women who work best in this way.

Therapists can support women to trust their intuitive judgment and help them go into the masculine world and implement their goals in their own way. By integrating their feminine knowing with their masculine assertiveness and goal-orientation, women are able to develop their own kind of power, a power that is unique to them and not an imitation of the male model.

In the next phase, women face a form of their own death and experience a spiritual rebirth. Preparation is needed for this intense task. Women need to develop in their own ways such masculine strengths as courage, goal-direction, determination, and ego. Ego, as Jung (1964/1982) describes it, is knowing what one wants and how to get it. It is necessary to have developed a strong sense of self and ego before embarking on the phase of spiritual development.

SPIRITUAL DEVELOPMENT

Psyche's third task is even more terrifying. She must go to the very center of the waterfall of the river Styx, which is physically inaccessible and guarded by monsters. Styx is the goddess of everything—the giver of death and rebirth. At this river, Psyche must fill a crystal goblet. An eagle, a symbol of spiritual intuition, appears and helps her. He dives into the depths of the waterfall (representing the unconscious), procuring the water for her.

This is a process of disintegration and rebirth. Women begin to experience themselves as dying during this stage, and, indeed, an old part of them is dying. They are letting go of an old way of life; they have stopped externalizing and begin to experience their own internal life. They can now value the unique feminine. When this process is over, even though it seems interminable at the time, they actually experience themselves as someone different. Through this phase of development, women gain the ability to go directly to the heart of an issue and return with astonishing wisdom. This is also the phase in which they develop the healing or spiritual abilities of the feminine.

Some degree of integration of the last two phases of development—acknowledgment of the feminine with integration of the masculine—must be achieved before a woman can approach this extremely intro-verted, intuitive process. Without enough development of the self and the will, entering this stage can be destructive. Women must first be grounded in their feelings and have their feminine powers integrated with their masculine reasoning abilities before they descend into this innermost place.

Power issues, both external interpersonal power and personal power, are being dealt with at this time. This type of power frightens people. Women must conquer their fear of being criticized or abandoned, since men are especially threatened by this deeper spiritual awareness.

> Yet a word that jumps out . . . is missing in . . . every article I've read on the subject. The word is FEAR. Is it possible our own unique strength has been held down by the superior physical strength in men over the ages, because men have been afraid?

> Afraid not that we will become more masculine—as the anti-feminist jargon goes—but that we will "become more feminine"? Is the archetypal woman subjugated by the archetypal man, not because she is weak, but because she is potentially so strong? (Lamm, 1984)

Ideally, feminist therapists will have experienced their own spiritual transformation before guiding other women through this phase of development. Therapists cannot take anyone where they have not been themselves (Jung, 1954). Evaluation of clients' ego strength is necessary before encouraging them into the spiritual phase.

This is a time of mourning for the younger, more naïve self that can never be again. The wisdom gained with awareness brings with it a deep sense of sadness for oneself, one's loved ones and the world. The therapist can comfort her client by understanding her need to mourn and being with her in the process. If the client has not already done body work, this would be an appropriate time to begin. Body work facilitates grounding and connection with sexual and spiritual energies, and releases painful memories stored in the body. With this grounding she can learn to speak from her own feminine reality while at the same time being aware of the masculine perspective (Woodman, 1985).

INTEGRATION

The fourth task Venus requires of Psyche is to go to the Underworld and obtain a cask of ointments. She is ready to throw herself from a tower, when the tower speaks to her. The tower (a symbol of the Great Mother) gives Psyche specific instructions for going to and from the Underworld. She must carry two coins in her mouth for Charon, the ferryman, who is to transport her across the river, Styx. She must also carry a loaf of bread in each hand to distract the two-headed dog Cerberus, who guards the entrance to Hades.

With the coins in her mouth, and the bread in her hands, Psyche begins her journey. She meets a beggar in need. This is the first test. She must not help him. She must keep her feminine generosity for her own self. This is the creative no. When she encounters the women weavers of fate, she cannot stop to talk, plan, and help others achieve their life plans.

The ferryman takes the coin from her mouth and ferries her across the Styx. A dying man reaches his arm out of the water to be saved. She cannot support an old, dying way of life or she will be stuck in her journey. She diverts Cerberus with the bread, and successfully obtains the cask of ointments.

It is important to understand the significance of the ointments. In the original myth, the purpose of the ointments was somewhat ambiguous. In the masculinized versions that began with Apuleius (second century, A.D.), this cask was said to contain "beauty" ointments (von Franz, 1980). Yet, no woman would spend years in self-exploration, pain and suffering to retrieve a box of beauty ointments. The fourth task of Psyche makes more sense from a feminine perspective if the cask is understood to contain *healing* ointments.

It is the task of the feminine to heal the wounds of a world disfigured by man's lack of awareness of the sacredness of nature. Psyche's integration of feminine and masculine energies in this last task is a symbol of their integration in the world. It is the magnitude of her responsibility that gives Psyche the courage to face this last set of dangers.

The goals of feminine development are for women to become healers and teachers. When they are absorbed in the lives of those closest to them, they do not have the time or energy to devote to larger purposes.

Through their evolution, the scope of their caring broadens until it embraces everyone and everything. This greater awareness cannot be denied; there is no way to not know what one knows. And the knowledge brings with it a responsibility to a greater cause—to the plight of humanity itself.

Psyche had to abandon her feminine generosity, and inclination to nurture and care for the ill and needy, because something more important was at stake. There could be no hesitation; had she hesitated, her mission would have failed. She had to have the resources to pay the ferryman, and the fortitude to stay out of the lives of others, and let them make their own mistakes.

Not many women are capable of, or willing to, encounter this last developmental task. It requires that a woman allow her family and loved ones to experience and manage their own lives. This is very difficult for the people she loves as well as for herself. However, this task is necessary in order for her to follow her own path in life. Fortunately, once this task has been accomplished, and she has learned to nurture herself as well as others (Gilligan, 1982), she will be more discriminating in the use of her natural generosity. She will also have the energy to contribute her wisdom to the culture. This is a marvelous resource which has previously gone untapped.

This developmental phase is reserved for middle or later life—an important opportunity for older women. They have acquired the wisdom that age brings to women. They know that if they begin to follow their own paths there is no turning back. We may look to actualized, older women for role models of those who have acknowledged their feminine truths, integrated them with their masculine skills, become autonomous and individuated, yet remained connected to others in a mystically feminine way.

Few women have actualized their potential, but studying the lives of those who have, such as Eleanor Roosevelt (Piechowski & Tyska, 1982), gives us some indication of the requisites. Eleanor had courage, depth, and commitment, as well as high intelligence. A lonely gifted girl, from early childhood, she exerted her will to conquer numerous fears, physical awkwardness, fatigue, depression, and loss of love (Piechowski, 1986). In the latter part of her life, she dedicated herself to furthering human rights and peace. She experienced severe losses and went through many periods of personal transformation. She rose above the ridicule and the prejudice of a culture that had no room for women's wisdom. It is such gifted women who give us the prophecy of the future. They pave the way for the evolution of society as a whole.

CONCLUSION

These developmental phases comprise a complete cycle of women's development; however, the phases need not be completed in a linear fashion. The process is cyclical, continually spiraling to deeper and deeper levels of awareness as a lifelong process. Each time a woman faces a crisis, she may revisit earlier phases in her development, gaining new insights. The evolving woman brings new wisdom to consciousness and contributes to the evolution of the entire culture.

In *The Sane Alternative,* James Roberts (1978) discusses the evolutionary leap our culture is experiencing. He is a proponent of the SHE future: Sane, Humane, Ecological.

When an individual or group first provides a synthesis able to attract most of the next generation, the older schools gradually disappear. In general, the paradigm shifts associated with the transition to the SHE future will reflect a shift of emphasis away from the overdeveloped, structured, exterior aspects of life towards the underdeveloped, unstructured, interior aspects. (p. 80)

What we see as the emerging consciousness of the developmental processes of women is being reflected in society as a macrocosm. "The woman of today is faced with a tremendous cultural task—perhaps it will be the dawn of a new era" (Jung, 1964/1982, p. 75). Tomorrow we will not lose the Ednas of the world.

REFERENCES

American Psychiatric Association. (1980). *Diagnostic and statistical manual of mental disorders* (3rd ed.). Washington, DC: Author.

American Psychological Association Task Force on Sex Bias and Sex-Role Stereotyping in Psychotherapeutic Practice. (1978). *American Psychologist, 13,* 1122–1123.

Brickman, J. (1984). Feminist, nonsexist, and traditional models of therapy: Implications for working with incest. *Women & Therapy, 3,* 49–67.

Burch, B. (1985). Another perspective on merger in lesbian relationships. In L. B. Rosewater & L. E. A. Walker (Eds.), *Handbook of feminist therapy: Women's issues in psychotherapy* (pp. 100–109). New York: Springer.

Cherry, L. (1975). The preschool teacher–child dyad: Sex differences in verbal interaction. *Child Development, 46,* 532–535.

Chodorow, N. (1978). *The reproduction of mothering: Psychoanalysis and the sociology of gender.* Berkeley, CA: University of California Press.

Chopin, K.O. (1899/1972). *The awakening.* New York: Avon.

Clance, P. (1985). *The imposter phenomenon.* Atlanta: Peachtree.

Culley, M. (Ed.). (1976). *Kate Chopin: The awakening. An authoritative text, contexts, criticisms.* New York: Norton.

Dabrowski, K. (1964). *Positive disintegration.* London: Gryf.

Darwin, C. R. (1859). *The origin of the species by means of natural selection.* London: Murray.

Darwin, C. R. (1871). *The descent of man and selection in relation to sex.* London: Murray (New York: D. Appleton & Co., rev. ed., 1897).

Downing, C. (1981). *The goddess: Mythological images of the feminine.* New York: Crossroad.

Dulit, E. (1972). Adolescent thinking a la Piaget: The formal stage. *Journal of Youth & Adolescence, 1,* 291–301.

Dweck, C. S., & Bush, C. S. (1976). Sex differences in learned helplessness: I. Differential debilitation with peer and adult evaluators. *Developmental Psychology, 12,* 147–156.

Dweck, C. S., Davidson, W., Nelson, S., & Enna, B. (1978). Sex differences in learned helplessness: II. The contingencies of evaluative feedback in the classroom, and III. An experimental analysis. *Developmental Psychology, 14,* 268–276.

Eichenbaum, L., & Orbach, S. (1982). *Understanding women: A feminist psychoanalytic approach.* New York: Basic Books.

Eichenbaum, L., & Orbach, S. (1983). *What do women want: Exploding the myth of dependency.* New York: Berkley Books.

Erikson, E. H. (1968). *Identity: Youth and crisis.* New York: Norton.

Firestone, S. (1970). *The dialectic of sex: The case for feminist revolution.* New York: Bantam.

Freud, S. (1925). Three contributions to the sexual theory. *Nervous and Mental Disease Monograph Series,* No. 7. New York: Nervous & Mental Disease Publishing Co.

Frey, K. S. (1979, March). *Differential teaching methods used with girls and boys of moderate and high achievement levels.* Paper presented at the Society for Research in Child Development, San Francisco.

Friedan, B. (1963). *The feminine mystique.* New York: Dell.

Galton, F. (1869). *Hereditary genius: An inquiry into its laws and consequences.* London (New York: D. Appleton & Co., 1870).

Gilligan, C. (1979). Woman's place in man's life cycle. *Harvard Educational Review, 49,* 431–446.

Gilligan, C. (1982). *In a different voice: Psychological theory and women's development.* Cambridge, MA: Harvard University Press.

Giovacchini, P. L. (1978). The psychoanalytic treatment of the alienated patient. In J. F. Masterson (Ed.), *New perspectives of the borderline adult* (pp. 1–19). New York: Brunner/Mazel.

Greenspan, M. (1983). *A new approach to women and therapy.* New York: McGraw-Hill.

Hall, G. S. (1916). *Adolescence* (2 vols.). New York: Appleton.

Holden, C. (1986, January 24). Proposed new psychiatric diagnoses raise charges of gender bias. *Science, 231,* 327–328.

Jung, C. G. (1923). *Psychological types. The collected works of C. G. Jung* (Vol. 6). (R. F. C. Hull, trans.). New York: Bollingen Foundation.

Jung, C. G. (1954). Marriage as a psychological relationship. *The development of personality. The collected works of C. G. Jung* (Vol. 17). (R. F. C. Hull, trans.). New York: Bollingen Foundation.

Jung, C. G. (1964/1982). Women in Europe. *Civilization in transition. The collected works of C. G. Jung* (Vol. 10). New York: Bollingen Foundation (as quoted in C. G. Jung, *Aspects of the feminine,* R. F. C. Hull, trans.; Princeton, NJ: Princeton University Press).

Kaplan, A. G., & Surrey, J. L. (1984). The relational self in women: Developmental theory and public policy. In L. E. Walker (Ed.), *Women and mental health policy* (pp. 79–94). Beverly Hills, CA: Sage.

Kernberg, O. (1975). *Borderline conditions and pathological narcissism.* New York: Aronson.

Kernberg, O. (1978). Contrasting approaches to the psychotherapy of borderline conditions. In J. F. Masterson (Ed.), *New perspectives of the borderline adult* (pp. 75–104). New York: Brunner/Mazel.

Kohlberg, L. (1964). Development of moral character and moral ideology. In M. L. Hoffman, & L. W. Hoffman (Eds.), *Review of Child Development Research* (Vol. 1, pp. 383–431). New York: Sage.

Kohlberg, L., & Kramer, R. (1969). Continuities and discontinuities in child and adult moral development. *Human Development, 12,* 93–120.

Lamm, D. (1984, August 26). Why do strong women threaten men? *Sunday Denver Post.*

Lysy, K. Z., & Piechowski, M. M. (1983). Personal growth: An empirical study using Jungian and Dabrowskian measures. *Genetic Psychology Monographs, 108,* 267–320.

Mahler, M. S., Pine, F., & Bergman, A. (1975). *The psychological birth of the human infant: Symbiosis and individuation.* New York: Basic Books.

Maslow, A. H. (1962). *Toward a psychology of being.* Princeton, NJ: Van Nostrand.

Masterson, J. F. (1976). *Psychotherapy of the borderline adult: A developmental approach.* New York: Brunner/Mazel.

Masterson, J. F. (1978). The borderline adult: Transference acting-out and working-through. In J. F. Masterson (Ed.), *New perspectives on psychotherapy of the borderline adult* (pp. 121–147). New York: Brunner/Mazel.

Miller, A. (1979). *The drama of the gifted child,* (R. Ward, trans.). New York: Basic Books.

Millett, K. (1970). *Sexual politics.* Garden City, NY: Doubleday.

Muus, R. E. (1975). *Theories of adolescence* (3rd ed.). New York: Random House.

Perry, S. (1986). Personal communication, February 7.

Piaget, J. (1932/1948). *The moral judgment of the child* (M. Gabain, trans.) New York: Free Press.

Piaget, J. (1950). *La psychologie de l'intelligence* (The psychology of intelligence; M. Piercy & D. E. Berlyne, trans.). London: Routledge & Kegan Paul.

Piaget, J. (1972). Intellectual evolution from adolescence to adulthood. *Human Development, 15,* 1–12.

Piechowski, M. M. (1975). Developmental potential. In N. Colangelo & R. T. Zaffrann (Eds.), *New voices in counseling the gifted* (pp. 25–57). Dubuque, IA: Kendall Hunt.

Piechowski, M. M. (1986). The concept of developmental potential. *Roeper Review, 8,* 190–197.

Piechowski, M. M., & Tyska, C. (1982). Self-actualization profile of Eleanor Roosevelt, a presumed nontranscender. *Genetic Psychology Monographs, 105,* 95–153.

Rawlings, E. I., & Carter, D. K. (Eds.). (1977). *Psychotherapy for women: Treatment toward equality.* Springfield, IL: Charles C. Thomas.

Roberts, J. (1978). *The sane alternative: A choice of futures.* St. Paul, MN: River Basin.

Rousseau, J. J. (1780/1911). *Emile* (W. H. Payne, trans.). New York: Appleton.

Rubin, L. (1983). *Intimate strangers: Men and women together.* New York: Harper & Row.

Searles, H. F. (1978). Psychoanalytic therapy with the borderline adult: Some principles concerning technique. In J. F. Masterson (Ed.), *New perspectives on psychotherapy of the borderline adult* (pp. 41–65). New York: Brunner/Mazel.

Sears, P., & Feldman, D. H. (1966). Teachers' interactions with boys and girls. *National Elementary Principal, 46,* 30–35.

Silverman, L. K. (1983). Personality development: The pursuit of excellence. *Journal for the Education of the Gifted, 6,* 5–19.

Silverman, L. K. (1986). What happens to the gifted girl? In C. J. Maker (Ed.), *Critical issues in gifted education, Vol. 1: Defensible programs for the gifted.* (pp. 43–89). Rockville, MD: Aspen.

Silverman, L. K., & Ellsworth, B. (1980). The theory of positive disintegration and its implications for giftedness. In N. Duda (Ed.), *Theory of positive disintegration: Proceedings of the third international conference.* Miami: University of Miami School of Medicine.

Sturdivant, S. (1980). *Therapy with women: A feminist philosophy of treatment.* New York: Springer.

Taube, S. S. (in preparation). *Who wrote this script? A woman's journey to self.*

Terman, L. M. (1916). *The measurement of intelligence.* Boston: Houghton Mifflin.

Terman, L. M., & Oden, M. H. (1959). *Genetic studies of genius: Vol. 5. The gifted group at midlife.* Stanford, CA: Stanford University Press.

Thorndike, E. L. (1910). *Educational psychology.* New York: Appleton.

Ulanov, A. B. (1971). *The feminine in Jungian psychology and in Christian theology.* Evanston, IL: Northwestern University Press.

von Franz, M. L. (1980). *A psychological interpretation of the Golden Ass of Apuleius, with the tale of Eros and Psyche.* Irving, TX: Spring Publications.

Van Gelder, L. (1984, January). Carol Gilligan: Leader for a different kind of future. *Ms. 12*(7), 37–40, 101.

Walker, L. E. A. (1984). Introduction. In L. E. A. Walker (Ed.), *Women and mental health policy* (pp. 7–19). Beverly Hills, CA: Sage.

Woodman, M. (1985). *The pregnant virgin.* Toronto: Inner City Books.

CHAPTER 4

Feminist Psychodynamic Therapies

Cynthia Daugherty
Marty Lees

An assumption inherent in this chapter is that theories of human behavior must be viewed as serving the function of explaining and defining the status quo. This assumption is important because it means that one must have some awareness of the sociocultural environment to appreciate the intent of any proposed model of human behavior. Throughout the literature review, readers are invited to explore in their own minds what each theoretical presentation was attempting to explain, justify, or to control.

The concept of evolution is another assumption that has guided this chapter. The most radical idea to be presented and supported is that feminist theories are a natural evolution of ideas presented in the original work of Freud. The evolution has resulted from, and is a reflection of, continued cultural evolution of the definition of what gives meaning to life. The industrial revolution of the 19th century gave way to the world wars, the Vietnamese war, and a technical/ electronic computer revolution. The role and status of women and children have changed. In the Western world, there are now single-parent families, blended families, and phenomenal numbers of divorce and remarriage. Birth control has been a major revolution. All of this is to say that what gives people meaning in life has changed. These changes have had a profound influence upon the field of psychotherapy and the definition of current treatment.

What this chapter will present is a review of Freud's original work defining psychodynamic therapy. Theorists who have evolved, advanced, and expanded Freud's concepts will be reviewed. The review section will conclude with descriptions of current feminist psychodynamic theories. Treatment techniques and outcome goals will be discussed. There will then be a discussion of conflicts and compatibilities between original psychodynamic theory and reformulated psychodynamic theory. A feminist model of psychodynamic theory will then be presented. The hope is that readers will come to share in the perspective that feminist psychodynamic therapies are a natural and logical evolution of the concepts originated by Freud.

EVOLUTION OF PSYCHODYNAMIC THEORY

Content of Theory

When Freud was 3 years old, the publication of the *Origin of Species* established that humans could become the object of scientific study. When Freud was 4 years old, Fechner founded the science of psychology. In the mid 1800s, Von Helmholz stated that energy is a quantity that could be transformed but not destroyed. While in medical school, Freud worked in the laboratory of Bruche, a great physiologist, who discovered the human organism to be a dynamic system amenable to the laws of physics and chemistry. Freud was a scientist, a logician, and a philosopher who applied dynamic principles of physics to mental processes. He developed a dynamic psychology that studied the transformation and exchange of energy within the personality (Hall, 1954).

Freud's ability to conceptualize about human behavior and to then apply those concepts to treatment has had a profound influence upon society. Freud constructed a comprehensive theory about human behavior to provide a framework for viewing and treating adult disorders of the psyche. The theory encompassed concepts of the unconscious, innate bisexuality, identification of a developmental process that revealed the unfolding of mental life, and a theory of causal factors in childhood leading to both normal and abnormal adult behaviors. His theory identified techniques for therapy as well as outcome goals. Freud's scientific data came from observation of self, intense introspection, and creative thought. A review of his work provides evidence of his own evolution of thought in attempting to construct a logically consistent theory.

The unconscious had central significance in Freud's psychodynamic theory (1900). Freud's study of symptoms led him to believe in the existence of dynamic forces operating in unconscious mental life. The subjective experience of anxiety was perceived to be the result of conflict among opposing forces. Freud believed that the uncovering of unknown forces in the unconscious would allow resolution of early childhood conflicts that would result in symptom reduction. The process could occur in the context of a therapeutic relationship in adult life.

Freud (1923) conceived of the human psyche as having three parts held in fluid dynamic equilibrium; the id, the ego, and the superego. Behavior was motivated by two groups of instincts: those in the service of life and those in the service of death (Hall, 1954, p. 58). These instincts resided in the id but were expressed through the work of the ego and the superego. The ego developed to obtain satisfaction of bodily needs and to protect and sustain life. The superego developed with the internalization of parental prohibitions. The ego and the superego were developed by displacement of id energies. The capacity for redistribution of psychic energy allowed for the development of personality. Individual differences, interests, attitudes, and values resulted from variations in the displacement and transformation of psychic energies.

Anxiety had an important role in the development and maintenance of a psychodynamic system. A primary ego function was to deal with anxiety that signaled intrapsychic conflict or external danger. The ego could master danger with "realistic problem solving methods" or it could use "methods that distort, deny, or falsify reality" (Hall, 1954, p. 85). These latter methods were called defense mechanisms. Defense mechanisms rendered the drives and conflicts unconscious, precluding their direct expression or conscious awareness. A compromise form of expression appeared in an indirect or disguised form known as a symptom which was viewed by the self or others as an unacceptable behavior pattern or character trait. Defense mechanisms impeded healthy ego development by consuming psychic energy needed for investment in growth-oriented pursuits. They simultaneously protected the developing ego from being overwhelmed by anxiety. The avoidance of anxiety led to the dual development of defenses and adaptive functioning.

Freud (1923, 1933a) identified three primary erogenous zones: the mouth, the anus, and the genitals. Each of these zones was associated with the satisfaction of a life need: the mouth with eating, the anus with elimination, and the genitals with reproduction. These zones were believed to be instrumental in personality development because they provided the infant with the initial experiences of irritation, excitation, and stimulation. These experiences also represented the child's first awareness of its ability to seek pleasure and to avoid pain. Freud outlined stages of psychosexual development calling them oral, anal, phallic, latency, and genital stages.

As the child progressed through these stages, the primary investment of psychic energy was focused on the erogenous zone commensurate with the child's developmental level. The child's ability to master bodily functions paralleled an increasing ability to neutralize and modulate strong libidinal and aggressive strivings. The uniqueness of each individual was attributed to the combination and interaction of primitive instincts, biological needs, ego strengths, and conflict resolution patterns during each of the psychosexual stages.

The oedipus complex of the phallic stage has received much attention. What made the oedipus complex so important was the belief that its resolution allowed the child to assume an appropriate heterosexual gender role (Freud, 1925, 1931, 1933a). Prior to the oedipus stage, Freud believed both male and female infants to be bisexual, meaning they inherited the tendencies of the opposite sex as well as those of their own sex. According to theory, both female and male children had to sever their primary attachment to their mother. This detachment process was postulated as being different for boys and girls, but similar in the sense that the focus was on the penis. The primary difference in the detachment process was described as resulting from fear of castration experienced by the males and envy of the penis experienced by the female child (Freud, 1925). For the boy, castration anxiety resulted in relinquishment of oedipal wishes for his mother and identification with his father.

For the girl, penis envy (her counterpart to fear of castration) connoted the beginning of her oedipal desires for her father. At around the age of 3, the female discovered her lack of a penis. She felt she had been deprived and possibly castrated by her mother, who herself lacked a penis. The daughter felt anger and fear toward her mother and turned away from her. The young girl ultimately replaced her wish for a penis with a wish for a boy baby. She then recognized that only males (fathers) could become love objects and provide her with a baby. She then began emulating her mother's behavior to learn how to have a husband and a child.

Castration fear was perceived to be a more severe subjective experience than penis envy. Castration fear motivated complete abandonment of oedipal desires. The oedipal resolution for girls was considered incomplete because the girl had no anxiety as strong as castration anxiety motivating her to relinquish her oedipal desires for her father. The incomplete resolution for girls resulted in psychic energies remaining bound up in oedipal conflict. Some psychic energy was therefore unavailable for further development of the superego and resulted in adult traits of passivity, masochism, and narcissism in women.

The latency stage was characterized by the lack of overt sexual and aggressive impulses. Children during this period were internalizing and identifying with parental prohibitions and societal values while they consolidated personality formation. With the onset of puberty, physiological maturation resulted in the resurgence of sexual and aggressive drives. The opposite sex became attractive and sexual drives sought objects (other people) as their aim rather than the self as was the case in the pregenital period. The tasks of the genital period were to marry, reproduce, establish a home and a family, and, for men, to engage in a vocation that furthered the advancement of civilization. For women the tasks of the genital period were accomplished when they had given birth to and raised a son.

Freud's construction of such an expansive theory of mental life stimulated thought and controversy. There has been a shift in psychodynamic theory from an emphasis on drives and the mastery of instincts and bodily functions to a focus on development of ego, emotional relatedness, and the mastery of human relationships. Currently there is a resurgence of interest in the cultural/environmental contributions to the differential psychological development of men and women. A brief overview of the major psychodynamic theory since Freud's time will be presented to demonstrate the evolutional process leading to the more current description of psychodynamic theory.

A major expansion of Freud's theory came from the British school of object relations, represented by theorists such as M. Klein (1932), Fairbairn (1952), Winnicott (1965), and Guntrip (1964). Each of these theorists contributed significantly to the rethinking of Freud's work. The focus of study and theorizing was on the pre-oedipal period and its contribution to ego development and personality formation. Klein postulated that instincts sought objects (the word she used for internal images of people or parts of people) as their aim rather than seeking pleasure. For Klein, the development of the ego was the focus of psychic life and the center of personality. Fairbairn took Klein's ideas further and renounced Freud's notion of instincts. He postulated that the seeking of human relationship was the primary motivator of human behavior and the driving force of psychic development. Object relations theory examines how the maturing infant forms internal images of the self and others while simultaneously beginning to separate the image of the other (the caregiver).

In 1936, Anna Freud expanded and elaborated Freud's concept of defense mechanisms postulating that the ego had repression and at least nine other defenses at its disposal. Her expansion led the way for a major shift in analytic technique from strict adherence to uncovering of id content to observation of defensive functioning to learn about the ego's functioning.

Hartmann (1939) was foremost among theorists classified as ego psychologists who saw a need to broaden Freud's structural/drive theory to explain more adequately relatedness between self and others. Hartmann proposed that selected ego functions such as perception, intention, thinking, and language develop outside the sphere of conflict. Thus, ego development was no longer regarded as resulting only from conflict between the id and the superego. Psychoanalytic theory began to focus on normal development as well as pathology as theorists were better able to define additional aspects of the developmental process.

Other theorists such as Kris (1951), Hartmann, Kris, and Lowenstein (1964) and Jacobson (1964) extended Hartmann's concepts to provide a more complete understanding of the development of psychic structure. Spitz (1965) and Mahler, Pine, and Bergman (1975) used observational data obtained from mothers and infants to link scientifically psychoanalytic concepts to human development. Their research demonstrated the importance and the essential nature of the reciprocal interchange between infant and caregiver in normal and pathological development. Mahler et al. (1975) delineated a sequence of developmental phases from birth to 36 months that experientially described the infant–caregiver relationship as it proceded from symbiosis through separation and individuation.

Kernberg (1975) and Kohut (1971) studied the impact of the developmental process on the individual's sense of self. This work led to the area of psychodynamic study known as self psychology, which examines the developmental visissitudes of narcissism.

The ideas of more recent feminist psychodynamic thinkers were enriched by the influential writings related to women's role in society. As hypothesized earlier, the psychology of women in its evolutionary description reflects cultural trends and changes.

Simone de Beauvoir (1952), an existential philosopher, proposed that the notion of women as second-class citizens was caused by patriarchal, power issues rather than internal, feminine characteristics. She viewed all humans as striving for freedom and viewed culture as imposing women's inferior social status. Women were viewed as failing to take responsibility for what could be changed in society, resulting in destructive sexual relationships and social ills.

The cultural school, represented by Reich (1963), Thompson (1941), Horney (1967) and others addressed the impact of culture on psychic development. These were the first writers to bring a feminist perspective to psychoanalysis. Reich identified the psychological, political, and economic functions of the family and its negative impact on women's development and female sexuality. Horney developed a female psychology. She identified power or the lack of power as a primary motivator for women's behavior. Female masochism was viewed as the result of repressive subordinating cultural practices. Thompson challenged many of Freud's concepts about femininity. She refuted Freud's notion that women have weaker superegos. Thompson identified that for women, security and social status are derived from establishment of a permanent love relationship with a man. Obtaining such a relationship was a culturally imposed mandate necessary for women's survival. Thompson reformulated the concept of penis envy to be women's symbolic desire for power and prestige.

Friedan (1965), Greer (1971), Firestone (1970), and Millett (1970) all challenged Freud's notions of penis envy and women's natural inferior status. Friedan and Greer were popular authors who brought to the public the first questioning of Freud's views of female psychology. When these authors addressed the lack of fit between Freud's theories and current culture, they became the theoretical founders of the women's liberation movement and offered justification for women's anger at feeling oppressed. These women said that to be human would be to be angry at male oppression. Culturally imposed sex roles were viewed as oppressive and resulted in much of what was defined as "pathology" in women.

Two major pieces of research introduced sex role theory into clinical application. Chesler (1972) provided data demonstrating that women were labeled "crazy" if they did not comply with patriarchal standards of women as caretakers and nurturers of men. She also demonstrated that women's freedom was even more limited if they questioned the validity of patriarchal norms of husbands and mental health professionals. Broverman, Broverman, Rosenkranz, and Vogel (1970) researched the attitudes of mental health professionals toward ideal characteristics of male and female clients. Their conclusion was that mental health professionals tried to mold women into patterns of behavior that even the professionals did not regard as healthy for adults.

The radical therapy movement, as exemplified by Wyckoff (1977), made a firm stand against the authoritarianism of traditional therapy relationships. The intrapsychic arena was discounted as a source of conflict. Her view of the therapist's role was that if the therapist was neutral, the therapist patronized the client and did not acknowledge environmental factors in creating conflict. Therapy was thus a re-creation of society's oppression of women. In Wyckoff's treatment model, the therapist was to be actively involved with the client and to join with the client in efforts to overthrow oppressive institutions. The affirmation of the oppression was regarded as the primary healing technique through validation of the client's personal experience of living. Wyckoff made a significant contribution to feminist therapy in challenging the techniques of treatment and calling into question the ethical issues of the therapist's role in deciding the focus of treatment.

Mitchell (1974) and Chodorow (1978) are considered current feminist psychodynamic theorists. They both embrace the psychodynamic concept of the oedipus complex as being explanatory of female development and gender identity. Mitchell believes that feminists have to understand Freudian concepts thoroughly and their relationship to the extended history of patriarchy in order for women to change their status in society. She views the female adoption of patriarchal norms as a natural consequence of the father's role in the oedipal triangle. The father represents information outside the mother–infant symbiosis. To separate from the caregiver, to continue psychological growth, and to participate in society, the child must adopt the patriarchal norms. Mitchell believes that patriarchy is not necessary for society's continuation and women no longer need to be the primary caretakers of infants. Mitchell's contribution is a reframing of the oedipal resolution.

Chodorow (1978) focuses on the oedipus complex as being the time when children resolve their gender identity. She believes Freud's description of the female resolution of the oedipus complex was male-biased. Chodorow provides a positive connotation to the female resolution. The girl's ability to maintain her attachment and identification with her mother results in the desirable characteristics of empathy and connectedness. She points out that male children must continually defend against their attachment to their mothers to fulfill the societal norms of masculinity. This results in male children learning to devalue feminine characteristics out of fear of their own dependent longings. Although male privilege is seen as desirable by both male and female children, girl children learn that they receive more societal reinforcement and attention for nurturing others (including their mothers) rather than addressing their own needs. Frustration related to fulfillment of these culturally determined sex roles creates the intrapsychic process that leads to women's fear of independence and men's fear of connectedness. Women's experiences of having participated in closer relational bonds with their mothers results in more complex relational needs and abilities. The role of mothering provides a re-creation of the early childhood experience of emotional distances; that is the mother–child relationship is closer, nurturing and gratifying, and the male (father)–child distance is further away. Fathers and males become idealized. Because women are the primary caretakers of children, stereotypical role behaviors are communicated to the children in the caretaker's efforts to be involved in close relationships.

Dinnerstein (1976) focuses on the preverbal phase of development as contributing to the differential outcomes of the oedipal resolution. Because women are the primary infant caregivers, women are identified with the initial experiences of frustration as well as the source of all goodness. Women are then internalized in a "chaotic pre-rational image" that includes the all-giving and the frustrating aspects of motherhood

(p. 250). The adult experience of this is to be fearful of the power of women. The male role defends against this power or fear by denying emotionality and embracing mechanistic rationality. The female role defends by colluding with the fear and supporting the men in their role. Women then avoid taking the responsibility and the risks involved in defining and running the world. Dinnerstein believes that characteristic female attributes of caring, expressiveness, and humanistic values must begin contributing to world making decisions because the male, mechanistic way will lead to the destruction of humanity. She hypothesizes that if men were providing care for infants, there would not be the internalized fear of women's power and women could contribute to world making decisions.

Miller (1976) explores the effects of having dominant subordinate roles in male and female relationships. Women carry the role of affiliation and do not achieve and enhance themselves. Men carry the role of self-enhancement and do not acknowledge emotional connectedness to others. Women give and sacrifice, anticipating that they will get their rewards in the end. However, because women do not have any power in this dominant–subordinate system, the women receive no rewards. Their options are limited, as is the ability to risk and to practice self-directed behavior. The dominant–subordinate roles are detrimental because neither males or females can become complete and authentic. Treatment goals as defined by Miller are that all people experience personal power without having power over others and that all people can serve others without being subservient.

The primary contribution of Gilligan's (1982) research is the inclusion of the women's "voice" and mode of thought to the theory of moral development. A complete theory of humanness and the ability to relate to others can be developed when the women's voice is included. She asserts that women's concerns about others is a strength to be valued in the decision-making process. She states that the complication for women in their personal development results from society's view that although goodness and caring are virtues, they are not rewarded with the measures of success (money, prestige). This devaluation of goodness places women in the bind of having to choose between what is morally right for them and what will be perceived as adult and successful. On a cultural level, the societal loss of the women's voice results in men carrying all the aggression with no modulation by the caring connected aspects of relationship.

Lerner (1980, 1982, 1983) writes about many facets of the treatment of women, including separation/attachment issues, client–therapist relationships, male/female roles, and stereotypical feminine qualities, such as anger and dependency. Lerner describes women's reluctance to verbalize anger to be a result of traditional affiliative role behavior. Women experience anger as separation and isolation. Lerner discusses the nonfeminist therapist's difficulties in seeing beyond proscribed displays of passive dependent behaviors to assess accurately the level of autonomy that women clients have achieved. The passive dependent stance is redefined as protective of love relationships. Lerner is respectful of the very real cost in terms of loss of traditional security in relationships if women choose to exercise their options for growth and authenticity. Lerner does remind clinicians that "the internal press toward growth is always more powerful than the wish to remain a dysfunctional child . . ." (1983, p. 702) and brings an optimistic note to the descriptions of female psychology and experiences.

Eichenbaum and Orbach (1983) contribute a comprehensive psychoanalytic view of the development of femininity as well as a descriptive explanation of techniques of psychoanalytic therapy with women. They concur with Freud that women are viewed as inferior, but they understand this to be a consequence of being raised a daughter in a patriarchal society. The mother–daughter relationship is viewed as the primary training ground for fostering the culturally desirable traits of nurturing others, self-denial and sacrifice. The mother's ambivalence about these traits and her anger and envy at male privilege are communicated to the daughter through their mutual identification as females. The mother must participate in teaching the child to deny her needs as unimportant and bad as she assumes her role of deferring to the needs of others. The result is that the female child feels inferior to others. Eichenbaum and Orbach believe gender role behavior is learned. They describe the learning process as beginning at birth. In their treatment model, the focus becomes the uncovering and the recreation of the mother–daughter relationship allowing the female client to experience validity of her needs and wishes.

Traditional and historical psychodynamic theorists define the psychology of men as the norm and the psychology of women as it differs from the psychology of men. Feminist theorists are discovering facets of development for both men and women that have been incomplete. There is the excitement of discovery with the positive connotations that women are not defective males. The developing psychology of women can contribute to a more complete understanding of all individuals as differences continue to be explored.

Techniques of Therapy

Psychodynamic psychotherapy attempts to reduce anxiety, to remove symptoms, to change maladaptive behaviors and patterns, and to improve one's ability to relate to others. It attempts to achieve these goals by uncovering and exploring the traumatic memories and painful affects associated with childhood that develop into symptoms and psychological conflicts. Repression is thought to bury the original forces and to remove conflict from awareness. With knowledge, clients can choose more adaptive conflict resolution. Freud developed the process of free association as the basic technique for gaining access to unconscious material. The use of free association led Freud to discover two phenomena that occurred in the therapeutic process that became primary treatment concepts in psychodynamic psychotherapy. These phenomena are resistance and transference.

Freud thought resistance was the visible end product of the defense mechanism's effort to keep painful, anxiety-provoking memories out of conscious awareness. In the process of free association, these memories would threaten to emerge. The ego then reasserted its defensive efforts. Identifying and interpreting resistance and defense mechanisms in the therapy process allowed the therapist and the client to uncover memories and conflicts that contributed to symptomology and anxiety.

Freud identified transference as another unconscious defensive effort in the therapeutic process. He found that clients related and reacted to him with deep feelings and desires that ignored the reality of the therapeutic situation. Those feelings repeated or transferred the loves and hates of earlier relationships onto the therapist. The source of those transference feelings remained hidden from the client, who experienced them as genuine emotions directed toward the therapist.

Countertransference refers to the complimentary feelings evoked in the therapist in response to the client. The therapist's awareness of her or his own subjective responses enables her or him to understand better and to interpret the client's transference issues. Countertransference is a vital tool of psychodynamic therapy.

Psychodynamic psychotherapies can be placed on a continuum of intensity and comprehensiveness. Psychoanalysis encourages the most intensity and results in the most comprehensive form of psychodynamic psychotherapy. Uncovering insight-oriented psychotherapy would be placed mid-range on the continuum. Supportive psychotherapy would be considered least intense.

Candidates for psychodynamic psychotherapy can also be placed on a continuum. Assessment of the client's psychodynamic structure determines the type of psychodynamic therapy most appropriate to meet the client's therapeutic need. Persons appropriate for both analysis and insight-oriented psychotherapy struggle with neurotic conflicts that encompass dyadic and triadic relationship issues of autonomy, competition, loss of approval or prestige, mastery, and achievement. Persons likely to benefit from insight-oriented therapy instead of psychoanalysis respond more effectively to a less intense and less regressive therapeutic process. Persons whose tolerance for anxiety and regression is limited, whose ability to delay gratification is minimal, and who have significant difficulty in relating to others need a supportive psychotherapeutic approach.

Psychoanalysis uses free association as the primary means of obtaining information to be analyzed. To foster free association, the analyst remains out of the client's view and offers limited verbal feedback. The associative process is disrupted by the analyst to ask questions that amplify or highlight resistance, or to clarify and confront recurrent attitudes, perceptions, or behavior patterns. When clarification has accurately identified the unconscious elements important in the client's symptoms and behaviors, these elements are presented through interpretations. The client must also have allowed defenses to relax enough that unconscious material can enter conscious awareness. Free association, clarification, confrontation and interpretation are the basic techniques used in analyzing resistance and transference in the analytic relationship. The intensity of the analytic relationship, regression, and affects are enhanced by having three to five analytic sessions per week. Variations and modifications of techniques originally developed for psychoanalysis are used in insight-oriented and supportive psychotherapy.

Clients in insight-oriented or supportive psychotherapy usually meet with the therapist once or twice a week in face-to-face dialogue. In insight-oriented therapy, interpretations are related to the patterns and underlying motivations of behavior. Transference is enhanced through attention to boundary issues. The therapist is more real and directive than in psychoanalysis but remains relatively neutral. The neutrality allows the client to use the therapy relationship to project, act out, and work through conflicts from the past and present. Free association and dream interpretation are used but less frequently than in psychoanalysis.

In supportive psychotherapy, few interpretations are made to the client. The content of the sessions has more of a problem-solving nature. The aim of supportive therapy is to strengthen defenses and to support the client's efforts to adapt and to interact effectively with the environment. Uncovering unconscious material to identify conflicts and to understand the unconscious motivations of behavior can be disruptive to clients who struggle with pre-oedipal issues of identity formation and separation from parental figures.

The therapeutic relationship has tremendous significance in the healing process of psychodynamic therapy. The client needs to feel understood and supported by the therapist. The treatment process involves the therapist's "lending ego" to the client during the regression that often occurs in the letting down of defenses. A major contribution by Freud was his effort to understand how the healing of early childhood conflicts can occur in the adult therapy relationship.

Outcome of Therapy

Traditional psychodynamic therapy focused on the intrapsychic conflict between the id and the superego. The desired outcome was that the ego function to mediate adequately between id, superego, and external forces. In psychoanalysis and insight-oriented psychotherapy, the exploration of the unconscious allowed original conflicts to become conscious and the client could then choose more satisfying behaviors for conflict resolution. In supportive psychotherapy, the goal was to strengthen defenses, to enable containment of basic drives, and to reduce the experience of conflict between primitive id impulses, superego prohibitions, and external forces.

CONFLICTS AND COMPATIBILITIES OF PSYCHODYNAMIC AND FEMINIST THEORY

Conflicts and Compatibilities of Theory Content

Freud's concept of the unconscious and its contribution to behavior, personality formation, and the therapeutic process is not disputed by a feminist psychodynamic perspective. Behavior is viewed as motivated to satisfy internal or external forces. Freud hypothesized that conflict between opposing forces or the imbalance between forces led to symptom formation. The "dynamic" part of psychotherapy addresses restructuring or rebalancing the oppositional forces.

Freud's structural divisions in mental life placed significant emphasis on instincts, drives, and conflict between internal forces. The feminist perspective places more emphasis on the functioning of the ego by examining its development from a cultural and interpersonal context as well as the intrapsychic context. External and cultural forces are seen as having a greater influence in creating conflict than in Freudian theory.

Freud identified instincts of sexuality and aggression as the primary motivators of behavior and their containment as the goal of mental life. Ego analytic and object relations schools of psychodynamic theory place less emphasis on the control and modulation of instinct. The seeking of relationships is viewed as the motivator of human behavior and the goal of mental life. The goal of satisfying relationships is more compatible with the feminist perspective.

Freud believed that the ego developed defense mechanisms to provide substitute gratification for id instincts and impulses. Feminist theorists expand Freud's original formulation and understand defenses as the ego's attempt not only to adapt to internal forces but also to external forces. The form of the defense mechanism is often societally imposed. For example, a prevalent symptom among women today is the eating disorder. The symptom defends against awareness or expression of underlying conflict most often connected to control issues in a relationship. The symptom is a caricature of a culturally imposed definition of women's beauty. Freud conceptualized symptoms as manifestations of inadequate defenses. Feminist theory would add that symptoms also present because of inadequate power or resources with which to resolve the underlying or overt conflicts. These conflicts can be as basic as having no validation of needs and desires.

Freud's concept of anxiety as the ego's way of signaling impending internal disequilibrium or external danger is not inconsistent with a feminist perspective. As noted earlier, feminist theorists recognize the significant cultural influences that lead to anxiety. Anxiety is not regarded as resulting primarily from internal conflicts.

Freud postulated that all people are born bisexual. He believed that appropriate resolution of the oedipus complex resulted in the acquisition of heterosexuality. Feminist thinkers have written extensively about the oedipus complex (Chodorow, 1978; Firestone, 1970; Horney, 1967; Mitchell, 1974; Thompson, 1964). These writers are in agreement that the notion of penis envy per se is inapplicable to women's development. There is relative agreement that women envy male privilege. The evolution of Freud's theory of development retains the concept of innate bisexuality. Feminist theorists propose, however, that gender identity originates much earlier in life than the oedipal period and is heavily influenced by the differential sex roles assigned to males and females in our culture.

The identification of sequential fixed stages of development leading to mastery of bodily functions and the ability to relate to others has remained constant in psychodynamic theory. It has been established by the object relations theorists that the ability to relate to others begins earlier than Freud postulated. Feminist psychodynamic thinkers expand the object relations viewpoint to describe internalized negative self-images for women as being culturally imposed. Those images are representative of the caregiver's experience (usually the mother) of being devalued by society (Chodorow, 1978; Dinnerstein, 1976; Eichenbaum & Orbach, 1983). This negative image is then communicated to the child.

Freud described women's primary character traits as passivity, masochism, and dependency. Feminist theorists have addressed these traits and differ with Freud's premise that these are innate traits. Feminist theorists describe these traits as culturally determined and developed in response to women being the subordinate population in society. These traits have positive connotations in the context of affiliation, nurturance, and male–female relationships. For example, women will appear dependent to preserve love relationships. Treatment and change of these patterns is often a goal of therapy. There is recognition that individual therapy cannot change society. However, reframing and identifying the source of conflict does change the individual experience which allows desired change to occur. Additionally, as women reclaim personal power and worth, societal change does follow.

The foundation of Freud's theory of female personality development was penis envy. He believed that penis envy resulted in the development of an inadequate superego. Women were viewed as unable to develop an internal sense of morals and ethics. Therefore, women could not control biological (sexual) needs and could not participate in important decisions. The concept of penis envy is male-oriented and has not proven to be valid in women's experience. Eichenbaum and Orbach (1983) note that breast envy would be a more logically consistent concept because infants usually have more contact with breasts than with penises. Horney (1967) raised the question of whether womb envy existed in men.

The concepts of Freud's early theory of female development which are incompatible with a feminist perspective, and are hypothesized to result from the female not having a penis are summed up as follows:

1. Female anatomy dictates destiny, for example, inferiority.
2. Women desire penises.
3. Female sexuality is solely related to reproduction with the goal of bearing a son.
4. Masochism, dependency, narcissism, and passivity are character traits resulting from normal female development.

A significant contribution by Freud was to identify the differential aspects of masculine and feminine development (1925, 1931, 1933b). However, rather than develop a completely unique psychology for women, Freud constructed a theory of female development based on what he believed were psychological consequences of anatomical differences between the sexes. His theory portrayed women as defective males. Women analysts of Freud's time (Horney, 1967) criticized Freud's view of women's development. As Freud continued his thinking and development of human psychology, he came to acknowledge the role of culture and socialization in fostering passivity and masochism (1933b, p. 76). Feminist theory has recognized the cost to men and humanity in not including women's traditional behaviors of caring and relationship consideration in the decision-making process (Dinnerstein, 1976; Gilligan, 1982; Miller, 1976).

Conflicts and Compatibilities of Techniques

Psychodynamic psychotherapies were discussed as being on a continuum of intensity and comprehensiveness. All use techniques evolved from original Freudian theory. Feminist therapists have addressed several issues and added some guidelines to the original techniques.

The radical therapy movement contributed in the area of the client–therapist relationship. Traditional psychoanalytic therapy was considered authoritarian and disrespectful of the client's knowledge of self. A more equalitarian relationship is considered consistent with feminist theory. The therapist informs the client of the process and techniques of therapy. The therapist respects the client as having expertise in defining the experience of her or his own conflict. When treatment is terminated, the client has the expertise and skills to resolve current and future conflicts.

The amount of self-disclosure by the therapist has been an issue in feminist therapy. Some feminist thinkers have regarded self-disclosure as a treatment technique to aid clients in depersonalizing negative internalizations of expected gender roles. A psychodynamic theory believes that the therapist's self-disclosure may rob the client of the opportunity to transfer on to the therapist issues that are present in the unconscious that contribute to conflict and symptom formation. However, it is essential that a feminist psychodynamic therapist identify and validate the negative psychological impact of the client's experience of living as a subordinate in a male-dominated, sexist society.

The APA Task Force on Sex Bias and Sex Role Stereotyping in Psychotherapy Practice (Brodsky, 1975) revealed that the psychoanalytic approach was perceived to be the most sexist of the therapeutic techniques. It was clear that all forms of psychotherapy and therapists that are less than knowledgeable about specific psychological processes and issues for women contribute to women receiving sex-biased treatment. These authors agree that classic psychoanalytic therapy is sexist and destructive to women. However, when modified, it can be nonsexist, feminist and an important catalyst for women's psychological growth.

Conflicts and Compatibilities of Outcome

Feminist theory does not take issue with the traditional psychodynamic goal of maximizing ego functioning. Feminist theory does disagree with the original description of how the superego is developed in women. In feminist theory, women are viewed as the primary source of superego for men by carrying the conscience. Men rely upon women to act on concerns for others and to be knowledgeable about the process of relationships and the "right" thing to do. Feminist thinkers view these qualities as needing to be shared by men and women and as innate potentials in all humans.

THEORY INTEGRATION AND NEW MODEL

Freud's process of psychodynamic therapy and many of its techniques are the foundations of the healing process in feminist therapy. The work in progress by current feminist psychodynamic theorists is an effort to identify and apply the concepts of the original theory that pertain to human development and the study of female psychology.

The proposed model of feminist psychodynamic therapy is evolving. It encompasses Freud's notion that personality unfolds from the dynamic interplay of internal/unconscious and external/conscious forces. External/cultural forces are strong determinants of behavior, which are internalized through the process of socialization. Because women are the primary caretakers (thus socializers) of children, the negative external/cultural images of women become internal and intrapsychic. Human behavior and development are motivated by one life force that impels humans to seek fulfillment and self-actualization in the context of relationships. The authors believe in the concept of the unconscious as containing a life force propelling growth and relationships. The unconscious also contains repressed conflicts of external demands and human needs and the individual's unique defense patterns used to ward off anxiety. The authors view the ego as the center of personality. The ego unfolds in the growth process and continues to expand its capabilities to mediate between internal and external demands. This is the evolving theory that guides the authors' model of feminist psychodynamic therapy.

The techniques for feminist psychodynamic therapy presented here attempt to incorporate the principles of feminist ideology with analytic technique. Strict adherence to classic analytic technique is relinquished. These authors do not see this as a violation of technique but rather as an evolutionary process that allows for expansion and development of psychodynamic therapy. The techniques representative of feminist ideology are:

1. The therapist conveys to the client her feminist values and orientation.
2. The goals of therapy are mutually determined.
3. There is respect for the client's knowledge of self and appreciation of the power differential between the therapist and the client.
4. The therapist identifies the cultural sources of the client's conflicts while maintaining awareness of the sociocultural barriers to self-enhancement. Financial constraints and loss of love relationships are examples of these barriers.
5. Demystification of the therapeutic process occurs through use of a mutually understood language (no jargon), sharing knowledge of the therapeutic process prior to a therapy contract, and, when appropriate, sharing literature germane to treatment issues.

The therapeutic relationship is the primary tool of the feminist psychodynamic model. Techniques are intended to enhance this relationship and to gain access to the determinants of the client's conflict. Techniques such as neutrality, parameter setting, clarification, interpretation of transference, etc., are useful only in the context of a positive therapeutic relationship and only when used in the appropriate phase of therapy. There is a progressive sequence in the therapy relationship that is characterized by varying amounts of trust and mistrust and dependence and independence. This progression is traditionally viewed in three parts as the beginning, the middle, and the termination phase of psychotherapy. In each of these phases, the tasks, quality, and intensity of the relationship changes, allowing the therapeutic process to unfold.

The beginning phase is characterized by the sharing of information. The therapist provides information about orientation, style, and the process of therapy. The client is asked to share reasons for seeking therapy. A beginning family and problem history is obtained with special focus on identifying the sex role constraints that interfere with the client's development and functioning. The feminist psychodynamic therapist is open, direct, and sincere while working with the client to identify and clarify the issues to be addressed in therapy. After one or more evaluation sessions, the therapist offers feedback consisting of the therapist's perception of the problem, focal issues, and the kind and process of therapy most likely to benefit the client. The client is encouraged to be an active participant in establishing a therapy contract with mutual goals and built-in treatment effectiveness measures. The beginning phase continues with a focus of identifying and resolving current problems while simultaneously establishing a therapeutic alliance. The therapeutic alliance will allow the client to feel there is an expert guide and companion through the psychological issues to be addressed. The beginning phase is oriented toward gathering and sharing information and developing a sense of trust in the context of a very important human relationship.

The middle phase can be characterized as being relationship focused. It is usually the longest in duration of the three phases. In the context of the relationship, the client works through the primary issues that interfere with self-satisfaction. "Working through" refers to the broad range of therapeutic exchanges that allow a client and therapist to experience, identify, and understand the client's issues and psychological barriers. These barriers emerge in a myriad of ways and need to be re-explored continuously in the therapeutic process. In this phase, the therapist may be less directive and more neutral to enhance transference of the client's early longings and unmet needs. This provides the client an opportunity to identify and work through conflictual material that was previously unconscious and contributing to psychological pain. The content of the child–caregiver relationship is the primary material of the transference. Virtually all the client's fears, needs, and conflicts become evident in the process of understanding and analyzing the transference. Dependence and independence are central issues in this phase. Through teaching, modeling, and analyzing transference and defenses, the therapist helps the client identify, express, and meet needs for caring and nurturance without sacrificing the boundary of a separate identity. In the middle phase, the client and the therapist explore in detail the client's internal and external relationship patterns through analyzing and understanding the therapy relationship.

The termination phase is characterized by mutual recognition that the work of therapy is nearing completion. The client's needs for support and help from the therapist decrease as the client understands and accepts her or his own needs as legitimate and worthwhile. The client's investment in the therapist and the relationship decreases with recognition of the boundaries of therapy. A natural progression of separation then follows. The client leaves therapy with understanding and acceptance of her or his own needs as well as awareness of the cultural impediments that hinder self-fulfillment.

There is recognition in feminist psychodynamic therapy that the therapeutic relationship mirrors the early child–caregiver relationship. The therapeutic relationship attempts reparation of unmet needs for nurturance and offers support for individual growth. A unique aspect of feminist therapy is that the therapist (mother figure) does not try to mold clients to gender roles. Feminist psychodynamic therapists recognize that all individuals have the same innate potentials. In the dual mother–therapist role, the therapist encourages the client to separate and to remain emotionally connected at the same time. The encouragement to grow can be more genuinely offered than with the mother because the therapist's self-identity does not hinge on the outcome of the client's development. The three phases of therapy offer a re-creation of the oral, anal, and genital phases as described by Freud; the taking in, the withholding, and the moving on to satisfying adult relationships.

There has been no one individual since Freud who has had such a profound impact upon thinking about human behavior. Much of Freud's theory has been adopted as gospel. This was particularly true of his early conceptualizations about female psychology. Because the theory affirmed that men were more able to make world decisions, men have been very reluctant to entertain notions about female psychology that differ from those of Freud. Patriarchy has been the modus operandi since long before the time of Christ. It is a fact of life that those in power do not surrender it easily. However, the very attributes that have been so denigrated, such as caring for others feelings, and morality, are the strengths that will bind women together and ultimately all humanity, to change the negative aspects of patriarchy.

The totality of Freud's theory is a theory of dynamic development, not a static description of women's personality traits. What is valuable is that Freud began a process of examining how gender roles are acquired.

A model that integrates a feminist perspective with psychodynamic theory is not yet complete. The authors believe that theories of human development are culturally determined. Accurate theories or descriptions of a culture can occur only after the culture has evolved on to something else. A complete theory of human behavior is a contradiction in terms. A more comprehensive psychology of women could have evolved had it not been for the very oppression that it seeks to address. In 10 years, the theory will be more complete, but always evolving.

All humans are participants in a cultural evolution. Traditional women's roles of caring and nurturing are coming to be valued by society. Women can experience the rewards of self-enhancement while men can express concerns for others. The goal of feminist psychodynamic theory is for therapy to advance beyond repairing results of stereotypical limiting sex role behavior toward a model of human development that acknowledges all individual's innate potentials.

ACKNOWLEDGMENT

As feminist authors, we acknowledge the clear heterosexual bias throughout the psychodynamic literature. Our hope is that future theory and research will be inclusive of all people.

REFERENCES

Beauvoir, S. de. (1952). *The second sex.* New York: Knopf.

Brodsky, A., Holroyd, J., Payton, C., Rubenstein, E., Rosenkrantz, P., Sherman, J., & Zell, F. (1975). Report of the task force on sex bias and sex-role stereotyping in psychotherapeutic practice. *American Psychologist, 30*(1), 1169.

Broverman, I., Broverman, D., Rosenkranz, P., & Vogel, S. (1970). Sex role stereotypes and clinical judgements of mental health. *Journal of Consulting and Clinical Psychology, 34,* 1–7.

Chesler, P. (1972). *Women and madness.* New York: Avon Books.

Chodorow, N. (1978). *The reproduction of mothering: Psychoanalysis and the sociology of gender.* Berkely, CA: University of California Press.

Dinnerstein, D. (1976). *The mermaid and the minotour: Sexual arrangements and the human malaise.* New York: Harper & Row.

Eichenbaum, L., & Orbach, S. (1983). *Understanding women: A feminist psychoanalytic approach.* New York: Basic Books.

Fairbairn, W. R. D. (1952). *An object-relations theory of personality.* New York: Basic Books.

Firestone, S. (1970). *The dialectic of sex: The case for feminist revolution.* New York: William Morrow.

Freud, A. (1936/1966). *The ego and the mechanisms of defense* (rev. ed.). New York: International Universities Press.

Freud, S. (1900/1953). *The interpretation of dreams.* London: Hogarth Press.

Freud, S. (1923/1947). *The ego and the id.* London: Hogarth Press.

Freud, S. (1925/1950). Some psychological consequences of the anatomical distinction between the sexes. In *Collected papers* (Vol. 5, pp. 186–197). London: Hogarth Press.

Freud, S. (1931/1950). Female sexuality. In *Collected Papers* (Vol. 5, pp. 252–272). London: Hogarth Press.

Freud, S. (1933a). *New introductory lectures on psychoanalysis.* New York: Norton.

Freud, S. (1933b). Femininity. In J. Strouse (Ed), *Women and analysis* (pp. 73–93.). New York: Grossman.

Friedan, B. (1965). *The feminine mystique.* New York: Penguin Books.

Gilligan, C. (1982). *In a different voice: Psychological theory and women's development.* Cambridge, MA: Harvard University Press.

Greer, G. (1971). *The female eunuch.* New York: McGraw–Hill.

Guntrip, H. (1964). *Personality structure and human interaction: The developing synthesis of psychodynamic theory.* New York: International Universities Press.

Hall, G. S. (1954). *A primer of Freudian psychology.* New York: American Library.

Hartmann, H. (1939). *Ego psychology and the problem of adaptation.* New York: International Universities Press.

Hartmann, H., Kris, E., & Lowenstein, R. S. (1946). Comments on the formation of psychic structure. *Psychoanalytic Study of the Child, 2,* 11–38.

Horney, K. (1967). *Feminine psychology.* New York: Norton.

Jacobson, E. (1964). *The self and the object world.* New York: International Universities Press.

Kernberg, O. (1973). *Borderline conditions and pathological narcissism.* New York: Aronson.

Klein, M. (1932). *The psychoanalysis of children.* London: Hogarth Press.

Kohut, H. (1971). Analysis of the self: A systematic approach to the psychoanalytic treatment of narcissistic personality disorders. *Psychoanalytic Study of the Child, 4.*

Kris, E. (1951). Ego psychology and interpretation in psychoanalytic therapy. *Psychoanalytic Quarterly. 20,* 15–30.

Lerner, H. (1980). Internal prohibitions against female anger. *American Journal of Psychoanalysis. 40*(2), 137–148.

Lerner, H. (1982). Special issues for women in psychotherapy. In M. Notman & C. Nadelson (Eds.), *The woman patient: Medical and psychological interfaces* (pp. 273–286). New York: Plenum.

Lerner, H. (1983). Female dependency in context: Some theoretical and technical considerations. *American Journal of Orthopsychiatry. 53*(4), 697–704.

Mahler, M. S., Pine, F., & Bergman, A. (1975). *The psychological birth of the human infant: Symbiosis and individuation.* New York: International Universities Press.

Miller, J. B. (1976). *Toward a new psychology of women.* Boston: Beacon Press.

Millett, K. (1970). *Sexual politics.* New York: Doubleday.

Mitchell, J. (1974). *Psychoanalysis and feminism.* New York: Pantheon Books.

Reich, W. (1963). *The sexual revolution.* New York: Farrar, Straus, & Giroux.

Spitz, R. A. (1965). *The first year of life: A psychoanalytic study of normal and devient development of object relations.* New York: International Universities Press.

Thompson, C. M. (1941). The role of women in this culture. In Strouse, J. (Ed.), *Women and analysis.* (pp. 245–277). New York: Grossman Publishers.

Thompson, C. M. (1964). *On women.* New York: New American Library.
Winnicott, D. W. (1965). *The maturational process and the facilitating environment.* New York: International Universities Press.
Wyckoff, H. (1977). Radical psychiatry techniques for solving women's problems in groups. In E. Rawlings & D. Carter, (Eds.), *Psychotherapy for women: Treatment toward equality.* Springfield, IL: Charles Thomas.

CHAPTER 5

Cognitive Behavior Therapy: Evaluation of Theory and Practice for Addressing Women's Issues

Iris Goldstein Fodor

INTRODUCTION

This chapter represents an attempt to synthesize theoretical and clinical writing, applying cognitive behavioral theories and practice to therapeutic work with women within a feminist framework. In reviewing this work, I will draw heavily on my own clinical experience and writings over the past 15 years. The early work was a first attempt to use a behavioral approach to address women's issues; the focus was on feminist understanding and treatment for phobia in women (Fodor, 1973, 1974). Later work added a cognitive component to behavior therapy and addressed a wider variety of women's problems, including eating disorders and assertiveness issues (Fodor, 1977; Wolfe & Fodor, 1975). More recent work argues for addressing recurrent, problematic patterns with a more interpersonal focus as well as interfacing with other therapeutic modalities for the most effective way of understanding and treating women's issues. (Fodor, 1987)

Basic Tenets of Behavior Therapy

Behavior therapy developed in the 1950s as the "application of modern learning theory to the treatment of clinical problems" (Wilson, 1984). In a recent, comprehensive overview of behavior therapy, Wilson speaks of three major approaches: (a) applied behavior analysis, (b) mediational stimulus–response model, and (c) cognitive behavior therapy/social learning theory. While this chapter will focus on the integration of the cognitive model and social learning theory as a form of feminist therapy, the author will briefly review some of the tenets of applied behavioral and mediational theory.

Applied Behavior Analysis

The applied behavior analysis methodology is based on the work of Skinner (1938) and his students who stress operant conditioning as primarily based on reinforcement and its consequences. Typically, there is a careful assessment of so called *adaptive* and *maladaptive* behaviors and their reinforcement contingencies are arranged to *shape* (increase) the desired behaviors and to *extinguish* (decrease) the undesired behaviors. Most work using applied behavior analysis has been done with individuals in group settings (institutions and schools). For example, the token economy is a reinforcement system that was developed in mental hospitals to reward patients for desirable behaviors (Wilson, 1984). Most self-control programs use variants of reinforcement contigencies to help clients alter behavior. This approach is the foundation of behavioral self-control procedures with women on weight issues. There is little theoretical writing on applying operant methodology to women's issues, although reinforcement is a central concept for socialization theory. Elaine Blechman (1984) has addressed the issue of female competence, using this model and her edited book on behavior modification with women has many chapters describing a behavioral model for addressing women's problems.

Mediational Stimulus–Response Approach

Clinical behavioral work in the mediational stimulus–response approach was developed by Wolpe (1958) and is based on the learning theories of classical or respondent conditioning developed by Pavlov and Hull. Wolpe's work emphasizes autonomic arousal and anxiety-based symptoms as the focus of treatment which mostly includes phobic and obsessive-compulsive disorders.

Most of the early behavioral work which addressed women's issues focused on phobias, which have a high prevalence rate for women. Between 85% and 95% of agoraphobics are reported to be female (American Psychiatric Association, 1980). Furthermore, the early symptoms of agoraphobia appeared to develop in young, married woman. Behavior therapists view symptoms as maladaptive behaviors that are learned and it is assumed that women's socialization experience puts them at high risk for the development of agoraphobic symptomology (Fodor, 1974). This is consistent with a feminist, theoretical analysis.

Lazarus (1966), using the behavior model accounts for phobic states arising from (a) a classically conditioned autonomic disturbance, (b) instrumental conditioning in the form of a habit of avoiding the conditioned stimulus, and (c) social reinforcement for engaging in the instrumental avoidance behavior.

Autonomic conditioning. Wolpe (1958) views phobias as relating to situations that evoke high intensities of anxiety. Many of his clinical examples focus on the stressful state of marriage and motherhood for young women along with their feelings of being trapped. The following is typical of the case histories that Wolpe cites to illustrate the autonomic conditioning aspects of phobia: "I was . . . very unhappy . . . always in a state of complete exhaustion trying to take care of the two children completely exhausted . . . resented my life. . . . One day when food-shopping . . . felt as if I wanted to erupt . . . to scream but didn't. A few days later, I went into Center City to meet my mother and sister and all of a sudden I began to feel very funny . . . told them I had to leave and that was the day I tried to walk home from the bus and I couldn't walk. . . ." (p. 302).

Wolpe (1958) also believes one can get a similar spread of anxiety to new stimuli based upon "symbolism." He writes about a 20-year-old woman who came for treatment of claustrophobia: "The onset of this turned out to be related to a marriage in which she felt 'caught' like a rat in a trap. Many years earlier she had a fearful experience in a confined space, and this had led to slight uneasiness in such places as elevators. Her marital situation now generated a chronic undertone of 'shut in' feeling, with which the physical enclosement of elevators now summated to produce a substantial fear reaction" (p. 99).

Avoidance behavior. The phobia constitutes the avoidance behaviors. The first patient avoids being out in the world, and the second avoids confined spaces, particularly elevators. Wolpe (1958) accounts for the avoidance behavior: ". . . the prospect of taking the action that would lead out the situation simply adds new anxiety to that which already exists and this is what inhibits action" (p. 80). Fodor (1974) stresses that these women are in conflict between their wish for freedom and independence and feeling dependent and trapped in their marital situation. The phobic symptoms arise from the stress of such a conflict and provide a solution. By becoming phobic and thus even more dependent, the woman does not have to resolve the conflict or learn how to become more independent.

Social reinforcement. Social reinforcement adds an additional factor to the development and maintenance of agoraphobia. Agoraphobia in women developed from a conditioned, autonomic reaction to the stress of perceiving being trapped in a relationship, following a lifelong history of social reinforcement for stereotypical feminine behavior. The ongoing, current reinforcement of avoidance behavior (by family members) is consistent with remaining in the more stereotypical female role.

Behavioral Treatment of Phobias

Behavioral treatment for remediation of stereotypical social conditioning, particularly in the case of phobias, has been construed as helping women by providing a structure to learn new ways of behaving, to aid in sex role integration and to provide different contingencies of reinforcement, this time for mastery and competency. (Fodor, 1973, 1974).

The early behavior treatment for phobias was the use of systematic desensitization, as developed by Wolpe (1958), which is based on the reciprocal inhibition principle: If a response inhibitory of anxiety can be made to occur in the presence of anxiety-evoking stimuli, it will weaken the bond between these stimuli and anxiety (Wolpe & Lazarus, 1966, p. 12). This procedure of systematic desensitization (which is a form of counterconditioning) employs a relaxation procedure to enable the patient to learn an alternative, incompatible response to the conditioned anxiety-producing stimuli. Once the client can relax (usually via a procedure that stresses alternating muscle tension with relaxation), the phobic scenes are visually presented in a graduated, imaginal fashion (called a hierarchy). What she learns is to associate these previously feared stimuli with relaxation instead of anxiety. To enhance the extinction of the avoidance response further, in vivo (real life) practice is usually carried out in conjunction with the desensitization procedure. In many respects, this treatment could be viewed as a training in how to cope with and face fears, the opposite of avoidance. (Goldfried, 1971). Recent, behavioral work in treating agoraphobics using this model stresses the real life practice ("in vivo exposure") as the essential ingredient (Foa & Kozak, 1986). For the past decade, anxiety disorders in general and agoraphobia in particular have been the target of programmatic behavioral research. Since, agoraphobics are primarily women, much of this behavioral work has stressed women's issues and trained women to be more independent, competent and to cope better (Brehony, 1980; Goldfried, 1980; Goldstein & Chambless, 1980).

However, the thrust for working on women's issues in the 1960s was focusing on behavior and behavioral retraining. In the early 1970s, at about the same time as the development of feminist therapy, cognitive techniques were added to the behavioral approach and cognitive behavior therapy became one of the most popular treatments for women's problems.

Cognitive Behavior Therapy

Historical and theoretical overview. Cognitive behavior therapy (CBT) resulted from the integration of three "schools": behavior therapy, cognitive therapy, and cognitive and social psychology. More so than any other therapeutic approach, CBT is an attempt to apply the latest theoretical and research findings from psychology to clinical issues (Mahoney, 1974). CBT developed at almost the same time as feminist therapy. Although most of the original developers of CBT were males (Michael Mahoney, Donald Michenbaum, Marvin Goldfried, and Aron Beck, among others), several feminist therapists began early on to apply CBT's basic theories and techniques to the development of feminist theory to address women's problems and to critique sexist practices. (Fodor, 1977; Jakobowski–Spector, 1973; Osborn & Harris, 1975; Wolfe & Fodor, 1975). Pioneering feminist therapists have used CBT to work with populations of women seeking assertiveness training (Jako-bowski–Spector, 1973; Wolfe & Fodor, 1975), for eating disorders, body image, and self-esteem problems (Fodor, 1983) and for sex therapy (Wolfe, 1976). CBT also offered many highly useful intervention techniques for women in crisis, becoming a basic foundation for a variety of programs. Walker's (1979, 1984) work with battered women and many of the rape crisis programs follow a CBT format.

CBT is built on the theoretical framework of social learning theory. Social learning theory is based on "a reciprocal interaction among three interlocking sets of influences: behavior, cognitive processes, and environmental factors" (Wilson, 1984). The basic tenet of social learning theory is that it is partly through their own actions that people produce the environmental conditions that can affect their behavior in a reciprocal fashion. The experiences generated by behavior also partly determine what individuals think, expect, and can do which in turn, affect their subsequent behavior" (Bandura, 1977b, p. 345).

Douglas (1985) argues that a cognitive behavioral perspective is particularly well to interface with a feminist philosophical approach to psychotherapy in that such a model provides for an understanding of the etiological and/or maintaining factors in a client's problems by reference to both social/political environments as well as to her/his own behavior. Accordingly, intervention can be viewed from the perspective of altering environmental events, the client's own behavior or both, whichever combination of factors based on clinical assessment, are causally related to the target problem and which are amenable to change (p. 6).

Much of the initial appeal of CBT in addressing women's issues in the mid-1970s was based on the assumption that by focusing on cognitions as well as teaching new behaviors it was possible for women to transcend the constraints of their prior socialization experience and to become the agents of their own change.

BASIC TENETS OF CBT

Wilson (1984) summarizes the basic assumptions underlying the cognitive/behavioral approach as follows:

1. There is an assumption that emotional problems are not caused by illness or abnormality, but viewed as problems in living or maladaptive ways of behaving.
2. Most so-called problematic behaviors are learned in the same manner as all other behaviors; hence, therapy can be construed as the same kind of relearning process involved in unlearning other kinds of behaviors.
3. There is an emphasis on the use of behavioral assessment to study the patterns of current problematic behaviors, rather than on historical antecedents and other assumed underlying causes.
4. Treatments are individually tailored and are typically broken into parts or groups, and there is a specificity of treatment approaches for the subproblems.
5. The therapist is viewed as a consultant/teacher/trainer, who is there to help clients learn as much about themselves as possible in order to alter their maladaptive behavior patterns. Behavior therapy emphasizes corrective learning experiences in which clients acquire new coping skills and improved communication competencies or learn how to break maladaptive habits and overcome self-defeating emotional conflicts.
6. Finally, CBT emphasizes pre- and posttreatment assessment, as well as follow-up.

Cognitive Behavior Therapy: Different Approaches

Cognitive behavior therapy (CBT) integrates behavior therapy and cognitive therapy. The underpinnings are based on behavioral concepts and techniques, with an added emphasis on identifying and changing maladaptive cognition. From the early 1970s on, the cognitive basis of CBT followed from the pioneering work of Albert Ellis (1962), who cites the stoic philosopher Epictetus (60 A.D.) Humans "are disturbed not by things, but by the views they take of them." That is emotional problems and maladaptive behaviors are viewed as a result of unproductive or irrational thought patterns. Central to the treatment of such maladaptive thought patterns is the concept known as cognitive restructuring. The aim of cognitive restructuring is to enable clients to think differently about their problematic situations. There are at least three different overlapping schools of cognitive behavior therapy which use variants of cognitive restructuring as a central therapeutic tool. They include:

1. *Rational Emotive Therapy (RET)* (Ellis, 1962), which places emphasis on the identification of irrational beliefs leading to emotional and behavioral disturbances, and on "challenging" or "disputing" these beliefs, preferably by a form of socratic dialogue.
2. *Cognitive therapy,* developed by Beck (1980) similarly emphasizes dysfunctional thinking underlying symptomatic behavior. Treatment is similar to Ellis's but tends toward empirical rather than evaluative disputation. Beck's approach has been most systematically applied to the treatment of depression.
3. *Self-management strategies.* These include self-instructional training developed by Meichenbaum (1977), which emphasizes training clients to teach themselves adapting coping self-statements and strategies. Similar work in self-control/self management training was developed by Mahoney (1974), Kanfer (1977), and Marlott & Gordon (1985). The major application of self-management strategies has been to problems of impulse control (i.e., impulsive children, weight disorders, alcoholic and drug problems).

CBT and women's issues: RET. The earliest, most fully developed and widely used form of CBT to address women's issues was RET. Feminist therapists have used RET concepts to work directly on women's issues. The therapeutic work of cognitive restructuring focuses on identifying and then remediating these messages to enable the clients to develop alternative, more adaptive belief systems. While the work in RET and feminist therapy covers the entire range of women's issues, the earliest work focused on assertiveness issues and serves as a model to illustrate how RET aids in challenging and changing sex role socialization messages.

Assertiveness training and RET. In 1975, this author's first use of CBT was in applying RET to the assessment of assertiveness and the development of assertiveness training programs for women within a feminist framework. (Wolfe & Fodor, 1975). This early work is typical of the social learning perspective on women's issues which stresses that maladaptive cognitions stem from sex role socialization messages. CBT focuses on the remediation of these messages to enable the client to develop more fully.

In 1975 we hypothesized:

> For many women, the stereotypes about the 'shoulds' and 'oughts' of sex role behavior and assertiveness function as internal belief systems or schemata through which their own and other's behaviors are evaluated. . . . And when their own behavior deviates from what they believe they ought to be, or from what others expect them to be, feelings of anxiety, guilt and confusion result. This in turn creates the low self-esteem, the low valuation of one's self and of one's human right that further perpetuate the vicious cycle of nonassertiveness . . . what appears to be the most important factor blocking women's effective assertion of their rights and feelings is a *welter* of irrational beliefs, inculcated early in life, that leaves them anxious and fearful of losing others, of hurting other's feelings, of being too aggressive or of unleashing a flurry of catastrophic retaliations . . . we have been convinced that any successful assertiveness training program for women must place its major focus on identification and challenging of these irrational belief systems" (Wolfe & Fodor, 1975, pp. 45–46)

RET was utilized as the form of therapy to help women change these irrational beliefs. This was done through a process of depropagandization: (a) Helping women become aware of what their irrational beliefs are and how they are self-perpertuating them, (b) directing them to test their beliefs against logical reality, then (c) replacing them with newer and more adaptive attitudes, feelings and behavior (Wolfe & Fodor, 1975, p. 46).

Irrational beliefs common to women. Ellis (1975) has pinpointed some core, irrational ideas which he believes are the root of most emotional disturbances. For women the following core beliefs may have special relevance (Wolfe & Fodor, 1975):

1. The idea that she must be loved by everyone for everything she does. (Everyone must love me).
2. Other people's needs count more than my own.
3. The idea that for her, it is easier to avoid than to face life's difficulties.

4. The idea that she needs a strong person to lean on or provide for her.
5. The idea that she doesn't have control over her emotions.

Ways of countering irrational beliefs that lead to unassertive responses. The following are examples of ways to dispute the specific belief systems:

> *Belief:* I must be loved and approved by every significant person in my life; and if I'm not it's awful. It would be terrible if someone called me a bitch; or thought I was terrible or selfish.
>
> *Disputation:* Why would it be terrible if the other person thought I was a bitch or rejected me? How does that make me a worthless, human being.
>
> *Belief:* It would be awful if I hurt another person. I was so mean not to go to my parents for Thanksgiving, what an uncaring daughter I am.
>
> *Disputation:* How can I really hurt another person or become a bad person simply by making my own well-being and comfort as important as theirs.
>
> *Belief:* The other person must be right, he sounds so sure of himself.
>
> *Disputation:* What do I really lose by telling my partner than I don't like the way he behaves toward me? If worst comes to worst and he leaves me, how would that make me a failure, a reject? And what's the evidence that if this relationship ends, I'll never find another person who treats me better. It might be nice to have someone to rely on, but what law is there that says even at this late stage I can't learn new coping skills and take care of myself, if necessary.
>
> *Belief:* Emotional misery comes from external pressure, and I have little ability to control or change my feelings; for example, he makes me feel anxious when he threatens to leave.
>
> *Disputation:* No one else can make me feel anxious. I make myself feel anxious by the way I view the situation. I can learn to control and change my feelings.

Variants of RET combined with consciousness raising have been used to address specifically the irrational beliefs related to various problematic behaviors. Janet Wolfe (1985) has recently reviewed the comprehensive work applying RET to women's issues.

Cognitive Behavior Therapy: The Treatment Package

Today, following the past decades' work, as outlined above, most cognitive behavior therapists use a combined treatment package that integrates the many variants of cognitive therapy with behavior therapy. A typical cognitive behavior approach to therapy includes the following steps:

1. *Specify the problematic behaviors.* Try to be as specific as possible in describing the symptomatic behaviors. Which behaviors are excessive and need to be extinguished (e.g., angry outbursts, overeating, too much dependency, avoidance or fearfulness)? Which behaviors are undeveloped and need to be shaped up (unassertiveness, too little independence, too little initiative)? For example, if we were working with an agoraphobic, we would want to study the precise nature of the anxiety attacks (When do they occur and not occur. Where she can and can't go and with whom).

2. *Collect data.* Data are collected from the therapist–client interactions as well as from the client's outside life. The technique of self-monitoring is central to CBT. The client is instructed to collect as much information as possible about her symptom via behavioral diaries, specially designed forms, thought-sampling questionnaires, etc. For example, in work with an agoraphobic we may want to know in detail the specifics of her day and the variation in anxiety levels. Anxiety is typically measured by means of the SUDS scale. (The SUDS scale, also called the subjective units of distress scale, asks a client to self-rate anxiety from least to most anxious on a scale of 0 to 100; Wolpe, 1958.) Other mood-rating scales may also be utilized.

3. *Identify patterns.* From the work in the therapy session as well as from the information acquired from self-monitoring, problematic patterns of behavior are identified. Certain patterns of irrational beliefs (Ellis, 1984) or maladaptive self-statements (Meichenbaum, 1977) are identified and how they tie into the problematic behaviors is highlighted. For example, an agoraphobic woman who avoids being alone in the street and is fearful of loss of control over anxiety may have the belief that in this context she is helpless and there are no ways she can control her anxiety.

4. *Goal setting.* Client and therapist work together to set goals for therapy. For example in the case of agoraphobics, this might involve setting up a hierarchy for exposure therapy learning to face fears, handle themselves when experiencing anxiety, as well as learning to become more independent.

5. *Cognitive behavioral treatment.* The work of helping clients change involves two interlocking treatment techniques: cognitive restructuring and behavior therapy.

a. *Cognitive restructuring.* Cognitive restructuring involves challenging the irrational beliefs (Ellis & Harper (1975) or using the Meichenbaum approach (1977) help the client substitute adaptive or coping self-statements for maladaptive or noncoping self-statements (e.g., an agoraphobic would learn to substitute the coping statement 'I can learn to control my anxiety' to counter the belief that she is helpless and can't control her anxiety.)

b. *Behavior therapy.* Behavior therapy enables the client to extinguish old, maladaptive behavior patterns and to learn new more adaptive ways of learning. This learning takes places as the old beliefs are being challenged and replaced by the new belief systems. The major behavioral techniques utilized at this stage are:

   i. *Instructional training for learning new behaviors.* The client is instructed in learning new adaptive behaviors to replace problematic behaviors. The client is taught new behaviors; e.g., assertive behaviors, how to diet, ways of confronting fears, etc.

   ii. *Behavior rehearsal.* The client practices the new behaviors (e.g., for the agoraphobic this may involve setting up a hierarchy of feared situations and slowing encountering these situations).

   iii. *Modeling.* The therapist teaches specific techniques that are not in the client's repertoire or are poorly developed (For example, the therapist may model relaxation breathing techniques to counter hyperventilation or assertive nonverbal behaviors, etc.).

   iv. *Self-control training.* Specific instruction to cope with the feelings of being overwhelmed. For example, the agoraphobic learns how to handle herself while having an anxiety attack.

   v. *Reinforcement for change.* The therapist and client both create opportunities for the client to get rewarded for the new behaviors. (For the agoraphobic, just engaging in previously feared behaviors is rewarding in itself. A women's group is often utilized at this point in therapy to provide support and encouragement for change.)

6. *Homework assignments.* Homework assignments in the form of further self-monitoring, specific behavioral assignments, etc., are standard features of CBT. (In working with agoraphobics, for example, at the beginning of each session, the therapist and client go over the encounters with feared situations, the week's stressful events, and rehash the successful and unsuccessful strategies. At

the end of each session, the therapist and client work out a new assignment.)

7. *Evaluation, follow-up.* One may give standardized self-report questionnaires, or encourage clients to keep behavioral diaries. Emphasis is on documenting change. Clients learn to be "their own scientist." Clients are encouraged to keep in touch with the therapist and to check in for periodic consultative or booster sessions around recurrent problematic issues.

8. *Family consultation.* While the above presentation focused on individual treatment, CBT often brings in significant others for work. It is also recognized that many clients' problems have an interpersonal focus. (For agoraphobics in particular, the problem needs to be construed as interpersonal in nature, and the therapist may need to work with a mate and or parents.) (Fodor, in press; Fodor & Wolfe, 1977).

Critique of CBT from a Feminist Perspective

CBT: An ideal integration with feminist therapy. In many ways, CBT seems ideally suited for an integration with feminist therapy.

- CBT is based on social learning theory. Problematic behavior is viewed as learned, shaped up by the environment.
- The therapist is seen as a consultant/teacher, not as an authoritarian doctor.
- CBT puts the client in charge. The emphasis is on using therapy as a vehicle for teaching the client about herself, setting her own goals, and learning techniques for change.
- CBT is optimistic about change. The therapy doesn't follow a medical model. The locus of change is on the individual. Any motivated client can learn how to combat irrational or unproductive thinking, substitute more rational and more productive coping strategies for less productive ones and learn to be in charge of one's life.
- Many of the techniques of cognitive behavior therapy (e.g., modeling, self-disclosure, teaching coping strategies) seem congruent with those used in feminist therapy.

The following illustration described presents an integrated CBT/feminist approach for treating a depressed client. It is an example of CBT as an ideal feminist therapy. (All cases are fictionalized composites of different clients treated over the past 10 years.)

Mary, a 52-year-old woman comes for therapy, depressed and un-happy. Her husband of 27 years, an academic, has just run off with a young female student. Her entire life has been wrapped around her husband, who is a prominent person in his field. She has been his secretary, research assistant, and traveling companion. Her social life was taken up with his professional colleagues and their wives. They have two sons in graduate school in far-off cities.

1. *Specify problem.* From the initial interview, Mary reports that she is lost without her husband. She has had little identity and life of her own and is clearly quite depressed. She admits to suicidal ideation, but she states that she has no wish to die, she just wants her husband back.
2. *Assessment.* She is given the Beck Depression Inventory (BDI) and scores high for depression (Beck, 1979).
3. *Identify patterns of behaviors.* Mary spends her time in the house alone; she sleeps most of the day. She doesn't return calls from friends. She has no work goals. Money is not an immediate problem since Mary has a small income from an inheritance.

Using the Ellis system, we see that Mary has the following irrational beliefs (These are also similiar to Beck's description of dysfunctional thinking in depression.) She believes that she is nothing without her husband. Life has no meaning without a man; she can't control her unhappy feelings. She believes she is responsible for her husband leaving, if she had been a better wife she should have known that he was unhappy and maybe she should have catered to him more. She feels very hopeless about a future without her husband and worries about being too old to be attractive to men. She doesn't see a way of being happy without a man.

Goal setting. Together, the therapist and Mary work out goals. The initial goals of therapy, may differ from the therapy goals later. The initial goal is to enable Mary to get through this difficult period and accept the loss. Mary agrees to this goal, but she would also like some help in winning her husband back, if that is possible. A later therapy goal might be to help Mary accept that she may have to be without her husband, learn to be alone, or search for another relationship and find some outside interest of her own as well as deal with growing older. Immediate behaviors which need to be changed are sleeping all day, lack of energy, initiative, and lack of social contact. Cognitive restructuring focuses on replacing her noncoping self-statements with the coping beliefs: "I can make myself feel better, by being more active."

Cognitive behavioral treatment: therapy techniques. Modeling. This takes the form of self-disclosure, a technique common to both CBT and feminist therapy. As Mary tells her story, her therapist gently tells her that she knows firsthand the type of pain she is experiencing; she, too, was married to an academic who left her for one of his students. This was done . . . not too early, not too detailed . . . but just enough to let Mary know that her therapist understand her loss. Later, on, the therapist may or may not provide the details of her own struggle and how she coped. The self-disclosure needs to be short, in tune with where client is at and used as both an empathetic bond and a building of hope. "It's not easy, I learned how to cope with my loss and you can too."

Cognitive restructuring. "I am responsible for my husband's leaving, I was not a good enough wife." The onus of responsibility for the failure of the marriage indicated by this belief needs to be replaced by a realistic appraisal of the difficulty all men and women have in making it together and the particular situation of academic men, who may take advantage of an available pool of adoring students. Therapist and client talk about the high percentage of academic men in midlife crises who leave wives in this way, as well as the fact that marriage between males and females is difficult. Mary is encouraged to read Lillian Rubin's *Intimate Strangers* to learn more about why men and women have such a hard time making it together. It is too early in therapy to question her need for a man. This is time to explore general heterosexual conditioning and specific problems that all men and women have together.

Development of assertive behavior. Mary has been very accommodating toward her husband. Mary is encouraged to get in touch with her anger and role play is used to express some of her outrage toward her husband. She is also encouraged to figure out how much contact she wishes to have with him. She does not feel ready to confront him in person, but does role play some assertive scenes. As we work, she is able to be in touch with her rage at her husband for insisting that she turn down a teaching job at a community college, because he was going on a sabbatical. Through the assertiveness work, she begins to experience the oppressive quality of the relationship with her husband and how she was not up to opposing him because of fear of losing him and a lack of assertiveness skills.

Working on independent behaviors. Mary has never lived alone or dealt with a single social life. We use behavioral diaries to capture what she is going through. She is spending a lot of time sleeping, rarely eating, makes few contacts with friends. Beginning work focuses on lifting the depression. She is encouraged to be more active, by walking, or going for a daily swim. As her spirits lift, we work on going out of the house, developing some plan for ways of socializing on weekends, and finally end up trying to help her find something she would like to do on an ongoing basis. She is also encouraged to read about women's lives. We begin with Simone de Beauvoir's biography, *The Prime of Life*. Mary is intrigued with the descriptions of Beauvoir's attempt to become an independent woman, doing things alone.

Working on self-nurturance. Mary was overly dependent on her husband to provide all her nurturant and sexual needs. She feels emotionally depleted, and cut off from what she believed was the only nurturance she had. She is encouraged to learn how to self-nurture. Mary has spent so much time pleasing her husband that focusing on herself is quite novel. Often, she is not sure what she wants. Gestalt awareness exercises are used to help Mary get more in touch with herself. (Nurturance training is used to counter the belief: I can only get what I need from a man; I can't learn how to nurture myself.) She is also encouraged to reach out to women and friends for nurturance, friendship, intellectual stimulation, and fun.

Work on career goals. At the beginning of therapy, Mary reports that her husband was "interesting" and she's a "nothing." For work on making herself interesting, we go back to premarriage fantasies about what she wanted to do with her life and explore her interests. Mary was an English major in college and she loved to read. While she has always enjoyed reading, she had never felt she could do much with a major in English. As we work on encouraging her to dream, she talks about the desire to write. After 6 months of therapy, Mary enrolls in a women's summer writing workshop. She begins to write short, humorous sketches about her life as an academic wife and makes new friends with women writers.

How CBT is not an ideal feminist therapy. While the above case (drawn from several real life histories) provides a positive example of the integration of CBT with feminist practice at its best, the situation for most women is more complex and certain ethical issues need to be addressed about the efficacy of such an approach. The following issues need to be addressed:

- CBT plays into a view of self as commodity and for the most part is a therapy geared to middle-class clients. Mary was a privileged woman, who was educated, had an income and was free to work on self-development. What if she were poor, alone with several young children to raise, and had little formal education or skills for self-support? Cognitive restructuring is often not enough for a client in a very difficult life situation. Adapting a more positive attitude may not be sufficient, when problems are overwhelming (e.g., a homeless woman may not have the strength to cope when she cannot find decent affordable housing, is living in a shelter and trying to comfort upset children). Social supports are necessary to bolster CBT strategies in working with such clients, and such supports are often unavailable.

- CBT, even though it is based on social learning theory, puts the onus of change on the client. It's up to you to change, we can help you undo poor parenting, bad prior conditioning, or sexist socialization practices. Such optimism, however, discounts both the difficult reality of women's lives as well as the ongoing sexist practices that exist in our society that make it hard for clients to change. For example, Mary's social life without her successful husband will most likely will be different, possibly less rich or exciting than before. Married couples often shun their friends when they divorce. Furthermore, Mary's chance of finding another academic husband or any husband at her age are slim. Older academic men do have a high divorce rate and do have an available pool of younger women for them. For all women there is a shortage of eligible men as they get older (Guttentag, 1983). Much more work needs to be done within CBT to redress the societal conditioning directly, and to prepare women to cope with the reality they face in a heterosexual world that places older woman at a disadvantage, rather than put the onus of change on individual women seeking therapy—that is, if you try hard enough there is a man out there for you. Other alternative choices for relationships need to be presented.

- While the therapist–client model for CBT is to have the therapist be a teacher/trainer, etc., we are assuming that the therapist will not impose his or her values on the client. Yet, given the instructional nature of CBT, the therapist is certainly in a powerful position through the use of cognitive restructuring to impose her or his world view on the client. Feminist cognitive behavior therapists may run into trouble with clients who seek help for traditional goals that are at variance with feminist goals. What if Mary really wanted to pursue the goal of getting her husband back or becoming an even more accommodating wife? Are we willing to do accommodation training? Would we be willing to do such work uncritically? Often feminist values are at variance with more traditional values. Since cognitive restructuring is often a powerful tool in the hands of a therapist who is perceived by the clients as powerful, we must be careful that we also have respect for who the client is, what her life-style preferences are and where she is in terms of her development, as well as how much she is willing to risk being at odds with her culture.

- Cognitive restructuring often adapts an intellectual, socratic mode of thinking that may reflect a male model of problem solving. More work needs to be done on addressing female ways of thinking through solutions.
- The model of CBT is currently under some attack and revision by theorists who feel there has been too much emphasis on the piecemeal, symptomatic approach to problems and not enough emphasis on underlying structures or patterns (Arnkoff, 1980; Arnkoff & Glass, 1982; Guidano & Liotti, 1983). This author has also argued for moving beyond addressing presenting symptoms and addressing more structural patterns. (Fodor, 1987). Is focusing on the presenting problem the best way to treat women? Maybe, it is time for feminist therapists to break down the barriers between psychodynamic and behavioral therapies and begin to construct a new, therapeutic system that focuses on structures and patterns, with concepts that can be objectively researched, and outcomes systematically studied.
- Cognitive behavior therapists for the most part do not examine the nature of the therapist–client relationship itself. This author feels much more work needs to be done in using the dyadic interactions of therapist and client for exploration of the client's more enduring patterns of behavior (Fodor, 1987). For example, do we really know how clients use our self-disclosure and modeling? How do they deal with our values?

Problems of Focusing on the Client as the Locus of Change

American culture places great value on individualism. In many ways behavior therapy, behavior therapists and the self-help/self-management movement of the past decade have played into this therapy goal of self-as-commodity. The message that we often give is that it's all up to you what you make of your life. If you enter our workshops, buy our books and work with us, you will become more assertive, or thinner, and more attractive and thereby more successful: You will become a better commodity, have better relationships, and get ahead in life (Fodor, 1983; Fodor & Thal, 1984). As therapists, we would do well to look into how much we are buying into the self-as-commodity aspect of therapy and using our cognitive behavioral techniques to enable our clients to live the best of all possible lives; and consider, instead questioning these societal values of maximal self-development, work achievement, and material rewards as the only routes to happiness.

Value polarities: CBT helps women to buy into stereotypes. Too often, CBT has been used to work with women to enable them to fit more into the traditional role which is often viewed as the optimal path to the good life. Programs are developed to enable them to be better wives, mothers, sex partners or to become more attractive or a more contemporary model, superwoman. Some of the worst abuses of CBT have occurred in the area of weight and attractiveness. A billion-dollar weight reduction, medical, pharmaceutical, and publishing industry is supported by 20 million overweight women, or roughly one-quarter to one-third of the American female population. Approximately 95% of the clients of overweight workshops are female and CBT has a very poor track record in enabling clients to lose significant amounts of weight and keep it off. Feminist therapy for the overweight woman must go beyond assuming that weight reduction is the desired goal. While this past decade has seen a mushrooming of behavioral weight control programs, such therapy at best can offer only short-term, minimal weight loss. Typically, a client, after repeated battles in weight-reduction programs, believes that she has two problems: One that she is overweight and therefore unattractive, and two that she is a failure because she lacks the necessary self-control to lose weight. Feminist therapy with such clients should challenge the standard CBT treatment package for weight reduction. It involves questioning the societally conditioned view of one's body weight.

For such work, clients are given a choice as to whether they wish to focus on weight loss at all or instead to increase self-acceptance of their body. Much more work needs to be done using CBT to enable professionals to see how much they buy into cultural stereotypes when they accept overweight women into weight control workshops and for women to learn to accept and deal with their own realistic body types (Fodor, 1983; Fodor & Thal, 1984). Also, many therapists, given the recent health and exercise craze, add an additional "should": "You should work on having a healthy body." We need to develop workshops for professionals to work on their own prejudices about being overweight and self-control. Therapists would do well to challenge the assumptions that there is a standard weight for each person, that moderate overweight is unhealthy and deadly, that self-control is easy—"it's up to you, you can do it," and that women are unattractive and undesirable when moderately overweight (Fodor, 1983).

Instead, a feminist CBT approach to weight might enable clients to understand that the problem is not "overweight" but their negative evaluations about it and themselves (e.g., "I can't stand to be over-weight" or "I'm a horrible person for being overweight"), which they have taken in from the culture. By cognitive restructuring, the client begins to understand that it is not the "overweight" that is the problem, but the negative evaluation of being overweight and the feeling that they can't stand to be overweight or are a horrible person because they are overweight that perpetuates the unhappiness and preoccupation with dieting. The goal is to help clients construct their own view of what is desirable and re-educate their social supports. We also need to use our skills to re-educate the media to present normal weight and large women in their advertisements and programs, to enable women of all body types to feel representative.

Problems in Using CBT to Enable Clients to Break Out of Cultural Stereotypes

This author has been aware of some of the contradictions inherent in feminist work using CBT. When we work with women seeking to transcend cultural stereotypes, it is important that we recognize that we may be creating additional problems for the client. For example, nonassertion has been conceptualized as a socially conditioned feminine trait associated with passive, submissive, helpless, and altruistic behaviors in women Osborn & Harris (1975). Assertiveness techniques were developed as an antidote to the traditional, feminine, nonassertive social programming.

Thus, as we saw earlier, women were encouraged to challenge the irrational beliefs stemming from their sex role socialization programming and replace them with more adaptive, assertive, enhancing belief systems. However, after more than a decade of work with women, it would appear that some of the beliefs inhibiting assertive behavior may not be so irrational or maladaptive (Fodor & Epstein, 1983; Lineham, 1984). Schwartz and Gottman (1976) speak of the deficit in nonassertive persons as the inability to estimate accurately the consequences of their assertion. In women, it may be the *accuracy* of their perception of the consequences that truly inhibits their behavior. There is now a growing body of research to suggest that there is bias against assertive women. (Solomon & Rothblum, 1985). For example, Rich and Schroeder (1976) report that expert and peer male and female judges both identified comparable noncoercible behaviors when enacted by men as assertive but aggressive when performed by women.

Not only is there bias, but behaviors encouraged by assertiveness training often are not rewarded but rather punished. A woman who is learning to be assertive may find that she was more highly valued by her spouse or employer when she was accommodating, self-denying and passive. Her assertiveness may increase her self-respect, but she may be unwilling to live with the negative reactions of others to her behavior and therefore may cease to use her skills. Thus, to maintain assertive responding and to continue developing an independent stance as a woman in a society that still values female accommodation presents some dilemmas for feminist therapists. We are training our clients to tackle a lonely and difficult path and we must begin to do research on how to effect change at the societal level, so that the burden of change is not solely on our individual clients. Assertiveness trainers need to work together to develop appropriate techniques to deal with the media and devise programs to effect attitudinal change. We will fail more women unless we can build a better societal reinforcement system. It is unfair to put the burden of change on the shoulders of individual women (Fodor, 1985; Fodor & Rothblum, 1985).

MOVING BEYOND CBT

My present view is that the basic foundation of CBT, which focuses on substituting adaptive for maladaptive belief systems, is too simplistic a view to encompass the complexity of people's problems and that people are remarkably resistant to substituting such rational adaptive thinking for their persistent, irrational, and maladaptive beliefs. Furthermore, after watching the emotional upheaval in many of my clients, I am convinced that affects cannot always be controlled by cognitions, but that they have patterns of their own which influence behavior and affect cognitions. There are more general schemata for processing beliefs (both rational and irrational) that reflect more central processes operating than the above formulation would suggest. We need to look at more than strings of irrational beliefs. "For change to be maintained and generalized the deep structure must be altered" (Arnkoff, 1980, p. 350).

Typically, when people come into therapy, it is because their old system is not working. Traditional CBT often attempts to shore the system by adding new coping strategies so that the client learns to manage new situations. When this works, it is the best work that behavior therapists do. However, for many clients the system may continue to break down, as we work piecemeal on anxiety management, assertiveness training, couples communication, self-control, etc. As we see the same problems occurring and recurring in the same clients over a period of time, we would do well to reconsider our basic assumptions. By maintaining a focus only on symptoms and not on patterns and processes as well, we are failing to enable our clients to understand some of the redundancies that contribute to their persistent problems. (Beck & Emery, 1985; Arnkoff & Glass, 1982; Mahoney, 1980).

Consider the following case seen over a 15-year span (Fodor, 1987). At age 25, the client seeks behavior therapy for public speaking anxiety. She is a young administrative assistant, highly stressed and a perfectionistic. We do a standard behavioral treatment for speech anxiety, which enables the client to conduct public demonstrations of her company's products and present her ideas at staff conferences. In 1970, we see her for 12 sessions, using desensitization, relaxation, and graduated practice. A textbook case, the client is now able to speak before her work colleagues and is satisfied with the outcome of her therapy; and, by most criteria, she would be considered a definite treatment success.

Five years later, the client returns with a serious marital problem. Her husband is drinking heavily and refuses to go for help. She has decided to leave him, but she is very anxious about supporting herself and living alone. She worries about breaking the news of the divorce to her Catholic parents. We work on anxiety management, and do assertiveness training, along with some feminist work on coping with being alone. Therapy lasts 12 sessions. We help the client restructure her beliefs that one needs a man to depend on to be happy, that a woman cannot live alone, take care of herself, etc.; countering them with "I can learn to take care of myself." She is encouraged to learn how to behave more independently (e.g., go to restaurants alone, etc.). The client uses therapy well. In 16 sessions over a 4-month period, her anxiety has leveled off, she can cope with the crisis of ending her marriage, and she looks forward to living alone and becoming more independent. She values her time alone, but still has few friends. The therapist urges her to go into a consciousness-raising group, but she declines, stating that she is a very private person and doesn't feel comfortable talking about her problems with strangers.

At age 35, in 1980, the client calls again, this time with a career crisis. She would like to return to graduate school for an M.B.A. She is worried that she may not be able to handle the stress of the prestigious school she wishes to attend. She is worried about finances, and her ability to juggle school, work, and social life. By the 1980s cognitive behavior therapists have developed techniques of stress management and training in coping skills. Again, the client responds well to the therapy and begins her M.B.A. At age 40, in 1985, she calls her therapist in a panic. She is exhausted from working full time and trying to finish her M.B.A. at night. She is being considered for a high-level management position, but she is panicking about getting through the job interviews. (The anxiety appears similar to the public speaking anxiety of 15 years ago.) The man with whom she has been living the past 3 years, has moved out, just when she was leaning on him for the first time.

In many respects, this woman could be considered a behavior therapy success. She comes for help every 5 years, requires only 3 or 4 months of therapy, and moves on with her life. Yet, the case can also be used to illustrate the failure of the piecemeal behavior therapy to assess or tap into a more central system, structure, or schemata that underlies the recurrent crisis (Arnkoff & Glass, 1982; Guidano & Liotti, 1983). For example, this client falls apart when she feels she is not in control of her life. Behavior therapy helps her cope with each crisis and achieve more control until the next overwhelming situation occurs. Furthermore, there appear to be potentially competing schemata operating, the most potent ones being out of client's awareness (and these are not so easily controlled by cognitions).

In appraising the 15-year pattern of the case, the following is apparent: This woman asks for help only in a crisis. At these times, she feels out of control about the situation that she is trying to deal with and about her own lack of control over her own anxiety. She picks unreliable, unsupportive men for her significant relationships. Her world view is to see herself always as independent and competent, always striving to become more independent and more competent. As she gets older, she increasingly picks bigger challenges as tests of her competency. When any anxiety breaks through, she feels as if the entire system is breaking down and she panics. Furthermore, in a city where psychoanalysts are everywhere, she seeks out a behavior therapist and short-term therapy. She appears reluctant to be dependent on a therapist, except in a state of panic.

Another way of asking the same questions in this case is: (a) Why is the symptom so aversive; why does being helpless, being alone or seeming incompetent, cause such panic? (b) How does the client use therapy? Does a cognitive behavioral therapist with a feminist orientation ally herself too early with the strong, independent part and not explore the underside of the conflict, the helplessness and dependency? (c) What relation does the achievement drive (work) have to shoring up competency? Why is the client less happy as she gets more successful? What would make this client really happy? The metaissue that was not addressed until age 40 was her pattern of handling her life—seeing life as a challenging test of her ability to cope, trying to handle the crisis alone and then often panicking when she can't cope, asking for short-term help and then going out to meet the challenges successfully until the next crisis. We also need to explore the key features of the competing systems and the conflicts they generate: Can I be strong if I ask for help? Can I be independent if I'm with a strong man? Why is competency more primary than nurturance as a goal?

Therapist client issues. Cognitive behavior therapists for the most part have avoided looking at therapist–client interactions. In the very act of carrying out our specific procedures, many of the problematic patterns experienced by clients in their lives are duplicated in their interactions with the therapist. Furthermore, in CBT the therapist is a powerful model. The therapist is an authority on coping strategies, is rational, able to argue, is an assertive role model and so on. I believe it is time for us to examine how we use these therapeutic interactions and their impact on the clients as important sources of data for both assessment and treatment. For example, if we examine the therapist–client interactions of the case presented above, we see that Maria was very compliant and deferent, the good student. She didn't like to reveal too much and was very troubled about showing the extent of her helplessness; yet, she depended on the therapist to "fix her" quickly. She also too readily accepted the values of the therapist and of behavior therapy values-independence and self-control, and never stopped to ask whether or not these goals or her therapy were really putting her on path of self-fulfillment or happiness. What we need then is a CBT that focuses on process and uses examination of that process as a learning tool in therapy.

A Focus on Therapist–Client Process: An Expanded CBT

The central issue that is rarely addressed within CBT and which is central to feminist therapy is the power of the therapist in directing cognitive restructuring. Often the therapist has very definite beliefs about how the client should change and these beliefs may be at variance with the client's prior social conditioning and current belief systems. Consider the case of an agoraphobic client who is carrying over into present interactions patterns of relating learned within a particularly restrictive familial socialization experience. From research on agoraphobic parenting practices (Brehony, 1983; Chambless & Goldstein, 1982; Fodor, 1974; Guidano & Liotti, 1983), we see that the world view of the family views arousal, independence, and mastery as not safe or viable for these clients. Since the clients are in a conflict over change and the therapist so often represents a very different perspective from the family's value systems, it is important for the therapist to recognize that the learning climate of therapy can be characterized as a conflict between two sets of beliefs or ways of being in the world. Since the parental and therapist's values are polarized, (for example, the parent may believe that the daughter is helpless, needs her mother or father nearby and cannot take care of herself) the therapist believes that the daughter can learn to be self-sufficient, rely on herself, and do without a protector. The client may buy into both those belief systems. It is important to explore fully the meaning of these various belief systems to the client and to enable the client to be clear about her own choices. In doing this work, it is also essential that the therapist be aware of her own power to influence and examine with the client the ways in which the client too readily is taking in the "new values" and becoming dependent on the therapist. (For a fuller discussion of these issues, see Fodor in 1987.)

CONCLUSION

It may be time for feminist therapists to put aside their own theoretical biases and begin to work together to develop a comprehensive therapeutic system that moves beyond adherence to particular models and ways of viewing client's problems to address the complexities of women's problems more fully. Such an integrated therapy would take into account prior socialization experiences, societal conditioning, individual personality, temperament, conflict, and patterns of behavior. An integrative system would ask clients what they really want out of life, what would make them happy and work toward a nonbiased system of therapy that enables clients to learn about themselves fully, to be in charge of their own lives and be strong enough to counter and change continuing societal inequities.

REFERENCES

American Psychiatric Association. (1980). *Diagnostic and statistical manual of mental disorders* (3rd ed.). Washington, DC: Author.
Arnkoff, D. B. (1980). Psychotherapy from the perspective of cognitive theory. In M. J. Mahoney (Ed.), *Psychotherapy process.* New York: Plenum Press.
Arnkoff, D. B., & Glass, C. R. (1982). Clinical cognitive constructs: Examination, evaluation, elaboration. In P. C. Kendall (Ed.), *Advances in cognitive-behavioral research and therapy, Vol. 1.* New York: Academic Press.
Bandura, A. (1977). *Social learning theory.* Englewood Cliffs, NJ: Prentice-Hall.
Bandura, A. (1977). Self-efficacy: Toward a unifying theory of behavioral change. *Psychological Review, 84,* 191–215.
Beck, A. K., & Emery, G. (1985). *Anxiety disorders and phobias: A cognitive perspective.* New York: Basic Books.
Beck, A. T. (1979). *Cognitive therapy and the emotional disorders.* New York: International Universities Press.

Blechman, E. (1984). Women's behavior in a man's world: Sex differences in competence. In E. Blechman (Ed.), *Behavior modification with women.* New York: Guilford Press.

Brehony, K. A. (1983). Women and agoraphobia: A case for the etiological significance of the feminine sex role stereotype. In V. Franks & E. Rothblum (Eds.), *The stereotyping of women: It's effects on mental health.* New York: Springer.

Chambless, D. (1982). Characteristics of agoraphobics. In *Agoraphobia: Multiple perspectives on theory and treatment.* New York: Wiley.

Chambless, D. L., & Goldstein, A. J. (1980). Agoraphobia. In A. J. Goldstein & E. B. Foa (Eds.), *Handbook of behavioral interventions.* New York: Wiley.

Chodorow, N. (1978). *The reproduction of mothering.* Berkeley, CA: University of California Press.

Douglas, M. A. (1985, April). A feminist cognitive-behavioral model: Taking feminist therapies to the mainstream. Unpublished manuscript.

Ellis, A. (1962). *Reason and emotion in psychotherapy.* Secaucus, NJ: Lyle Stuart and Citadel Books.

Ellis, A., & Harper, R. A. (1975). *A new guide to rational living.* Englewood Cliffs, NJ: Prentice Hall.

Ellis, A. (1984). Rational-emotive therapy. In R. J. Corsini (Ed.), *Current psychotherapies.* Itasca, IL: F. E. Peacock.

Emmelkamp, P. M. G., & van de Hout. (1983). A failure in treating agoraphobia. In E. B. Foa & P. M. G. Emmelkamp (Eds.), *Failures in behavior therapy.* New York: Wiley.

Fiedler, D., & Beach, L. R. (1978). On the decision to be assertive. *Journal of Consulting and Clinical Psychology, 46,* 537–546.

Foa, E. B., & Kozak, M. J. (1986). Emotional processing of fear: Exposure to corrective information. *Psychology Bulletin, 99*(1), 20–35.

Fodor, I. G. (1974). The phobic syndrome in women. In V. Franks & V. Burtle (Eds.), *Women in therapy.* New York: Brunner-Mazel.

Fodor, I. G. (1974). Sex role conflict and symptom formation in women: Can behavior therapy help? *Psychotherapy: Theory, Research and Practice, 11*(1), 22–29.

Fodor, I. G. (1977). Cognitive/behavior therapy for the overweight woman. *Scandinavian Journal of Behavior Therapy, 6*(4), 60.

Fodor, I. (1983). Behavior therapy for the overweight woman: A time for reappraisal. In M. Rosenbaum, C. M. Franks, & Y. Jaffe (Eds.), *Perspectives on behavior therapy in the eighties.* New York: Springer.

Fodor, I. G. (1985). Assertiveness training in the 80's: Moving beyond the personal. In L. Rosewater, & L. Walker (Eds.), *Handbook of feminist therapy.* New York: Springer.

Fodor, I. G. (1987). Moving beyond cognitive behavior therapy: Integrating gestalt therapy to facilitate personal and interpersonal awareness. In N. Jacobson (Ed.), *Psychotherapists in clinical practice: Cognitive and behavioral perspectives.* New York: Guilford Press.

Fodor, I. G. (1987). Cognitive behavior therapy for agoraphobic women. Toward utilizing psychodynamic understanding to address family belief systems and enhance behavior change. In M. Braude (Ed.), *Women, power and psychotherapy.* New York: Hayworth Press.

Fodor, I. G., & Epstein, R. (1983). Assertiveness training for women: Where are we failing? In E. Foa & P. Emmelkamp (Eds.), *Failures in behavior therapy.* New York: Wiley.

Fodor, I. G., & Rothblum, E. D. (1985). Strategies for dealing with sex role stereotypes. In C. Brody (Ed.), *Women therapists treating women.* New York: Springer.

Fodor, I. G., & Thal, J. (1984). Weight disorders: Overweight and anorexia. In E. Blechman (Ed.), *Behavior modification with women.* New York: Guilford Press.

Fodor, I. G., & Wolfe, J. (1977). Assertiveness training for mothers and daughters. In R. Alberti (Ed.), *Assertiveness, innovations, applications, issues.* San Luis Obisbo, CA: Impact.

Goldfried, M. R. (1980). Psychotherapy as coping skills training. In M. J. Mahoney (Ed.), *Psychotherapy process: Current issues and future directions.* New York: Plenum.

Goldstein, A. J. (1982). Agoraphobia: Treatment successes, treatment failures, and theoretical implication. In D. L. Chambless & A. J. Goldstein (Eds.), *Agoraphobia: Multiples perspectives on theory and treatment.* New York: Wiley.

Goldstein, A. J., & Chambless, D. L. (1978). A reanalysis of agoraphobia. *Behavior Therapy, 9,* 47–59.

Guidano, V. F., & Liotti, G. (1983). *Cognitive processes and emotional disorders.* New York: Guilford Press.

Guttentag, M. (1983). *Too many women.* Beverly Hills, CA: Sage.

Hafner, R. J. (1982). The marital context of the agoraphobic syndrome. In D. L. Chambless & A. J. Goldstein (Eds.), *Agoraphobia: Multiples perspectives on theory and treatment.* New York: Wiley.

Jakobowski-Spector. (1973). Facilitating the growth of women through assertive training. *The Counseling Psychologist, 4,* 76–86.

Kanfer, F. H. (1977). The many faces of self-control, or behavior modification changes its focus. In R. B. Stuart (Ed.), Behavioral self-management. New York: Brunner/Mazel.

Lazarus, A. (1966). Broad-spectrum behavior therapy and the treatment of agoraphobia. *Behavior Therapy Research, 4,* 95–97.

Lineham, M. (1984). Interpersonal effectiveness in assertive situations. In E. Blechman (Ed.), *Behavior modification for women.* New York: Guilford Press.

Mahoney, M. J. (1974). *Cognition and behavior modification.* Cambridge, MA: Ballinger.

Mahoney, M. J. (1980). Psychotherapy and the structure of personal revolutions. In M. J. Mahoney (Ed.), *Psychotherapy process: Current issues and future directions.* New York: Plenum Press.

Marlott, A., & Gordon, J. (1985). *Relapse prevention.* New York: Guilford Press.

Meichenbaum, D. (1977). *Cognitive-behavior modification: An integrative approach.* New York: Plenum Press.

Munby, M., & Johnson, D. W. (1980). Agoraphobia: The long-term follow-up of behavioral treatment. *British Journal of Psychiatry, 137,* 418–427.

Osborn, S. M., & Harris, G. G. (1975). *Assertive training for women.* Springfield, IL: Thomas.

Padawer, W., & Goldfried, M. (1984). Anxiety-related disorders, fears and phobias. In E. Blechman (Ed.), *Behavior modification with women.* New York: Guilford Press.

Rich, A. R., & Schroeder, H. E. (1976). Research issues in assertiveness training. *Psychological Bulletin, 83,* 1081–1096.

Schwartz, R. M., & Gottman, J. M. (1976). Toward a task analysis of assertive behavior. *Journal of Consulting and Clinical Psychology, 44,* 910–920.

Skinner, B. F. (1938). *The behavior of organisms: An experimental analysis.* New York, NY: Appleton-Century-Crofts.

Solomon, L., & Rothblum, E. (1985). Social skills problems experienced by women. In L. Abate & M. Milan (Eds.), *Handbook of social skills training and research.* New York: Wiley.

Thorpe, G., & Burns, L. (1983). *The agoraphobic syndrome.* New York: Wiley.

Walker, L. (1979). *The battered woman.* New York: Harper and Row.

Walker, L. (1984). *The battered woman syndrome.* New York: Springer.

Wilson, G. T. (1984). Behavior therapy. In R. J. Corsini (Ed.), *Current Psychotherapies.* Itasca, IL.: F.E. Peacock.

Wolfe, J. (1976). *How to be sexually assertive.* New York: Institute for Rational-Emotive Therapy.

Wolfe, J. L. (1985). Women. In A. Ellis & M. Bernard (Eds.), *Clinical applications of Rational-Emotive Therapy.* New York: Penum.

Wolfe, J. L., & Fodor, I. G. (1975). A cognitive/behavioral approach to modifying assertive behavior in women. *The Counseling Pyschologist, 5*(4), 45–59.

Wolpe, J. (1958). *Psychotherapy by reciprocal inhibition.* Stanford, CT: Stanford University Press.

Wolpe, J. (1970). Identifying the antecents of an agoraphobic reaction: A transcript. *Journal of Behavior Therapy and Experimental Psychiatry, 1,* 299–304.

Wolpe, J., & Lazarus, A. (1966). *Behavior Therapy Techniques.* New York: Pergamon Press.

CHAPTER 6

Power, Gender, and the Family: Feminist Perspectives on Family Systems Theory

Michele Bograd

The relatively recent development of family therapy and family systems theory provided a new paradigm by which to understand human behavior and psychopathology. Initially, this paradigm seemed nonsexist and gender-neutral. Growing out of a base of liberal social action, family therapy challenged the biases of traditional psychodynamic individually oriented theory and practice. Although the progenitors of family therapy were all men, women have risen to prominence in the field and have expanded the stereotypical "feminine" therapeutic repertoire to include directive, overtly powerful, and active intervention styles. But recently, feminists have drawn attention to sexist biases in systems theory and practice. Controversy rages in the field, since a radical feminist critique challenges the structure and goals of the simplest clinical intervention, as well as the most abstract epistemological axioms of family systems theory.

Because the feminist analyses of family therapy are in early stages of development, it is premature to draw final conclusions about the variety of ways that feminism and family therapy can be integrated. On one end of the continuum, it seems possible to assimilate a feminist consciousness into family therapy as it now stands. On the other, a clearly articulated feminist framework requires a radical reconstruction of family systems theory and clinical practice. The possibility of integration depends both on how radical a feminist framework is employed to account for male–female relations, and on the particular theoretical axioms and practices of a specific school of family therapy. Regardless of how or whether this integration evolves, it is necessary to highlight the profound questions posed by a feminist perspective. Although there are a variety of family systems frameworks, discussion will focus on the implications of a feminist perspective on family therapy in general.

BASIC COMPONENTS OF FAMILY SYSTEMS THEORY

Although many different schools of family therapy exist, they share some basic theoretical assumptions. Instead of examining the internal world of the individual, family therapists focus on the individual as an element of a family system. Systems are a complex of interacting elements and the relationships that organize them, in which the whole is greater than the sum of its parts (Nichols, 1984). Systems are regulated by feedback or the exchange of information and energy between elements of the system, and between the system itself and the surrounding environment. Crucial to systems theory is the notion of circular causality. Most models of human behavior assume that the past determines the present through linear cause and effect. In contrast, systems theorists analyze how elements are interrelated or how every part influences the others and is reciprocally influenced in turn. Systems are described by reference to processes and structures. Rather than focusing on static individual traits or characteristics, family therapists examine sequences of behavior that are recurring elements of the present transactional context. If the interactional patterns endure over time, they organize family subunits into somewhat constant relationships or structures. Although the term "structure" denotes a fixed entity, family therapists define structures as dynamic, ever-evolving patterns.

These fundamental beliefs about systems are common to the variety of family therapy models, but considerable differences between schools exist regarding the therapist's role; the family structures or processes of most clinical interest; whether the therapist facilitates change through a primary focus on behavior, insight, cognition, or emotion; if and how the past is taken into account; the treatment techniques employed; and the nature of desired therapeutic goals. In spite of the proliferation of numerous family therapy models, popular typologies categorize them into five major approaches, to be briefly summarized (for more detailed description and comparison, see Hoffman, 1981; and Nichols, 1984).

Experiential family therapy, one of the earliest family therapy approaches, developed out of the humanistic movement. As such, therapeutic goals include a commitment to personal fulfillment and individual growth, with special focus on the facilitation of spontaneous expressive experience in the here-and-now. Experiential family therapists, such as Whitaker (Napier & Whitaker, 1978; Whitaker, 1976; Whitaker & Keith, 1981) and Satir (1967, 1972), are often creative and self-disclosing, using their personal relationships with families and gestalt techniques, such as family sculpture, to expand the family's member capacities for intense, playful, and emotional experiences and to further congruent clear communication.

Transgenerational family therapy approaches place more emphasis on the past and on the social context beyond the nuclear family. Transgenerational family therapists examine interactional and emotional patterns over three or more generations in an effort to uncover family myths, legacies, and patterns that restrict adaptive functioning in the present. For example, Bowen (1974, 1976, 1978) analyzes how well differentiated individuals are from their families-of-origin and coaches clients to achieve a rationally detached and emotionally modulated connectedness to their families.

In the *structural family therapy* approach, the therapist takes an active, directive role in guiding the family toward functional family structures characterized by relatively clear hierarchical relationships between parents and children and by flexible, permeable boundaries between various family subsystems (Minuchin, 1974; Minuchin & Fishman, 1981; Minuchin, Rosman, & Baker, 1978; Umbarger, 1983). Structural family therapists assume that individual symptoms are a product of dysfunctional family organization, which includes dimensions such as boundaries, hierarchies, coalitions, and alliances. Structures are defined as the relatively enduring interactional patterns that arrange family subunits into somewhat constant relationships regulating the flow of information and energy. The goals of structural interventions include repositioning family members into more appropriate subsystems with more functional boundaries, inducing crisis and flux to challenge rigid, stuck patterns and developing new behavioral sequences.

The *strategic family therapists* are less concerned with changing family structure than with providing symptom relief. Based in communication, cybernetic, and general systems theory, strategic family therapists address the interactional sequences maintaining the presenting problem. Strategic family therapy is often short-term, pragmatic, and problem focused. Goals include behavior change rather than insight, symptom resolution rather than structural transformation (Fisch, Weakland, & Segal, 1982; Haley, 1973, 1976, 1980; Madanes, 1983; Watzlawick, Beavin, & Jackson, 1967; Watzlawick, Weakland, & Fisch, 1974). To these ends, strategic family therapists take direct responsibility for designing specific interventions to resolve the presenting problem, and utilize a range of direct and indirect techniques, including symptom prescription, paradoxical techniques, and rituals.

As family therapy theory has grown more sophisticated with special focus on epistemology, the *systemic family therapy* approach has become increasingly popular (Selvini–Palazzoli, Boscolo, Cecchin, & Prata, 1978; Tomm, 1984a,b). Systemic family therapists define the nature of systems in new and different ways from more traditional family therapists. A distinguishing feature of this approach is the emphasis on cognition or on the belief systems by which family members construe events and behaviors. Systemic family therapists utilize special techniques, such as circular questioning, to illuminate the patterns of relationships in families. The focus of treatment is on information of differences, rather than on behavior. The role of the therapist is facilitative rather than directive. By maintaining careful neutrality, the therapist constructs hypotheses about family interactions with the goal of introducing new information into the system so that the family can discover its own solutions.

Given the range of family therapy schools, the feminist analysis is still in its beginning stages. With the exception of Ault–Riche (1986), feminist clinicians have not carefully addressed the specific strengths and weaknesses of a particular family therapy school. To set the context for such future work, this chapter will examine the biases and potential liabilities common to most family therapy approaches, after briefly suggesting some of the compatibilities between family systems and feminist perspectives.

COMPATIBILITY OF FEMINIST AND FAMILY SYSTEMS PERSPECTIVES

Considerable overlap exists between feminist and family systems clinical frameworks, which may partly account for why some time elapsed before feminists began a critical examination of family systems theory. In somewhat simplified terms, the social context is viewed as a prime determinant of behavior in many family therapy and feminist theoretical frameworks (Libow, Raskin, & Caust, 1982). Both feminist and family therapists tend to distrust the use of static psychiatric diagnostic labels. Psychopathology is not approached as a deficit intrinsic to the individual, but as an adaptive function of how the individual is interrelated to other people and the broader environment. For example, a woman's passivity is defined as responsive to a man's control or as an indirect method for accomplishing her goals without upsetting a relationship, rather than as a character flaw established in her early infancy. Clinical interventions are then geared to changing the structural and interactional components of the relationship, with the goal of increasing role flexibility. Feminist and family therapists both value concrete, observable behavior change as an outcome criterion.

In spite of these common parameters, however, there are important differences between feminist and family systems frameworks. Discussion will focus on the theoretical challenges that feminism poses for family systems theory, specifically the nature of certain basic family systems constructs, the interrelationship of families and the broader social context, the analysis of the typical current family structure, and a multidimensional approach to the construct of gender.

FAMILY SYSTEMS THEORY: MAN-MADE LANGUAGE

Drawing from the sciences of biology and cybernetics, family systems theory appears objective, scientific, and neutral. Family systems theory corrects many of the biases inherent in more individually oriented intrapsychic frameworks. But careful examination of certain systems constructs and of how they are used descriptively reveals that the technical, organizational language of systems theory can highlight male-defined realities (Spender, 1980), ignore or distort women's experiences, and smuggle in biased content (James & McIntyre, 1983). Since clinical theory provides the direction for clinical intervention, these concerns are not simply esoteric but inherently practical and political.

The most basic question is: How are things named or categorized in family systems theory? In general, many basic family systems terms reflect prototypically male attributes and sometimes define them as standards of healthy family functioning (Hare–Mustin, 1978). Families are commonly assessed for their degree of hierarchy, differentiation, or autonomy. In contrast, prototypically female attributes are devalued: Interdependence becomes undifferentiation; intense relatedness becomes enmeshment. The issue here is not that certain "male" characteristics are valued, but that they are placed on a bipolar continuum where the more stereotypical female pole is defined as less healthy or viable (Women's Project in Family Therapy, 1982). Although the description of interactions is a distinguishing characteristic of family systems theory, family therapists have yet to develop a language that reflects and validates woman-based experiences of relationships in the family context.

The male bias in family systems language goes beyond the presence of discrete terms to how this language is employed in the description of behavioral sequences. Aided by the abstract, mechanistic terminology of family systems theory, clinical formulations of transactional patterns appear as detached, nonjudgmental observations. Yet, many formulations draw on stereotypical, culture-bound ideals of men and women that, in very subtle ways, denigrate women and perpetuate traditional assumptions about male–female interactions (Bograd, 1986b; Margolin, Fernandes, Talovic, & Onorato, 1983). For example, take the common and simple formulation: She nags, he withdraws. Built into this simple interactional description is the image of woman as a demanding bitch or shrew. Her requesting attention or compliance is framed as shrill, repetitive complaint; his response seems understandable and is subtly condoned. The hidden bias become more evident in examining a formulation, descriptive of the same behavior, rewritten from a woman's perspective: She asks a simple question, he abandons. A truly neutral description might read: She makes a request, he becomes silent and does not respond.

Family therapists often employ implicit images of typical couples, which shape what is highlighted and what is ignored by family therapists as they capture the complexity of family transactions (Margolin et al., 1983; Women's Project in Family Therapy, 1982, 1983). Family therapists note if a woman has more status than her husband, while male dominance is typically taken for granted. By emphasizing female status in a given family, the formulation implies that this contributes to symptom maintenance: Female dominance is pejoratively described. Language can also be employed in ways that elicit different responses to a behavior, depending upon whether it is enacted by a man or a woman: "father absence" conveys very different meanings than "maternal deprivation" (Hare–Mustin, 1978). Family systems terms can also obscure or distort fundamental social realities of family life. For example, fathers are often described as "peripheral" or "powerless" in relationship to the domestic domain. This ignores that many "powerless" fathers hold pivotal decision-making roles in the family, are able to control and strongly influence the direction of family life, and have financial and social power because of how they are situated in the public domain (Women's Project in Family Therapy, 1983).

The mystification of male–female relationships in family systems theory is not simply a result of the careless misuse of a "value-free" language, which can simply be corrected by more sensitive terminology and careful construction of systemic formulations. Inequality in families cannot be addressed by family therapists, given their adherence to a particular theoretical approach to the construct of power.

POWER: FEMINIST VS. SYSTEMS DEFINITIONS

The analysis of the unequal power relations between men and women is the conceptual pivotal point of any feminist theory. The greatest theoretical disagreement between family therapists and feminists concerns the definition and even the existence of power. Theoretical controversy exists in the family therapy field concerning the epistemological underpinnings of systems models. The reality and nature of power is central to this debate. To oversimplify the abstract and complex discussions influencing how family therapists are defining and understanding systems, in one systems framework, there is no such thing as "real" power; in the other, there is no such thing as real "power." Traditional family systems theory or first-order cybernetics states that men and women in families constitute systems characterized by circular relationships where their behaviors mutually shape and constrain one another. Since each part influences the other, no one family member has unilateral or greater control over the system than any other. Unequal power relationships then are not what they seem. They are simply complementary: the powerless play as significant a part in their oppression as do the powerful. The newer "evolutionary" models challenge the basic assumptions of first-order cybernetics models. In these second-order cybernetic models, power is defined as theoretically irrelevant because it reflects the erroneous application of a linear epistemology (Keeney, 1983). Power is defined as a nonuseful metaphor, a way of punctuating experience that leads to clinical interventions and conceptual distinctions that are neither ecologically pure nor pragmatically effective.

From a feminist perspective, major problems exist with these theoretical premises of systems theory. First, the denial or neutralization of power contributes to minimizing the consequences of the abuses of power. This is most evident in cases of violence against women (Bograd, 1984, 1986a). Family systems conceptualizations of incest, for example, frame the abusive incident as just one step in the mutually regulated dance between husband, wife, and daughter (Bograd, 1986a; Brickman, 1984). When incest is redefined as a distance regulator or as a homeostatic mechanism, the traumatizing and coercive quality of the husband's behavior disappears. Second, responsibility for maintenance of inequality is diffused, given the theoretical axiom that every family member contributes equally to maintaining the system. Family therapists commit a conceptual error when they confuse functional description of a system with the moral allocation of responsibility. While family therapists are often quick to argue that systemic description is not equivalent to blame, in practice such formulations lead to a primary treatment focus on female family members. For example, the wife of an alcoholic is guided to be less "enabling" since she presumably plays as significant a role in maintaining the husband's drinking as he does. Family therapists are just beginning to grapple with the difficult theoretical and clinical questions regarding how to acknowledge the systemic interrelationship of family members while holding one individual morally responsible for abusive or coercive behaviors. Lastly, although family therapists address the balance of power in families in certain ways, systems theory obscures aspects of domination. Systems theory suggests either that men and women in families are in harmoniously balanced, complementary relationships or that men and women are equally oppressed by their respective positions (Goldner, 1985a). Yet there can be no true complementarity if there is not parity of power to begin with (Women's Project in Family Therapy, 1983). And while it is clear that roles of the powerful have detrimental consequences for individual males, men as a class are not as oppressed as women. This suggests that clinical interventions that attempt "fairness" or nondifferential treatment of men and women penalize the family members with the least power (Brickman, 1984; Jacobson, 1983; Margolin et al., 1983).

Feminists acknowledge that there is a transactional component that maintains inequality between men and women (Henley, 1977; Miller, 1976), yet do not deny the reality of oppression. Family therapists are clearly aware of injustice and domination, but our language, stripped of connection to the social field, guides us to talk about these phenomena in abstract and mechanistic terms (Goldner, 1985a,b; James & McIntyre, 1983). This, in turn, is related to how family therapists conceptualize the interrelationship of the family and society.

THE FAMILY AND SOCIETY: WHAT IS THE BOUNDARY?

While family therapists acknowledge that the larger social context shapes the family and is reciprocally related to it, most family therapists draw a boundary around the family to examine its internal structure and processes. While this conceptual boundary was necessary to develop family systems theory, the feminist critique of systemic notions of power suggest that the family needs to be examined in context, that family therapists have not been systemic enough (Goldner, 1985a; MacKinnon & Miller, 1987; Taggart, 1985). The most radical feminist analysis suggests that family therapists oversimplify or misrepresent the multiple forces shaping family process.

For example, family by family, clinicians examine the common dynamic of overfunctioning man/underfunctioning woman. Each family is approached as a novel interpersonal event; certain transactional sequences are attributed to the current, interactional context or perhaps to the individual histories of family members. While such an analysis can beautifully illuminate the internal workings of the family, it ignores that family structure does not evolve by chance. It is no coincidence that, in most families, men control the resources, hold certain status, and interact in predictable ways, and that women are relatively disempowered, hold a devalued status, and interact in predictable ways. These structures and patterns are not created de novo in each family, but result from the socially structured and predetermined interrelationships of men and women as a class (Gillespie, 1971). By ignoring these factors, family therapists cannot adequately account for the nature of family interaction, nor for the factors that constrain how families can change.

Because of the theoretical decision to focus primarily on intrafamilial life, family therapists may also incorrectly diagnosis certain family structures or processes maintaining symptomatic behavior. For example, family pathology is commonly linked to the structure of disengaged father, overinvolved mother, and symptomatic child. But when we broaden our lens, it is clear that this is not an unusual social structure, but prototypical of families in Western culture. Furthermore, although individual factors may lead to the father's disengagement or the mother's so-called overinvolvement, powerful social forces contribute to and maintain this normative structure.

These external social forces may also contribute to intrafamilial conflicts. Because family therapists examine only the internal workings of each family, husband–wife tension may be attributed to the mother's intense involvement with her school-phobic child or to unresolved issues in each spouse's family of origin, rather than to the changing structure of male and female roles or to the multiple pressures on mothers entering the workforce. Although social forces contribute to intrafamilial conflict, feminists go one step further by arguing that our society may require a certain type of family structure that is inherently "dysfunctional" and ultimately not to the benefit of its individual members (Goldner, 1985a,b; James & McIntyre, 1983). If family therapists continue to promote traditional family forms, they may be perpetuating the structures that help maintain the symptomatic behavior they are trying to ameliorate. The examination of this possibility requires a critical analysis of the family as a social institution.

CAN FAMILY THERAPY PROVIDE A CRITICAL ANALYSIS OF THE FAMILY?

Family systems theory cannot address fundamental questions about family structure and process. To understand the family, family therapists examine only its current functioning and transactional patterns—not its historical development or genesis. Within the systems definitional framework, the family is viewed as a subtype of an organizational system that is a cohesive whole, functioning to attain goals adaptive for each of its members. But if families are defined as qualitatively different human systems (James & McIntyre, 1983), then we must account for how the family as a societal institution is socially constructed (Taggart, 1985).

Feminists have analyzed the family as a system that perpetuates male domination, that best suits the needs of men as a class, and that requires the personal self-sacrifice of women (James, 1985). In contrast to current systems views of the family as a coherent and harmonious whole, Goldner (1985a,b) suggests that the family is a system characterized by internal contradictions, which have evolved over time in complex ways, given the historical development of the private and public domains. Her sophisticated analysis suggests that power is not shared in a complementary fashion by men and women, nor do men simply dominate and oppress women. Instead, because of the systemic transaction between family and society, the interrelationship of gender, power, and family roles is paradoxical and contradictory. For example, since the industrial revolution, the domestic sphere has had a separate but not equal existence from the public domain. Within the home, women are indeed central and "powerful" figures, but this power is ambiguous, since women and their domestic roles are socially degraded. Coupled with this, in most "normal" families, wives do not share equal power with their husbands but are in a relatively subordinate position. Although family therapists examine the appropriate hierarchical relationship between parents and children, they assume that husbands and wives share equal power and rarely address the hierarchical structure of the marital subsystem, much less how it is influenced by the power and resources available to men and women in extrafamilial roles.

Because family therapists have not critically examined the family as an oppressive social institution, interventions are usually geared to helping solidify or stabilize the typical family form. When it is assumed that the family functions for the good of all its members, interventions that aid the system as a whole are presumed to benefit individuals as well. But if the family is a social structure founded on the subordination of women, the goals of the relational system may not be compatible with the goals of the individual woman (Hare–Mustin, 1980; Jacobson, 1983; Margolin et al., 1983). Family therapists may then unwittingly help the woman adjust to a basically exploitative context (Gurman & Klein, 1980). Because family therapists rarely articulate the ideal family structure informing their clinical interventions or assume that the relationship structure is simply a matter of the spouses' personal tastes (Jacobson, 1983), the political position of family therapists is determined by default.

The potentially conservative function of family therapy could be modified if therapists paid greater attention to the macrosystemic social dimensions that organize family processes and structures. But a feminist analysis suggests that the relationships between men and women in families are also determined by the psychological arrangements of gender—a topic not yet addressed by family therapists.

FAMILY THERAPY AND GENDER AS AN INDIVIDUAL, INTERPERSONAL AND SOCIAL CONSTRUCT

Historically, family therapists have examined interacting elements of a system: Whether these elements were male or female was not of theoretical importance (Layton, 1984). Gender differences are not taken into account by family therapists in most analyses of dominant/subordinate patterns, common and painful impasses between husbands and wives, and prototypical male–female interactional patterns. Yet conventional notions of male and female roles are an implicit part of most family therapy models. Healthy family functioning is often linked to the allocation of instrumental roles to men and expressive roles to women (Hare–Mustin, 1978), and criteria of successful treatment outcome often relate to the fulfillment of normative gender-based behaviors (Gurman & Klein, 1980).

Feminist theoreticians have broadened the definition of gender beyond stereotypical family roles to address gender on two levels not yet adequately integrated into family systems theory: the social and the intrapsychic. Feminists define gender as more than an individual or interpersonal phenomenon. It is approached as a macrosystem dimension organizing society as a whole. At this level of analysis, it can be seen that men and women are not equally limited by their gender roles. Gender is organized at the social level in ways that maintain male dominance over women as a class, a pattern that is replicated in the family, which, in turn, maintains this social structure.

For example, a defining characteristic of the traditional female sex role is that women are primarily responsible for the harmony of the domestic sphere. In order to gain therapeutic leverage into the family system, family therapists often focus on the wife, who is usually more committed to therapy, more adept at verbalizing feelings, and more willing to modify her behaviors. We enlist the wife's aid and reinforce her centrality to the family, even as systemic formulations define this centrality as pathogenic and clinical interventions serve to reduce her involvement. By simultaneously utilizing but devaluing women's family roles, family therapists can perpetuate the social norm that women should adapt themselves to the family context and subordinate their own needs to those of the husband and children. But a paradox exists: While family therapists may intervene to guide women toward perfecting stereotypical gender roles, adherence to these roles is diagnosed as dysfunctional or problematic. The overinvolved mother who indirectly expresses her power is following the dictates of the maternal female role. When family therapists do not analyze this role, they hold individual women accountable for behaviors that are socially prescribed (Goldner, 1985b; Taggart, 1985).

When family therapists do not openly name and label the ideal gender roles that inform their clinical interventions, they can unwittingly perpetuate traditional and restrictive sex roles and so, by default, serve a conservative function by maintaining the status quo (Goldner, 1985a; Hare–Mustin, 1978, 1980; Jacobson, 1983; James & McIntyre, 1983; MacKinnon & Miller, 1987; Margolin et al., 1983; Taggart, 1985; Women's Project in Family Therapy, 1982, 1983). Because family therapists do not question the socially constructed nature of male–female relations, even gender-sensitive interventions may be of limited efficacy. For example, family therapists can try to redefine static roles and increase individual flexibility by helping the woman develop more instrumental rational ways of relating and the man to experiment with expressive nurturant behaviors. While such clinical interventions can be useful, they beg the larger question of the structure of male–female relationships. Moving pieces on the board does not challenge the rules of the game itself: We are "shifting chairs on the Titanic" (Carter, 1985).

Family therapists treat family members as if gender roles can be easily switched, changed or transcended (Goldner, 1985b). But the transformation of gendered roles cannot be accomplished simply by the modification of family structures and processes. Feminist theoreticians have provided a careful analysis of the interrelationship of social structure, family roles, and individual gender identity (Chodorow, 1978; Goldner, 1985b; James & McIntyre, 1983). By virtue of the social (not biological) fact that sole women are the primary caretakers of children in nuclear families, boys and girls develop intrapsychic structures that help maintain the family as we know it and the class relationships of society as a whole. Because of its theoretical axioms, family systems theory cannot address the intrapsychic psychological reality of gender. But these internal structures may limit the effectiveness of clinical

interventions that focus primarily on behavior and interpersonal transactions.

For example, take a conventional couple in which both spouses work.
The wife is angry because she is still primarily responsible for domestic
duties. The family therapist helps the couple negotiate a behavioral
contract in which the husband takes over some household chores. But
he constantly forgets things at the store and procrastinates before
washing the dishes. The wife gets more aggravated, not understanding
why her spouse can't keep all these things in mind, when she is able
to do so even though she also holds a full-time job. On the interpersonal
level, this sequence can be analyzed with the popular systems formulation of "pursuer and distancer": The more the wife requests of
the husband, the more he withdraws, which serves as a way of regulating
the closeness between them. On the social level, the husband is being
asked to attend to tasks he considers beneath him. Though he tries to
share power within the home, he has greater professional status outside
of it, which influences the power dynamics between the couple. Even
though the husband tries to take more responsibility at home, by virtue
of his gendered personality, he cannot easily attend simultaneously to
duties and to his relationship in a way that is prototypically easier for
women. His lack of ability to fulfill the therapeutic contract is con-
strained by extrafamilial forces, by how the roles of husband and wife
are ideologically constructed in our culture, by the interactional patterns
with his wife, and by his own gendered psychological characteristics.
Because family systems cannot adequately account for this complexity,
Goldner (1985a) has called for a reform of the construct of gender in
family therapy: The conceptual map of systems theory does not fit the
terrain of family life.

REFORMATION OR RECONSTRUCTION?: CONCLUSIONS

Family systems theory is a conceptually useful framework for capturing
the complexity of interpersonal relations. Many of its axioms are
consonant with feminist beliefs and family therapy techniques are
potentially potent tools for transforming the relationships between men
and women. At the same time, a feminist critique raises a fundamental
question: What are the social costs of a theoretically parsimonious and
clinically expedient model? A feminist analysis of family systems theory
suggests that these costs are quite high, particularly for women, until
family therapists can adequately account for the unequal distribution
of power in systems; for the structure of the contemporary family and

its interrelationship with society at large; and for the individual and social dimensions of gender. While some of the shortcomings of family systems theory are a function of how it is employed, it is clear that systems theory itself precludes asking (much less answering) questions deemed crucial from a feminist perspective.

Modification or extension of extant family systems constructs can partly ameliorate current theoretical limitations. For example, the interdependence of family and social context could be elucidated by family therapists with relative ease. However, systemic description of inequality will necessitate a radical restructuring of fundamental systems axioms, including those of circular causality, power, and the very definition of the system itself. Such an effort will be strengthened by adding a critical analysis of the family as a historically situated and culturally perpetuated social institution.

This kind of analysis will bring us straight to the question of gender itself. Acknowledgment of the pervasive effects of gender on language, thought, the structure of social relations, and individual development will challenge family therapists to address the multiple levels of the intimate relationships between men and women. Such an experience will also be quite humbling. Although the primary task of family therapists is addressing the distress of a particular family, all family problems are not simply clinical problems. They are related to the heart of family life and to the structure of our society, founded on the subordination of women to men.

REFERENCES

Ault–Riche, M. (1986). A feminist critique of five schools of family therapy. In M. Ault–Riche (Ed.), *Women and family therapy* (pp. 1–15). Rockville, MD: Aspen Systems Corp.

Bograd, M. (1984). Family systems approaches to wife battering: A feminist critique. *American Journal of Orthopsychiatry, 54,* 558–568.

Bograd, M. (1986a). A feminist examination of family systems models of violence against women in the family. In M. Ault–Riche (Ed.), *Women and family therapy* (pp. 34–50). Rockville, MD: Aspen Systems Corp.

Bograd, M. (1986b). A feminist examination of family therapy: What is women's place? In D. Howard (Ed.), *The dynamics of feminist therapy.* New York: Haworth Press.

Bowen, M. (1974). Toward the differentiation of self in one's family of origin. In F. Andres & J. Lorio (Eds.), *Georgetown family symposia (Vol. 1).* Washington, D.C.: Georgetown University Medical Center.

Bowen, M. (1976). Theory in the practice of psychotherapy. In P. Guerin (Ed.), *Family therapy: Theory and practice.* New York: Gardner Press.

Bowen, M. (1978). *Family therapy in clinical practice.* New York: Gardner Press.

Brickman, J. (1984). Feminist, nonsexist, and traditional models of therapy: Implications for working with incest. *Women & Therapy, 3,* 49–67.

Carter, B. (1985). Ms. Intervention's guide to "correct" feminist family therapy. *Family Therapy Networker, 9,* 78–79.

Chodorow, N. (1978). *The reproduction of mothering: Psychoanalysis and the sociology of gender.* Berkeley: University of California Press.

Fisch, R., Weakland, J., & Segal, L. (1982). *The tactics of change: Doing therapy briefly.* San Francisco: Jossey–Bass.

Gillespie, D. (1971). Who has the power? The marital struggle. *Journal of Marriage & the Family, 33,* 445–458.

Goldner, V. (1985a). Feminism and family therapy. *Family Process, 24,* 31–47.

Goldner, V. (1985b). Warning: Family therapy may be hazardous to your health. *Family Therapy Networker, 9,* 18–23.

Gurman, A., & Klein, M. (1980). Marital and family conflicts. In A. Brodsky & R. Hare–Mustin (Eds.), *Women and psychotherapy.* New York: Guilford Press.

Haley, J. (1973). *Uncommon therapy.* New York: Norton.

Haley, J. (1976). *Problem-solving therapy.* San Francisco: Jossey–Bass.

Haley, J. (1980). *Leaving home.* New York: McGraw–Hill.

Hare–Mustin, R. (1978). A feminist approach to family therapy. *Family Process, 17,* 181–194.

Hare–Mustin, R. (1980). Family therapy may be dangerous for your health. *Professional Psychology, 11,* 935–938.

Henley, N. (1977). *Body politics: Power, sex and nonverbal communication.* Englewood Cliffs, NJ: Prentice–Hall.

Hoffman, L. (1981). *Foundations of family therapy.* New York: Basic Books.

Jacobson, N. (1983). Beyond empiricism: The politics of marital therapy. *American Journal of Family Therapy, 11,* 11–24.

James, K. (1985). Breaking the chains of gender: Family therapy's position? *Australian Journal of Family Therapy, 5,* 241–248.

James, K., & McIntyre, D. (1983). The reproduction of families: The social role of family therapy? *Journal of Marital & Family Therapy, 9,* 119–129.

Keeney, B. (1983). *Aesthetics of change.* New York: Guilford Press.

Layton, M. (1984). Tipping the therapeutic scales—Masculine, feminine, or neuter? *Family Therapy Networker, 8,* 20–27.

Libow, J., Raskin, P., & Caust, B. (1982). Feminist and family systems therapy: Are they irreconcilable? *American Journal of Family Therapy, 3,* 3–12.

MacKinnon, L., & Miller, D. (1987). The new epistemology and the Milar approach: Feminist and sociopolitical considerations. *Journal of Marital & Family Therapy, 13,* 139–155.

Madanes, C. (1983). *Strategic family therapy.* San Francisco: Jossey–Bass.

Margolin, G., Fernandes, V., Talovic, S., & Onorato, R. (1983). Sex role considerations and behavioral marital therapy: Equal does not mean identical. *Journal of Marital & Family Therapy, 9,* 131–145.

Miller, J. (1976). *Toward a new psychology of women.* Boston: Beacon Press.

Minuchin, S. (1974). *Families and family therapy.* Cambridge, MA: Harvard University Press.

Minuchin, S., & Fishman, C. (1981). *Family therapy techniques.* Cambridge, MA: Harvard University Press.

Minuchin, S., Rosman, B., & Baker, L. (1978). *Psychosomatic families: Anorexia nervosa in context.* Cambridge, MA: Harvard University Press.

Napier, A., & Whitaker, C. (1978). *The family crucible.* New York: Harper & Row.

Nichols, M. (1984). *Family therapy: Concepts and methods.* New York: Gardner Press.

Satir, V. (1967). *Conjoint family therapy.* Palo Alto, CA: Science & Behavior Books.

Satir, V. (1972). *Peoplemaking.* Palo Alto, CA: Science & Behavior Books.

Selvini–Palazzoli, M., Boscolo, L., Cecchin, G., & Prata, G. (1978). *Paradox and counterparadox.* New York: Jason Aronson.

Spender, D. (1980). *Man made language.* Boston: Routledge & Kegan Paul.

Taggart, M. (1985). The feminist critique in epistemological perspective: Questions of context in family therapy. *Journal of Marital & Family Therapy, 11,* 113–126.

Tomm, K. (1984a). One perspective on the Milan systemic approach: Part 1. Overview of development, theory and practice. *Journal of Marital & Family Therapy, 10,* 113–125.

Tomm, K. (1984b). One perspective on the Milan systemic approach: Part 2. Description of session format, interviewing style and interventions. *Journal of Marital & Family Therapy, 10,* 253–271.

Umbarger, C. (1983). *Structural family therapy.* New York: Grune & Stratton.

Watzlawick, P., Beavin, J., & Jackson, D. (1967). *Pragmatics of human communication.* New York: Norton.

Watzlawick, P., Weakland, J., & Fisch, R. (1974). *Change: Principles of problem formation and problem resolution.* New York: Norton.

Whitaker, C. (1976). The hindrance of theory in clinical work. In P. Guerin (Ed.), *Family therapy: Theory and practice.* New York: Gardner Press.

Whitaker, C., & Keith, D. (1981). Symbolic-experiential family therapy. In A. Gurman & D. Kniskern (Eds.), *Handbook of family therapy.* New York: Brunner/Mazel.

Women's Project in Family Therapy. (1982). Mothers and daughters. *Monograph Series, 1.*

Women's Project in Family Therapy. (1983). Mothers and sons, fathers and daughters. *Monograph Series, 2.*

PART II

Application of Feminist Therapies

CHAPTER 7

Feminist Therapies with Women

Lynne Bravo Rosewater

INTRODUCTION

The double bind that women psychotherapy clients face was first identified 15 years ago by the classic Broverman study (Broverman, Broverman, Clarkson, & Rosencrantz, 1970), which found that a woman could not be considered a healthy female and a healthy person at the same time. One would hope with the passage of time mental health professionals' view of women would have changed. Unfortunately, the latest research to replicate the Broverman study (Rosencrantz, DeLorey, & Broverman, 1985) shows that the bias still exists.

Russo and Denmark (1985), in an essay on women, psychology, and public policy, state the case clearly: "Despite the past century, sexism still pervades American public policies and still exists in institutions at the federal, state and local levels" (p. 1161). One major issue they point out is "the persistent disparity between policy assumptions and the realities of women's lives" (p. 1161). For minority and disabled women, this disparity is the widest.

It is clear that research findings and policy recommendations alone are insufficient to create change. The actual *implementation* of policy is essential. Feminist therapy is a means of achieving this transition from policy to practice, as feminist therapy in itself is a way of translating abstract philosophy to concrete practice. Feminist therapy, built on feminist philosophy, advocates political, social, and economic equality for women and men (Rawlings & Carter, 1977). A belief in equalitarian relationships and appropriate therapist self-disclosure moves feminist therapy away from an authoritarian, hierarchical model. How feminist therapy is practiced is a model for translating theory to action: There is congruence between what is said and what is done.

GETTING STARTED

That congruence between principle and practice is initially demonstrated by the process of selecting a therapist. Feminist therapists view the client as a consumer who actively chooses her therapist. Clients are encouraged in the initial contact (usually a phone call) to ask questions about the therapist: her philosophical orientation, her location, her availability, her fees and her flexibility in negotiating fees, her areas of expertise and her knowledge regarding the issues with which the client wishes to work. The client is encouraged to question other therapists as well to feel that she is making an informed selection.

On the basis of her screening process, the first appointment is an opportunity to negotiate the specifics of the therapeutic relationship. Some therapists do not charge for this first interview, while others do. It is important to clarify whether or not the client will be charged and the exact fee if a charge is made. At this first interview both client and therapist present their goals. For a client these goals may include her preference for working style (how active she wants her therapist to be), what issues she wishes to work on, her ability to pay, her scheduling needs and any other relevant issues for the therapy. The therapist needs to state her philosophical beliefs, her working style, how and why she schedules appointments, her policy for fees and fee collection, her ground rules (advance notice about breaking appointments, how emergency calls are handled, etc.) and her expertise about the areas the client wishes to address. Furthermore, both client and therapist must discuss how the therapy will be evaluated, with an emphasis on the notion that a dissatisfied consumer is free to go elsewhere.

For lesbian clients the importance of seeing a lesbian therapist needs to be discussed. Some state categorically that a lesbian client should see only a lesbian therapist (Escamilla–Mondanaro, 1977), while others feel that a lesbian therapist is preferable (Sang, 1977). Clearly, lesbian clients want and deserve a nonhomophobic therapist. The ability and sensitivity of a heterosexual therapist working with lesbian clients has been eloquently discussed by Siegel (1985). For further information on lesbian clients, see Brown's chapter.

This negotiating session reflects the egalitarian relationship explicit in feminist therapy, a relationship that has been defined as "based on mutual respect for each other's skills" (Rosewater, 1984, p. 270). The importance of validation is essential to any therapy labeled as "feminist," as is prowomen values.

Part of that negotiation process is discussing the use of diagnosis. Many clients are covered by third-party payment. While such insurance allows many more individuals to afford therapy, it also requires a diagnosis to receive reimbursement. The sexist bias of DSM-III has been articulated by Kaplan (1983), which sexism is even more blatantly revealed in the new diagnostic categories proposed for the revision of DSM-III. The decision to use a diagnosis, along with its ramifications, must be discussed with a client. If a diagnosis is to be used, discussing which diagnosis and why that diagnosis is suggested is also necessary. It is also possible to use diagnosis as an example of empowerment, such as using Post-Traumatic Stress Disorder to describe the behavior of survivors of violence (battered women, rape victims). Of feminist concern is the creation of diagnostic categories which would expand the posttraumatic stress disorders into categories that describe the consequences of abuse (Walker, 1985b). Such diagnostic categories reflect the consequence of victimization: victimization causes pathology, rather than pathology creates victimization.

HOW WOMEN ARE VIEWED

DSM-III (APA, 1980) and its proposed revision mirror the stereotyping and devaluing of feminine roles. Typical feminine behavior is often labeled as characteristic of a personality disorder (for example, histrionic, dependent and the newly proposed self-defeating personality disorder). Defining female-learned behavior as pathological is misogynist, another way of victimizing women (Rosewater, 1985b). Learning to value female traits is one step used by feminist therapists to eliminate the bias of sex role stereotyping and its subsequent second-class status for women. Smith and Siegel (1985) argue that empowerment includes helping women be aware of and valuing the power they already have. In this context there is equal affirmation for indirect, invisible "feminine" power as there is for visable, direct "masculine" power. Further, empowerment includes helping women be aware of their potential to create change—working toward social, political, and economic equality—and a more caring world. Dr. Helen Caldicott, a pediatrician and leader of the Women's Action for Nuclear Disarmament (WAND), models this role of competency and caring.

WORKING TOWARD WHOLENESS: RESPECTING THE CLIENT

Feminist therapy challenges some basic assumptions of traditional psychotherapy—that clients are "sick" and that the doctor knows more than the patient. Based on a presumption of health rather than illness, feminist therapy sees an individual's behavioral as a function of being oppressed rather than confused or sick (Rosewater, 1984). Thus feminist therapy does not embrace the medical model but rather fosters an educational, positive growth model of human behavior. Therapy is not aimed at adjustment, as defined by some authoritative therapist; it becomes an ongoing process of facilitating change, as that change is defined by the client. The "expert" about her own life experience is the client not the therapist. What the client says about her life is both heard and believed. Long before Masson's (1984) exposé of Freud's original seduction theory, feminist therapists were hearing women talk about childhood incest and accepting that account as factual and not imagined.

Striving Toward an Egalitarian Relationship

In addition to believing the client, the feminist therapist is sensitive and responsive to feedback from the client. Recognizing and acknowledging mistakes is both a way of modeling humanness and according the client the respect that she deserves.

Striving toward an egalitarian model, the feminist therapist recognizes and respects her own competence without devaluing the client's ability to teach her. By advocating on her client's behalf and teaching her client how to advocate on her own behalf, the feminist therapist works for social change and uses her power and privilege in a manner that equalizes, rather than exaggerates power differential.

Avoiding Labels

The changes that go on in therapy, both the client's feelings toward herself, her therapist, and others, are not labeled. Such terms as "transference" and "countertransference" are psychoanalytical labels, imbued with many connotations that are antithetical to the tenets of feminist therapy. These feelings need to be explored in an educational fashion that help the client be aware of her own empowerment. Labels tend to perpetuate an hierarchical model, as the therapist "knows what you are doing" and "tells" you. Respecting the client's own knowledge and intuitions, the therapist respects the client's readiness to deal with issues in therapy. "Resistance" is a therapist-defined interpretation; "readiness" is client-defined.

Avoiding Revictimization

Closely allied with not hearing (or believing) women is blaming them. Traditional therapies, geared to cause and effect, often view women as the source of their own problems. Battered women were/are seen as masochistic, both evoking and enjoying the violence in their lives (Symonds, 1979). Rape victims were/are seen as provocative; rape was/ is seen as an act of sex rather than an act of violence (Brownmiller, 1975). Feminist therapy has placed the responsibility for his actions on the aggressor, not the victim. Before the growth of rape crisis centers, rape victims were revictimized by the insensitivity of their treatment in the emergency room, the therapist's office and the courtroom. Feminist therapy has not only denounced such revictimization, it has emphasized women's strength through such crises by relabeling victims as survivors as a way of conveying this image of power (Walker, 1985a).

MEDICATION AS AN ADJUNCT

The medical model, used in some traditional psychotherapy, such as psychoanalysis, not only views clients as "sick," but sees medication as the remedy. Treating symptoms rather than the source of the problem, women are freely given prescriptions (Walker, 1984a), most frequently antianxiety or antidepressant drugs or major tranquilizers.

Drugs tend to reinforce the notion that "something is wrong with me." All too frequently chemotherapy is the only therapy used; the time spent talking with the therapist is about what is happening with the pills rather than what is happening in the woman's life.

The feminist backlash against the indiscriminate use of drugs with women was to decry medication. However, the realization that medication may be a useful adjunct to therapy is now more accepted (Hendricks, 1985b). How the decision about medication is made is one way feminist therapy differs from traditional therapy. Sharing the reasons for suggesting medication and the pros and cons (especially the potential side-effects) of a particular medication, the decision about medication is a joint one. Medication doesn't replaces the need for finding alternative ways of coping that lessen stress and which may eventually lessen the need for the medication. Nor does the use of medication eliminate the need to examine what life realities are causing or complicating the symptoms being treated.

Freud's legacy to therapy was his ideal of therapist objectivity. The removal of the therapist from the therapy process clearly delineated the doctor from the patient. As women working with women, we share the commonality of gender-related oppression. By appropriate self-disclosure about our own struggles and process of growth, we feminist therapists blur the distinction between "healthy" therapist and "sick" client (Smith & Siegel, 1985).

Feminist therapy is a reframing of what therapy is and how it works. Moving away from a medical, hierarchical model, it sees emotional problems as the consequence of external as well as internal problems. The emphasis on behaviors as symptoms of oppression rather than illness makes it a more optimistic therapy.

WORKING WITH WOMEN CLIENTS

The usual application of feminist therapy is with women. In a world defined and run by men, women are second-class citizens. The status of women as a minority group creates its own unique set of problems, including group self-hatred and a feeling of culpability (Hacker, 1976).

While all women are members of a minority group because of their lack of power and privledge in society, the problems for women vary for different types of women. Bernard (1984) makes the distinction between "traditional" and "modern" women. The stress for traditionalists, Bernard found, pertained to the changing family values, which made traditionalists feel that they were now the "out" rather than the "in" group. For modernists, the stress related to the changing role relationships, which made these women feel they had to undertake even more and subsequently feel overburdened.

For other women the major focus of life is survival. Women are becoming a majority in the ranks of the poor, a phenomenon labeled as the "feminization of poverty" (Pearce, 1979). This group of poor women is made up of increasing numbers of minority women (Belle, 1984). Poverty enhances the likelihood of stress. Low-income women are more likely to experience "chronic stressful conditions" (such as "inadequate housing, dangerous neighborhoods, burdensome responsibilities, and financial uncertainties") and "acute stressful events" (such as greater crime and violence, discrimination and losses) (Belle, 1984, p. 138).

If the focus is on the realities of the woman client's life, the role of the feminist therapist is to help effect change by enhancing individuals' problem-solving skills and political awareness (Wycoff, 1977). Listening is a key ingredient, as is respecting the client's own expertise about her life. In this context, failure to attain goals is never assumed to be the individual's failure. The broader social context must always be assessed. Feminist therapy is respectful of the inclination of women, because of their lesser power and privledge, to accept self-blame. What differentiates feminist therapy from many traditional therapies is this sensivity to revictimization. Starting with the supposition that mental health problems originate within the society and not just within the individual, feminist therapists are more likely to look for alternative explanations to individual inadequacy. Kaplan (1983) summarizes this issue: "It is difficult to say when society should be labeled as 'unjust' and when an individual should be labeled as 'crazy' " (p. 789). Yet, the role of the feminist therapist is to do just that. There is scrutinizing of every issue raised in therapy for sex role bias.

Sex Role Stereotypes: The Fallout

Many of the issues women face in therapy are the sequelae of sex role stereotypes. As Chesler (1973) found, women are often labeled as crazy for either underconforming or overconforming to sex role stereotypes. This double bind for women of either being unfeminine or unhealthy (Broverman, et al., 1970) is central to many treatment issues, including anger, power issues, self-nurturance, relationships, divorcing, and mothering.

Anger/Power Issues

Girls learn to be "nice" and to take care of others. The expectations that accompany such nurturing behavior preclude the luxury of anger. Many women come to therapy immobilized in their expression of anger and fearful of being seen as "bitchy." Feminist therapists must help women both to express their anger and to be willing to deal with the negative reactions such anger may cause (Fodor, 1985). In addition, as mentioned earlier, feminist therapists encourage women to acknowledge the ways in which they have already expressed their anger.

Anger and power are two sides of the same coin. Acknowledging anger and finding viable means of correcting inequity are the basis of feminist empowerment.

Self-Nurturance

Owning anger and dissatisfaction is the beginning of the ability to self-nurture. Feminist therapists give permission for women to learn to take care of themselves. Such permission does not mean that woman can no longer take care of others. Having to choose between total self-sacrifice or total selfishness is a setup, another double bind for women. From a feminist perspective, helping women value their special "morality of concern" (Gilligan, 1982) means acknowledging that such concern is as important for ourselves as is for others.

Relationships

Women have learned to define themselves by the quality of their relationships. They have been taught to equate success with finding (and keeping) a man. Maintaining a relationship becomes an affirmation of a woman's capacity to nurture. Traditional therapies reinforce this notion that it is a woman's role to please her man. Women who are dissatisfied with how men were treating them are asked to examine "What are you doing to displease him?" or "What could you do that would make him happy?" Feminist therapy does not assume that any relationship is better than none or that a woman's self-worth is judged by the length of her relationships. DeHardt (1985) provocatively asks: "If my observations are correct that women often become less rather than more the persons they are capable of being when struggling to develop or maintain a relationship with a man, how can I, a feminist therapist, committed to empowering women, facilitate my client's heterosexual relationships?" (pp. 170–171). A feminist therapist helps her client work on standards to judge the healthiness of a relationship, to question why this relationship is important for her and to decide on the appropriateness of maintaining the relationship. These standards apply also to other relationships—to friends, to individuals with whom a woman works, and to her family members.

This chapter deals primarily with the problems of heterosexual relationships. The different dynamics of lesbian relationships, including boundaries and merger, create unique problems in these relationships. See Brown's chapter for an in-depth discussion.

Divorcing (Leaving)

Divorce represents failure. "I'm sorry your dreams didn't come true," one divorced friend was told. Such failure is difficult, especially for women who are acculturated to believe that it is her job to keep the marriage together.

Working on divorce issues involves three major tasks: identifying and facilitating the grieving process, helping women resolve their guilt feelings, and educating women about their legal rights.

A divorce is similar to a death. In a society that values a woman who can keep her man, being a divorcee is less prestigious than being a widow. In addition, a divorce lacks the formal religious and social support that exists for a death. Yet the grieving process for a divorce is similar to that for a death: a sense of sadness, loss, and anger. The woman is grieving both the loss of her husband and the loss of her relationship. While she may be ready to "let go" of the husband, she is often more reluctant to "let go" of the relationship. The anger centers on whatever behavior led to the ending of the marriage. Respectful of the magnitude of loss, a feminist therapist is supportive and facilitative of the typical grieving process by labeling this behavior as appropriate "mourning." Anger is a legitimate part of that mourning process. A feminist therapist helps her client acknowledge and value her anger as a means of surviving her loss and growing.

Along with grief, many women experience tremendous guilt about the breakup of a relationship. Having been socialized to accept the responsibility for maintaining relationships, women accept the dissolution as their failure. This guilt is often intensified for women with children, who feel their children will be cheated by not having a full-time father. A feminist therapist labels divorce as a two-party failure or simply a growing apart of two individuals. Furthermore, that divorce is an ending of the husband–wife relationship, not the parent–child relationship. Fathers are encouraged by feminist therapists to remain in frequent contact with their children, except when there is danger of psychological, physical and/or sexual abuse. Batterers who use child visitation as a means of harassing or attacking their ex-wives may lose their rights to participate in their child's upbringing if they don't learn nonviolent communication skills. It is especially important that women work through their guilt feelings before agreeing to terms for a dissolution, as many women make major concessions that are not in their best interest because of their guilt. Mediation, a new approach to division of property and children, has been viewed with skepticism by feminists, who fear traditional not feminist values will be the standard used.

Many divorcing women have incorrect or inadequate information about their legal rights. Helping educate women about their legal rights is part of the advocacy process of feminist therapy. This instruction comes from the feminist therapists' own learning and from referral to appropriate feminist resources that have expertise in issues of child support, custody, division of marital assets (including pension plans) and appropriate resources for lesbian mothers.

Women clients need to know: "All of your fears are justified about divorce. There is no easy or pleasant way to get divorced." However, most women survive divorce, often gaining better appreciation of their own strength and independence in the process.

Motherhood

"To be or not to be . . ." is the question of the 1980s. Motherhood has historically represented a fixed role of woman as nurturer/housewife. Women were told that we were "incomplete" without children, as they make us feel "fulfilled." The ambivalence about motherhood is a common therapeutic subject. For women the ever-present double bind presents itself once again: Women with children are overwhelmed by the responsibility, while women without children are either ostracized for their decision not to have children or pitied for their infertility (Hendricks, 1985a).

Many women seek therapy because they are feeling inadequate as mothers. They are not living up to their idealized image of themselves (nor are their children). Creating more realistic role expectations helps lessen this feeling of incompetence. In addition, learning to set rules and consequences helps women feel more in control by recognizing the considerable power they have as parents. Therapists who have the humbling experience of being a mother themselves help clients accept that no one is a perfect mother.

There are women who seek therapy because of their agony about their inability to be mothers. It has been estimated that as many as 25% of the couples who want to have children are infertile. The immense psychological strain of infertility is just beginning to be studied by feminists (Hendricks, 1985a). As Hendricks points out, the grieving process for infertility is monthly, each menstrual period a reminder that pregnancy has not been accomplished. Respecting the importance of choice, a feminist therapist is attuned to the immense pain and the indignity of the medical processes that infertile women encounter is recognized and addressed.

Many women enter therapy to help them make a choice about whether or not to have children. These women include partnered and single women (heterosexual and lesbian). The focus in feminist therapy is on teaching women to examine and rank the issues necessary for any decision-making process. Helping the woman network with other women who are of similar age and who have faced similar circumstances gives her an opportunity to make a more informed choice. The feminist therapist is less concerned with what the decision is, than with how the decision has been reached. A tenet of feminist philosophy, of course, is the expansion of alternatives from which a woman can choose.

Some woman come to therapy to help them make the choice about motherhood due to an unplanned pregnancy. These women have no good choices: Either they must decide to have a child they are not ready to have or decide to terminate the pregnancy. Feminist therapists have special sensitivity for women who must make a decision. This becomes especially critical when the client is a teen-ager. It is important to help each woman decide what is the right decision for her. If she does choose to have an abortion, it is important to refer her to a clinic that is concerned more about the trauma to the individual woman than about the economic gain from performing an abortion. The welfare of the woman, whatever her decision, is always of prime concern.

Warning: Women at Risk

Being female may be dangerous to your mental health! There are certain typical high-risk mental disorders that are found with women including violence/victimization, depression, substance abuse, eating disorders, and anxiety disorders.

Violence Against Women

Many women come to therapy to deal with some kind of personal violence in their lives: incest, rape, or battering. Others come to therapy to deal with the long- and short-term effects of violence without ever linking the cause to violence. Some women are victims of multiple kinds of violence. Walker (1984b) found that 49% of the battered women in her study had been physically and/or sexually abused as children. Unfortunately, traditional therapists contribute to the victimization and sexually exploit their clients. A study in California has found that in 90% of the cases, sex occurred between a male therapist and a female client (Bouhoutsos, 1984.) Harm to the female client was reported by a second therapist in 90% of these cases (Bouhoutsos, Holyroyd, Lerman, Forrer & Greenberg, 1983). Feminist therapists are not immune from this abuse of the power relationship in therapy. Several of the large financial settlements by the American Psychological Association Insurance Trust were to compensate women clients who sued their women therapists for sexual abuses in therapy.

An important consideration in working with these women is to avoid revictimization. It is essential to listen to what they say and to respect their pace for change. These tales are often told in what may appear to be a rambling and confused manner. Recognizing that the symptoms presented by victims of violence helps the therapist identify the battered woman syndrome, a subcategory of the DSM–III's diagnosis of Post-Traumatic Stress Disorder, rather than misdiagnose the woman as schizophrenic or a borderline personality disorder (Rosewater, 1985a). Denial and minimization are often used in the therapist's office as they have been used at home as a means of self-protection.

In addition much of the reporting includes self-blame. Incest survivors have been taught to feel that they must have been sending some kind of "signals" that encouraged the sexual encounters. Rape survivors also feel a similar sense of guilt, especially if their attacker was someone they knew. Battered women often feel it is their inadequacy as a wife/lover that caused the beatings. In all these cases, a feminist therapist helps her client to realize that her anger belongs not with herself but with the perpetrator. She must also help the client deal with the tremendous amount of anger and rage that the therapy process stirs up for her.

One major task for the feminist therapist is to assess the danger that a woman still residing with a violent man may face. Ironically the predictors of lethality are based primarily on the man's behavior (Browne, 1983). Like Walker (1985a), I rehearse an escape plan with any woman client still residing with a violent man. (See Walker, 1985a, for an excellent chapter on dealing with victims/survivors of interpersonal violence.)

Walker (1985a) sums up a major dilemma in treatment:

> No matter how hard the victims have tried, they know they have failed in keeping themselves totally safe from harm. While they do view the violent acts as the responsibility of the man, they also feel guilt for not having done whatever it would have taken to prevent him from unleashing his violence toward them personally. These feelings are far more complicated than originally were theorized. In feminist therapy, their complexity can be more easily revealed, accepted and validated and the implications for how such feelings influence cognition and behavior can be better understood. (pp. 206–207)

Feminist therapy provides the needed elements for healing: respect, honesty, caring, and competency. In a safe atmosphere, victims can make the transition to survivors, acknowledging their strength and skills.

Depression

Certainly marriage licenses should contain a warning label: Married women are two to three times more likely to develop depression than married men (Radloff & Cox, 1981). It is evident that trying to live up to her sex role expectations can cause women to experience symptoms of depression. Kaplan (1983), in a feminist critique of this phenomenon, questions whether a woman's unhappiness and her being labeled as "depressed" might "be manifestations that she is scapegoated for society's illness, its unjust sex-role imperatives" (p. 789). Radloff and Cox (1981) theorize that depression for women is a sequential model of learned susceptibility and precipitating factors. This author (Rosewater, 1984) has written that a feminist treatment of depression

> centers on examination of the environmental impact on the woman in treatment, historically and currently. Depression may be viewed as a coping skill (Kaplan, 1983) or as a healthy reaction to an unjust situation. But that doesn't make the depression go away! The role expectations for women in our society and whether a given role is right for any particular woman needs to be critically examined. Feminist therapy aids in the reevaluating of specific roles and the rules governing those roles. (p. 273)

Some feminist therapists have found the use of tricyclical antidepressants to be helpful adjuncts in the treatment of depression (Hendricks, 1985b). It is important when treating depression to help women learn how to direct their anger outward rather than inward.

Addictions

For many women growing up has been a process of learning to hate themselves and to suppress their anger. Substance abuse is a natural progression, as chemicals of many kinds—alcohol, food, drugs—serve to numb anger. Identifying addictions as such is an important part of treatment, as successful therapy is impossible if someone is abusing alcohol or other drugs. This author will only continue therapy with clients unable to stop such drug and/or alcohol abuse on their own, if they seek residential treatment. The usual 28-day treatment program offers the woman an opportunity to acknowledge and end her dependency. Since Alcoholics Anonymous is male-based, it is important to help women in recovery find a woman's group or a woman's modeled group that recognizes the unique problems of women in recovery.

Stopping the addictive behavior is the beginning not the end of treatment. The recovery process is usually the most difficult, because with the cessation of the numbing chemical, intense anger often begins to surface rapidly. Helping women to learn to identify, respect, and appropriately direct their anger are all issues to be addressed in recovery.

Obesity

Eating disorders, such as bulimia and anorexia, are also addictive-based disorders that likewise require residential treatment for the women unable to stop their distructive eating (or noneating) patterns. A feminist analysis of the pressure on women to be thin (Orbach, 1978; Wooley & Wooley, 1980) is an essential part of the treatment for these diseases.

Separate from but allied to the issue of eating disorders are the problems of obesity. The stereotype for women is that they cannot be "too rich or too thin." The fear of obesity is often the origin of eating disorders. Obese women are oppressed (Wooley & Wooley, 1980). Conditioned to hate themselves as others hate them for their excess poundage, they are unacknowledged victims. The feminist therapist helps obese women to love and accept their bulk and to recognize that their unhappiness is created by societal expectations and negative behavior toward them. The assumption that everyone can be thin is untrue. Brown (1985) makes the feminist observation that fat women defy stereotyped expectations for women to be small, as they take greater space and are perceived as more threatening. Some women are left with the double bind of either perpetually starving or being heavy. It is important to identify this double bind and to give support for the anger it engenders, as well as their anger about the oppression to which fat women are subjected. Body self-hatred is epidemic for women; helping heal the split between mind and body can be accomplished by feminist body psychotherapy (See Moss, 1985, for a discussion of this work).

Other Developmental Issues

There are other issues frequently addressed by feminist therapists that are not covered in this chapter. Some are addressed in other chapters of this book (aging, lesbian life-style, third-world/minority populations). Two others not covered expressly in either this book or this chapter are phobias and sexual dysfunction. The exaggeration of the stereotypical expectation for women to be fearful is the development of phobias. An excellent discussion on anxieties for women, including hysteria and agoraphobia, can be found in Chambless and Goldstein (1980). Likewise, sexual dysfunction can represent the fulfillment of the injunction that "good girls don't like sex." Two outstanding chapters on feminist analysis of sexual dysfunction are available in Cammaert (1984) and Seidler–Feller (1985).

Obstacles to Delivering Service

Feminist therapy is built on idealism that must function in an imperfect world. What goes on in therapists' offices comprises a minute fraction of women's lives. In the growing conservatism of American society, every few steps forward seems to be met with a step backwards. As Russo and Denmark (1985) make clear, we must be concerned with the realities of women's lives, which include tremendous obstacles: poverty, disability, racial discrimination, and homophobia. You can't eat idealism! The National Women's Mental Health Agenda (Russo, 1985) puts forth these feminist concerns.

The lack of unity among women is often discouraging. While we can understand the impact of membership in a minority group (Hacker, 1976), the reality of the Phyllis Shafly's in our lives is difficult. In our zeal to be "politically correct," feminist therapists, like other feminists, have alienated many women. Like any philosophically based group, feminist therapists need to learn from our mistakes. The importance of valuing feminine traits, of finding a basis of solidarity for both "traditional" and "modern" women, of expanding past white, middle-class issues is a challenge to which feminist therapists are rising.

Perhaps the most hopeful model feminist therapists have to offer in contrast to "male" behavior is the public acknowledgment of "mistakes," of a willingness to accept imperfection as human and necessary for growth. The concept of egalitarian relationships and appropriate self-disclosure in therapy is a way of modeling this female behavior. Acknowledging imperfection in the therapist's office is a start to acknowledging the imperfections in the world at large.

What Does Work!

While discouragement is an inevitable part of the feminist process, feminist therapists have made incredible progress in the treatment of women. Feminist therapists have successfully impacted the treatment of rape victims, created new insights about the widespread incidence of incest, and raised the country's awareness about the epidemic of family violence. Feminist therapists have created shelters for battered women and their children and developed expertise to help victims in criminal and civil courts. In addition, feminist therapists have addressed the issues of inadequate child support and in many states passed laws to enable women and their children to collect the money due them. Feminist therapists have created alternative women's support groups for recovering alcoholics and confronted the cause and effect between eating disorders and the pressure placed on women to be thin.

The most successful techniques in the treatment of women have come from our grassroots evolution. Feminist therapy started as women helping women. Concerned about inadequate (and abusive!) treatment that women were receiving, feminist therapy set out to develop a healthier, more holistic model. The feminist/collective approach eliminated hierarchical structure. Using, rather than abusing, power and privilege is a way of acknowledging our expertise without confusing that expertise for superiority.

The essence of the Talmud, the basis for Jewish law, has sometimes been simply explained as, "Do not do onto another what you would not have them do unto you." Feminist therapy models this admonition. There is congruence between the therapist's behavior and her expectations of her client's behavior. It is not surprising that the techniques used inside the therapist's office are similar to the ones used outside. Modeling political activism, the therapist encourages her clients to find a suitable way to help create change: Being involved is an appropriate way to experience empowerment.

Networking is a powerful technique. With the permission of both clients, I often give one woman who is working on a problem the number of another who has had a similar experience. I also let the one seeking help know that at sometime she will be the one I ask to provide the help. Networking also consists of linking women with existing groups that are addressing the problems a given client is facing.

The use of group therapy is very effective to help women address the commonality of the problems that they face. Furthermore, the use of groups adds to the sense of personal expertise and de-emphasises the therapist as expert.

CONCLUSION

Feminist therapy provides a different viewpoint from traditional psychotherapy. This viewpoint emphasizes health rather than pathology, empowerment rather than dependence, egalitarianism rather than condescension, and an active rather than a passive quality of interaction. The expert is seen as the client rather than the therapist. The congruence between behavior and rhetoric add a level of consistency and credibility. The therapist is a model and guide helping other women explore familiar terrain with a positive belief about recovery from oppression.

REFERENCES

American Psychiatric Association. (1980). *Diagnostic and statistical manual of mental disorders (3rd ed.)*. Washington, DC: Author.

Belle, D. (1984). Inequality and mental health: Low income and minority women. In L. E. Walker (Ed.), *Women and mental health policy* (pp. 13–150). Beverly Hills, CA: Sage.

Bernard, J. (1984). Women's mental health in times of transition. In L. E. Walker (Ed.), *Women and mental health policy* (pp. 181–195). Beverly Hills, CA: Sage.

Bouhoutsos, J. C. (1984). Sexual intimacies between psychotherapists and clients: Policy implications for the future. In L. E. Walker (Ed.), *Women and mental health policy* (pp. 207–227). Beverly Hills, CA: Sage.

Bouhoutsos, J., Holroyd J., Lerman, H., Forer, B., & Greenberg, M. (1983). Sexual intimacies between psychotherapists and patients. *Professional Psychology: Research & Practice, 14* (2), 185–196.

Broverman, I. K., Broverman, D. M., Clarkson, F. E., Rosencrantz, P., & Vogel, S. R. (1970). Sex-role stereotypes and clinical judgements of mental health. *Journal of Consulting and Clinical Psychology, 34,* 1–7.

Brown, L. (1985). Women, weight and power: Feminist, theoretical and therapeutic issues. *Women & Therapy,* 3(1), 61–71.

Browne, A. (1983). *When battered women kill.* Doctoral dissertation for the Union of Experimenting Colleges and Universities.

Brownmiller, S. (1975). *Against our will: Men, women and rape.* New York: Bantam Books.

Cammaert, L. P. (1984). New sex therapies: Policy and practice. In L. E. Walker (Ed.), *Women and mental health policy* (pp. 247–266). Beverly Hills, CA: Sage.

Chambless, D. L., & Goldstein, A. J. (1980). Anxieties: Agoraphobia and hysteria. In A. M. Brodsky & R. Hare-Mustin (Eds.), *Women and Psychotherapy* (pp. 113–134). New York: Guilford Press.

Chesler, P. (1973). *Women and madness.* New York: Avon Books.

DeHardt, D. C. (1985). Can a feminist therapist facilitate clients' heterosexual relationships? In L. B. Rosewater & L. E. A. Walker (Eds.), *Handbook of feminist therapy* (pp. 170–182). New York: Springer.

Escamilla-Mondanaro, J. (1977). Lesbians and therapy. In E. I. Rawlings & D. K. Carter (Eds.), *Psychotherapy for women* (pp. 256–265). Springfield, IL: Charles C. Thomas.

Fodor, I. G. (1985). Assertion training for the eighties: Moving beyond the personal. In L. B. Rosewater & L. E. A. Walker (Eds.), *Handbook of feminist therapy* (pp. 257–265). New York: Springer.

Gilligan, C. (1982). *In a different voice.* Cambridge, MA: Harvard University Press.

Hacker, H. M. (1976). Women as a minority group. In S. Cox (Ed.), *Female Psychology* (pp. 156–170). New York: St. Martin's.

Hendricks, M. C. (1985a). Feminist therapy with women and couples who are infertile. In L. B. Rosewater & L. E. A. Walker (Eds.), *Handbook of feminist therapy* (pp. 147–158). New York: Springer.

Hendricks, M. C. (1985b). *The medication of clients in a feminist therapist practice.* A paper presented at the annual Advanced Feminist Therapy Institute, Bal Harbor, FL, April.

Kaplan, M. (1983). A woman's view of DSM-III. *American Psychologist, 38*(7), 786–792.

Masson, J. (1984). *The assault on truth.* New York: Farrar, Strauss, & Giroux.

Moss, L. E. (1985). Feminist body psychotherapy. In L. B. Rosewater & L. E. Walker (Eds.), *Handbook of Feminist Therapy* (pp. 80–90). New York: Springer.

Orbach, S. (1978). *Fat is a feminist issue.* New York: Paddington Press.

Pearce, D. (1979). Women, work and welfare: The feminization of poverty. In K. W. Feinstein (Ed.), *Working Women and Families* (pp. 103–124). Beverly Hills, CA: Sage.

Radloff, L. S., & Cox, S. (1981). Sex differences in depression in relation to learned susceptibility. In S. Cox (Ed.), *Female Psychology* (2nd ed., pp. 334–363). New York: St. Martin's.

Rawlings, E. I., Carter, D. K. (Eds.), (1977). *Psychotherapy for women.* Springfield, IL: Charles C. Thomas.

Rosencrantz, P. S., DeLorey, C., & Broverman, I. K. (1985). *One half a generation later: Sex-role stereotypes revisited.* A paper presented at the annual convention of the American Psychological Association, Los Angeles, August.

Rosewater, L. B. (1984). Feminist therapy: Implications for practitioners. In L. E. Walker (Ed.), *Women and mental health policy* (pp. 267–279), Beverly Hills, CA: Sage.

Rosewater, L. B. (1985a). Schizophrenic, borderline or battered? In L. B. Rosewater & L. E. A. Walker (Eds.), *Handbook of Feminist Therapy* (pp. 215–225). New York: Springer.

Rosewater, L. B. (1985b). *A critical statement on the proposed diagnosis of masochistic personality disorder.* A paper presented to the American Psyciatric Association's Work Group to Revise DSM-III, New York, November 18.

Russo, N. F. (Ed.). (1985). *A woman's mental health agenda.* Washington, DC: American Psychological Association.

Russo, N. F., & Denmark, F. L. (1985). Women, psychology and public policy: Selected Issues. *American Psychologist, 39*(10), 1161–1165.

Sang, B. E. (1977). Psychotherapy with lesbians: Some observations and tentative generalizations. In E. I. Rawlings & D. K. Carter (Eds.), *Psychotherapy for women* (pp. 266–275). Springfield, IL: Charles C. Thomas.

Seidler-Feller, D. (1985). A feminist critique of sex therapy. In L. B. Rosewater & L. E. Walker (Eds.), *Handbook of feminist therapy* (pp. 119–129). New York: Springer.

Siegel, R. J. (1985). Beyond homophobia: Learning to work with lesbian clients. In L. B. Rosewater & L. E. A. Walker (Eds.), *Handbook of feminist therapy* (pp. 183–190). New York: Springer.

Smith, A. J., & Siegel, R. F. (1985). Feminist therapy: Redefining Power for the Powerless. In L. B. Rosewater & L. E. Walker (Eds.), *Handbook of feminist therapy* (pp. 13–21). New York: Springer.

Symonds, A. (1979). Violence against women: The myth of masochism. *American Journal of Psychotherapy, 33*(2), 161–173.

Walker, L. E. (1985a) Feminist therapy with victims/survivors of interpersonal violence. In L. B. Rosewater & L. E. Walker (Eds.), *Handbook of feminist therapy* (pp. 203–214). New York: Springer.

Walker, L. E. A. (1985b). *Statement on proposed diagnosis of masochistic personality disorder.* A paper presented to the American Psychiatric's Work Group to Revise DSM-III, New York, November 18.

Walker, L. E. (Ed.). (1984a). *Women and mental health policy.* Beverly Hills, CA: Sage.

Walker, L. E. (1984b). *The battered woman syndrome.* New York: Springer.

Wooley, S. C., & Wooley, O. W. (1980). Eating disorders: Obesity and anorexia. In A. M. Brodsky & R. Hare-Mustin (Eds.), *Women and psychotherapy* (pp. 135–158).

Wycoff, H. (1977). Radical psychiatry for women. In E. I. Rawling & D. K. Carter (Eds.), *Psychotherapy for women* (pp. 370–391). Springfield, IL: Charles C. Thomas.

CHAPTER 8

Feminist Therapy With Divorced, Single, Female Parents

Edna I. Rawlings
Dee L. R. Graham

FEMINIST THERAPY WITH DIVORCED, SINGLE, FEMALE PARENTS

An increasing number of children are being raised in single-parent families. In spite of public and media interest in the single-male-parent phenomenon (e.g., films such as *Kramer vs. Kramer*), single-parent families are overwhelmingly headed by women. While the proportion of children living with their fathers after divorce has tripled since 1960, only one-tenth of children live in father-custody families following divorce (Glick & Norton, 1978). There are 24 million women who head single-parent households, compared with only 800,000 men.[1] The percentage of women-headed families has risen from 10.7% in 1970 to 15.4% in 1983. It is even higher for ethnic minorities; for example, in 1983, 41.9% of Black families were woman-headed, compared with 28% in 1970 (Coalition on Women and the Budget, 1984). Woman-headed families are created through divorce, widowhood, and never-married mothers. However, the exponentially increasing divorce rate is generally credited with the dramatic increase of woman-maintained families over the past decade (Hetherington, Cox, & Cox, 1976). Glick (1979) has

---

[1] The statistics on women-headed families were cited by Carl T. Rowan, a nationally syndicated journalist in an article, "Measuring a 'female job'," which appeared in *The Cincinnati Enquirer*, June 27, 1985, p. A–19. The statistics on single, male parents appeared in an article by Peter Francese, "Numbers of dads dwindle with lifestyle changes," which appeared in *The Cincinnati Enquirer*, June 16, 1985, p. E–1.

projected that one-third of the children 18 years of age in 1990 will have lived with a divorced parent.

This chapter will focus on feminist therapy with women who are heads of families as a result of divorce. About 80% of all divorced women have children (Brown, Feldberg, Fox, & Kohen, 1976). The older research literature on single mothers and their families has created biases in therapists as well as the public at large. Therefore, it is useful for therapists to be aware of the limitations of this literature. Much of the older research was methodologically flawed and, from a feminist perspective, politically misguided. Such studies conceptualized the single-parent homes as deviant, homogeneous, and invariably causing dysfunction in children (Levitin, 1979). More recent studies such as Hetherington, Cox, and Cox (1979, 1982), Kelly and Wallerstein (1975, 1976) and Kazak and Linney (1983) reflect increased methodological sophistication and less of an antidivorce slant. However, the most recent literature still has a white, middle-class bias and lacks a feminist perspective.

PSYCHOSOCIAL ADJUSTMENT IN WOMEN-HEADED FAMILIES: A BRIEF, CRITICAL LOOK AT THE LITERATURE

The antidivorce ideology that permeates our society leads us to believe that divorce and single parenting is an unmitigated tragedy for parents and children. Many clinicians who write about divorce view it as symptomatic of emotional illness. Mother-headed families have received the brunt of criticism from many social scientists and mental health professionals who have joined politicians and religious leaders in decrying the demise of the traditional family and predicting the destructive effects of "broken homes" or "father absent homes" on children (Gettleman & Markowitz, 1974).

A number of mental health experts have perpetuated the myth that divorce is a symptom of personal maladjustment (e.g., Despert, 1962). There is, of course, ample documentation of emotional distress among divorced women. To cite one example of a study of psychopathology in divorced women, Bloom, Asher, and White (1978) found separation and divorce to be associated positively with rates of psychiatric disorders, motor vehicle accidents, disease morbidity, suicide, homicide, and disease mortality. A study of a nonclinical population of divorced mothers by Hetherington et al. (1976) found that immediately following divorce, women heads of households expressed feelings of depression, anxiety, anger, rejection, and incompetence to a greater extent than a control group of married women and divorced men. They also found that social adjustment problems were greater for women than for men.

Many researchers have been concerned with the effect of father absence on children, especially male children. Evidence of greater antisocial and delinquent behavior (e.g., Hetherington, Cox, & Cox, 1978) and cognitive learning disabilities (e.g., Santrock, 1972) in male children is reported in the literature. Fewer studies have looked at the effects of father absence on girls; however, Hetherington, Cox, & Cox (1978) noted greater dependency behaviors in girls from mother-headed homes. In an earlier study, Hetherington (1972) observed increased proximity and attention seeking from males by teen-age daughters of divorced women.

The Hetherington, Cox, & Cox (1979, 1982) study was unique in making direct observations of mother–child interactions, as opposed to relying on self-report data. Sons showed high rates of noncompliance and other aversive behaviors in interactions with their mothers. Daughters, in contrast, were more whiny, complaining, and dependent. Problems in the family interaction were significantly correlated with both rates of deviant child behavior and mothers' feelings of self-esteem, competence, anxiety, and depression. Based on these observations, Hetherington and associates concluded that dysfunctional interactions between divorced mothers and their children were bidirectional. Both mothers and children who were under stress mutually reinforce each other's maladaptive behaviors, creating a vicious cycle.

The ominous references to pervasive emotional distress in divorced women and their children found in the literature are open to alternative interpretations. Most of the studies are correlational in nature and do not tell us what in the divorce situation leads to the emotional distress or deviancy. The tension and distress in the marriage prior to the divorce may be a contributing factor. Also, divorce creates a crises situation. Hetherington and Camara (1984) point out that the response to divorce will be modified by having adequate resources available for stress management. These authors suggest that the single-parent family's resources need to be studied systematically in relation to coping with divorce. These resources include personal resources (financial, educational, health, and psychological), family resources (cohesion, adaptability, communication, and problem-solving skills) and social supports (neighbor, kin, and friendship networks, and self-help groups).

In one of the few longitudinal studies, Hetherington, Cox, & Cox (1979, 1982) found a reduction of symptoms in mothers and children over time. These investigators discovered poor adjustment in women heads of household immediately after divorce. Even 1 year after divorce, these mothers complained that they felt "walled in" and "trapped" with their children. Two years later, however, their distress symptoms were much alleviated and the women were reporting fewer social adjustment problems. The children of these women also showed symptomatic improvement over the 2–7 year period, but some were still having behavioral problems. This was particularly true for male children. This study suggests that the initial adjustment period is stressful for divorced women and their children but as they learn to cope with life-style changes, their mental health improves.

The belief that father absence has a detrimental effect on children also needs to be re-evaluated. As Pedersen (1976) pointed out, the typical paradigm of comparing children from father-absent homes with children from two-parent nuclear families yields meager information on the psychological processes that affect the development of children's behavior when fathers are present or absent. There is evidence, for example, that marital tension and discord are more strongly associated with antisocial behavior of children than the mere fact of father absence due to divorce (cf. Rutter, 1971). Nye (1957) discovered that children from marriages broken by divorce showed better adjustment with respect to psychosomatic illness, delinquent behavior, and parent–children relations than children from unhappy, unbroken marriages. The behaviors of the absent fathers who are not living with the children on a daily basis nevertheless may be actively contributing to the stress of both the mother and the children, exacerbating the dysfunctional interactions within the mother-headed family. As documented below, the mental health of divorced women and their children is affected by how supportive the ex-spouse is, the amount of friction between ex-spouses around custodial and financial matters, and by the extent to which the ex-spouse manipulates the children for revenge.

One of the most serious methodological problems in the studies of the emotional adjustment of divorced mothers and their children is the biased nature of the samples used. The majority of past studies have had a pathology bias and concentrated on clinic populations (Gettleman & Markowitz, 1974). The multitudes of divorced women and their children who make successful adaptations to the dissolution of their nuclear family typically are not the object of investigation. In spite of the deficit focus in the literature, some investigators (e.g., Hunt, 1966) find many divorced persons reporting positive feelings of relief, newfound freedom, and personal growth as a result of separation and divorce.

We need more research to explore moderating variables which may reduce the extent of trauma or examine growth-producing aspects of successful adaptation to the divorce. The research we do have on women's positive adaptation to divorce indicates that it is associated with social and economic supports (Goode, 1956; Weiss, 1975), an active social life (Raschke, 1977; Spanier & Casto, 1979) and nontraditional sex roles (Brown & Manella, 1978). Factors associated with poor adjustment include having two or more children (Goode, 1956), male children (Hetherington et al., 1982), being ambivalent or not wanting the divorce (Goode, 1956; Spanier & Casto, 1979), being older, and having had a longer marriage (Chiriboga, Roberts, & Stein, 1978; Goode, 1956; Hetherington, 1981).

Jacobson (1978) looked at factors associated with children's positive adjustment to divorce. These included more communication from the mother about the divorce, and being aware of parent's marital problems for a longer period of time. Given these conditions, children are less likely to feel guilty and blame themselves for the divorce. This interpretation is supported by earlier findings of Kelly and Wallerstein (1975, 1976). Continued parental conflict around custody and financial factors, maladaptive parent–child interactions, and inconsistent and coercive types of discipline are factors that contribute to poor adjustment in children (Kelly & Wallerstein, 1975, 1976; Hetherington et al., 1979, 1982).

A FEMINIST PERSPECTIVE ON MOTHER-HEADED FAMILIES

From a feminist perspective, the pathology model of divorce described in the previous section is analogous to viewing the independent woman as deviant. As Rich (1977) notes:

> What we did see, for centuries, was the hatred of overt strength in women, the definition of strong independent women as freaks of nature, as unsexed, frigid, castrating, perverted, dangerous; the fear of the maternal woman as "controlling," the preference for dependent, malleable, "feminine" women. (p. 55)

When one examines the politics of the research in the older literature the real issues seem to center around male control of women and children in the home, the basic socialization unit. Bemoaning the demise of the traditional father-headed family reflects anxiety over the erosion of an important socializing institution for the patriarchy. Research shows that fathers play a primary role in the sex role socialization of both girls and boys (Johnson, 1975). One of the reasons for researchers concentrating on male children may be that male children have more problems in mother-headed families. However, a feminist explanation would be that males are more valued, hence, their problems are taken more seriously.

Women-headed households are a viable alternative family arrangement, not a deviant or disorganized family, or even a second best alternative to the traditional family. Gettleman and Markowitz (1974) quote Goreman as saying that, "at the very least, divorce must be understood as part of the 'passing of patriarchism, familialism, and of the revolt of women'" (p. 213).

Brown et al. (1976) referred to divorce as the "chance of a new lifetime" and Douvan (1976) noted that it is often the beginning of new growth in women and families. Following divorce, single, female parents often discover for the first time in their lives that they can break out of their dependent roles and function as autonomous individuals, who can competently exercise choice and control in all spheres of their lives. New avenues of self-development and relationship growth are available to single mothers and their children. This is particularly true if women do not immediately seek refuge in a new relationship or marriage.[2] Among the benefits the single mother discovers are increased personal autonomy and a greater sense of competence (Otto & Otto, 1976). Although many adjustment problems exist for these newly structured families, women discover that they have more say in the management of their domestic responsibilities, the discipline of their children, and their social and sexual activities (Brown et al., 1976). While the literature focuses on difficulties in mother–child interactions in these mother-headed families and the adjustment of children from these families, the possibility for closer emotional ties with the children and enhanced maturity in the children also exist (Bach, 1974; Douvan, 1976; Weiss, 1979).

In spite of a positive attitude toward alternative families, feminists are aware of the enormous problems facing these families. Feminists, however, view the difficulties faced by single, female parents and their children as primarily by-products of societal values that are hostile to women's independence. In our society, divorced women are stigmatized. There is considerable pressure on divorced women to remarry. Traditional sex role socialization for women stresses economic dependency

---

[2] Wattenberg and Reinhardt report that 67% of divorced women remarry and the highest rate of remarriage is within the first year after a divorce. Approximately, 33% of divorced women remain on their own. Also, 44% of remarriages end in divorce (E. Wattenberg, & H. Reinhardt, 1981, Female-headed families: Trends and implications, In E. Howell & M. Bayes, (Eds.), *Women and Mental Health*, pp. 347–356. New York: Basic Books.)

and underdeveloped instrumental behavior, which is reinforced by traditional marital roles (Dowling, 1982).

The protraditional family and antiwomen bias of our society is apparent in many aspects of post-divorce life. Divorced women are often shunned socially by a couple-oriented society, as they are often seen as competitors by their still-married women friends and thus lose former social supports and outlets. Sexual and racial oppression reflected in narrow job opportunities and low wages for women and minorities have meant real financial hardships for women-headed families.

The economic disadvantage of being female in this society is reflected in the fact that, whereas only approximately 15% of all families are woman-headed, half of families below the poverty level are women-headed (Coalition on Women and the Budget, 1984). Women and their families become poorer after divorce; this is not true for men (Hetherington & Camara, 1984).

In spite of the increasing numbers of women-headed families, societal services to assist these families lag behind (Benedek & Benedek, 1979). The slow development of supports and services for women-headed families especially when viewed against the magnitude of the need for such services also reveals lack of social legitimacy of these families. The current conservative political climate is threatening the few services available (Coalition on Women and the Budget, 1984). The long-term feminist solution to the problems of mothers who are heads of household would be social reforms that would eliminate the major forms of oppression facing women in today's society (e.g., flex time, employer funded on-site child care, comparable worth pay, job-training programs, etc.). However, the divorced, single mothers who come to therapy need some immediate remedies for the problems they encounter daily.

Thus, while mother-headed families created by divorce represent opportunities for personal growth in women and their children, divorce is unquestionably a major life crisis for them. For women to be thrust suddenly, often without preparation, into total family responsibilities is scary. This difficulty is often compounded by financial hardship, social isolation, and lack of supportive services. A "worst case" scenario would be the following: emerging from the cocoon of the nuclear family is the newly divorced woman who has not been socialized to be self-sufficient, feeling guilty about depriving her children of a "normal" two-parent family, and possibly endangering their mental health, experiencing challenges to her authority as head of household from her children and society, encountering hostile, social stigmatization, loneliness, and poverty, and lacking marketable work skills and training.

Single-female parents are most likely to seek therapy during times of crises when old roles and coping strategies are no longer adequate.

At these times of crises the human organism is more open to change than at other times (Otto & Otto, 1976). Therapists can maximize the opportunities for divorced, single-female parents and their children to experience the "chance of a new lifetime" by helping these clients develop more effective role identities and coping strategies and utilizing whatever support services that do exist.

One of the strengths of feminist therapy is placing personal behavior in a socio-political context. With the aid of a feminist therapist, divorced women in the process of developing single-parent families can come to view their personal changes as part of a larger pattern of social change in family structures of which they are innovators.

A FEMINIST DEVELOPMENTAL APPROACH TO PSYCHOTHERAPY WITH SINGLE, FEMALE PARENTS

From the standpoint of therapy with single, female parents, it is important to keep in mind that most of the issues that single-parent families face are developmental. Divorce is not a single life event; rather, it involves a whole series of changes in life circumstances. Hetherington (1981) pointed out two phases: (1) the crises of divorce itself, and (2) the reorganization of the family into a single-parent unit. At different stages of the process members of the single-parent family must cope with different tasks, using different strategies. Following divorce, not only does the family structure change, but the roles, the stresses and the social supports also change. Age of the children at the time of the divorce is an important variable in understanding the life cycle of the single-parent family (cf. Hetherington, 1981).

Aslin (1976), following a scheme developed by Bohannan, outlined the following six major areas in which changes take place during and following divorce: (1) emotional, (2) legal, (3) economic, (4) parental, (5) community, and (6) psychological (autonomy). Carter (1977) indicated that the most pressing problems facing divorced women were financial hardship (economic), loneliness (community), and autonomy (psychological). Kazak and Linney (1983) chose to investigate the following three role changes in single, female parents who were divorced: parental, self-supporter (economic), and social participant (community). The participants in their study were 47 divorced, middle-income women, 27 to 49 years old, who had been separated for varying amounts of time. The investigators examined the women's perceived competence in three of these role changes with respect to reported life satisfaction. They found that 3 years after separation women expressed the least perceived competence in the role of social participant, and competence in that role was the greatest predictor of life satisfaction. However, more than 3 years after separation, perceived competence in all three roles was equal, but perceived competence in the role of self-supporter was the best predictor of life satisfaction. This study does highlight the developmental aspect of the divorce process; however, similar studies need to be carried out, using women from different income levels and racial groups.

Aslin's six categories will be used in describing the changes facing the single, female parent that need to be addressed in therapy. In describing changes in these six areas, it is clear that there is often overlap and conflict between the areas.

Emotional Changes: Achieving Emotional Stability and Independence

During the divorce process and within the first 2 years post divorce the mother and her children may experience considerable emotional stress. Coping with the emotional aftermath of divorce tends to be the primary focus of therapy. Overlapping with emotional factors are practical problems of financial stability, loneliness, and parenting which exacerbate or moderate the emotional reactions, depending on how successful a woman has been in resolving these issues. There appear to be three stages that women go through emotionally in response to divorce: depression and grief, anger, and anxiety due to confusion (cf. Collier, 1982).

Dealing with depression and grief. The intensity of negative feelings following divorce may be surprising and disconcerting to women, especially if they had expected only positive feelings following the severing of an unhappy marital bond. Contradictory feelings may be felt alternatively or simultaneously. A woman who experiences a roller coaster of feelings may fear that she has made a serious error in obtaining a divorce or that she is having a nervous breakdown. While most women experience many negative feelings immediately preceding and following divorce, they may continue to experience distress for as long as 2 years after divorce. These negative feelings may be the result of marital tension that led to the divorce, the stress of legal battles around the divorce, as well as part of the "separation distress syndrome" (Parkes, 1972). Depression is commonly experienced at this stage. If her children are simultaneously expressing high level of distress, she may also feel guilty about the psychological damage that she has caused them by divorcing.

Using cognitive restructuring or reframing (e.g., Beck, 1976), the feminist therapist can label the client's feelings and/or those of her children as a "separation distress syndrome" (Parkes, 1972), which represents a natural grieving process following loss (Otto & Otto, 1976). The negative feelings following divorce can be conceptualized as grief reaction to the loss of whatever positive features in the relationship were given up, one's fantasy or dream of what a good marriage or family would be like, and one's former role or identity. Collier (1982) and Otto and Otto (1976) suggest some techniques for working though the losses and developing a new postdivorce identity. Both these sources stress "choice" and "control" as key issues for a woman going through a major life crises. Feminist therapy supports women's need for choice and control.

The children's emotional distress can also be reframed as a temporary reaction to loss and change, rather than evidence that they have been psychologically damaged by the divorce. In most cases the children can be helped by the mother to deal with their grief; only in extreme cases do these children need professional help. Being understanding and responsive to her children's distress and communicating love in the context of consistent discipline will aid the children in making adjustments to the new family situation. The intensity of emotional distress and the forms that it takes vary with the ages of the children involved, with younger children experiencing more distress than older ones (cf. Hetherington, 1981). For the first year following divorce, some mothers experience such great stress that it is difficult for them to be as emotionally available to their children as their children need. By assisting the mother in reducing her own stress as described above and helping her bring some order to her life and household, feminist therapists can moderate these early strains on the single-parent family. Placing the changes the family is going through in a developmental framework can reassure the mother that with time there is hope for a positive family adjustment.

Although there are not as many support services for single-parent families as there are needs for services, feminist therapists who work with divorced, single mothers need to know the resources available to single-parent families and make referrals when appropriate. For example, some cities have organizations with programs to strengthen families after divorce. Support groups for children of different ages and sexes, and for single parents, help single-parent families deal with many of the stresses they face.

Dealing with anger. A positive adjustment to divorce and to her new identity as a single mother is facilitated by a woman learning to handle anger. Women are discouraged or even punished for expressing anger. Hence they may learn to fear even their feelings of anger (Miller, 1976). Consequently, women often turn their anger on themselves, which leads to depression. Women who are angry at their ex-spouses, especially if the woman did not want a divorce and is unable to express that anger, can remain psychologically stuck in their past relationship. If this is the case, the woman may have little energy to construct a new life for herself until her anger has been expressed and integrated. Sex role analysis (Rawlings & Carter, 1977) is a good place to start in helping a woman understand why anger is such a problematic emotion for her. After she has a context for understanding her anger phobia, she needs to be taught some mechanism for getting in touch with her anger and expressing it constructively. Carter (1977) suggested using role play, the Gestalt empty chair technique and creative fantasy as mechanisms for helping women get in touch with and work through disruptive angry feelings. Burtle (1985) outlined an approach to using anger as a treatment tool for women. The purpose of these exercises is not to purge all angry emotion, but to aid a woman in channeling anger so that she directs her energy in ways that promote her survival and growth.

Anxiety and confusion. Divorced women experience the greatest amount of stress at the times when (1) their marriages are being dissolved, and (2) they are establishing their new postdivorce identities (Spanier & Casto, 1979). After letting go of her former identity, the woman who has not yet developed a new one may experience anxiety and confusion (Collier, 1982; Otto & Otto, 1976). She may feel insecure about her ability to take control of her life, to make decisions for herself and to assume new responsibilities. Even day-to-day routines may feel overwhelming. She may try to get the therapist to take over for her and tell her what to do. Women in the *confusion stage* appear helpless and it is tempting for the therapist to play the game of "Mother (or Father) Knows Best." At this stage she definitely does not need rescue. What the woman going through a major life transition needs most of all is to exercise choice and control in her life (Collier, 1982). Feminist therapists are less likely than other therapists to slip into an authoritarian parental role.

Techniques such as sex role analysis (Rawlings & Carter, 1977) can be used for value and role clarification. Sex role analysis can facilitate the client's understanding of the price she has paid for the privileges associated with the traditional role and what costs and benefits accrue from rejecting that role. Using sex role analysis, the divorced woman can engage in self-defining her own roles—as a mother, a self-supporter, and a social participant. For women who are new to feminism, having them read feminist books such as Miller's *Toward a New Psychology of Women* (1976) helps them creatively rethink their roles.

Legal Changes: Achieving a Favorable Divorce Settlement

Women clients amidst the emotional turmoil of divorce frequently make such statements as, "I don't want any of *his* money or property; I just want out of the marriage," "It's his money; he earned it; all I did was stay home with the kids," or "I don't deserve anything because I'm the one who wants the divorce." Later these same women will feel cheated or "ripped-off" if they did not ask for an equitable settlement. Having the woman who is reacting in a self-negating manner out of guilt or depression to examine and dispute her own irrational beliefs helps her replace irrational beliefs with more rational ones.

Some assertiveness training (e.g., Phelps & Austin, 1975) may be necessary to help these women deal with lawyers and hostile husbands in obtaining a fair settlement. Women who fight for their financial, property, and custody rights during legal proceedings generally feel enhanced self-esteem. However, the cautions recommended by Fodor (1985) do apply.

In the authors' experience, divorce lawyers are paternalistic toward women but give them poor service. In part the lawyers, including some women lawyers who claim to be feminist, do not like to deal with the emotional distress of their women clients. One of the first author's clients who called her lawyer in an agitated state seeking advice only after her husband had repeatedly violated a separation agreement, was icily told by her lawyer, who was allegedly a feminist, "I can't hold your hand over every little thing!" This client subsequently fired this lawyer and hired another feminist lawyer who was more responsive and respectful to her.

Women who are traditional in their sex roles have enough difficulty being assertive of their rights; however, when faced with the power of the male-dominated legal system they may become virtually immobilized. Women are most emotionally vulnerable at a time when they must make extremely important legal decisions and provide important information to their attorneys. They must also be very clear with attorneys about their expectations and wishes.

While providing emotional support, the therapist needs to help the woman going through the legal maze of divorce remain task-oriented. Control of decisions should always remain in the hands of the client; however, the feminist therapist can provide information and alternatives that will assist her in making informed decisions. The therapist can share some of her own experience and those of other clients who have gone through the divorce process. These, if relevant, can help clients become aware of and able to avoid choices that might have been very financially costly to them or produced unhappy custody agreements.

Financial and property settlement. In doing therapy with a single, female parent going through the divorce process, the feminist therapist can often function as a consultant to help the woman do realistic planning in asking for alimony and child support. Being ignorant of family finances in a marriage and unaware of financial realities puts women at a disadvantage in negotiating a favorable financial and property settlement. Women who initially refuse to look after their own best financial interest are more likely to do so if reminded that they are not just negotiating for themselves but also for their children. If the woman needs additional training for the job market, she can be encouraged to make support for this training part of the financial arrangement of the divorce. For women that are financially naïve, helping them work out a budget may alleviate some of the distress of a lowered income. Although many middle-class women consider help from their husbands or welfare demeaning or constraining, the therapist can help them look at such financial arrangements as temporary measures until they obtain the necessary training or retraining to become financially independent (Brown et al., 1976). Encouragement toward financial independence is often an important part of therapy with women going through divorce, considering that fewer than one-half of all men ordered to pay child support do so; even fewer pay court-ordered maintenance or alimony. The new laws on garnishment are proving to be inadequate in a large number of cases.

Child custody and visitation. Custody issues can often be the most painful aspect of the divorce settlement. Theoretically, the court decides custody based on the best interests of the children. Actually, prejudicial attitudes which do not coincide with the best interests of the children often prevail (Rand, Graham, & Rawlings, 1982). Sex role stereotyping generally ensures that women who want custody are successful and in most situations the mother is the primary psychological parent. Occasionally the court awards custody of the children to the father against the wishes of the mother. Sometimes the basis for the decision is rational; for example, the children are older and elect to live with the father. If one of the parents is emotionally or sexually abusive to a child that parent should not be given custody and visitation should be severely curtailed and responsibly supervised.

Unfortunately, there are instances when the basis for the custody decision is irrational. For example, although there is no evidence that a woman's sexual behavior or sexual orientation is correlated with her parenting ability, sexually active women and lesbian mothers frequently lose a custody battle solely on that basis (Chesler, 1986; Rand, Graham & Rawlings, 1982).

When the female parent is denied custody against her wishes, some grief work with her may be necessary (see *Emotional Changes* above for therapeutic techniques for grief work). In addition, the woman may need to find ways to channel the expression of her anger, that she feels toward her ex-spouse or at her children who may have decided to live with their father, along constructive lines. For example, a lesbian mother who has been denied custody of her children may want to organize or join a social action group working for the rights of lesbian mothers. A woman whose children have elected to live with their father may put her energy into developing a satisfying social network to reduce her feelings of loneliness and rejection. Cognitive reframing can help mothers understand that custody decisions are rarely permanent and children change over time.

For some women deciding not to be the custodial parent may be in the best interests of themselves and their children. Society puts intense pressure on women to be mothers (Trebilcot, 1983). The social stigma attached to women who prefer not to have custody of their children is considerable. There are many reasons why a woman may not seek custody of her children after divorce; for example, she may need to complete a degree or devote her energies to a new career. She have many fewer financial resources than her ex-spouse. Emotionally, she may not find full time child care congenial. Whatever her reason, a woman should be able to opt out of the custodial parent role, temporarily or permanently, without guilt. The therapist should support a woman's decision not to be the custodial parent if that is her choice. Not being the custodial parent does not mean that a woman is abandoning her children. Being an involved, caring non-custodial parent is an important role. Feminist therapy can help women explore this new role which does not have the benefit of role models.

ECONOMIC CHANGES: ACHIEVING ECONOMIC INDEPENDENCE

Women who head households need to be self-supporting. Divorce forces most women to be more economically independent and to provide most—if not all—of the support for their families. Many women neither expect nor are trained to take care of themselves financially. Women who are divorced with dependent children must assume the responsibility for both deciding what they want in life and devise the means to achieve these goals within a realistic framework. The financial burden of maintaining a single-parent family may be the single most important challenge facing a divorced woman. For example, Kazak & Linney (1983) found that feeling competent in the role of self-supporter was the greatest predictor of life satisfaction among single, female parents.

Recently divorced women without marketable skills and those whose job training prior to marriage have been rendered obsolete by absences from the job market due to childrearing face special hardships. Even women with good job credentials are often faced with difficulty getting jobs and promotions commensurate with their merit, due to sexist attitudes in the marketplace. Assistance from the former spouse in the form of alimony or child support, even when ordered by the court, may be unreliable or inadequate (Hetherington, 1981).

Because most single mothers must work to support their families, career counseling is another important adjunct treatment. For a client struggling with career decisions, reading *What Color is Your Parachute* (Bolles, 1985) or *The Three Boxes of Life* (Bolles, 1981) and doing the relevant exercises outlined in the texts can be beneficial. These books contain a philosophy of making choices and taking control of one's life that is very beneficial to women faced with the complexities of single parenthood. In some cases formal vocational or career counseling may be necessary.

In addition to obtaining satisfying career and income, the single mother may need assistance in developing a supportive environment that makes work possible. This involves problem-solving and providing information on practical matters, for example, obtaining adequate child care.

PARENTAL CHANGES: ACHIEVING GOOD, SINGLE PARENTING SKILLS

In general, single female parents seem to feel most competent about their parenting role (Kazak and Linney, 1983). This is probably because many mothers were already shouldering most of the parenting responsibilities pre-divorce. Most single female parents function very adequately in their parenting role. Some women need reassurance post-divorce that they are parenting effectively since their children may try to make them feel guilty when discipline is enforced. A feminist therapist needs to be aware of typical behavior of children of different ages and to understand how children of different ages are apt to respond to the stress of divorce (cf. Hetherington, 1981). This information can help the mother discriminate between temporary adaptations and serious chronic behavioral problems that may require professional intervention.

Post-divorce stress may disrupt the interaction of some women and their children, particularly in the first year or two following divorce (Hetherington, Cox, & Cox, 1979). One of the ways children, especially young children, communicate their distress is through behavioral disturbances. Hetherington (1981) has reported that both sons and daughters are less compliant to mothers than to fathers and this is especially true of sons. Thus, some women who are in the process of establishing a single, parent family may seek guidance from the therapist in setting realistic expectations and establishing constructive discipline.

Establishing authoritative parenting. The development of social competence in children from intact families is associated with a pattern of discipline which Baumrind (cited by Santrock & Warshak, 1979) described as authoritative parenting. Santrock and Warshak (1979) found that authoritative parenting in both mother-custody and father-custody homes was also linked with increased social competence in children. Authoritative parenting involves considerable verbal give and take between parents and children, warmth and the enforcement of control and rules in a non-punitive manner. However, Lewis (1981) has reinterpreted the variable "firm control" as measuring the child's willingness to obey rather than the parents' tendency to exercise control. She concludes that, "the behavior of well-socialized children may be due to the variables that accompany firm control rather than to firm control per se; deleting firm control from the authoritative parenting package is not associated with less well-socialized behavior" (p. 547). Helping the single parent whose children are exhibiting behavior problems to develop authoritative parenting can aid the well-being of children and the mother.

Eliminating coercive interactions. In contrast to authoritative parenting, coercive interactions between parents and children have been observed in single family homes in which children show behavioral disturbance (e.g., Hetherington, Cox, & Cox, 1982; Kelly & Wallerstein, 1975, 1976). Coercive interaction refers to interactions in which the aversive behavior of one family member is terminated by the aversive behavior of another. Thus the aversive behavior of each is reinforced by the termination of that behavior in the other. Positive behaviors remain at a low level of frequency because they are not reinforced. These maladaptive interactions between mothers and their children have been shown to be bidirectional (Hetherington, Cox, & Cox, 1982).

Hetherington, Cox, & Cox (1982) found that the most negative interactional problems were observed between divorced mothers and their sons. In trying to explain these findings, Hetherington (1981) has suggested that boys' behavior in general has been observed to be more disruptive than girls'; also, due to sex-role stereotyping, boys may not be seen as needing as much emotional support as girls following divorce. Santrock and Warshak (1979) report that children living with the different sex parent are less well adjusted than those living with the same sex parent. Whatever the explanation, coercive interactions are painful for both parent and child and destructive to family harmony and the child's social development. The mothers whose sons had behavioral problems were less consistent with their sons, communicated less effectively with and used more negative commands and sanctions and fewer positive commands and sanctions than with their daughters. Difficulty with discipline peaked one year after divorce; there were fewer discipline problems at a two year follow-up but some persisted (Hetherington, Cox, & Cox, 1982).

From a social learning perspective, the remedy for coercive interactions is to increase the reinforcement of positive behaviors through such rewards as praise, privileges and attention, while at the same time extinguishing aversive behaviors through a variety of aversive contingencies (e.g., time-out, response cost, ignoring) for undesirable social behaviors (cf., Patterson, 1974a, 1974b). If it appears that coercive interactions are taking place between mothers and their children, the therapist can teach these behavioral techniques to the mother. When practiced consistently, these techniques generally reduce the children's destructive behaviors. In cases of severe behavioral problems, family therapy or individual psychotherapy for the child may be indicated.

Supporting children's independence. There is evidence that middle-class, single-female-parent families make fewer maturity demands on their children than two-parent families, lower-class, single-female-parent, or single-male-parent families (Hetherington, 1981). Most of these mothers work and are increasing the stress on themselves by this behavior. These mothers may try to make up for deprivations they feel they have inflicted on their children through divorce by spoiling them with material things and/or not demanding that they do their fair share in the family. Such misguided altruism not only is detrimental to the child but increases the burden on the single parent.

Sex role analysis described above is one way of getting women to assess the costs and benefits of self-sacrifice. If the woman is acting out a martyr role with respect to her children out of guilt, the feminist therapist can suggest that she experiment sharing household responsibilities with them. Most women quickly discover that children who are given responsibilities in the family commensurate with their age are happier, as they become more self-reliant and feel like they are making a significant contribution to the family. The mothers are also much happier with this arrangement.

For a single-parent family to function effectively, especially if the mother is working and has several children to care for, sharing responsibility with the children is virtually a necessity for a well-functioning home environment. Weiss (1979) has described shared decision making and the absence of a hierarchy among single parents and their children. These give children new rights, new authority as well as new responsibilities which can lead to growth and early maturity.

On the negative side, there are some overburdened mothers who reverse roles and expect children to take on age-inappropriate task and/or to become her primary emotional support at the expense of their own development. Weiss has found that such role reversals tend to be of brief duration since the mother generally recognizes the inappropriateness of the situation. In extreme cases in which the mother and child appear stuck in role reversals, the feminist therapist can help the mother clarify family roles and help her identify alternative resources to cope with her emotional needs.

Additional skills which facilitate healthy interactions between a mother and her children come under the headings of communication training (e.g., Gordon, 1970) and assertiveness training (e.g., Phelps & Austin, 1976). Bibliotherapy can be a useful adjunct to feminist therapy. Books that the author has recommended to single mothers include *Growing Up Free* by Letty Cottin Pogrebin (1980) and *The Single Mother's Handbook* by Elizabeth S. Greywolf (1984).

Providing nonsexist role models. Single, female parents often worry that their sons will be deprived of male role models due to the father's absence. Indeed, the literature review cited earlier indicates that a father's absence is an important social concern. Having two loving parents is a bonus; however, there is no compelling scientific evidence that the presence of a father is essential for the development of healthy children of either sex. Abusive or inadequate fathers are undoubtedly worse than none at all. Many children continue to interact with their fathers after divorce and may actually spend more time with them than before. This is more likely to be true for sons than daughters (Hetherington, 1981). There are generally many males in a boy's environment with whom he can identify and emulate.

When a woman brings up the issue of providing male role models, the feminist therapist can generally inquire further into what her actual concerns are. The therapist can ask her what values she wants male role models to communicate to her sons and daughters? What attributes does she want her male and female children to emulate? The therapist can share with her the belief that her interactions with her children and the values she communicates to them are important factors in their sex role development and also communicate that mothers can model and reinforce instrumental and nurturant behaviors for both their sons and daughters. Having the mother read books on nonsexist child rearing, for example, *Growing Up Free* by Pogrebin (1980) can be helpful.

Eliminating power struggles and manipulations. Hess and Camara (1979) discovered that relationships between family members for both traditional and divorced families appeared to have a more potent effect on child behavior than did marital status. Positive relationships between a mother and father in the postdivorce period greatly mitigated the negative effects of the divorce. However, when one or both parents use the children as pawn in their power struggles during and following divorce, the results can be disastrous for the children. There are, of course, violent men who will not stop power struggles until they get what they want, whether it be custody of their children or even return of the woman to the relationship. In dealing with an extremely destructive ex-spouse, a woman may have to seek legal assistance to protect herself and her children.

However, even well-meaning parents often get caught up in "divorce wars" and do not realize how their actions are affecting their children. Children often take advantage of this situation and attempt to play one parent off against the other, thus escalating the fight. When the therapist becomes aware that children are caught between two angry parents, she should confront the maladaptive behavior of her client to increase the client's self-awareness and to make the client aware of the consequences of continuing this behavior. If the client is motivated to change the behavior, the therapist can teach the client direct communication skills (Gordon, 1970) and behavioral principles (Patterson, 1974a,b).

Sometimes, but not always, when one parent stops playing the manipulation games, the other will also stop. In any event, the child can benefit from at least one mature parent to buffer the destructive effects of an immature or emotionally disturbed parent. When clients are reluctant to give up the manipulation games, it may be because they find these games satisfying ways to vent their anger, a way to stay emotionally involved with their ex-spouse and/or they are afraid the parent who continues to manipulate (e.g., by bribing the children with presents and privileges) will win their children's affection away from them. Helping the woman deal with her anger (cf. Emotional Changes, above) can get the client unstuck from the negative relationship with her ex-spouse. Confronting the client with her refusal to go through an "emotional" as well as a legal divorce and working through the loss associated with the emotional divorce can also be a way to get the client unstuck.

Some clients fear that giving up the manipulations involves a risk of losing the children's affection. An effective technique for overcoming this fear is asking clients to try an experiment. The experiment requires that they unilaterally cease their manipulations and refuse to respond in kind to manipulations by the spouse or the children for a period of time. They are instructed to observe the effects of their "unilateral disarmament" on the children's behavior. Conscientiously undertaking this experiment generally leads to a gradual improvement in mother–child relationships over a period of time.

Some clients think they must always present a united front with their ex-spouses in front of their children even when they actually disagree with the ex-spouses' decisions or behavior. They may even try to cover or make excuses to the children for their ex-husbands' behavior. For example, one client repeatedly told her children their father, who was in excellent health but behaviorally unstable, was ill when he repeatedly failed to show up for his weekly visits. When it appears that such distortions are occurring, the feminist therapist can point out the risk the woman is taking in denying or distorting reality: possibly losing the respect and trust of her children and modelling dishonest behavior. Assertiveness training may be useful in helping a woman express her true feelings to her ex-spouse and to the children in appropriate ways and insist that her rights and the rights of her children are respected.

Eliminating child abuse. The most serious lapses of responsible parenting are emotional, physical, or sexual abuse of the children. Such behavior has long-term, destructive consequences. There are instances in which a mother may divorce a husband who has emotionally, physically, or sexually abused her and/or her children and the abuse continues under court-sanctioned visitation.

If the mother has reason to believe that the children are being physically or sexually abused by the father while he is visiting with them, she should be encouraged to report his behavior to legal authorities and to file legal charges against him. Of course, therapists have a responsibility to report their suspicions of child abuse. Fortunately, legal authorities are taking complaints of physical and sexual abuse of children more seriously than in the past. Children who have experienced emotional, physical, or sexual abuse often require professional help.

If the therapist has knowledge that the mother is abusing her children the therapist should immediately inform the client that the law requires the therapist the report the abuse. A feminist therapist who has handled several cases of this type makes a phone call to the Human Services Department while the client is in her office so that the client may hear whatever the therapist says. The therapist, with the client's permission, sets up a meeting with the human services worker and the client in her office. The therapist negotiates a contract with the client concerning the type and frequency of future reports to the department. These reports generally consist of informing the department on a routine basis that the mother is still in treatment and a progress statement at the end of treatment. In the experience of this particular therapist, this procedure has facilitated rather than hindered a good, working, therapeutic relationship with the client.

COMMUNITY CHANGES: ACHIEVING FRIENDSHIP, SUPPORT SYSTEMS, AND INTIMACY

Feeling competent in the role of social participant is important to the life satisfaction of divorced, single, female parents (Kazak & Linney, 1983). For most women, divorce means separation not only from the former spouses but from the community and other meaningful relationships. Unlike other significant life changes (e.g., marriage, bereavement, etc.) there are no *rites de passage,* no rituals, no standardized roles for friends and families when a marriage dissolves. Unattached women are less welcome than unattached men in couple-dominated activities. Women who work may only interact with coworkers on the job and the nonworking single mother may find herself virtually isolated from adult companionship. Creating a satisfying social life is not a luxury but a necessity for the good mental health of the mother (Kazak & Linney, 1983).

Building friendships and support networks. When interviewing a new client, feminist therapists generally inquire into environmental supports. If a woman does not have a support network or lacks satisfying social outlets, the therapist can make it part of the therapy contract to work with her to develop this aspect of her life. The actual strategies depend on the woman and her circumstances. The therapist needs to be aware of community resources for varied interests and life-styles. For example, during the past year, the author has had single mothers request information on the lesbian community, a singles social organization, parents without partners, college continuing education classes, a volunteer social agency, and a women's summer camp. In addition to resources, social skills, communication, or assertiveness training may be needed by some women in order to make and maintain good interpersonal relationships.

The divorced, single mother needs a support network. Due to her own independence needs the mother's family of origin may not be the best source of support. Single mothers need several sources to call on in times of crises since overtaxing any one source can cause that source to be less willing to help in the future (Hetherington, 1981).

Overton and Avery (1984) found that most single women's support came from other women. By becoming involved with other women who share her circumstances, she has the opportunity for companionship, affection, and emotional support. Women can also offer each other practical advice and help in coping with loneliness, child care, and other problems common to divorced women. Important learning takes place between women: for example, learning that one can obtain intimacy from women as well as men, that one can be affirmed as a worthwhile person in one's own right. Such knowledge reduces a woman's dependency on men as a source of support, self-esteem, and identity. Women can model strength, competency, and problem solving for each other in addition to providing support and nurturance. The feminist therapist begins this process.

Single female parents who are not too emotionally distressed can benefit immensely from an all women's group, e.g., a women's support group, a women's therapy group, a C–R (consciousness-raising) group, a divorced women's group, or a single mother's group. The first author has had clients who were able to make important interpersonal contacts with other women by joining a women's organization as a participant or volunteer. Sometimes even trading child care and other activities with other mothers in one's neighborhood has reduced loneliness for a single mother. Recently Overton and Avery (1984) developed relationship enhancement training for single, female friendship pairs, which is a positive step toward legitimizing and strengthening female bonding.

Expressing intimacy and sexuality. Another aspect of being a social participant is developing relationships of psychological and sexual intimacy. Mothers who head households are sexual beings who have the right to express their sexuality in any ways that they choose. Female socialization teaches women to use sex as a tool to manipulate and/ or please men rather than as a natural expression of their sexual feelings and needs. Our society has a contradictory way of looking at divorced mothers. On the one hand, there is the stereotype of the divorcee as a loose, sex-starved female who is easy prey for male exploitation; on the other hand, there is the stereotype of the mother as asexual. This madonna–whore duality is our society's way of defining women on the basis of their sexuality. Most women find themselves conflicted over the double messages society sends them about sexuality and this is often exacerbated when a woman becomes a single parent.

The area in which these women may initially experience the greatest loss is in the area of intimacy (Hetherington et al., 1977). In the past, intimacy has been synonomous with marriage. However, the feminist therapist who does not believe that marriage is the only legitimate avenue to achieving intimacy can support single, female parents' exploration of alternate life-styles, such as group and communal living, cohabitation, and lesbianism as opportunities for women to develop intimacy outside of marriage. A reconstituted family that involves communal living or a live-in lover can be a positive environment in which to raise children.

Women are often concerned about how their children will be affected and react to their expression of their sexual selves. Sometimes women fear that their children will disapprove of their sexually intimate friends; or their children may have actually communicated disapproval. Alternatively, some children try to pressure their mothers into remarriage. Once again, sex role analysis can be a useful for helping women to sort out their own values and become self-defining and authentic in their sexual expression. The feminist therapist can share her own values that an important aspect of the healthy personality is an acceptance of one's own body, one's sensuality, and sexuality. The therapist can also explain that how children will be affected by the mother's expression of sexuality will depend on the quality of communication and interaction between the mother and her children. The mother can be reminded that she is the adult in the family and that she did not get divorced to relinquish control of her life to her children. Additionally, children's lives can be enriched by being exposed to different personalities, values, discipline, and life-styles of significant others in their mother's life, provided that these significant others are mature and caring in their interactions with the children. There may, of course, be adjustment problems as children adapt to having a new person share their lives, but with patience and good mother–child communication, most of these problems can be solved. Sometimes mothers and their adolescent daughters are beginning the dating process at about the same time. In the first author's experience, being able to share this experience actually made the mothers and daughters emotionally closer.

Women going through divorce sometimes fear that being sexually active will affect their custody and financial settlement. Chesler (1986) reports that these fears are not without foundation when fathers wage custody battles. In the case of lesbian mothers, the court has sometimes forced a woman to choose between her lover and her children (Rand, Graham, & Rawlings, 1982). Women on welfare often find welfare workers prying into their intimate lives to determine if they are living with a partner (Brown et al., 1976). For the mother who has concerns about reprisals from the court, welfare, the ex-spouse, or relatives, she and the therapist can go through a decision-making exercise in which the woman weighs the costs and benefits of various options and chooses the contingencies with which she feels comfortable. While the client is the person who must make the final decision, the therapist can pose alternatives and provide information which can help make any decision an informed one. For example, a lesbian mother who hides her lesbianism from her children because she fears losing custody of them or even losing their love should be made aware that she may be risking her own psychological growth and may be creating an unhealthy atmosphere of deceit in her family that could be detrimental to her children's psychological development (Rand et al., 1982). A divorced woman known to the author was threatened with a custody battle by her ex-husband when he discovered that she was in a lesbian relationship. This woman agreed to give him custody provided that he face the children and explain to them why he would not let them live with their mother. At that point he dropped his threats. Not all women in a similar situation would take the risk that this woman did and there is no guarantee that the results of similar action would be positive. Each woman has to examine her own situation and decide what risks she is willing to take.

PSYCHOLOGICAL CHANGES: ACHIEVING AUTONOMY

Achieving psychological autonomy means becoming a self-actualized person, i.e., a person who is a mature, complete human person (cf. Maslow, 1968). From a feminist perspective, a self-actualized, single, female parent is one who is able to nurture oneself, to be able to balance one's own needs with those of others, to find ways of creatively handling multiple roles and the inevitable conflicts this involves and having one's identity centered in oneself.

Becoming androgynous. Women and children who form single-parent families must become more independent and assume new responsibilities that were previously performed by men. Women who formerly may have felt competent only in performing expressive and communal activities come to feel competent in agency and instrumental tasks as well. This allows them to be more fully functioning human beings. Males who become single parents probably have a similar growth experience in developing their expressive, communal aspect. Some of the ways that therapists facilitate the development of androgyny in single, female parents that have been discussed in this chapter include sex role analysis (Rawlings & Carter, 1977), assertive training (e.g.,

Phelps & Austin, 1975), anger therapy (Burtle, 1985; Carter, 1977); career counseling and life planning (Bolles, 1985), and social learning skills training (Patterson, 1974a,b) and cognitive approaches such as reframing (Watzlawick et al., 1974).

Nurturing oneself. An important part of achieving psychological autonomy is learning to nurture oneself. Women are taught to be nurturant to significant others, e.g., men and children, but not to themselves. Most women have experienced a nurturance deprivation throughout their lives. Chesler contended, "Female children are quite literally starved . . . for physical nurturance and a legacy of power and humanity from adults of their own sex ("mothers")" (1972, p. 18). Single mothers who are experiencing considerable emotional and physical deprivation need permission to use their own capacity for nurturance for themselves and to share this with other women.

Therapists can encourage a woman to find ways of nurturing herself no matter how difficult her financial circumstances. Otto & Otto (1976) present a list of ways in which women can provide self-nurturance. When therapy for women is conducted in an all female group setting, self-nurturance, and nurturance of other women is facilitated by direct encouragement and modeling of group members (Carter, 1977).

Balancing needs. Women have been socialized to be concerned about others; therefore, when they focus on their own needs they may feel selfish (Gilligan, 1982). A woman may experience conflict between the needs of her children and her own needs for career development and an active social life. Rather than continue to conceptualize the dilemma as a win/lose situation, she can be taught to reframe it as a balancing problem in which her needs and the needs of her children should be given equal priority.

Reducing role conflict. In developing all the new roles and identities a woman needs in her single-parent role, she may experience role conflict; i.e., she finds she cannot meet the demands of all roles simultaneously. In dealing with role conflict, the therapist can have her examine what strategies she is using for dealing with multiple roles. Hall (1972) has developed a schema of the different ways that people deal with interrole conflict. According to Hall, one can engage in *structural role redefinition,* i.e., change external role demands (Type I), *personal role redefinition,* i.e., internally redefine one's role (Type II), or *re-active role behavior,* i.e., work harder in all roles (Type III). Many single, female parents adopt Type III, strategy, which can be frustrating and draining. Being aware of Type I and Type II strategies gives women more choices in the ways in which they carry out their roles. Time management techniques (e.g., Lakein, 1973) can help a woman cope with the many demands in her busy life more effectively.

Self-centering. From a feminist perspective, women should center their lives around themselves rather than others, including their children. Society affirms as "feminine" women who negate themselves in relationships with significant others including husbands, lovers, and children (Miller, 1976). Women often confuse self-centering and self-interest with selfishness, egocentricity, and lack of femininity. This aspect of the traditional role greatly contributes to the pervasiveness of depression in women (Radloff & Cox, 1981). There is a danger that the single, female parent who derives her primary identity from her children will consequently "smother" them. Sex role analysis and feminist bibliotherapy are techniques that feminist therapists frequently use to aid single, female parents to become self-centered. When a woman becomes centered in herself, she experiences a sense of personal power and identity. She can then afford to view her children as separate persons who enrich her life rather than provide the primary meaning for her existence. Having to provide meaning for a parent is too great a burden for any child. A woman who is centered in herself has the greatest potential for being a happy, effective, single parent.

CONCLUSION

The traditional nuclear family is rapidly becoming just one of many types of families. As women revolt against oppressive roles and press for more personal and financial autonomy, divorce rates increase along with the numbers of single-parent, mother-headed families. From a feminist perspective, this trend is not deplorable but a welcome disintegration of patriarchial versions of marriage and family institutions. Social attitudes always lag behind social change. The needed social reforms are not in strengthening traditional institutions but creating supporting structures for the changing realities of single-parent family life. In the interim, therapists who hold feminist values can ease the strains on women and children caught in personal and societal transition by using a wide variety of techniques and strategies to assist divorced women going through changes in six major areas: (1) emotional, (2) legal, (3) economic, (4) parenting, (5) community and (6) psychological, to develop new, effective roles and identities.

REFERENCES

Aslin, A. L. (1976). Counseling "single again" women. *Counseling Psychologist.* 6, 37–41.

Beck, A. (1979). *Cognitive therapy and emotional disorders.* New York: International Universities Press.

Benedek, R. S., & Benedek, E. P. (1979). Children of divorce: Can we meet their needs? *Journal of Social Issues. 35*(10), 155–169.

Bloom, B. L., Asher, S. J., & White, S. W. (1978). Marital disruption as a stressor: A review and analysis. *Psychological Bulletin, 85,* 867–894.

Bolles, R. N. (1981). *The three boxes of life.* Berkeley, CA: Ten Speed Press.

Bolles, R. N. (1985). *What color is your parachute? A practical manual for job-hunters & career changers* (rev. ed.). Berkeley, CA: Ten Speed Press.

Brown, C. A., Feldberg, R., Fox, E.M., & Kohen, J. (1976). Divorce: Chance of a new lifetime. *Journal of Social Issues, 32*(1), 119–133.

Brown, P., & Manella, R. (1978). Changing family roles: Women and divorce. *Journal of Divorce, 1,* 315–327.

Burtle, V. (1985). Therapeutic anger in women. In L. B. Rosewater and L. E. A. Walker (Eds.), *Handbook of feminist therapy: Women's issues in psychotherapy* (pp. 71–79). New York: Springer.

Carter, D. K. (1977). Counseling divorced women. *Personnel & Guidance Journal, 551*(9), 537–542.

Chesler, P. (1972). *Women and madness.* New York: Doubleday.

Chesler, P. (1986). *Mothers on trial.* New York: Macmillan.

Chiriboga, D. A., Roberts, J., & Stein, J. A. (1978). Psychological well-being during marital separation. *Journal of Divorce, 2,* 21–36.

Coalition on Women and the Budget. (1984). *Inequality of sacrifice: The impact of the Reagan budget on women.* Washington, DC: National Women's Law Center.

Collier, H. (1982). *Counseling women: A guide for therapists.* New York: Free Press.

Despert, J. L. (1962). *Children of divorce.* Garden City, NY: Dolphin Books.

Douvan, E. (1976). The single parent: Challenges and opportunities. In R. K. Loring & H. A. Otto (Eds.), *New life options—The working woman's resource book* (pp. 325–344). New York: McGraw–Hill.

Dowling, C. (1982). *The cinderella complex.* New York: Summit Books.

Fodor, I. G. (1985). Assertiveness training for the eighties: Moving beyond the personal. In L. B. Rosewater and L. E. A. Walker (Eds.), *Handbook of feminist therapy: Women's issues in psychotherapy* (pp. 257–266). New York: Springer.

Gettleman, S., & Markowitz, J. (1974). *The courage to divorce.* New York: Ballantine Books.

Gilligan, C. (1982). *In a different voice: Psychological theory and women's development.* Cambridge, MA: Harvard University Press.

Glick, P. C. (1979). Children of divorced parents in demographic perspective. *Journal of Social Issues, 35*(4), 170–182.

Glick, P. C., & Norton, A. J. (1978). Marrying, divorcing and living together in the U.S. today. *Population Bulletin, 32,* 3–38.

Goode, W. J. (1956). *After divorce.* New York: Free Press.

Gordon, T. (1970). *Parent effectiveness training.* New York: Peter H. Wyden, Inc.

Greywolf, E. S. (1984). *The single mother's handbook.* New York: Quill.

Hall, D. T. (1972). A model of coping with role conflict: The role behavior of college educated women. *Administrative Science Quarterly, 17,* 471–486.

Hess, R. D., & Camara, K. A. (1979). Post-divorce family relationships as mediating factors in the consequences of divorce for children. *Journal of Social Issues, 35*(4), 79–96.

Hetherington, E. M. (1972). Effects of father absence on personality development in adolescent daughters. *Developmental Psychology, 7,* 313–326.

Hetherington, E. M. (1979). Divorce: A child's perspective. *American Psychologist, 34*(10), 851–858.

Hetherington, E. M. (1981). Children and divorce. In R. W. Henderson (Ed.), *Parent-child interaction* (pp. 33–58). New York: Academic Press.

Hetherington, E. M., & Camara, K. A. (1984). Families in transition: The processes of dissolution and reconstitution. In R. D. Parke (Ed.), *Review of child development research.* (Vol. 1, pp. 398–440). Chicago: University of Chicago Press.

Hetherington, E. M., Cox, M., & Cox, R. (1976). Divorced fathers. *Family Coordinator, 25,* 417–428.

Hetherington, E. M., Cox, M., & Cox, R. (1979). Play and social interaction in children following divorce. *Journal of Social Issues, 35*(4), 26–49.

Hetherington, E. M., Cox, M., & Cox, R. (1982). Effects of divorce on parents and children. In M. E. Lamb (Ed.), *Nontraditional families: Parenting and child development* (pp. 233–267). Hillsdale, NJ: Erlbaum.

Hunt, M. (1966). *The world of the formerly married.* New York: McGraw–Hill.

Jacobson, D. S. (1978). The impact of marital separation/divorce on children: III. Parent-child communication and child adjustment, and regression analysis of findings from overall study. *Journal of Divorce, 2,* 175–194.

Johnson, M. M. (1975). Fathers, mothers, and sex typing. *Sociological Inquiry, 45,* 15–26.

Kazak, A. E., & Linney, J. A. (1983). Stress, coping and life change in the single parent family. *American Journal of Community Psychology, 11*(2), 207–220.

Kelly, J. B., & Wallerstin, J. S. (1975). The effects of parental divorce: I. The experience of the child in early latency. II. The experience of the child in late latency. *American Journal of Orthopsychiatry, 45,* 253–254.

Kelly, J. B., & Wallerstein, J. S. (1976). The effects of parental divorce: Experiences of the child in early latency. *American Journal of Orthopsychiatry, 46,* 20–32.

Lakein, A. (1973). *How to get control of your time and your life.* New York: Signet.

Levitin, T. E. (1979). Children of divorce. *Journal of Social Issues, 35*(4), 1–25.

Lewis, C. C. (1981). The effects of parental firm control: A reinterpretation of findings. *Psychological Bulletin, 90*(3), 547–563.

Maslow, A. (1968). *Toward a psychology of being* (2nd ed.). New York: Van Nostrand.

Miller, J. B. (1976). *Toward a new psychology of women.* Boston: Beacon.

Nye, F. I. (1957). Child adjustment in broken and in unhappy unbroken homes. *Marriage & Family Living, 19,* 356–361.

Otto, H. A., & Otto, R. (1976). Maximizing the positive in separation, divorce, and widowhood. In R. K. Loring & H. A. Otto (Eds.), *New life options— The working woman's resource book* (pp. 427–449). New York: McGraw-Hill.

Overton, D. H., & Avery, A. W. (1984). Relationship enhancement for single females: Interpersonal network intervention. *Psychology of Women Quarterly, 8*(4), 376–388.

Parkes, C. M. (1972). *Bereavement.* New York: International Universities Press.

Patterson, G. R. (1974a). Intervention for boys with conduct problems: Multiple settings, treatments, and criteria. *Journal of Consulting Psychology, 42,* 471–481.

Patterson, G. R. (1974b). Retraining of aggressive boys by their parents: Review of recent literature and follow-up evaluation. In F. Lowey (Ed.), Symposium on the Seriously disturbed Preschool child, *Canadian Psychiatric Association Journal, 19,* 142–161.

Pedersen, F. T. (1976). Does research on father-absent families yield information on father influences? *Family Coordinator, 25*(4), 459–464.

Phelps, S., & Austin, N. (1975). *The assertive woman.* San Luis Obispo, CA: Impact Press.

Pogrebin, L. C. (1980). *Growing up free.* New York: McGraw-Hill.

Radloff, L. S., & Cox, S. (1981). Sex differences in depression in relation to learned susceptibility. In S. Cox (Ed.), *Female psychology: The emerging self* (2nd ed., pp. 334–350). New York: St. Martin's.

Rand, C., Graham, D. L. R., & Rawlings, E. I. (1982). Psychological adjustments and factors the court seeks to control in lesbian mother custody trials. *Journal of Homosexuality, 8*(1), 27–39.

Raschke, H. J. (1977). The role of social participation in postseparation and postdivorce adjustment. *Journal of Divorce, 1,* 129–140.

Rawlings, E. I., & Carter, D. K. (Eds.). (1977). *Psychotherapy for women: Treatment toward equality.* Springfield, IL: Charles C. Thomas.

Rich, A. (1977). *Of woman born: Motherhood as experience and institution.* New York: Bantam.

Rutter, M. (1971). Parent–child separation: Psychological effects on the children. *Journal of Child Psychology & Psychiatry, 12,* 233–260.

Santrock, J. W. (1972). Relation of type and onset of father absence to cognitive development. *Child Development, 43,* 455–469.

Santrock, J. W., & Warshak, J. W. (1979). Father custody and social development in boys and girls. *Journal of Social Issues, 35*(4), 112–125.

Spanier, G. B., & Casto, R. F. (1979). Adjustment to separation and divorce: An analysis of 50 case studies. *Journal of Divorce, 2,* 241–253.

Trebilcot, J. (Ed.). (1983). *Mothering: Essays in feminist theory.* Totowa, NJ: Rowman & Allenheld.

Watzlawick, P., Weakland, J. H. & Fisch, R. (1974). *Change: Principles of problem formation and problem resolution.* New York: W. W. Norton.

Weiss, R. S. (1979). Growing up a little faster: The experience of growing up in a single-parent household. *Journal of Social Issues, 35*(4), 97–111.

CHAPTER 9

Feminist Therapy with Male Clients

Anne L. Ganley

INTRODUCTION

For many people, the term feminist therapy is typically associated with the image of a feminist therapist counseling women clients in individual, group, couples, or family sessions. Such an image is based on the assumption that feminist therapy by its nature is solely for the female client. Supposedly, if men are involved at all as clients in the therapy, it is because they are in relationship as lover or family member to a female client. Yet in spite of this image of feminist therapy, the reality is that men are also consumers of this psychotherapeutic approach. Some men intentionally seek out feminist therapists while others are in feminist therapy because it was available. These men may have sought a qualified therapist or, more specifically, a female therapist only to discover later that she is a feminist therapist. At an agency or counseling center these men may have been assigned to their therapist, unaware of the therapeutic approach used by that therapist.

This reality that men are consumers of feminist therapy is not reflected in the literature of the new field of feminist therapy. While there has been much written about feminist therapy and women as well as about feminism and men, there is a noticeable gap in articles about the applications of feminist therapy with male clients. The primary contribution of feminist therapy to therapy with men stems from its power to redefine the norms for the mental health of the adult male and the adult female, and to assert that these norms are the same for both men and women. This androgynous model of mental health for both men and women, by definition, changes the very nature of the therapeutic issues male clients will deal with in feminist therapy. This chapter will consider each of these issues in light of this model.

Moreover, it will review the practices and principles in feminist therapy that must be reconsidered to avoid their becoming obstacles to using this approach with male clients.

TRADITIONAL MODELS OF THE MENTALLY HEALTHY ADULT

Traditional approaches to therapy have attempted to address the needs of male clients. The sheer volume of literature that forms the basis of these therapies with men prohibits a detailed review or a feminist critique of each in this chapter. However, the central difference between these nonfeminist approaches to therapy with men and a feminist approach is not so much in the strategies used, but in their definition of what it is to be a mentally healthy adult male or mentally healthy adult female. What traditional approaches have in common are their limited models for normal human behavior. Some approaches rely on a double standard model whereby men and women are treated differently, while others employ an androcentric model for both men and women.

For many years there has been a double standard of mental health, one for men and one for women. Descriptions of the mentally healthy male were considered synonymous with those of the mentally healthy adult. As the Broverman et al. (1972) study revealed, the characteristics seen as appropriate for a mentally healthy woman were not seen as synonymous to being a healthy adult. Furthermore, the adult woman was characterized by more negative qualities. Under this double standard, women either had the characteristics of an adult and were considered "unfeminine" or they had the characteristics associated with being "feminine" and were considered less than an adult. As long as they had the stereotypical masculine qualities, they were considered healthy adults. Unfortunately this double standard is still used as the norm in much clinical practice.

Even when this model is challenged, it is too often replaced by an androcentric model, which endoreses stereotypical masculine traits as ideal for all persons (Brown & Liss–Levinson, 1981). The androcentric model defines the healthy adult as being achievement-oriented, rational, instrumental, independent, aggressive, and individualistic, etc. Neither the double standard of the mentally healthy adult nor the androcentric model affirms the typically feminine attributes, such as being relational, interdependent, empathetic, or nurturing. Neither affirms pluralistic models of mental health.

In the past decade and a half, criticisms of the male model for mental health have come from multiple sources. Feminists within psychology (Chesler, 1972; Kaplan, 1976; Rosewater & Walker, 1985) and feminists outside psychology (Ehrenreich, 1983) have questioned the negative impact of the unchallenged androcentric model on both women and men. Some of the challenges to the model have come from writings and research on the psychology of women (Gilligan, 1982; Miller, 1976) where a more complete understanding of women's development underscores the inadequacy of the androcentric model. Building on feminism, the men's liberation movement has also questioned the model's relevance to men, and it has called on men to develop further their "feminine" qualities of being more emotionally expressive, nurturing, and empathetic (Fasteau, 1974; Goldberg, 1976; Pleck & Sawyer, 1974; Welch, 1985). Some of the criticism comes from scholarship outside of feminism where the definition of mental health is expanded by a better understanding of white racism (Schwartz & Disch, 1970), race/ethnicity/culture (McGoldrick, Pearce, & Giordano, 1982), sexualities (Bell & Weinberg, 1978; Zilbergeld, 1978), economic class (Sennett & Cobb, 1972), aging (Fisher, 1986), and differences in physical abilities. In the face of this ever-growing body of knowledge, the androcentric model for mental health is inadequate at best and is damaging at its worse.

It is not surprising that women's mental health suffered under these standards. Too often, therapy based on such models mislabeled women who had either traditionally masculine or feminine attributes as being deviant, pathological, inappropriate, or irrational. When being measured against such limited models, women in therapy were expected to adjust to the status quo. What is also not surprising is that all who did not fit these narrow models were also stigmatized by those norms of mental health: persons of color, persons of lower economic class, lesbians, gays, bisexuals, the elderly, and those differently abled.

Furthermore, even those who supposedly do fit, i.e. men, are limited by that mental health norm. While the androcentric model reinforces men's positions of economic and social power, it is a mixed blessing. As discussed later in this chapter, such a model also cripples their understanding of themselves in the past and present, and it limits their ability to change in the future. Traditional therapeutic approaches to counseling men reinforce an androcentric norm and assist clients only in adjusting to the status quo. In so doing, they fail to meet the therapeutic needs of both those men who fall outside that norm and those whose issues are the direct result of ascribing to that norm.

AN ANDROGYNOUS MODEL OF MENTAL HEALTH

Feminists look to an androgynous model for mental health to move beyond the deficits of the androcentric model (Bem, 1974; Cox, 1982). Rawlings and Carter suggest that "to think of traits in terms of the masculine–feminine dichotomy perpetuates the old set" (1977, p. 28). They prefer Bakan's concepts of agency (self-protection, self-assertion, self-expansion) and communion (being at one with the organisms) for their definition of an androgynous model. They stress that Bakan's major contribution is in defining the central developmental task as being the one of integrating and balancing agency with communion. A feminist analysis also brings to this androgynous model an awareness of the pluralism in how this norm of the healthy adult is lived out. This pluralism results from differences in race/ethnicity/culture, age, economic class, sexualities, and physical abilities. The androgynous model for the healthy adult says that men and women can be both relational and achieving, instrumental and expressive, rational and emotional, self-nurturing and other-nurturing, assertive and receptive, independent and dependent, individualistic and collaborative. Androgyny calls for a flexibility of roles and life-styles, egalitarian rather than power-based relationships, and a sensitivity to human rights.

DEFINITION OF FEMINIST THERAPY WITH MEN

As discussed in detail in the second chapter, feminist therapy is a philosophy as well as a particular school of therapy. The philosophy, based on feminist theory, guides the use of a wide variety of assessment and therapeutic techniques. Central to the philosophy is the assumption that ideology, social structure, and behavior are interwoven: Hence, women's and men's behavior stem more from socialization and institutional sex roles than from biology (Cammaert & Larsen, this volume, Chapter 2). A feminist analysis highlights the harmful effects of such sex role stereotyping for both women and men while also being clear that women's economical and political status is more negatively affected than men's.

Feminist therapy involves the resocialization of women (Forisha, 1981) and of men. It uses the androgynous model of mental health for both men and women to assist clients in identifying goals for therapy. This is a model of health, growth, and development rather than one based on illness. As evidenced by the preceding four theory chapters, feminist therapy draws on a variety of personality theories in understanding human behavior. The feminist therapist employs psychoeducational approaches, choosing to incorporate strategies from radical psychiatry, humanistic psychology, cognitive behavioral approaches, etc. Some even attempt to use psychoanalysis within the feminist conceptual framework. In sex role analysis, the external and internal constraints to change are identified. While feminist therapy stresses individual responsibility for change, it deals with the issues of choice, control, and power within the current social structures. The process of feminist therapy draws on the phenomenological experiences of both therapist and clients as women to guide the changes (Brown, 1984). Furthermore, feminist therapy is recognized as not being solely a change process for an individual, since it calls upon both client and therapist to change society's institutions, including the structures of psychotherapy itself.

Such a definition of feminist therapy distinguishes it from two closely related approaches to therapy: nonsexist therapy by male and female therapists and profeminist therapy by male therapists. In nonsexist therapy there is the use of sex role analysis and the androgynous model of the mentally healthy adult. However, little attention is given to the need to restructure social institutions, either by the therapist or the client. Oftentimes nonsexist therapy practice reflects traditional methods and procedures; little attempt is made by the therapist to be accessible to varieties of persons or to empower clients both in therapy and in their communities. Inclusive language may be used, traditional sex roles challenged, and individual change supported, but these nonsexist approaches appear to focus solely on the progress of individuals to the exclusion of social change. The primary difference between feminist therapy and nonsexist approaches is that the nonsexist approach addresses the personal but overlooks the political.

Profeminist therapy is similar to feminist therapy in its sex role analysis of human experience, its understanding and use of power, its use of the androgynous model of mental health, and its recognition of the need for social change. The difference between the two rests solely in the gender of the therapist. In feminist therapy the therapist is a female who uses her phenomenological experiences as a woman to understand her clients and to enrich her therapeutic strategies. In profeminist therapy the therapist is male. Since he does not have the phenomenological experience of being female, he uses his experiences as a male and particularly a male whose understanding of himself, of all men, and of women has been transformed by feminist analysis. The recognition that feminist therapy is a phenomenological process clarifies that men cannot be feminist therapists. Male therapists can and do use feminist analysis to provide nonsexist therapy *and* to bring about social change: In doing so they are profeminists therapists. This description of the difference does not devalue them or their work. At this time and in this social context it is merely different from feminist therapists.

Feminist therapy with men is a particular kind of feminist therapy shaped by the gender of the client. A feminist analysis underscores the point that men in this culture have different experiences than women: This reality alone makes all the difference in the application of feminist therapy to male clients. Rather than discuss all the similarities and differences between feminist therapy with men and that with women, the remainder of the chapter will focus on those particular client and process issues raised by feminist therapy with male clients.

CLIENT ISSUES IN FEMINIST THERAPY WITH MEN

The use of the androgynous model for mental health in therapy with male clients brings into focus certain specific issues which otherwise might not be identified. In addition, such a model reframes some of the traditional counseling issues presented by male clients. To illustrate these points, each of the common themes raised in feminist therapy with male clients are discussed separately, although in practice they are often interwoven. Specifics from a variety of cases and practice settings are used in the examples in order to provide some breadth to the particular theme. The examples also illustrate how a particular theme may appear in a very dysfunctional and obvious way with one client, whereas it would result in less dysfunction for another person. To a greater or lesser degree some combination of these issues are presented by most male clients in feminist therapy.

Relationship/Achievement Values

One of the major developmental tasks for the adult is the integration and balance of relationship and achievement needs in one's life. Sometimes characterized as the balance between love and work, this issue for most men involves the integration of the whole range of relationships: acquaintances, friends, lovers, and family members with multiple aspects of doing work. On no other issue is the impact of sex role socialization so disparate for men and women. As the work of Miller (1976) and Gilligan (1982) reveal, women have been socialized to value relationships and to measure their self-worth and that of others in terms of one's ability to develop and maintain relationships. Men on the other hand are socialized to value achievement and production and to measure their self-worth and that of others accordingly.

Men assess their own worth in terms of their achievements, which in turn are determined by quantitative standards of how much, how many, how often, and how big. Whether it is football, corporate sales, sexual activity, surgical procedures, legal cases, farming, manufacturing, selling illegal drugs, or philanthropic work, the push for men is to be bigger or better than other men. They tend not to value relationships except in terms of the way those relationships improve or detract from their achievement goals. Historically, even family relationships for men signified property relationships. In fact the word family originally means having to do with the property and slaves of a particular man. Relationships are entered into and dissolved according to men's achievement needs. Oftentimes what has been described as great models of male–male friendships have been those of being "comrades in arms," where the relationship is actually a means to a task. In addition to that military setting, the friendships may now take place on the racquetball court or in the pool hall. However, the emphasis still remains on these relationships being vehicles for conducting business rather than being experiences shared between intimates.

The change in times may have modified some of the particulars in the way the theme is manifested, but for men in therapy the struggle between relationship and achievement values remains. Some men describe this conflict solely in terms of a sense of failure about achievement goals. For example, they may be unemployed due to disability, aging, changes in the job market, imprisonment, or by choice. Or they may be employed, but they are filled with anxiety about performance or they are dissatisfied when the work does not fit their dreams. In either case the despair or anxiety is centered solely with discomfort about work and achievement. There is hardly any mention of relationships. Men's emphasis on achievement at expense of relationship usually means that their relational needs are not even acknowledged. Occasionally the theme is expressed solely in terms of relationships: a troubled marriage, a lack of friends, or a sense of alienation. Yet seldom do men recognize their needs to be both relational and achieving.

In feminist therapy, the sex role analysis of the issues as presented by the client make the dimensions of the relationship/achievement conflict apparent. This aspect of feminist therapy allows the individual male client to become aware of the specific nature of his strengths and weaknesses in integrating those two parts of his life. It also encourages a valuing of the relational side of his life as an end in itself. Thus, as he makes changes in one aspect, he will not inadvertently ignore the other. By identifying the gender-specific nature of his conflict, he may be better able to strategize the steps for change. Sometimes this may initially involve developing more realistic expectations in terms of work and then focusing more on developing relationships. Sometimes the approach would be reversed. A feminist analysis contributes to the resolution of this particular conflict the reminder that gender socialization for men emphasizes achievement to the detriment of relationships. Both are needed for a sense of well-being and healthy functioning.

Intimacy Avoidance

For some men one result of the devaluing of relationships in their socialization is their avoidance of intimacy. This intimacy avoidance is manifested in many ways. Men may demonstrate a fear of intimacy through excessive anxiety and/or anger in any relationships which pose even the possibility of intimacy. In such relationships they may swing from times of intense demands for reassurance that a partner "loves" them to times of extreme anger at the partner for inconsequential events. With either behavior the result is to drive the partner away; thus avoiding the possibility or actuality of intimacy. The avoidance of intimacy may also be expressed in the excessive emphasis on sexual behavior in one or multiple relationships. For these men there is the appearance of intimacy through sex but without the emotional involvement. With others this issue is revealed in what they call their anxiety about meeting women. With either the Don Juan or the timid man, the intimacy avoidance is totally focused on their relationships with women or the lack of relationships with women. They do not even express intimacy issues as they pertain to friends, children, or work associates. Others may experience the intimacy avoidance by being the classic workaholic or substance abuser which allows them to avoid all opportunities for intimate relationships with friends, lovers, and family members.

For clients dealing with the issue of intimacy avoidance, feminist therapy is particularly useful. It reframes the issue in terms of gender role socialization, rather than in terms of one particular past negative event, such as abandonment by mother, rejection by previous girl friend, or a bad marriage. A sex role analysis of this particular issue assists both client and therapist in understanding both the social rewards that determine this behavior as well as the negative events that contributed to it. Only then will the changing of intimacy avoidance become more than finding one good woman. In feminist therapy with men the goal becomes the process of increasing intimacy in a variety of relationships: parent–child, friend–friend (both sexes), colleague–colleague, and lover–lover. The change also involves a process of building social reinforcers for being intimate. Intimacy requires a lot of risk taking and one cannot be successful without sometimes failing. Too often traditional therapies have focused exclusively on trying to avoid the failures rather than on how to use them as a learning experience.

Self-disclosure/Insight/Empathy

Given the emphasis on achievement rather than on relationships in the gender socialization for men, it is not surprising that deficits in relationship skills appear. One such deficit is in self-disclosure. In order to have relationships one must be able to reveal oneself to another. Yet sex role socialization holds up as the ideal for men the man who is strong, nonemotional, striving, achieving, better than others. Here the emphasis becomes revealing only part of the self to avoid the display of any "weaknesses," i.e. emotions. Consequently, men become skilled at avoiding self-disclosure. This serves them well in certain achievement tasks such as war and production. However, this avoidance of self-disclosure has its price, both for the psychological and physical well-being of men as well as for their relationships with others.

Men suffer personally from this constraint on expressing emotions by the self-perception that there is part of who they are that they must keep hidden. This "secret" part is perceived as being negative and not experienced by other normal men. Such thinking leads to decreased self-esteem and to the perception that others would misuse the information against them. Masking and monitoring of thoughts and feelings become the norm and consume physical and psychic energy. Some suggest that this results in stress and stress-related illnesses (Jourard, 1974).

Men's lack of self-disclosure also impairs their relationships with others. As Jourard (1974) points out, men's failure to self-disclose limits their insight into themselves and blocks their ability to empathize with others. Men do not reveal feelings and thus do not get feedback about those emotions or the perceptions that accompany those feelings. They often do not identify certain emotions in themselves. This lack of information about themselves leads them to misperceive the thoughts and feelings of others. Consequently their attempts to respond to another are often inappropriate or miss the mark. Jourard uses the self-disclosure process of therapy itself to illustrate this breakdown in insight and empathy due to the lack of self-disclosure. With increasing self-disclosure (in therapy), the client becomes more aware of feelings and more skilled in labeling them. With this increased insight into self comes the increased ability to identify the feelings and thoughts of others and to consider as real the differences and similarities in the other. This is empathy.

Feminist therapy's sex role analysis of this theme assists men in identifying the multiple ways they are limited by the failure to self-disclose. In supporting changes for men in this characteristic, the value of self-disclosure must be integrated with both achievement and relationship needs. Clients may need to learn to discriminate the types and timing of self-disclosure to use in the workplace and in social relationships. For change to occur, the male client needs to develop a support system with others, which affirms his growing abilities in self-disclosure and in empathizing with others. In feminist therapy this can be accomplished through the encouragement of either therapeutic groups or social change groups which are committed to this process goal.

Anger as Mask/Identifying All Emotions

While much has been written in the men's liberation field about men being socialized to avoid expressing emotions, less attention has been given to the reality that men are oversocialized to use the emotion of anger as a mask for other emotions. The issue is not so much that they do not express feelings, but that they usually express all feelings as anger. Women are socialized to be emotional and men are socialized to be angry. This has particularly serious consequences when this emotional pattern is paired with the behavioral pattern of violence (Ganley, 1981). While all men do not physically batter their partners or children or strangers, most misuse anger. When experiencing the full range of human emotions, such as happiness, sadness, fear, and anger, men tend to identify and express the negative emotions of sadness and fear in all their varying degrees as upset/anger. Consequently, guilt, anxiety, hurt, disappointment, etc., result in inappropriate angry expressions.

Tavris (1982) examines how culture shapes human emotions, specifically anger, and challenges the simplistic acceptance of human emotions as being innate. Men's expression of anger is in keeping with their socialization to be instrumental rather than relational. Anger is used by men to intimidate, to control, and to punish others—to accomplish a task. Women's expression of their emotions is in keeping with their relational priorities. Women express feelings to maintain relationships rather than to accomplish a task.

Given the centrality of this emotion in men's sex role socialization, anger is a major theme in feminist therapy with male clients. The writings of Brown and Liss–Levinson (1981), Forisha (1981) illustrate that the issue of anger is also a central theme for women in feminist therapy. However, this is true for very different reasons and the feminist therapist working with both male and female clients has to deal with the anger theme in very different ways according to the gender of her client. Anger in women is not synonymous with anger in men. Anger is not anger is not anger. A male client's experience and expression of anger must be routinely assessed by the therapist. Because of their gender socialization, men usually do not acknowledge that their anger or its accompanying violence may even be a problem. A routine assessment of anger reveals where an individual male's anger expression is on a continuum of misuse to abuse (Ganley, 1981). Furthermore, the assessment allows both therapist and client to recognize when crisis intervention strategies may be necessary, due to the lethal nature of the way the client is expressing anger. As anger is explored further as a theme in feminist therapy, the male client can learn to identify and to express constructively the other human emotions which lie beneath that mask of anger.

Communication Skills: Listening, Reflecting, and Facilitating

Given the devaluation of relationships in men's socialization, it is understandable that certain communication skills are overdeveloped and others overlooked. Men tend to have the communication skills necessary to their instrumental roles. They give orders, state demands, provide facts, interrupt others, and interrogate others clearly and easily. While there is a cultural myth that women are more verbal, the experience of men in mixed groups is that they dominate the conversation in both length, frequency, and volume of comments. What is evident is that men are verbal, but they use certain verbal skills more than others. They often appear blocked or tongue tied when attempting to use the communication skills that are more typically associated with developing and maintaining intimacy in relationships. In addition to the previously discussed poor self-disclosure skills, men have problems with the listening and facilitating skills due to their sex role socialization. When "listening," men often hear only a portion of the message before interpreting it and preparing their responses. They usually do not ask for clarification nor do they utilize the active listening skills of paraphrasing or reflecting. In groups they do not take the role of facilitating; they don't draw others out or summarize what has happened, or make process comments. They will be very verbal in conversations, but the content and types of comments reflect their gender socialization.

In feminist therapy with men, the issue of these communication deficits need to be addressed to make the therapeutic process possible. Most therapies will involve the clients in increased self-disclosure and communication of emotions. What is important in feminist therapy with men is the awareness that the men also traditionally have deficits in listening and facilitating skills. Unless this is kept in mind, insight-oriented therapies can occur without assessing for deficits in listening or facilitating communication skills. As with other issues, feminist therapy is useful in identifying the source of the deficits while also promoting client responsibility for developing those skills. The emphasis in feminist therapy on two-way communications between the therapist and the client in individual therapy as well its emphasis on group therapy provide the male client an immediate laboratory for change. Male clients need encouragement to apply these skills in both intimate relationships and work relationships. For some clients, the skills have already been learned in management classes. Here the communication skills are taught to enhance being instrumental, not relational. Without a feminist analysis, the skills are utilized only in the typically masculine world of work and they are not generalized to personal relationships.

Models for Relationships: Mutuality vs. Dominance; Collaborative vs. Competitive

Although men's socialization devalues relationships, it does offer a model for work, social, and family relationships. This model is one of competition and dominance. Since men enter relationships to meet achievement needs, men seek a position of power or control in those relationships. Their primary model for relationships appears to be a hierarchical one. Since each relationship must have a one up and a one down, then each relationship is entered with some jostling for position. No man wants to be in the one-down position, since it becomes a threat to his ideal of being independent. In collegial and social relationships, men are competitive. Even so called male–male bonding develops out of a dominance model in which too often men bond with each other to be against another, e.g., team sports, all-male clubs to be "away from women," military units, gangs, etc.

A feminist analysis not only places value on relationships, but it offers new models for relationships: collaboration rather than competition; mutuality rather than dominance. In collaborative relationships, information, resources, and power are shared. Mutuality in relationships requires respect for the other as having equal worth to oneself as well as the respect for differences in resources. Developing mutuality in work, social, and family relationships becomes a process of maximizing cooperation rather than competition, of giving rather than hoarding, of sharing oneself rather than withholding oneself, and of valuing the differences of the other rather than defending against those differences. Each of the above becomes a theme for reframing many of the issues presented by male clients in feminist therapy.

Nurturing: The Self and The Other

Even though the androcentric model sets a standard for men to show limited emotions and to be independent, men as human beings have emotional and intimacy needs. In the development and maintenance of their sense of self, they, like women, need affirmation and acceptance. Typically they look for and expect this nurturing to come from women but not from men. There are various theories to explain this: the reality of women as the primary nurturers in childhood establishes this pattern, the association of nurturing with emotions and relationships means nurturing is women's work, etc.

What is important in feminist therapy with men is to look at the consequences of this expectation of woman as being the only nurturer: Men do not learn to do this for themselves or for others. Nurturing involves being aware of and responding to emotional needs. In self-nurturing, it is the nourishing of one's spirit. In therapy the male client needs to be challenged to do this for himself. Like the female client in feminist therapy, the male client needs to accept the importance of one's own emotions and the responsibility for attending to them. Unlike the female client, who has been socialized to nurture others and has only to learn to apply this to herself, the male client has to be taught basic nurturing skills. In addition to nurturing oneself, men need to learn to nurture others. To break that self-defeating cycle of always looking to women to do nurturing, men must be expected to give and receive nurturing with other men. In addition they need to develop skills in providing nurturing to women without immediate demand for reciprocity. Men's nurturing skills need to be developed in a variety of relational contexts: work, social, and intimate.

Consensual vs. Nonconsensual/Coercive Sex

Gender socialization has a major impact on men's sexuality. A primary operative assumption in male heterosexuality is that the male take the initiative, be dominant, and overcome the expected resistance of a female partner.[1] The expectation of the female is that she "says 'no' when she means 'yes'."This expectation can become erotically charged for the male, so that his erotic interest becomes dependent upon the "conquest." Operating with a nonconsensual model of sexual interaction bypasses the need for listening, negotiation and mutual choice, and disregards the lack of interest or ambivalence of the partner. In addition, this sexual interactive style is counterproductive for the male because it emphasizes his sexual performance expectations while it minimizes genuine relational interaction and the benefits of sexual intimacy (Fortune, 1982).

The impact of sex role socialization on sexuality is illustrated by the continuum of resulting dysfunctions. For some men this gender socialization puts them at risk to be sex offenders. David Finkelhor (1984) discusses traditional masculinity and its relationship to child sexual abuse as other authors have done with its relationship to sexual violence against adults, i.e., primarily women (Groth, 1979; Russell, 1982). With male clients the therapeutic issues of sexuality range from the nonconsensual, to the coercive, to violently abusive. A feminist analysis challenges men to develop consensual, relational models for sexuality.

Acceptance of "No": Disappointment vs. Anger

A recurring theme in feminist therapy with men revolves around their perception (real or imagined) of being turned down, hearing no, or being rejected by family members or women. Their typical response is one of anger and a desire to punish the other. And for many this desire to punish is acted upon. This response in part stems from the previously discussed issue of identifying all emotions as anger. However, this issue is also associated with men's socialization to the concept of entitlement in relationships with women or family members. Men expect that things will go their way in such relationships. When they do not, they perceive the other as intentionally harming them and therefore deserving of punishment. Women on the other hand typically experience those no's as a rupture in the relationship and respond with hurt and attempts to re-establish the relationship. Given the nature of adult–adult relationships and family life, there are bound to be many no's and rejections in the course developing intimacy. After all women are adults with

---

[1] Some of these comments also apply to homosexuality as well, but there are some differences. In order to avoid doing injustice to these variances, space requires the author to limit her comments to heterosexual males.

their own needs and wants, and relationships of mutuality have to be negotiated. Too often in therapy men's statements of anger about rejection are validated without exploring men's socialization to entitlement. In order to better meet their intimacy needs, men need resocialization to accept no's from women and family members, to experience disappointment rather than anger at those times, and to perceive those no's as being acts of autonomy rather than as acts of attack against them.

Noncoercive Problem Solving

Due to cultural norms of masculinity which socialize men to be solely instrumental rather than instrumental *and* relational, men regard control, coercion, and violence as the only tools available to accomplish problem solving. This is a natural outcome of the overemphasis on achievement to the detriment of relationships. If relationships have equal value to accomplishments, more attention would be given to the problem-solving skills of listening, brainstorming, negotiation, and compromise in order to sustain relationships. The increased interest in mediation, "yes–yes" negotiation, and other such nonadversarial models of problem solving is in part due to the recognition that while coercion or violence may work to accomplish an immediate task, it destroys the relationship in the process.

In feminist therapy, the teaching of any noncoercive, problem-solving skills attends not only to the skills themselves but also to their function, i.e., relationship maintenance. Otherwise the acquisition of these new skills (assertion, mediation, etc.) can simply further enhance the client's ability to control or coerce others. For example, teaching men assertion skills too often has simply increased their ability to exert power over others in order to achieve their goals, disregarding others' needs. In feminist therapy, assertion training would always be viewed as a means to the end of enhancing and sustaining relationship through good communication.

Attitudes and Beliefs about Women

Just as the androcentric model of mental health has misled men in their understanding of themselves, it also misleads them in their understanding of women. Feminist therapy on this issue with men involves re-education of men about who women are now and what their potentials are as adults. This re-education requires the client to utilize resources of books, films, music made by women about women as well as to listen with a "new ear" to their experiences of the women in their lives. Obviously feminist therapy has a unique contribution to make to men dealing with these issues since the feminist therapist herself has the phenomenological experience of being female, has the knowledge about women in general, and is one model of the androgynous adult embodied as woman.

PROCESS ISSUES IN FEMINIST THERAPY WITH MALE CLIENTS

There are certain process issues typically associated with feminist therapy that have to be reconsidered in light of a male client population. Reconsidering these issues enables the feminist therapist to avoid their becoming obstacles to the therapeutic goals of the male clients. The two primary process issues are the use of therapist as model and the use of power in the therapy. These are complex issues in any type of therapy and it is beyond the scope of this article to delineate them in detail. However, this introductory discussion of them is a reminder that feminist therapy with men is not the same as feminist therapy with women.

Therapist as Model

Therapist as model has been accepted as being important in many therapeutic encounters and particularly so in feminist therapy with women. Here, the feminist therapist as model directly demonstrates with the female client the reality that the personal is political, that being female is valuable, and that growth in the direction of autonomy does not necessarily result in loss of relationships. The client is both taught and affirmed by the therapist as model.

In feminist therapy with men, therapist as model shifts in somewhat different directions, since the feminist therapist is female. Here the therapist can provide modeling of specifics skills, such as communication skills, nurturing skills, and nonviolent, problem-solving skills. However, there are limits to such modeling because males also need to experience other men who have these skills. Furthermore, there is a danger that modeling of certain skills by a female therapist will reinforce a male client's self-defeating cycle of relying solely on women to provide these skills. Obviously these limits can be overcome by doing feminist therapy with men in groups where men can learn from each other's positive gains or by referring the client to a profeminist therapist. Another strategy would be to raise this limitation directly in the therapy and to expect the client to build male support networks for the changes he is seeking. This benefits the client in moving the issues out of the rarefied atmosphere of the therapy sessions and into his daily world.

Female therapist as model provides substantive learnings for men in feminist therapy. First, the client experiences a woman as an androgynous adult who is competent, independent, rational, and instrumental while also demonstrating the more typically feminine qualities of being relational and nurturing which challenges and rectifies the client's sexist attitudes about women. Secondly, the therapy sessions for male client can be the laboratory where he learns to discard the seductive or dominating interactive patterns of relating to women and to replace them with the communication skills necessary to relate to women as authorities or as valued peers, depending on the circumstances. Gender of therapist is salient to the process issue of therapist as model.

Power

To provide feminist therapy for men, the therapist must be cognizant of a variety of power issues that are manifest in the therapeutic process. Douglas (1985) discusses power and feminist therapy by highlighting the multiple issues related to power: the different bases of power (reward, coercive, informational, expert, legitimate), the inequality inherent in the client–therapist roles in therapy, the use of direct and indirect power, and gender as power. In her discussion she accepts the feminist therapy principle of minimizing the power differential between therapist and client and suggests that implementing this principle must take into consideration all the power issues she raises.

In feminist therapy with women the therapeutic goal is to equalize the power differential between client and therapist by a variety of process strategies (demystifying therapy, psychoeducational approaches, etc.) as well as by the use of particular techniques (having the client call the therapist by the first name, the use of touch, placement of office furniture, etc.). Careful thought is given to these issues because women generally enter therapy feeling very powerless. This powerlessness is at least in part due to their experiences in a culture that devalues women and ascribes differential power solely based on gender.

In feminist therapy with men, the situation is different. Due to sex role socialization, male clients will often assume a position of power over the female therapist even if they feel powerless at that time in other areas of their life. This assumption of power is based on their gender vis-à-vis the female therapist. Even though the roles in therapy between client and therapist would give greater weight to the therapist, the gender power differential is more salient to the client. Utilizing strategies prematurely to de-emphasize therapist's power based on role may inadvertently foster this inappropriate client response and block therapeutic change. It may be more effective with certain male clients to expect them to use titles or other standards of behavior to establish and reinforce the female therapist as authority, i.e. to indicate the differential in power based on role and to de-emphasize power inequality based on gender.

Another therapeutic practice which needs to be reconsidered in light of power and gender is the use of touch in feminist therapy with men. The use of certain kinds of touch can establish power differentials or equality. In feminist therapy with women a hug or touch is used to convey warmth, support, and a sense of being present to the other. These are done in the context of minimizing the power differential between female therapist and female client. In feminist therapy with men these types of touch must be used carefully because of the way men have been socialized to sexualize touch between men and women and/or to use touch from a base of having power over another. One type of touch that restructures power issues with the male client is the handshake initiated by the female therapist. It conveys a feminist therapist's assumption that therapy is both a relational and instrumental process. It also conveys to men that the woman as therapist is there to share equal power with men but not to be intimidated (fear of touch) or to be seduced (sexual touch).

Feminist therapists with male clients must also deal with their own issues of having power over men. In a significant number of situations involving therapy with men (sex offenders, batterers, etc.), it is therapeutic for the client to experience women as having power over them. The major therapeutic issue in therapy with offenders is teaching accountability. That requires having the power to hold the person accountable and being willing to use that power. The feminist therapist who prematurely attempts to equalize the power between the male client and herself can prevent change from occurring. Clearly feminist therapy with men requires a re-evaluation of the practices and procedures generally associated with feminist therapy with women.

CONCLUSION

It is difficult at times to discuss concepts of feminist therapy with male clients without the appearance of reducing the topic to simplistic generalities. It can begin to sound like a paraphrase of comedian Bill

Cosby's comment on his 20-year marriage ("my wife has given me a machoectomy"): doing feminist therapy with men is performing a machoectomy. However, the reality is that the mental health of all persons is severely damaged by sex role socialization and sexism. An important contribution to changing this reality is feminist therapy with male clients. To provide this, feminist therapists are called upon to rethink their understanding of feminist therapy, of men as clients, and of themselves. This chapter is one part of that ongoing process.

ACKNOWLEDGMENTS

The author wishes to acknowledge the substantive contributions to this article by Marie M. Fortune and Laura S. Brown.

REFERENCES

Bem, S. (1974). The measurement of psychological androgyny. *Journal of Consulting & Clinical Psychology, 42,* 155–162.

Broverman, I., Vogel, S., Broverman, D., Clarkson, F., & Rosenkrantz, P. (1972). Sex-role stereotypes: a current appraisal. *Journal of Social Issues, 28,* 59–78.

Brown, L., & Liss-Levinson, N. (1981). Feminist Therapy I. In R. Corsini (Ed.), *Handbook of innovative psychotherapies* (pp. 299–314). New York: Wiley-Interscenic Publication.

Brown, L. (1984). Feminist assemssment and therapy. Workshop conducted at the Washington State Psychological Association Continuing Education Program.

Chesler, P. (1972). *Women and madness.* New York: Doubleday.

Cox, S. (Ed.). (1982). *Female psychology—the emerging self.* New York: St. Martin's.

Douglas, M. (1985). The role of power in feminist therapy: a reformulation. In L. Rosewater & L. Walker (Eds.), *Handbook of Feminist therapy: Women's issues in psychotherapy* (pp. 241–249). New York: Springer.

Ehrenreich, B. (1983). *The hearts of men.* Garden City: Anchor Press/Doubleday.

Fasteau, M. (1974). *The male machine.* New York: McGraw-Hill.

Finkelhor, D. (1984). *Child sexual abuse.* New York: Free Press.

Fisher, K. (1986). Demographics beckon young to maturing field. *APA Monitor, 17,* 18–19.

Forisha, B. (1981). Feminist Therapy II. In R. Corsini (Ed.), *Handbook of innovative psychotherapies* (pp. 315–332). New York: Wiley-Interscenic Publications.

Fortune, M. (1982). *Sexual violence: the unmentionable sin.* New York: Pilgrim Press.

Ganley, A. (1981). *Court mandated treatment for men who batter.* Washington, DC: Center for Women Policy Studies.

Gilligan, C. (1982). *In a different voice.* Cambridge: Harvard University Press.

Goldberg, H. (1976). *The hazards of being male.* New York: Signet Books.

Groth, A. N., & Birnbaum, H. J. (1979). *Men who rape.* New York: Plenum Press.

Jourard, S. (1974). Some lethal aspects of the male role. In J. Pleck & J. Sawyer (Eds.), *Men and masculinity* (pp. 21–29). Englewood Cliffs, NJ: Prentice-Hall.

Kaplan, A. (1976). Androgyny as a model of mental health for women: From theory to therapy. In S. Kaplan & J. Bean (Eds.), *Beyond sex-role stereotypes: readings toward a psychology of androgyny* Boston: Little, Brown.

McGoldrick, M., Pearce, J., & Giordano, J. (Eds.). (1982). *Ethnicity and family therapy.* New York: Gilford Press.

Miller, J. (1976). *Toward a new psychology of women.* Boston: Beacon Press.

Pleck, J., & Sawyer, J. (Eds.). (1974). *Men and masculinity.* Englewood Cliffs, NJ: Prentice-Hall.

Rawlings, E., & Carter, D. (Eds.). (1977). *Psychotherapy for women: Treatment toward equality.* Springfield, IL: Charles C. Thomas.

Rosewater, L., & Walker, L. E. (Eds.). (1985). *Handbook of feminist therapy: Women's issues in psychotherapy.* New York: Springer.

Russell, D. (1982). *Rape in marriage.* New York: Macmillan.

Schwartz, B., & Disch, R. (1970). *White racism.* New York: Laurel Edition.

Sennett, R., & Cobb, J. (1972). *The hidden injuries of class.* New York: Vintage Books.

Tavris, C. (1982). *Anger—The misunderstood emotion.* New York: Simon & Schuster.

Welch, D. (1985). *Macho isn't enough! Family man in a liberated world.* Atlanta: John Knox.

Zilbergeld, B. (1978). *Male Sexuality—A guide to sexual fulfillment.* Boston: Little, Brown.

CHAPTER 10

Feminist Therapy with Lesbians and Gay Men

Laura S. Brown

INTRODUCTION

Feminist therapy was probably one the the first approaches to psychotherapy that was built on the premise that lesbians and gay men were not per se pathological. It remains one of few models of behavior change that intentionally perceives the variability of sexual orientations in human beings as a simple fact, rather than a matter for concern and intervention. In that regard, a feminist therapy perspective on psychotherapy with any lesbian or gay male client is almost always a preferred one. Just as feminist therapy was revolutionary in refusing to see the norms of women's lives as deviant from an androcentric model, so it is revolutionary in seeing lesbian and gay male identities as different yet equal to the sexual orientations of heterosexual women and men. For the lesbian or gay client not to need to prove that important aspect of her or his life to be nondeviant removes an unnecessary burden from the client's shoulders and speeds the process of change for which psychotherapy is sought.

In addition, feminist therapy is perhaps the only approach to psychotherapy that counts large numbers of open, self-identified lesbians among its practitioners and theoreticians. This is not to say that lesbians (and gay men for that matter) are necessarily feminist therapists. Rather, it indicates how different feminist therapy is in its inclusion of the lesbian and gay phenomenological perspective in the development of theory and practice. Although sexual minority individuals have always been therapists, few have approached their work with the consciousness of homophobia and comfort with sexuality that marks feminist therapists who are openly lesbian and gay; additionally, many heterosexual feminist therapists who have dealt consciously with homophobia in themselves share the positive perspective on lesbian and gay issues in psychotherapy held by openly lesbian and gay feminist therapists (Siegel, 1985). Consequently, the view from within provided by lesbian feminist therapists is one that affirms the concept of the normative, rather than deviant, nature of lesbian and gay sexual orientations.

This chapter will briefly review earlier approaches to psychotherapy with lesbians and gay men from other psychotherapeutic theoretical perspectives. Those views will be critiqued from the perspective of feminist therapy. Finally, specific applications of feminist therapy theory with issues common to lesbian and gay male therapy clients will be described. It is important to note in all of this writing that the population of lesbians and gay men not in therapy has been poorly described and defined. This invisibility of the population is an artifact of the severe discrimination against lesbians and gay men, and the frequent penalties attendant on any individual so identified. Lesbians and gay men of color, working-class lesbians and gays, aging sexual minority women and men, and other subgroups within the lesbian and gay population are most inadequately described. In consequence, inferences should be carefully made from examples in this chapter to lesbians and gay men in general. In addition, examples describing a population of psychotherapy clients cannot be construed as describing the population as a whole. Although in the case of heterosexual therapy clients that statement is taken quite for granted, the opposite has historically been true with lesbians and gay men, and rather grandiose generalizations have been made from psychotherapy patient groups to lesbians and gay men as a whole. It has been one of the strengths of feminist therapy that this overinclusive perspective has not been embraced; the caveat, nonetheless, remains important for the reader new to the concept of sexual minorities as mentally healthy human beings.

NONFEMINIST APPROACHES TO PSYCHOTHERAPY WITH LESBIANS AND GAY MEN

Two of the traditional and well-established approaches to psychotherapy have directly addressed the issue of psychotherapy with lesbians and gay men (although one extremely obscure approach to therapy, Aesthetic Realism, has the conversion of homosexuals to heterosexuality as its goal and primary claim to effectiveness, it is so little known and used as to not require comment here. Readers are directed to a chapter by Baird & Reiss in Corsini, [1981] for details). Both classical psychoanalytic theories of personality and psychotherapy and early operant conditioning models of behavior therapy dealt with lesbians and gay men as a class of deviant individuals and each of these radically different approaches to psychotherapy had as its goal for therapy with sexual minority individuals the conversion to heterosexual patterns of behavior.

A variety of psychoanalytically oriented writers since Freud have addressed the question of the causes and "treatment" of homosexuality. Freud himself wrote very little on the topic; his famous "Letter to an American Mother," often quoted during the debates over the American Psychiatric Association's classification of homosexuality as mental illness, implied that he held a somewhat benign view of homosexuality, certainly not seeing it as a more serious form of pathology than others that he addressed. Psychoanalytic theory classifies homosexuality as a "perversion," that is, an acting out, rather than a repression of an arrest or trauma in normal development. However, psychoanalytic thinkers since Freud, moved by a somewhat homophobic cultural *Zeitgeist,* have singled out homosexuality, particularly in men, as a singularly severe and pathological form of behavior. Socarides (1968, 1972) has been a particularly vocal proponent of this view of homosexuality. His descriptions of the diffuse and extreme pathology that he claims to have observed in his homosexual sample (all patients in psychoanalytically oriented psychotherapy) are echoed by other psychoanalytic theorists (Bergler, 1965; Caprio, 1953; Deutsch, 1933). None of the psychoanalytic writers prescribes any particular variant upon psychoanalysis as a therapy technique for lesbian and gay male clients. Rather, the emphasis is on the use of psychoanalysis to effect a "conversion" to heterosexuality, with cautions to the analyst that homosexuals will resist treatment and cling to their pathology, thus proving difficult as patients.

Aside from other feminist critiques of psychoanalytic theory on the grounds of general misogyny and cultural bias, feminist therapists have diverged sharply from psychoanalytic explanations of both the etiology of homosexuality and the appropriate goals for therapy with lesbian and gay clients. Feminists have argued that the psychoanalytically based "close-binding mother/absent weak father" theory of the etiology of homosexuality in men advanced by Bieber et al. (1962), and a concomitant study by Kaye et al. (1967) that found lesbians to have similarly disturbed parental gender role models, are seriously flawed, both methodologically and philosophically. Brown (1975) points out that both sets of researchers obtained their data on lesbians and gay men by polling the psychoanalysts who were treating lesbians and gay men, resulting in a badly skewed sample. Brown also commented, as have other writers (Gonsiorek, 1982; Morin, 1977, 1978; Moses & Hawkins, 1982) that the assumptions regarding "appropriate" and "inappropriate" gender role modeling in the parents of these lesbians and gay men reflected sexist bias then prevalent in psychoanalytic models of mental health. A feminist perspective on the development of sexual object choice would of necessity not include such rigidly gender role stereotyped concepts. Rather, a feminist therapy perspective construes gender roles to be flexible, and places a variety of behaviors that have historically been assigned to one or the other gender within the purview of both. This androgynous view of mental health stands in sharp contrast to the analystic perspective that sees nurturing, gentle behaviors in men, or overtly powerful ones in women, as suspect for violation of gender role norms.

From the perspective of treatment, a feminist therapy approach contains certain assumptions about the nature of the relationship between clients and their therapists that would stand in sharp, and critical contrast to psychoanalytic approaches to therapy with lesbians and gay men. For instance, since in feminist therapy treatment goals are mutually negotiated and agreed upon by client and therapist, the unilateral setting of a goal of sexual orientation change by a therapist would not occur. Thus the picture described by Socarides and others of the resistant homosexual therapy patient would be unlikely to emerge, since the therapist would not be engaged in the imposition of her or his values about "normality" onto the client. Nor is it likely that a feminist therapist would agree to undertake this task of the conversion of an individual from lesbian or gay to heterosexual as a goal of psychotherapy. Even though the current (at time of writing) version of the Diagnostic and Statistical Manual of Mental Disorders (DSM–III) contains a diagnostic category for "Ego-Dystonic Homosexuality," a feminist therapist would be very unlikely to utilize such a diagnosis. Rather, the assumptions underlying such a diagnosis would be called into question, and the fact pointed out that people of all sexual orientations may be, at some point, dissatisfied with that orientation. It is an assumption within feminist therapy that the sole reason that therapists have taken on the task of "converting" homosexuals to heterosexuality has been a homophobic devaluation of a homosexual object choice.

A feminist analysis would begin with the assumption that a lesbian or gay male client's desire to change sexual orientation, should that exist, is a reflection of that client's internalization of homophobic messages from the surrounding culture. Rather than participate in the oppression of the client by cementing those self-hating messages firmly in place, a feminist therapist would challenge the homophobia. Psychoanalysis, with its unswerving view of lesbians and gay men as pathological can easily be critiqued from the feminist perspective as simply serving as a means of social control, implementing the homophobia of society rather than challenging it. From the viewpoint of feminist therapy, psychoanalysis is a poor choice for therapy with lesbians or gay men, because of both the sexism and the homophobia embedded in psychoanalytic thinking on sexual minority individuals.

Behavior therapy also addressed questions of etiology and conversion of homosexuals early in theory development. Behavior therapy with homosexual individuals was often aversive therapy, performed in penal settings. Several weak learning models of the development of homoerotic object choice were advanced during this period in the early 1960s; these primarily revolved around a theoretical scenario in which early experiences of arousal were associated with same-sex persons, leading to a classical conditioning of arousal to a same-sex stimulus (Ovesey, 1969; Saghir & Robins, 1973). These explanatory models lacked supporting data, and appear for the most part to have been attempts to fit the existence of homosexuality into a model that could be explained by learning theories; the volume of literature on the development of homosexuality from a behavioral personality theory perspective has been quite sparse. This was not the case with literature on behavioral approaches to sexual orientation conversion were done without regard to etiological factors; e.g., there was treatment of the "symptom" of homosexual arousal without inquiry into how that "symptom" had been established.

In 1976, Gerald Davison, then president of the Association for the Advancement of Behavior Therapy, and originally one of the practitioners of aversive therapy with homosexuals, delivered a presidential address in which he called for the end of such interventions by behavior therapists. Citing and critiquing the behavior therapy literature on behavioral approaches to conversion of sexual object choice, Davison pointed out the massive failure of behavioral techniques of any sort to effect lasting changes in the sexual orientation of adults. He suggested that it might in fact be unethical for behavior therapists to contract with a client to work for a change of sexual orientation, given the high failure rate of behavioral approaches to reach such a goal (Davison, 1976, 1977).

Since Davison's challenge to his own profession, behavior therapy with sexual minority individuals has shifted direction. For instance, behavior therapists working with gay affirmative models have used techniques such as modeling and desensitization to aid clients in reducing their homophobia. Cognitive behavioral techniques have been effectively used in challenging homophobic cognitions in lesbian and gay male clients. Behavior therapy has moved from a position not dissimilar to that of psychoanalysis to one where the conversion of a lesbian or gay man's sexual orientation is not typically promoted as an end goal for treatment.

From the perspective of feminist therapy, Davison's critique of earlier behavioral efforts to change sexual orientation should suffice, in that the issues raised by him mirror those raised by feminist therapists. Behavioral and cognitive behavioral techniques are commonly part of the repertoire of some feminist therapists, and when used in conjunction with a feminist philosophy of treatment can be powerful tools for change.

Various other theories of psychotherapy have commented on homosexuality, usually briefly, and usually in a manner that reflects cultural homophobia. Ellis (1955, 1962, 1964), writing from the theory of Rational Emotive Therapy, posited that lesbians and gay men suffer from irrational ideas about sex with the opposite gender, and would likely be heterosexual were those irrational ideas to be challenged successfully in therapy. Jackins, the founder of Re-evaluation Cocounseling, described homosexuality as a form of "distress" (RC jargon for neurosis) that would change in response to appropriate emotional discharge (Jackins, 1962), although recently the cocounseling movement has responded to the advent of lesbian and gay liberation by removing the label of "distress" from homosexuality. The feminist critiques applied earlier to psychoanalytical thinking hold here as well, in that both Rational Emotive Therapy and Re-evaluation Cocounseling have assumed homosexuality to be a pathology, rather than a normal variant of human behavior, and in so doing, uncritically introjected the homophobic and sexist norms of society at large into their theorizing.

In the past several years, lesbian and gay therapists, writing from a perspective that, while not necessarily nor explicitly feminist, embodies many of the concepts and philosophies of feminist therapy, have begun to develop a model of therapy called "gay affirmative psychotherapy." As with feminist therapy, gay affirmative therapy has developed from a political as well as a psychological base. It works from the perspective that lesbians and gay men are an oppressed minority, rather than a psychologically deviant group, and that an important component of psychotherapy for lesbians and gay men is the examination of the impact of their oppression on their psychological functioning. Malyon (1982) has described the manner in which a dynamically oriented, gay affirmative therapist would work, and focuses on the ways in which homophobic oppression acts to reduce opportunities for the performance of normal developmental tasks for lesbians and gay men. Gay affirmative practitioners have particularly spoken to the issue of how homophobia deflects adolescent development for lesbians and gay men, and have devised treatment models that view common problems in functioning of lesbian and gay clients as outgrowths of that oppressed adolescent period. Gay affirmative psychotherapy also attends to the issue of coming out, that is, the process by which an individual develops and then declares a lesbian or gay identity. Gay affirmative models of psychotherapy have primarily been developed by therapists working with a gay male population; it appears that lesbian affirmative psychotherapy has been long subsumed under feminist therapy theory, which was developed with a consciously lesbian affirmative, nonhomophobic perspective.

FEMINIST THERAPY WITH LESBIANS AND GAY MEN

A feminist therapy perspective on working with lesbians and gay men looks to the cultural, social, and emotional environment for clues to the etiology of problems brought into therapy by lesbian and gay male clients. Although lesbian and gay male clients can and do exhibit the range of symptoms and psychopathology exhibited by heterosexual clients, certain sociocultural issues are more likely to be explored by a feminist therapist in making an assessment and developing an intervention strategy. This is likely to be the case for any client seen by a feminist therapist. Commonly, a feminist therapist will observe issues of gender role socialization, race, class, disability, and age in the process of creating a feminist conceptual framework for understanding intrapsychic conflict. However, with lesbian and gay male clients, the impact of homophobia, and its interaction with other forms of cultural oppression and self-alienation is of specific concern, and will be dealt with as primary here.

Homophobia refers to the irrational fear and hatred of same-sex sexual and affectional preferences, individuals who manifest those preferences, and behaviors associated with those individuals. As a cultural phenomenon, homophobia enlarges to include negative stereotypes regarding lesbians and gay men, their lives, and their relationships. All North Americans grow up in cultural settings that are, to one degree or another, homophobic. Sometimes, the homophobia manifests itself simply by the invisibility of lesbians and gay men; in other settings, it takes an active, negative form. Whatever shape homophobia takes, it is highly likely that a lesbian or gay man will have learned to view himself or herself through a homophobic lens long before being aware of and identifying herself or himself as lesbian or gay.

Consequently, a feminist therapist, in assessing a lesbian or gay male client, will explore how it is that this person currently construes the meaning and value of her or his homosexuality, as well as how that may have changed over time. A feminist therapist will collect data regarding the degree to which a client's past and current social and emotional environments were homophobic. This often includes developing a sense of how invisible lesbians and gay men were in the client's early environment, and the effect that invisibility might have had on the client's developing awareness of her or his own homosexuality.

Race, class, and culture, while important contextual determinants by and of themselves, may interact with cultural homophobia in particular mixtures that are helpful or harmful to the particular lesbian or gay male client. Lesbians and gay men of color are often oppressed by their racial group for their homosexuality, and by white lesbians and gay men for their ethnicity (Moraga & Anzaldua, 1981). Some upper-class white lesbians and gay men may find themselves less negatively impacted by cultural homophobia because of experiences in same-sex environments where homosexuality is tolerated, or because class acts as a buffer against the stigma associated with homosexuality in some manner (Cruikshank, 1985).

An analysis of gender role socialization and gender role compliance is also essential to the development of a feminist therapy contextual framework for understanding lesbians and gay men. In most aspects of North American cultures, as well as in many other cultural milieus, there is a blurring of distinction between gender role and sexual orientation. Assumptions are often made that "masculine"-appearing women or "feminine"-appearing men are homosexual. This assumption is so strongly fixed in American psychology that Scale 5 of the Minnesota Multiphasic Personality Inventory, which purports to measure masculinity and femininity, was developed by using the interest and attitudes of gay men as the mmeasure of femininity. Writers such as Green (1974) have reported their attempts to make "feminine" young boys more masculine in their behaviors, with the stated intention of averting homosexuality in those boys.

This cultural confusion regarding the relationship of gender role to sexual orientation affects lesbians and gay men no less than heterosexual women and men. Assessment of the rigidity of a lesbian or gay client's gender role socialization, and exploration of the penalties for gender role deviance contained within that socialization process is thus essential with sexual minority clients. The interaction of sexism, in the form of rigid gender roles, with homophobia becomes another important point of focus.

Without the careful examination of these sociocultural factors and their interactions, therapy is not likely to be feminist. In examining common issues brought into therapy by lesbians and gay men, the importance of understanding homophobia, sexism, race, class, and other cultural phenomena becomes apparent. It appears that these issues are particularly well addressed by a feminist therapy perspective. They include:

1. Coming out to self, family, and community;
2. Internalized homophobia and coping with cultural homophobia, racism, classism, and sexism;
3. Sexuality and sexual functioning;
4. Couple relationship problems;
5. Gender role concerns and their interactions with other socio-cultual phenomena.

Coming Out

Coming out is a process that occurs in stages; a lesbian or gay man comes out to self first, naming one's self as lesbian or gay, integrating that awareness and title into pre-existing self-concepts. The person who is out to her/himself then faces a series of questions regarding whom else to come out to, and how. Being out carries both risks and benefits. In some places, being out can mean loss of job, home, and children. In others where the rights of lesbians and gay men are more securely protected, being out can mean a fuller, more complete integration of the public and private spheres of life. In many circumstances, a person who faces no external penalties for being out will remain closeted, so great has been the fear of eventual negative consequences. Lesbians and gay men are constantly in the process of coming out, as well. Every new setting, every new person raises the question again for a lesbian or gay man. Do I come out here? Why? Why not?

A feminist analysis brings a number of strengths to the therapy client who is struggling with issues of coming out, either to self, or to family and community. A starting point is the concept of the normative nature of same-sex sexual and affectional attraction. The therapy client who begins the process of coming out in therapy, or who enters feminist therapy during the period of questioning and self-doubt, is more likely to encounter in a feminist therapist an attitude toward homosexuality that is accepting and supportive. A feminist therapist is likely to be informed of the difficulties many persons have in distinguishing between sexual orientation, gender role, and quality of sexual function.

Thus, the person who describes herself as attracted to other women while continuing to adhere to a somewhat traditionally feminine gender role will not encounter disbelief or devaluation of her sexual feelings from a feminist therapist on the erroneous (yet often cited by traditional therapists) grounds that she is "too feminine to be a lesbian." Women and men in the process of coming out to self may be caught in dilemmas regarding what they perceive to be badness of fit between their own self-concept and the homophobic stereotypes they have learned regarding lesbians and gay men. For instance, sexual minority people with strong religious faith may feel that they must choose between one and the other. This sense of being pulled between two parts of the self is also often true for ethnic minority lesbians or gay men. Lesbians or gay men with career plans that are typical for their gender may feel that, in order to be truly lesbian or gay, they must move into vocations that are stereotypically associated with gayness, e.g., truck driving or coaching for women, hairdressing or interior design for men, whether these fit their vocational needs or not. A feminist approach can be of enormous help, both in sorting out the differences between gender role and sexual orientation, as well as in creating an opportunity to examine and question the validity of sexist and homophobic stereotypes. A feminist analysis constantly calls into question taken-for-granted notions regarding "appropriate" male and female behavior, and is an important part of facilitating an exploration of sexual orientation in therapy.

A feminist analysis can also become important in supporting a lesbian or gay male client in assessing risks and benefits of coming out to family and community. A lesbian or gay male client may, for whatever reason, have unreasonably good or bad fantasies of the outcome of such action. A feminist analysis goes beyond assessing the risks of being open to explore equally fully the risks of the closet to mental health, intimacy, and general well-being. In exploring these risks, discussions of coming out in therapy lead invariably to explorations of homophobia, both internal and external.

Homophobia

An important aspect of exploring sexual orientation and the developmental process of coming out in therapy is the examination of how lesbians and gay men have internalized cultural homophobia. The effects of internalized homophobia can be seen in many of the issues that lesbians and gay men bring into therapy. One of the tasks of a feminist therapist is to help clients understand how they have been trained to participate in their own oppression. The theoretical construct of internalized oppression can be used here to illustrate how individuals learn and identify with cultural and social norms that are oppressive to themselves, and to explain some of the difficulties people encounter in dealing with the "gut feeling" that what they are doing and being is wrong, even when there is the cognitive understanding that the old strictures are not useful.

Lesbians and gay men have been among those most carefully taught to engage in this cooperation with societal messages that they are "flaunting" themselves when speaking of their relationships, "hurting their families" by being honest with them about sexual orientation, or being "unnecessarily fixated on their homosexuality" by being out in work settings. A feminist analysis of heterosexual privilege in society can be shared with clients by a feminist therapist; the fact that heterosexual women and men are continually "flaunting" heterosexuality by references to spouses, celebrations of weddings and anniversaries, holding hands in public, kissing partners hello and goodbye, or that in coming out to families, lesbians and gay men are not sharing bad news, but rather increasing intimacy through greater self-disclosure. A feminist analysis can clarify how certain privileges of the dominant class (in this case, heterosexuals) can be shared with the oppressed class, rather than given up as some sort of inevitable penalty for a homosexual object choice. These viewpoints flow very naturally from the feminist therapy concept that all sexual orientations are equally normative and mentally healthy.

Consequently, feminist therapists working with lesbians and gay men will find themselves continually identifying and challenging aspects of the client's own internalized homophobia. As mentioned earlier, this is likely to occur first during explorations of coming out, when homophobic stereotypes regarding the relationship between gender roles and sexual oreintation or mental health and sexual orientation must be challenged for the lesbian or gay client to adopt a positive lesbian or gay identity. Issues of how race, culture, class, and other group memberships interact with homophobia are also likely to come under examination at this point in the feminist therapy process. A feminist analysis will lead to further awareness of how internalized oppression functions. For instance, extrapolating from feminist analysis of the impact of sexism on women's functioning, an analysis of how lesbians and gay men are shamed for behaviors that are stereotypically lesbian or gay can be developed, parallel to analyses of how women are shamed for womanly attitudes and behaviors.

A paradigm similar to that developed by Gilligan (1982) in studying gender differences in moral development can be applied to the understanding and re-evaluation of lesbian and gay lives. Gilligan's model observes differences and attempts to give them meaning in the cultural context without attempting to assign excess value to one set of behaviors over another, different one. For instance, lesbian or gay clients may complain of feeling "adolescent," e.g., uncertain, awkward, unskillful in approaching a potential partner, easily limerent, in their approach to sexual relationships, and apply a homophobic analysis to this observation, drawing the conclusion that lesbians and gay men are incapable of mature adult relationships. A feminist therapist, applying a political analysis, might observe that homophobia acts as a barrier for adolescent lesbians and gay men to engage in normal adolescent dating and sexual experimentation during teen-age years, and that the common phenomenon of the middle-aged lesbian or gay adolescent is not a sign of arrested development, but rather oppressed and stopped opportunities. It is not uncommon for single status to weigh more heavily on lesbians and gay men because of the underdevelopment of same-sex courtship skills, and the absence of culturally approved and modeled same-sex courtship rituals. Because many lesbians and gay men are laboring against the internalized stigma associated with their sexual orientation, there is a tendency to want relationships to be immediately perfect and functional, and a lack of tolerance for what, in heterosexual relationships, may be awkward or uncomfortable, but rarely proof that the gender of the beloved is wrong.

Finally, feminist analysis and awareness of the impact of homophobia might lead to an examination of how sexual minority individuals have learned to oversexualize their relationships as a response to cultural homophobia, and that skills in same-sex dating and courtship do not develop well in homophobic contexts. Attending to the ways in which context shapes the meaning of behavior is central to feminist analysis and can go far in reducing the stigma from many behavior patterns common among lesbians and gay men.

This analysis of the presence, and subtle yet far-reaching effects of internalized homophobia is best done with a clear, feminist comprehension of the oppression of lesbians and gay men. Therapists working with a feminist perspective are uniquely equipped to address this concern because of the power that feminist political analysis lends to the understanding of the nature and function of homophobia in sexist society. Pheterson (1984) has particularly commented on how the stigmatized status of certain groups of women, lesbians among them, and the threat of stigma against women not in those groups, has been a means by which sexist societies control women, as well as divide them. Brannon (David & Brannon, 1976), a man writing from a feminist perspective, has made similar observations regarding the function of homophobia as a means of socially controlling men via fear and shame.

Gender Role Concerns

Problems related to gender role expectations are common ones for
lesbians and gay men seeking therapy, perhaps because they perceive
themselves as falling outside the boundaries of the correct role behaviors
for their gender. For some, this is a source of pride; for many seeking
therapy, it is a source of intense discomfort and feelings of alienation
and isolation. Gender roles, unquestioned and unchallenged, become
a focal point for early feelings of wrongness and outsider status for
many lesbians and gay men during childhood and adolescence. A
common thread in the histories of lesbians and gay men, in therapy
and out, is that of feeling incapable of "fitting it" with gender role
expectations. Even those who superficially conformed, behaviorally,
e.g., were neither "tomboys" nor "sissies" still are likely to express this
sense of feeling themselves outside of and uncomfortable with their
assigned gender role. At the same time, there is discomfort for some
adult lesbians and gay men regarding the degree to which they may
conform to gender role expectations. This seems particularly to be the
case for lesbians, where there is a devaluation of femininity (reflecting
cultural sexism and misogyny) coincident with a ban on appearing
overly masculine and "butchy," and for feminine-appearing gay men.
   Feminist therapy theory is a very useful guide for interventions with
clients presenting with such concerns, although clearly this is not limited
to lesbian and gay male clients. As previously mentioned, feminist
theory provides a basis on which to critique and comprehend gender
roles, and to remove the stigma associated with noncompliance. It also
gives a therapist a model of health and functioning that can identify
the strengths of noncompliance with gender roles. In addition, feminist
analysis speaks to the question of social desirability of gender roles.
This is particularly important in working with clients who devalue
themselves because of their perceived adherence to the less socially
desirable female role. Calling that judgment of lesser worth into question
opens the possibilities for lesbian and gay male clients to re-evaluate
and assign new importance to previously disowned and devalued aspects
of themselves.

Sexuality and Sexual Functioning

Another aspect of concerns brought into therapy by lesbians and gay
men that is well addressed by a feminist therapy perspective is that of
sexuality and sexual functioning. The sexual behavior of lesbians and
gay men has been the target of much homophobic myth. Sexual re-

lationships between two women or two men were portrayed in fiction and psychiatric literature as squalid, bestial, or perverted, happening under the influence of drugs or alcohol, and only in the context of a pickup or one-night stand (Loulan, 1985). Same-sex sexuality has also been romanticized as reflecting "intragender empathy" (Masters & Johnson, 1979), with the notion being presented that lesbians and gay men have no problems in sexual functioning because they are so well aware of what their partner wants due to shared gender. In either case, there has been little that supports lesbians or gay men in the development of personal norms of sexual functioning, or that makes sense of problems in desire, arousal, or performance sexually in a same-sex setting.

Feminist therapy theory operates from a perspective on sexuality that confronts gender-linked norms and myths regarding sexual desire and performance. Well-functioning sexuality is perceived as consisting of behaviors that are mutually satisfactory, in a context where power is reasonably equal between partners, and where coercion is not present. Specific behaviors, e.g., having an orgasm, performing particular sexual acts, having particular fantasy content, are not valued per se, but rather only as they reflect the needs of the individual. This is not a libertarian model; nonconsensual sexual activities and sexual activities between persons greatly unequal in power, e.g., adults and children, therapists and their clients, teachers and students, fall outside the feminist definition of well-functioning sexuality. Instead, this construct promotes the development of a sexual sense of self that reflects an individual's own desires and limits. In addition, feminist therapists have been in the forefront of those describing the impact of childhood sexual abuse on sexual functioning in adult women and men.

Thus a feminist analysis of sexuality would call into question the notion of male sexuality as object-focused, of female sexuality as always existing only in the context of emotional intimacy, of high male rates of sexual desire and low female interest in sexual activity. In addition, feminist therapists have redefined and broadened the definition of sexual activity, moving away from a definition of sex as genitally focused and orgasm-oriented to one that includes that definition along with others (Seidler–Feller, 1985). For instance, to the therapist operating within a feminist therapy framework, "good sex" may be defined as a mutually pleasurable experience of nongenital caressing and petting between partners, or having one partner masturbate to orgasm while being held and caressed by the other. It might include genital love making in which orgasm is not necessarily a component of what occurs, but where what happens is pleasurable. Loulan (1985) refers to a "willingness" model of lesbian sexuality, in which the openness to sexual activity is the necessary precondition, rather than the actual presence of sexual arousal in one or both women.

For lesbians and gay men, who have long lacked any clear information about what is "normal" sexually, feminist definitions of sexuality and confrontations of mythology such as described above can be highly effective approaches to therapeutic interventions. The task for the feminist therapist again involves separating out sexist gender role norms from the concept of "healthy and normal." A feminist therapist can support a lesbian or gay male client in defining that which is sexually "right" for her or him in a manner that is based upon feminist norms of self-respect, power equality, and noncoerciveness in sexual encounters, and can facilitate the client in an awareness of how she or he is imposing sexist norms on her or his own sexuality.

Feminist therapy theory also can provide a vehicle for examining the impact of homophobia on sexual functioning for lesbians and gay men. In the case of disorders of sexual desire in sexual minority clients, the symptoms of lack of desire are often interpreted by the client, and by nonfeminist therapists, as indications that the client must not be "really lesbian or gay." A feminist therapy perspective proceeds more cautiously than this, and instead first examines the impact on lesbian and gay sexual functioning of the homophobic mythologies discussed earlier. A feminist therapist would aid a lesbian or gay client in examining what messages she or he has internalized regarding the shameful or dangerous nature of same-sex sexuality, and would support an exploration of the environments in which learning about the client's own sexuality took place. Early sexual experiences in settings that were not conducive to arousal and sensuality, and that may have been frankly antisexual (e.g., restrooms, army barracks) are explored in terms of their meaning for later sexual activities.

Additionally, a feminist therapy perspective creates a context for exploring gender role myths and norms regarding sexuality, e.g., that men always initiate, that women who are sexually aggressive are "bad" or "dirty," that receiving stimulation implies passivity, that men only want orgasms or that women only want closeness. Such gender role norms regarding sexual behavior often act in a negative synergy with homophobia; a feminist therapy perspective on sexual dysfunction thoroughly explores that relationship in the process of intervening in sexual problems of lesbians or gay men. A sexually dysfunctional individual may fear that she or he is not a "real woman" or "real man," confusing sexual functioning with gender role. In working on sexual concerns with same-sex couples, an awareness of gender role related norms for sexual behavior can be essential in untangling problems in communication and sexual interaction. Often the most useful intervention is one of educating the couple regarding the lack of usefulness of the gender role stereotypes for sexual behavior, and supporting them in developing their own norms that move beyond gender roles. Lesbians, for example, may need additional support for initiating sex, or techniques for reframing their rates of sexual desires and activity as their own rhythms, rather than lower or higher than the rate "should be" according to some previously introjected standards of (heterosexual) sexual activity. Gay men, conversely, may need support for seeking nonsexual cuddling, and for differentiating sexual desire from needs to be held. Examining the fear of being a "sissy" (read: acting "like a woman"), or "passive" via cognitive restructuring and reframing can flow very easily from a feminist analysis of sexuality where sexual and affectional behaviors have been appropriately separated from gender roles.

It is worth noting that the parallel situation, the heterosexual individual with a disorder of desire, is unlikely to be told that she or he is not "really heterosexual." Although Kaplan (1979) describes all homosexual sexuality as a disorder of sexual desire, thus illustrating the degree to which nonfeminist sex therapy can be homophobic, the devaluation of same-sex sexuality is so great in nonfeminist approaches to sex therapy that the possibility that a woman or man experiencing problems with heterosexual arousal might be homosexual is not a concept commonly advanced in the standard sex therapy literature. Masters and Johnson (1979) do prescribe conversion to heterosexuality as a treatment for sexual minority clients with disorders of desire and arousal; they do not prescribe the converse for heterosexual women and men with disorders of desire.

Couple Relationship Problems

A problematic relationship between two people of any gender can benefit from a feminist analysis. This is particularly the case in therapy with lesbian and gay male couples. In addition to problems that any couple faces, lesbian and gay male couples must deal with the problematic juxtaposition of two individuals' similar experiences of gender role socialization, leading to similar gender role related sets of expectations and skills for couple relationships. A feminist analysis provides that which is crucial; an understanding of the societal milieu in which a same-sex couple must function. McCandlish (1982), McWhirter and Mattison (1982) Brown and Zimmer (1985) and Clunis and Green (1988) have all commented upon the ways in which dealing with gender role issues often becomes the major focus of therapy with lesbian and gay male client couples.

Lesbian couples commonly come to therapy with complaints of difficulty expressing anger, maintaining boundaries, avoiding fusion, initiating and acting, both in the sexual and nonsexual realms. Gay male couples tend to bring the complementary set of gender role-generated complaints, such as difficulty maintaining relationships, versus initiating them, barriers to intimacy, overly tight boundaries, and problems in the expression of tender feelings.

In a situation such as couple relationships, where many problems for couples of any sexual orientation are so closely tied to the sexism inherent in current gender roles, a feminist theoretical perspective is a necessary component of effective intervention. Feminist therapy theory has been consistent in expanding the parameters of behavior beyond gender roles; thus feminist therapy with lesbian and gay male couples can be quite powerful in seeing behavior beyond the gender roles as acceptable and appropriate. Aiding sexual minority couples in understanding how their problems are gender role-related also tends to remove an onus of failure from the shoulders of couples already burdened by homophobic expectations that their same-sex relationship is doomed to failure.

Race, Class, and Culture

Because feminist therapy theory is concerned with the varieties of cultural settings in which gender roles and attitudes toward homosexuality develop, feminist therapists also bring to their analyses of the concerns of lesbian and gay male clients an awareness of how race, social class, age cohort, and other demographic factors interact to influence gender role development and homophobia. This awareness of how racial and class differences lead to differences in how gender roles are construed can be particularly important in therapy with same-sex couples. Occasionally, the presumption of similarity based on gender is made by clients whose class or cultural backgrounds have given widely variant interpretations to the gender role. For instance, two women may have difficulty at first seeing that the fact that they are both female had different meanings in the families in which they grew and developed because the race, class, or cultural backgrounds of those families may have been different. This can particularly be the case where both gender and race are the same, but class and other cultural factors are different. The nonobvious variable of class, which is often blurred in North American culture with its myth of a classless society, can be an important source of conflict, as well as of strength once the conflicts are resolved.

Feminist therapy theory leads to a knowledge and appreciation of cultural variations in the social construction of gender, and thus to a fuller comprehension of what on the surface appears confusing to many lesbian and gay male clients entering therapy. The issue of being lesbian or gay and ethnic, and the challenges that this dual identity presents to ethnic minority lesbians and gays, are also better comprehended from the perspective of feminist therapy theory. The importance of attachment and positive identification with one's ethnic community, while struggling with the homophobia that may be present there, and at the same time dealing with racism in the lesbian or gay community where one's sexual orientation receives affirmation and support, is validated by the feminist emphasis on the importance and meaning of culture and community. Feminist analysis creates the possibilities for therapists to engage in a more complete and far-reaching assessment of the problems confronting their lesbian and gay male clients who are not white, middle-class, highly educated, young, or able-bodied, in part simply by mandating attention to the realities created by these minority group memberships. Such an analysis also aids lesbian and gay male clients in making better sense of their own behaviors and feelings by facilitating the process of sorting out which behaviors are internally motivated, and which are more likely to be responses to external, environmental oppression, and the need to survive that.

SUMMARY

Beyond the issues of specific, common presenting problems of lesbian and gay male clients that are addressed well from the perspective of a feminist theory of therapy is the feminist therapy emphasis on the integration of personal growth and political change. For many lesbians and gay men, therapy can only strengthen the armor and provide the tools necessary to survive a world that continues to be hostile toward sexual minorities and deny them their civil rights. It can be very difficult for lesbians and gay men to maintain a positive self-image, no matter how clear the feminist analysis of their therapy, if they are constantly assaulted by the attacks on them that range from the subtle (e.g., "queer" jokes), to the fatal (e.g., "queer bashing," a phenomenon in which gangs of heterosexual youths seek out and physically attack gay people). The more recent phenomenon of the AIDS epidemic has made the tenuousness of legal gains made by sexual minorities more clear; the calls for registration and quarantine of people with AIDS (and by implication, all gays) cannot be ignored by lesbian and gay men, nor by their therapists. A feminist analysis, however, may be most useful here in sorting out what is actually there to fear, and what can still be done in self-advocacy.

Feminist therapists, understanding the very concrete opportunities for empowerment and personal healing available in political action, may discuss with lesbian and gay male clients the possibility of involvement in lesbian or gay civil rights groups, doing anything from stuffing envelopes to speaking out publically on issues. A feminist therapist will lend support to measures aimed at changing laws that discriminate against lesbians and gay men, often making herself available to educate the public or testify at hearings on legislation. Lerman's (1979) paper suggesting that feminist therapists have an ethical obligation to work for the passage of the Equal Rights Amendment so as to provide legal and societal confirmation of the equal value of women can be extrapolated to the obligation on the part of feminist therapists to work similarly in support of legal rights for lesbians and gay men. Feminist therapy is unique in philosophies of psychotherapy by supporting the ethical concept of political action on the part of therapists, and unique in the degree to which political action and behavior promoting social change are seen as intergral to the therapy process rather than a diversion from the "real" intrapsychic work of therapy. In feminist therapy with lesbians and gay men, this joining of the political and the personal is particularly apt and necessary.

It is difficult to see what concerns brought into therapy by lesbians and gay men would not be more full and adequately addressed by a therapist working from a feminist theoretical perspective. This would particularly be the case for those lesbian and gay male clients who are struggling with overt issues of their own homophobia, e.g., desire to change sexual orientation or become more securely closeted. Because a feminist therapy ethic empowers clients to choose and clarify their own goals for therapy, a feminist therapist can facilitate the client's exploration of why they have adopted homophobic goals for themselves. This goodness of fit between the needs of lesbian and gay clients and the philosophies of the feminist therapies is indicated by anecdotal evidence suggesting that lesbian clients in particular tend to seek out therapists who identify themselves as feminist therapists. In this author's experience as a referral resource, the request that a therapist being referred to be feminist occurs in almost all of the cases where the prospective client is a lesbian.

This mutual attraction does not seem to be as strong between feminist therapy and gay men. Several reasons for this can be postulated. The most likely is gender-related. Most feminist therapists are women; many therapists who identify themselves as nonsexist or gay affirmative are men. It appears that gay men seeking a therapist who has a feminist analysis, or one similar to it, are seeking nonsexist and gay affirmative male therapists rather than feminist therapists who are women. A second reason may be that gay men, as men, may still be bound up in issues of their own sexism in ways that might lead to a devaluation of women, or of feminism, and thus feminist therapy. Those gay men who do actively seek out female feminist therapists often seem to do so with a stated goal of working on their own internalized gender role restrictions, particularly their attitudes toward their own femininity.

As feminist therapy theory continues to develop, and as the limited body of knowledge about the lives and realities of lesbians and gay men expands, it is likely that more specific applications of feminist therapy to this population will present themselves. Lesbian and gay adolescents, for instance, would hypothetically be a client population that would benefit from therapy done with a feminist theoretical perspective. However, little data exist on work with this client population at this time, as it is a difficult population to identify. Also lacking is information on feminist therapy with lesbian and gay elders and people of color. This lack of information reflects the status of general information in the psychotherapy literature regarding elders or people of color, as well as the inhibiting effects of multiple oppression regarding seeking therapy. In addition, as most feminist therapists at this time are white and young or middle-aged, lesbian and gay people of color and lesbian and gay elders may not see feminist therapists as potential resources, inasmuch as many people of color or elders have difficulty seeing a white, young, therapist as a potential support. Despite these lacunae, a feminist theory of therapy continues to appear to be the perspective of choice for any therapist working with lesbians and gay men.

REFERENCES

Baird, M., & Reiss, E. (1981). Aesthetic realism. In R. Corsini (Ed.), *Handbook of innovative psychotherapies*. New York: Wiley.

Bergler, E. (1956). *Homosexuality: Disease or way of life?*. New York: Hill & Wang.

Bieber, I., Dain, H., Dince, P., Drellich, M., Grand, H., Gundlach, R., Kremer, M., Rifkin, A., Wilbur, C., & Bieber, T. (1962). *Homosexuality: A psychoanalytic study*. New York: Basic Books.

Brown, L. S. (1975, August). *An investigation of the stereotypic picture of lesbians in the clinical literature.* Paper presented at the convention of the American Psychological Association, Chicago.

Brown, L. S., & Zimmer, D. (1985). An introduction to therapy issues of lesbian and gay male couples. In N. Jacobson & A. Gurman (Eds.), *The clinical handbook of marital therapy.* New York: Guilford Press.

Caprio, F. S. (1953). *Variations in sexual behavior.* New York: Citadel Press.

Clunis, D. M., & Green, G. D. (1988). *Lesbian couples.* Seattle: The Seal Press.

Cruikshank, M. (Ed). (1985). *The lesbian path.* San Francisco: Grey Fox Press.

David, D., & Brannon, R. (Eds.). (1976). *The Forty-nine percent majority.* New York: Addison–Wesley.

Davison, G. (1976). Homosexuality: The ethical challenge. *Journal of Consulting & Clinical Psychology, 44*(2), 157–162.

Davison, G. (1977). Homosexuality and the ethics of behavioral intervention. *Journal of Homosexuality, 2*(3), 195–204.

Deutsch, H. (1933). Homosexuality in women. *International Journal of Psychoanalysis, 14,* 34–56.

Ellis, A. (1956). Are homosexuals necessarily neurotic? In D. Cory (Ed.), *Homosexuality: A cross-cultural approach.* New York: Julian.

Ellis, A. (1962). Are homosexuals really creative? *Sexology, 29*(2), 88–93.

Ellis, A. (1964). The truth about lesbians. *Sexology, 30*(10), 652–655.

Gilligan, C. (1982). *In a different voice.* Cambridge, MA: Harvard University Press.

Gonsiorek, J. (1982). Present and future directions in gay/lesbian mental health. In J. Gonsiorek (Ed.), *Homosexuality and psychotherapy: A practitioner's handbook of affirmative models.* New York: Haworth.

Green, R. (1974). *Sexual identity conflict in children and adults.* New York: Basic Books.

Jackins, H. (1962). *Fundamentals of co-counseling manual.* Seattle: Rational Island Publishers.

Kaplan, H. S. (1979). *Disorders of sexual desire.* New York: Simon & Schuster.

Kaye, H., Berl, S., Clare, J., Eleston, M., Gershwin, B., Gershwin, P., Kogan, L., Torda, C., & Wilbur, C. (1967). Homosexuality in women. *Archives of General Psychiatry 17*(5), 626–634.

Lerman, H. (1979, August). *Failure to pass the Equal Rights Amendment could be hazardous to your mental health.* Paper presented at the convention of the American Psychological Association, New York.

Loulan, J. (1985). *Lesbian sex.* San Francisco: Spinsters, Ink.

Malyon, A. K. (1982). Psychotheraputic implications of internalized homophobia in gay men. In J. Gonsiorek (Ed.), *Homosexuality and psychotherapy: A practitioner's handbook of affirmative models.* New York: Haworth.

Masters, W., & Johnson, V. (1979). *Homosexuality in perspective.* Boston: Little, Brown.

McCandlish, B. (1982). Therapeutic Issues with lesbian couples. In J. Gonsiorek (Ed.), *Homosexuality and psychotherapy: A practitioner's handbook of affirmative models.* New York: Haworth.

McWhirter, D. P., & Mattison, A. M. (1982). Psychotherapy for gay male couples. In J. Gonsiorek (Ed.), *Homosexuality and psychotherapy: A practitioner's handbook of affirmative models.* New York: Haworth.

Moraga, C., & Anzaldua, G. (Eds.). (1981). *This bridge called my back: Writings by radical women of color.* Watertown, MA: Persephone Press.

Morin, S. F. (1977). Heterosexual bias in psychological research on lesbianism and male homosexuality. *American Psychologist, 32,* 629–637.

Morin, S. F. (1978). Psychology and the gay community: An overview. *Journal of Social Issues, 34*(3), 1–6.

Moses, A. E. & Hawkins, R. O. (1982). *Counseling lesbian women and gay men: A life-issues approach.* St. Louis: C. V. Mosby.

Ovesey, L. (1969). *Homosexuality and pseudohomosexuality.* New York: Science House.

Pheterson, G. (1984, April). *Alliance between whores, wives, and dykes.* Paper presented at the Third Advanced Feminist Therapy Institute, Oakland, CA.

Saghir, M. T., & Robins, E. (1973). *Male and female homosexuality: A comprehensive investigation.* Baltimore: Williams & Wilkins.

Seidler–Feller, D. (1985). A feminist critique of sex therapy. In L. B. Rosewater & L. E. A. Walker (Eds.); *Handbook of feminist therapy: Women's issues in psychotherapy.* New York: Springer.

Siegel, R. J. (1985). Beyond homophobia: Learning to work with lesbian clients. In L. B. Rosewater & L. E. A. Walker (Eds.), *Handbook of feminist therapy: Women's issues in psychotherapy.* New York: Springer.

Socarides, C. W. (1968). *The overt homosexual.* New York: Grune & Stratton.

Socarides, C. W. (1972). Homosexuality: Basic concepts of psychodynamics. *International Journal of Psychiatry, 10.*

CHAPTER 11

Feminist Therapy with Ethnic Minority Populations:
A Closer Look at Blacks and Hispanics*

Vickie M. Mays
Lillian Comas–Diaz

The integration of a feminist philosophy into the theory, practice, and ethical standards of traditional psychotherapies with ethnic minorities deserves close examination, for it offers a potentially rich, philosophical orientation from which to conduct therapy. Most theories of human behavior and methods of therapeutic practice have failed to take into account cultural variables relevant to ethnic group members (Solomon, 1982). Traditional clinical intervention strategies have had varying degrees of effectiveness with Black (see Jackson, 1983, for review) and Hispanic clients.

Increasingly, ethnic minority practitioners have questioned the application of traditional theory and methods to ethnic group members because traditional approaches lack congruence with their experiences, life-styles, and culture (Jackson, 1983; Mays, 1985). The authors believe that there is a definite need for developing theories and methods appropriate to the culture and life-style of the various ethnic groups. Until these theories have been developed and empirically tested, it is necessary in current practice to take into account the unique experiences of ethnic minorities, considering the influence of the external social world on their personalities (Lerman, 1985; Solomon, 1982). This

---
*Completion of this chapter was partly funded by an Academic Senate grant from the University of California to the first author.

orientation must modify traditional theory and practice to accommodate the interaction between the social world and inner reality and the consequent impact on the etiology, presentation, and approach to treatment of ethnic group members. Feminist philosophy offers the potential of such a perspective.

FEMINIST PHILOSOPHY

Early feminist philosophy was questioned and in many instances rejected by ethnic scholars (Smith, 1985). Rejection was based explicitly on the primacy of gender division in feminist philosophy, which was most strongly expressed in two tenets. The first was the belief that the oppression of women was the most fundamental oppression. The second was a belief in a sisterhood in which a woman has more in common with another woman of a different ethnic, racial, or class group than with a man of the same ethnic, racial, or class group. Primacy of gender division tended to ignore the strong realities of ethnicity, race, culture, and class bonds in the lives of ethnic minority group members. It relegated to second-class status the racial and ethnic bond that many ethnic minorities perceive as critical to the continuation of their groups.

However, as feminist philosophy has grown and has continued to prioritize the pluralistic and integrative aspects of its philosophy, its relevance as a philosophical foundation for psychotherapeutic treatment of ethnic minorities has increased. The greatest asset of current feminist philosophy is its belief in a dialectical relationship between its theory and practice. As experiences occur that challenge its theory, the theory is refined to adapt to those experiences, keeping both theory and practice accountable to each other (Stanley & Wise, 1983). This dialectical process within feminist therapy challenges the practitioner to examine those aspects of theoretical and applied traditional therapies that are speculative and concerned primarily with abstract knowledge. A feminist philosophy mandates the practitioner to engage in ethical therapeutic practices grounded in experiences that reflect the client's social reality. Inherent in this philosophical orientation is the demand that practitioners monitor ways in which their individual, internalized value systems operate on the outer world of their clients' lives (Gilbert, 1980). The necessity for social change as well as inner psychological changes in order to promote well-being among ethnic groups is an implicit challenge of a feminist perspective (Lerman, 1985). For the ethnic client, feminist therapy encourages understanding the intricate and complex social realities and the effect of economic, social, and biological systems in their lives.

SOCIALIZATION AND DEVELOPMENTAL ISSUES

A great deal has been written about the impact of the differential socialization of women and men on the development of personality, character traits, styles of relating, and sense of self in relation to the world (Chodorow, 1978; Gilligan, 1982; Schlachet, 1984). However, the impact of differential socialization among ethnic minorities has been examined very little; instead, it has been assumed that the same detrimental effects have been suffered. This volume espouses that feminist philosophy recognizes the process whereby the socialization of women differs from that of men and regards the process and effects as destructive and oppressive to women. Let's examine the application of this premise to two specific ethnic minority groups: Blacks and Hispanics.

Blacks

The socialization process of Blacks originates in a value base that has been transmitted from generation to generation. It is characterized by a strong ethnic identity, a sense of community, the rejection of materialism and competition as basic values, and a strong sense of spirituality (Ward, 1981). In Black culture individuals belong to a racial/ethnic community by virtue of skin color and may feel that they owe their survival to other people, both past generations and contemporaries who sacrifice and strive each day to make their lives better (Mbiti, 1969). The community is responsible to a large extent for the individual's sense of identity; it instills attitudes and beliefs regarding the self, the community, and the larger society that ensure development and survival of the self.

For Black Americans the family and the community are critical to the individual's physical and emotional survival. Blacks live in a community under attack by the values, beliefs, and attitudes of an Euro-American culture. Hence, the socialization of Blacks has been shaped by an antagonistic environment (Ward, 1981). In maintaining their culture in the face of antagonism, Black women and men have developed cultural/gender-specific patterns of socialization in order to lighten their feelings of oppression, enhance group solidarity, sustain hope and build self-esteem and satisfying survival-based interpersonal relationships (Billingsley, 1976). The sex role demarcations in Black culture are often confusing to nonethnic minorities as they do not follow those of Anglo culture and in some ways differ from those of other ethnic groups.

Black women are described by such characteristics as: self-reliant (Robinson, 1983), self-assertive, independent, strong, possessive of a fighting spirit, contrary, and erotic (Christian, 1985). At the same time Black women have suffered from the stereotypical images of Sapphire, Aunt Jemima, the Black mammy, the sex kitten, and evil woman; although the labels are not overtly in use, Black women continue consciously to refute them in their physical appearance, manner of dress, and behavior. In attempts to help disprove these images, Black men, particularly believers in Nationalism, idealized the Black woman and her relationship to Black men by viewing her as Queen or Mother of the Universe, responsible for the survival of the Black race (Christian, 1985). Indeed, in the past the Black community would not have survived if Black women had not taken on the roles of supportive wives and mothers. Black women are the keepers of the moral conditions of Blacks and hold the key to physical survival by bearing children to create a new nation.

Clearly, sexism and racism have critically affected the social and psychological spheres of Black women and men's lives. The impact for both is felt most strongly in their identities as men and women. The Black man is often characterized as sexually promiscuous, macho, lazy, slick, handsome, experienced in the ways of life, a protector and endangered (Gary, 1981). Some Black men, in struggling to live the role of a man in American society, are filled with anger, self-hatred, or depression for they are powerless, instead of powerful, as men are expected to be. The Black man's displays of his (limited) power, or rather his maleness, most often must rely on the cooperation of the Black woman. His mate becomes a visual representation of his financial success and access to power and resources in society. Her appearance, her sophistication and savvy in social spheres, her level of education, her employment, and other signs of achievement are benchmarks for his success in the world. The Black woman is critical to his display because racism limits his physical and economic access to other displays of power, such as owning property in exclusive neighborhoods and the ability to participate in leisure activities that require private membership or prestigious employment. Hence racism by its restrictions reinforces the need of some Black men to imitate the white man's conventions for power displays (Christian, 1985).

When a Black woman opposes this symbolic role in a relationship, a Black man feels betrayed and not supported in his efforts to be "a man." Other Black women, conditioned by years of selfless behavior (Mays & Howard, 1986a) and responsibility for the survival of the race, often feel a part of the failure that Black men experience when denied their status as men (Christian, 1985). In a true ethnic/gender-appropriate mode, some Black women compromise their own dreams and ambitions to assist the men who, because of society's sexism, are more likely to bring in greater resources and status to their families than are the women. But the struggle by Black women not to subjugate their individual selves to family or community survival is an old one. Women often have been caught between their own personalities and desires and the life expected of them as Black mothers in a racist and sexist society.

The Black women who refuse this role, who define themselves outside of the gender, class, and racial/ethnic definitions of the Black society, are viewed as *contrary,* a term used in Black culture (Christian, 1985). "Contrariness" in Black women often reflects attempts at self-definition and maintenance of integrity in the face of race, class, and gender definitions by the larger society and gender and class restrictions of behavior within the Black community.

Black women not only bear the traditional definition of women in their culture but also must confront the limiting sexist myths of another race that oppresses them (Christian, 1985). The conventions that are expected to hold are not even conventions of their own communities (Christian, 1985). Black women fall especially short of fulfilling the role of woman when the model is the Southern white woman. As Christian (1985) points out, it is no wonder that these Black women seem mad or their behaviors irrational whenever they are being themselves. Their contrariness is an insistence on being spontaneous, characteristically themselves, momentarily human beings without the societal constraints of either the Anglo or Black community, which have planned their paths regardless of their individual personalities, dreams, or desires (Christian, 1985).

The Black woman who chooses not to be a wife or mother, who chooses to be in an interracial relationship, who fights with others regarding their assessment of her, or who places her self-development as a priority before the many needs of her family or the Black community is "contrary." The Black woman who says "no" to a Black man regarding his expectations of her relationship to him is "contrary" (Christian, 1985). The Black woman who chooses a path of development not typical of most Black women's planned destinies is "contrary" and her behavior is dismissed as irrational. The further she moves from society's prescribed roles for her the more she is viewed as angry or, from the Black male's perspective, as having a "chip on her shoulder." Black women are viewed by whites as different because they are Black and by Black men as different because they are female. Consequently, this "other" status often leads to dismissal of attempting to truly understand their behavior (Christian, 1985). Instead, such behavior is dismissed as the woman's own problem.

Although these "contrary" women maintain a sense of integrity, they can pay a price for it ranging from loneliness to being targets of physical violence. Solace and empowerment are often found in relationships with other Black women, from which a new perspective in self-identity and roles within the Black community emerges. The amount of courage to challenge the Black woman's limiting role in a society with a racist and sexist definition of her is tremendous. Yet seldom within the therapeutic context of assessing psychological strengths is this acknowledged.

In understanding the life of the Black American, a therapeutic paradigm that encourages exploring the role of culture and the impact of migration is important. Many of the cultural mores and ethos embraced by Black Americans find their roots in a Southern tradition—a culture that flowed from a rural life-style—where societal conventions have much to do with the conduct of relationships between man and woman, young and old, and Black and white (Christian, 1985). Memories linger of a united community which sustained its members even under the hardest times. It was a culture where mobility was restricted, work was for survival, motherhood usually occurred within the confines of marriage, and pain and sorrow were trivialized as legitimate states for Christians.

Movement to the urban life-styles of the present challenged the notions which were passed on as legacies by previous generations. Stories of suffering, hard times, the necessity of struggle, the placement of the family (and, thus, the race) above all else by the Black woman and the equation of Black manhood with a well-paying, steady job are legacies creating present-day "ghosts" for many Blacks.

Myths, memories, and folklore combine with the events of the present to cause some Blacks to live constantly in the shadow of these "ghosts." For those never explicitly told the myths that everyone else operates from they strive to intimately understand the nuances of Black culture. In a time in which a steady, paying job is unobtainable by a large segment of the Black male community and when Black women who constantly give of themselves suffer depression from the lack of respite from their roles, these legacies are significant factors in current intrapsychic states. Even those not knowing their history or understanding the intricacies of Black culture wrestle with the ghosts of invalid stereotypes from 100 years ago (Christian, 1985). Practitioners need to understand that the legacies of the past which help form identity are best handled by neither denying them nor becoming fixated on the past, but rather by renewing those aspects of heritage that are nurturant, sustaining, and culturally defining. Practitioners must help their ethnic clients not allow their cultural or ethnic heritage to function as an abstraction to which they subordinate their individual lives. Instead, they should grasp the past as a living idea that helps to chart the future.

The Southern tradition taught many Blacks, especially Black women, an "I-can-do" ethos, in which righting a wrong means attacking the problem head on, not waiting, and not "meeting to meet" about the problem, but rather naming the problem and solving it (Mays, in press). Such strategies may conflict with those of an urban, Euro-American tradition.

As generations live their lives in urban, Northern culture, moving into new cultures and transcending the old class structures, tensions have developed as to the existence of a Black culture or identity among the heterogeneous Black population. The questions, as posed by Christian (1985), are:

> whether there is a functional Black culture in the present day society, a contemporary Black community that is held together by bonds that work. Are Blacks essentially upwardly mobile and taking on an amalgamated cultural identity? Is color merely camouflage? Or is race/ethnicity in America operating as a communal bond, a source of rich support and positive identity or is it merely a marker of a past history once functional but no longer perceived by contemporary blacks as operative in their response to each other? (p. 69)

These are crucial questions with which many Black Americans struggle intimately today. The questions manifest in many disguises in the therapy room. For example, a typical issue is how to be assured that children of professional Blacks who have lived and attended primarily white and middle-class schools can be given a Black identity and the skills and experiences to interact positively with other Blacks from less privileged backgrounds. Another disguise is feelings of frustration and depression among professional Black women whose occupations propel them into a middle-class environment where they find few eligible Black men for long-term relationships. Feelings proud of their career achievements nagging feeling sometimes loom that this achievement was at cost of potential Black male marriage partners. Or there is the issue of the young, Black, teen-age gang members who rob and assault other Blacks and express no sense of common fate with their victims. The sense of community based on ethnic identification appears lost.

As Blacks struggle against the racist, sexist, classist definitions that society has promulgated for Black men and women, it is critical that we have a therapeutic philosophy that examines behavior as it relates to the social structure. There is movement to a new class with few role models showing how to maintain elements of the Black culture, which seem out of place in certain class activities. Given the changing realities of Blacks, a therapeutic philosophy is necessary in which hetereogenity is viewed as positive. In the 1980s there are many life-styles and ways of approaching issues that confront Blacks as Blacks, as Americans, and as individuals. This creates a real struggle for Blacks facing a legacy passed on by parents and the community—a dream and mandate for the survival of that family or community's image.

HISPANICS

Hispanics like Blacks embrace cultural values that often differ from those of White Americans. Within the traditional Hispanic culture, sex roles are clearly demarcated. Men are expected to be cold, intellectual, rational, profound, strong, authoritarian, independent, and brave, while women are expected to be sentimental, gentle, intuitive, impulsive, docile, submissive, dependent, and timid (Senour, 1977). These attributes are encouraged early in the socialization process, where boys and girls are taught two very different codes of sexual behavior. Boys are given greater freedom of movement, are encouraged to be sexually aggressive, and are not expected to share in domestic or household responsibilities. On the other hand, girls are expected to be passive, obedient, and homebound. Furthermore, men are seen as strong by nature and not needing the protection required by women, who are perceived as weak by nature and vulnerable to the sexual advances of men. This rigid demarcation of sex roles encourages a double moral standard for the sexes and is epitomized in the concept of machismo.

Machismo literally means maleness or virility and stipulates that by virtue of their gender, men are superior and are to be treated as authority figures. Culturally, it means that the man is the provider and the one responsible for the welfare of the home and the family. Machismo tends to be manifested in a man's sexual freedom, affective detachment, physical dominance over women, and excessive alcohol consumption (Giraldo, 1972). Although it has been argued that machismo is more prevalent among lower socioeconomic classes (Kinzer, 1973), it is nevertheless believed to influence behavior in all strata of Hispanic society (Giraldo, 1972).

The cultural counterpart of machismo is marianismo. Based on the Catholic worship of the Virgin Mary, who is both a virgin and a madonna, the concept underlying marianismo is that women are spiritually superior to men and, therefore, capable of enduring all suffering inflicted by men (Stevens, 1973). Using the Virgin Mary as their role model, unmarried Hispanic women are expected to be chaste and virginal, and not to demonstrate interest in sex even once they are married. When they become mothers, Hispanic women attain the status of madonnas and, accordingly, are expected to deny themselves in favor of their children and husbands. The image of the "Mater Dolorosa" is quite prevalent among Mexican-American women by arguing that these women, without being masochistic, appear to get satisfaction and fulfillment from suffering. Stevens (1973) associates this with Catholicism, which offers guidance on how to suffer and emphasizes its benefits. In noting the high incidence of somatic complaints among low-income Hispanic women in psychotherapy, Espin (1985) suggests that these complaints may well be a reaction to the self-sacrificing dictum, especially since somatization is a culturally accepted mode of expressing needs and anxieties.

At first sight, these sexual codes seem to condone the oppression of one group (women) by another (men) and thus coincide with the feminist precept that the socialization process is destructive and oppressive to women. However, the dynamics involved in male–female relationships are very complicated and as a consequence, the power relationship between the sexes is not straightforward. For example, Stevens (1973) asserts that the marianista code rewards women who adhere to it. Due to the sacredness of motherhood, women who bear children enjoy a certain degree of power despite the outward submissiveness of their behavior. Stevens further posits that as women grow older, they attain a semidivine status. Adult offspring tend to fight their mothers' struggles, especially against their fathers. Furthermore, the children are manipulated into doing what their mothers want. Hence, power is achieved through passivity and conformity to the marianista role.

Another way in which Hispanic women obtain power is by emphasizing their culturally ascribed feminine role. Historically, women in most cultures have resorted to healing and magic as a means of empowerment (Bourguignon, 1979). Similarly, Hispanic culture assigns the healing role to women: *curanderas* among Mexican-American women, *espiritistas* among Puerto Ricans, and *santeras* among Cubans are overrepresented by females. Espin (1985) states that Hispanic female healers obtain power through the use of supernatural forces that cannot be resisted. She asserts that Hispanic female healers are transformed, by virtue of their healing powers, from powerless members in the family (due to cultural sex role expectations) to powerful members. Moreover, they obtain control over their lives, performing behaviors that are usually associated with women who espouse feminist values. These behaviors include leaving their family in order to pursue their healing "careers" and, as a consequence, achieving social mobility, financial independence, and community prestige.

Furthermore, Comas–Diaz (in press) asserts that within the Puerto Rican culture, women enjoy a powerful, albeit passive position, because the task of communicating with the spirits is still a predominantly female one, dating back to the Taino Indian society, characterized by the belief in spirits, where women had the power of invoking the spirits. Similarly, Canino (1982) found that when she studied sex roles among Hispanics, both husband and wife reported traditional patriarchal attitudes. However, when the same couples were interviewed extensively and observed during decision making, the most prevalent marital transaction was a shared process. Thus, this suggests that the cultural context needs to be taken into consideration when denoting a "socialization process that is oppressive to women."

Feminist philosophy can be useful in assessing Hispanic women's behaviors. For example, cultural dynamics discourage women's direct expression of their feelings and rights. As a consequence, feelings of inferiority, premature marriages, and motherhood among Hispanics have been related to their traditional female roles (Canino, 1982). Moreover, Lopez–Garriga (1978) describes the use of indirect and/or covert manipulation among Puerto Rican women in order to exert power in a culturally acceptable manner. She indicates that these manipulative strategies are characteristic of oppressed people of different sexes and ethnicities. Clearly the feminist paradigm can properly address these issues.

Oppression is a relevant paradigm in using a feminist framework with Hispanics. Hispanic women are observed to defend and perpetuate machismo as a way of coping with the oppression that ethnic minorities face in the United States. For example, Senour (1977) claims that Chicanas reinforce machismo in their men to compensate them for their lack of status in the majority society. Similarly, Steiner (1974) cites Puerto Rican women who defend machismo as an understandable response to socioeconomic deprivations as well as to racism: Men take their frustrations out on women because they are oppressed. In utilizing a feminist perspective, the therapist needs to take these issues into consideration.

Another paradigm that the feminist therapist needs to observe while working with the Hispanic population is acculturation. Hispanics in the United States exhibit diverse degrees of acculturation, which is directly related to gender roles. Traditional sex roles are undergoing change among Hispanic emigrés. The Hispanics' native culture, including its machismo/marianismo codes, is not reinforced by the new dominant culture, which is more influenced by the impact of the women's liberation movement. However, cultural transition itself often presents Hispanic men and women with a sex role reversal in terms of public interactions. For example, studies of immigrant families reveal that the family member who most often deals with the dominant culture assumes the instrumental role, thus becoming autonomous and more acculturated, while the one who assumes the affective role becomes increasingly isolated (Sluzki, 1979).

In many cases, the instrumental role is filled by the man and the affective one by the woman. However, among Hispanics instrumental/affective role taking is not always respectively male/female. The pressures of economic survival in the United States, as well as the types of skills that are in demand, have contributed to the role reversal among Hispanics. This role reversal is common, as it is often easier for low-income female immigrants to obtain employment in the United States than it is for male immigrants. Indeed, the woman may have no choice but to assume the instrumental role because she is able to sell her sewing and domestic skills, while her partner's ability to farm is not marketable and therefore is irrelevant in the city. This situation is typical among most ethnic minorities who immigrate to the U. S. (Immigrants, 1985). Ethnic minorities may present themselves in therapy struggling with the consequences of sex role reversal. Feminism, with its emphasis on power-balanced relationships, can be used effectively to address these issues.

First-, second-, and even third-generation Hispanics continue to face acculturation conflicts. For example, sex roles among Hispanic women can be complicated by the expectations imposed by the two different cultural contexts in which they live. The Anglo culture tends to apply masculine criteria to the evaluation of women's performance, ascribing the greatest value to those who distinguish themselves occupationally or professionally. Yet this tendency is contradicted enough to send mixed messages to the women. For example, a consequence of this is that the Chicana is far surer of her role within traditional Mexican culture than she is in the mainstream, where her role is ambivalent (Senour, 1977). Apparently, this sureness of role that her ethnic culture provides has not stopped the Chicana, nor other Hispanic women, from exploring the behavioral alternatives available to her. This exploration can lead to conflict within the nuclear unit as well as within the extended family. Again, feminist therapy is equipped to best deal with these contradictions and help the woman separate the societal pressures of her ethnocultural reality from her personal dynamics.

The degree of acculturation needs to be carefully monitored. For instance, a first-generation Hispanic woman would present a different clinical picture than a third-generation one, who in turn would be placed at a different point of the acculturation spectrum from the recent immigrant. In addition, regardless of acculturation, gender roles should be assessed and the socioeconomic context considered. For instance, it is common to see a middle-class, second-generation Hispanic woman professing progressive and even feminist views regarding education and employment of women, while holding traditional values on family and marital relationships. The following vignette illustrates some of these issues.

Susana is a 22-year-old Cuban-American woman. She lives at home with her parents and a younger brother 18 years old. Susana is enrolled in a nearby college, where she pursues a bachelor's degree with plans to later become a lawyer. She is a first-generation Hispanic within an upper-class family. Her father, a physician who emigrated from Cuba with his family, has a successful practice in the United States. Her mother, a college professor in literature, was unable to find a comparable job and decided to "stay home and take care of things." Susana is fully bilingual and highly acculturated to the mainstream. Both parents have reinforced her pursuing a professional career and allowed her a significant amount of autonomy.

Susana was referred to psychotherapy after a suicide attempt with an overdose of pills (Valium from her father's supply). This was her first contact with the mental health system. The whole family was seen in evaluation. The family assessment revealed a patriarchal system, with the mother bearing indirect influence and power. Although Susana was the elder, she was treated as a child by all family members, including her younger brother.

Individual sessions revealed that the precipitant event for Susana's suicide attempt was the anniversary of her abortion. Susana became pregnant by her boyfriend, a Black American classmate, during her first year at college. Susana had wanted to get married and establish her own nuclear family. Her parents, however, stated that Susana's pregnancy would impede her future career as a lawyer. Thus, they pressured Susana into having an abortion. Later Susana realized that her parents' real motivation for the abortion was a racial one; they did not want Susana to have a Black child. Susana, who was raised as Catholic and viewed motherhood as sacred, had extreme difficulties dealing with these inconsistencies.

During therapy Susana was able to mourn the loss of her pregnancy and to work through her guilt. Feminist orientation was used in therapy aiming at empowering Susana by expanding her options. Treatment also addressed Susana's coping with cultural inconsistencies.

CLINICAL ISSUES

Basically, ethnic minorities function psychologically similar to any other group of people (Block, 1981). What differs and what the practitioner needs to take into account is their manner of expression or intensity of symptoms (Block, 1981). Because of the racial, ethnic, cultural, class, and gender struggles of ethnic minorities, they do develop different personality structures, defense hierarchies, and symptomatologies in response to their social, political, and individual life conditions (Block, 1981). These differences have clear implications for help-seeking behavior, climical presentation in therapy, and the client's attitudes and expectations of mental health services.

Help-Seeking

Ethnic minorities continue to underutilize traditional mental health services (Kitano, 1969; Mays, Howard, & Jackson, 1988; Neighbors, 1984; Neighbors & Jackson, 1984). When they do enter the traditional service system, they tend to receive inpatient treatment, more crisis intervention services, and fewer psychotherapy sessions, and they fail to keep appointments and terminate therapy early (Griffith, 1977; Jackson, 1976; Jones, 1974, 1978; Sue, McKinney, Allen, & Hall, 1974; Warren, Jackson, Nugaris, & Farley, 1973; Yamamoto, James, & Palley, 1968). The fault for this underutilization is often placed on demographic characteristics (such as lower income and less education) of the ethnic group. Some believe that it is a mistake to focus on these factors in isolation from the total context of how ethnic group members define mental health problems, where they go for help, and when it is deemed appropriate to seek professional treatment (Mays, Howard, & Jackson, 1988; Snowden, Collinge, & Runkle, 1982). It is a mistake that may cause practitioners to overlook valuable opportunities for interventions that may reduce or eliminate low utilization or early terminations by ethnic group members (Snowden, Collinge, & Runkle, 1982). The pluralistic orientation of feminist therapy may have some impact in changing this pattern.

For the most part ethnic minorities do not perceive mental health services as the most relevant avenue for coping with their problems unless those problems have reached the stage of a "nervous breakdown" (Block, 1981; Neighbors, 1984). Coping styles within most ethnic group communities follow a tradition of independence and self-reliance (Robinson, 1983) in which intrapsychic problems are handled alone, within the family, or in extended kinship/friendship networks (Block, 1981).

For example, in the Black culture there is an emphasis on accomplishing tasks with "no sweat" (Block, 1981). The no-sweat attitude is particularly characteristic of ethnic men, who in times of stress may display a cool indifference toward their problems. Complaints or attitudes of "can't" are viewed as inappropriate according to the legacy of a people who have sacrificed and overcome many apparently dramatic traumas.

Even in everyday occurrences, the number of serious survival based problems that some segments of the ethnic community struggle with cause the seriousness of intrapsychic conflicts to pale in comparison. Seeking treatment in a formal setting for such problems is viewed as a self-serving luxury that is not appropriate. When problems are encountered, informal networks are the primary choices for help seeking. Among Black Americans informal networks (e.g., friends, minister) are used to a greater extent in coping with problems than are the traditional mental health services (Mays, Howard, & Jackson, 1988; Neighbors & Jackson, 1984). The young Black man who after a marital disagreement calls his friends to play basketball may be viewed as indifferent or not upset by the marital dispute. But within a cultural/gender-appropriate perspective, this behavior reveals that he is seeking informal help. This young Black man will discuss his marital problems within a context that is informal but typical of Black male, help-seeking strategies.

Asians follow a pattern somewhat different from that of Blacks as they are less likely than Blacks to handle problems alone or to seek the services of a community mental health center. They are less inclined than Blacks or Hispanics to utilize ministers. They rely most often on family, friends, physicians, and hospitals for help with emotional or personal problems (Ossirio, Aylesworth, & Lasater, 1979). The Chinese help-seeking pattern is one in which there is persistent family involvement, extensive use of general health care systems, and extreme delays in mental health contact and entry (Lin, Inui, Kleinman, & Womack, 1982; Lin & Lin, 1981). In most Asian cultures, the family rather than the individual is viewed as the basic social unit. The mental illness of an individual is taken as a threat to the homeostasis of the family unit (Lin, Inui, Kleinman, & Womack, 1982). Therefore the involvement of the family in seeking help and the attempts at containing the problem within the family tend to be persistent (Lin, Inui, Kleinman, & Womack, 1982). According to Lin et al. (1982), because the shame and failure is shared by all of the family, the family promotes denial of the problem as a psychiatric one. The individual is more likely to somaticize, which allows the behavioral aberrations and psychological suffering to be viewed more comfortably as having a medical basis. Hence, it is important to recognize how cultural norms and networks that are often presumed to be supportive may influence the symptoms presented.

In addition, the therapist may need to take into account the conflict, feelings of shame, and embarrassment or traitor status that ethnic group members feel when they turn to professional sources. These feelings may be exacerbated when the therapist is Anglo. Sensitivity regarding how the cultural dynamics may impact the entry into treatment of ethnic group members may help in maintaining them in treatment.

Typically, ethnic group members do not enter the formal mental health system until their problems are severe or symptoms are very distressing (Howard, 1984; Mays, Howard, & Jackson, 1988; Neighbors, 1984), which may account for why they more often need crisis intervention.

Symptoms and Presenting Factors

Somaticization is one culturally acceptable mode used by ethnic minorities to express some of their psychological distress. For some segments of the ethnic community there is little differentiation between physical and mental concerns (Lin & Lin, 1981; Padilla & Ruiz, 1973). Among Asians this lack of differentiation has much of its origin in East Asian (especially Chinese and Japanese) language in which there is somatopsychic terminology for psychological problems, psychocultural coping processes that emphasize suppression and denial of emotion, and the traditional Oriental (Chinese) medical concepts (Lin, Inui, Kleinman, & Womack, 1982). Examples are yin–yang imbalance, obstruction of the circulation of vital energy (ch'i), and disturbances of harmony, with natural as well as supernatural powers being regarded as reasons for physical problems, the somatic bases for psychological disturbances.

Blacks tend to express psychological stress through such problems as headaches, stomach ailments, backaches, and general nervousness, with little understanding of the psychological determinants of these ailments (Block, 1981). Hispanics follow much the same pattern as Blacks, with the same gender pattern of greater prevalence of somaticization among women. Hispanic women tend to report somatic complaints as a means of expressing their needs and thereby obtaining support from significant others (Hynes & Werbin, 1977). A study by Comas–Diaz, Geller, Melgoza, and Baker (1982) revealed that, despite this cultural tendency, Hispanics requesting services at a community mental-health clinic did present complaints of a psychological nature: depression, anxiety, concentration problems, obsessions and compulsions, fears, and sleep problems. In addition, they also complained of physical and financial problems.

It is not unusual that when ethnic minorities enter therapy their major complaints are disguised (Block, 1981). In fact, Black clients may verbally deny the depth of the problem and their need for help (Block, 1981) because of their cultural style of not being dependent and helpless in the face of problems. As Block (1981) points out, what the therapist must remember is that they do *not* feel under control and *do* sense that something is seriously wrong. Thus, in examining the presenting symptoms of ethnic clients it is important to remember that their life situations may result in somewhat different styles of coping and psychosocial competence (Evans & Tyler, 1976; Tyler & Gatz, 1976). A feminist paradigm for therapy of ethnic minority group members would be highly appropriate, for feminist philosophy regards individual behavior as best understood by examining the social structure.

Expectations

Many ethnic groups are more accustomed to a style in which directive help is given by telling the person the necessary course of action to quickly remedy a problem (Carter, 1979; Sue & Sue, 1972; Vontress, 1971). Ethnic minorities live in an environment in which mistakes are more costly to them because of society's negative expectations. Due to the racist, sexist, and classist tendencies to homogenize ethnic subgroups, a mistake by one individual may have repercussions for all members of that subgroup. Because it is so important to "get it right" the first time, the authority will often spell out exactly what is to be done. Mothers concerned about the welfare of their children are very directive in explaining what the child's behavior is to be if that child is to survive successfully in a racist society. The child also learns that this authoritative approach comes from love and caring. Thus, Blacks, for example, when entering mental health services for their physical problems, experience impatience and frustration at the lack of direct intervention aimed at their medical problems.

Unaccustomed to the therapy process and consistent with cultural experiences, they expect the therapist to be assertive, to ask questions, and to come up with an answer as a physician does when physical symptoms are presented (Carter, 1979). In talking about a problem, a client may expect that the therapist will label the seriousness of the problem and the degree to which it is affecting the client. A study conducted by the second author (Comas–Diaz et al., 1982) revealed that Hispanics expected the therapist to be decisive and give advice while viewing themselves as active participants and assuming an active personal responsibility for the outcome of therapy. Therapists who were not assertive, directive, and decisive were viewed as uncaring.

In establishing a therapeutic relationship it is necessary for practitioners to understand in what way individuals will give them permission to be an influence in their lives (Solomon, 1982). Solomon (1982) describes urban middle-class individuals as relating to others out of a *gesellschaft* orientation in which they look at a person's place in the hierarchy of social statuses and decide what is appropriate behavior in relationship to that status or position. Therefore they become more concerned with the credentials, location, and looks of the office. On the other hand, Solomon views ethnic group members as relating to others from a *gemeinschaft,* a highly personal orientation. This orientation sanctions roles based on personal attributes, so the client's interest is in the attributes identifying the practitioner in the role of person, not therapist. Hence questions arise as to the marital or parental status of the therapist. Differences in orientation call for an involvement of the personal self rather than the professional self as usually advocated by traditional therapies.

Many American psychotherapies emphasize self-disclosure, active participation, openness, decision making, and growth in independence (Wong, 1983). These culturally laden goals may not be the best approach within some ethnic groups such as Asians (Sue & Sue, 1977). For the new Vietnamese immigrant accustomed to a structured society in which one is often the passive receiver of knowledge dispensed by an authority, pushing for active participation, decision making, and independence in the treatment setting would be contrary to cultural expectations (Wong, 1983). Ethnic minorities require culturally informed and relevant services addressing the complex nature of their expectations and attitudes toward treatment (Comas–Diaz et al., 1982). These issues should be carefully examined when delivering psychotherapy within a feminist perspective. Again, feminist therapy, with its pluralistic and integrative orientation, can accommodate and address the complexity of ethnic group members' attitudes and expectations of mental health services.

APPLICATION OF FEMINIST THERAPIES

Blacks

The philosophy of feminist therapy allows for a positive view of the cultural life-styles of Blacks, which promote kinship and friendship patterns, the exchange of favors and gifts, and the ethic of mutual obligation (Bailey & Perkins, 1982). It promotes insight into the interdependence of the past in both its historical and personal realms in coping with the present and moving adaptively into the future.

While there is a multitude of therapies aimed at helping individuals with psychosocial problems, several have common goals: increased skills in coping with everyday events, greater self-insight into the consequences of one's actions in the world, and greater willingness to accept responsibility for one's feelings and actions (Solomon, 1982). It is likely that for Black Americans problems in these areas may be due in part to feelings of powerlessness induced by the negative valuation they experience in society (Solomon, 1982). Thus effective therapy with many Black Americans may need to be directed toward empowerment. Solomon (1982) defines empowerment as "a process whereby the individual is assisted in utilizing interpersonal relationships effectively to enhance self-esteem and obtain basic social supplies, such as health care, employment, or financial assistance" (p. 177). Within the context of psychotherapy she sees this accomplished by:

1. Helping clients to perceive themselves as causal agents in reaching solutions to their problems or problems;
2. Helping clients to perceive the practitioner as having knowledge and skills which they can use;
3. Helping clients to perceive the practitioner as a peer and a colloborator in the problem-solving effort; and finally,
4. Helping clients to perceive opportunities to change the responses from the wider society. (p. 177)

It is also crucial to deal with Black anger and experiences of self-hatred and degradation imposed on Black Americans (Trotman, 1984). Both legacies and current climates have left psychic wounds and scars that have a tremendous influence on the psychological well-being of Blacks in this country. Intra- and intergroup conflicts regarding gradations of skin color, hair texture, and physical features often leave deep pains and feelings of rejection and self-hatred.

Practitioners must be sensitized to the "cultural depression" often brought into therapy by Black clients (Trotman, 1984). In a Black culture which stresses the ability to "do it" and manage difficult situations without showing signs of stress (Block, 1981), the typical presentation signs of psychomotor retardation, weight loss, increases in sleep, and inactivity may not be present. Instead one is more likely to see weight gain from overeating, greater activity, and in the case of Black women, an increase in selflessness behaviors (Mays & Howard, 1988).

Inclusion of the content of Black Americans' experiences may demand a reordering of the thinking and procedures of traditional therapies (Ward, 1981). The collective orientation of feminist therapy will result in the most effective mental health services because it recognizes the need for weighing the Black individual's own goals as well as family responsibilities and obligations against the consequences for the global Black community and against reactions in wider society (Jackson, 1983; Ward, 1981).

Hispanics

Feminist therapy that incorporates an orientation cognitive of Hispanic culture can be successful. It has been argued that when mental health services are culturally relevant, Hispanics utilize them (Abad, Ramos, & Bryce, 1974). Several theoretical orientations and modalities have successfully been employed with Hispanics (Acosta & Yamamoto, 1984). The common denominator of successful treatments is the integration of a sociocultural perspective. For example, all-female groups have been used successfully with Hispanic women, due to the women's willingness to confide in an all-female group matters that they would not discuss elsewhere (Hynes & Werbin, 1977). In a similar format, assertiveness training has been effectively used with Hispanic women (Boulette, 1976). Moreover, a cultural component has been incorporated into assertiveness training in order to "translate" culturally the concept to Puerto Rican women (Comas-Diaz & Duncan, 1985). These attempts have been used by the therapist while applying a feminist perspective to Hispanics.

Feminist therapy, with its precepts of empowering the client, can help Hispanics to better identify and utilize their resources. For instance, support systems are available within the Hispanic culture. The extended family, for example, can be a source of both frustration and support. Feminist therapy, with its emphasis on the collective, can help individuals negotiate this complex network. Feminist therapy, with its aim of achieving meaning in the individual's life, allows Hispanics to examine their ethnocultural identity in the treatment process. This is crucial because regardless of ethnicity, race, or gender, cultural identification is a process that is pervasive (Helms, 1985). Furthermore, the dialectic of feminist therapy enables Hispanic clients to address the dynamic and evolving process of acculturation and its subsequent impact on identity. Many Hispanics have a bicultural identity. Feminist therapy can help Hispanic women, who have multiple, often conflicting roles, to negotiate conflictive demands and achieve meaning through an awareness of increased choices.

SUMMARY

A therapeutic approach that integrates the interpersonal politics of race, ethnicity, culture, and class into its perspective will be most useful for effectively treating ethnic minority group members. This therapeutic approach, rather than focusing on self-awareness and the ego in abstraction, ought to center on family, community obligations and responsibilities, and the cultural/socioeconomic realities of ethnic group members (Wong, 1983). Feminist therapy is such a perspective. It recognizes the legitimacy of healing that can occur through examining how the outer realities of the social world influence intrapsychic feelings. Other cultural considerations that are important in the treatment of ethnic minorities include attention to the heritage of the client, degree of acculturation or migration experiences, age (generation), circumstances surrounding departure from the client's homeland and separation from loved ones, presence or absence of family, extended family, friends, and community supports, and proximity of these sources of support (Wong, 1983).

As long as traditional theories and methods of application in psychology continue to be predicated on philosophical orientations that are inconsistent with the social and inner realities of ethnic minorities, they remain invalid, and their use is unethical in the treatment of these individuals (Pedersen & Marsella, 1982). Practitioners are facing ethnic minority clients who present patterns of behavior inadequately addressed by many traditional theories of behavior. Practitioners are dutybound to embrace a philosophy that can help them integrate the experiences of ethnic group members into their behavior theories. Feminist philosophy offers such an opportunity and may be the catalyst for new empirically derived theories of personality and psychotherapy that will result in effective mental health services for ethnic group members.

REFERENCES

Abad, J., Ramos, J., & Bryce, E. (1974). A model for delivery of mental health services to Spanish-speaking minorities. *American Journal of Orthopsychiatry, 44,* 584–595.

Acosta, F. X., & Yamamoto, J. (1984). The utility of group work practice for Hispanic Americans. *Social Work with Groups, 7*(3), 63–73.

Bailey, M., & Perkins, W. E. (1982). Afro-American feminism: Problems and prospects. *Black Sociologist, 9*(1), 88–95.

Billingsley, A. (1976). *The evolution of the black family.* New York: National Urban League.

Block, C. B. (1981). Black Americans and the cross-cultural counseling and psychotherapy experience. In A. J. Marsella & P. B. Pedersen (Eds.), *Cross Cultural Counseling and Psychotherapy.* New York: Pergamon Press.

Boulette, T. R. (1976). Assertiveness training with low income Mexican American women. In M. R. Miranda (Ed.), *Psychotherapy with the Spanish speaking: Issues in research and service delivery.* Los Angeles: Monograph No. 3, Spanish Speaking Mental Health Research Center.

Bourguignon, E. (1979). *A world of women: Anthropological studies of women in the societies of the world.* New York: Praeger.

Canino, G. (1982). The Hispanic woman: Sociocultural influences on diagnoses and treatment. In R. M. Becerra, M. Karno, & J. Escobar (Eds.), *Mental health and Hispanic Americans.* New York: Grune & Stratton.

Carter, J. H. (1979). Frequent mistakes made with black patients in psychotherapy. *Journal of the National Medical Association, 71*(10), 1007–1009.

Chodorow, N. J. (1978). *The reproduction of mothering: Psychoanalysis and the sociology of gender.* Berkeley, CA: University of California Press.

Christian, B. (1985). *Black feminist criticism: Perspective on black women writers.* New York: Pergamon Press.

Comas–Diaz, L. (in press). Mainland Puerto-Rican women: A sociocultural approach. *Journal of Community Psychology.*

Comas–Diaz, L., & Duncan, J. W. (1985). The cultural context: A factor in assertiveness training with mainland Puerto Rican women. *Psychology of Women Quarterly, 9*(4), 463–475.

Comas–Diaz, L., Geller, J. D., Melgoza, B., & Baker, R. (1982, August). *Attitude expectations about mental health services among Hispanics and Afro-Americans.* Paper presented at the 90th annual meeting of the American Psychological Association, Washington, DC.

Espin, O. M. (1985). Psychotherapy with Hispanic women: Some considerations. In P. Pedersen (Ed.), *Handbook of cross-cultural counseling and therapy.* Westport, CT: Greenwood Press.

Evans, D., & Tyler, F. B. (1976). Is competence enhancing for the poor? *American Journal of Community Psychology, 4,* 25–33.

Gary, L. (1981). *Black men.* Beverly Hills, CA: Sage.

Gilbert, L. (1980). Feminist therapy. In A. M. Brodsky & R. Hare–Mustin (Eds.), *Women and psychotherapy: An assessment of research and practice* (pp. 245–265). New York: Guilford Press.

Gilligan, C. (1982). *In a different voice: Psychological theory and women's development.* Cambridge, MA: Harvard University Press.

Giraldo, D. (1972). El machismo como fenomeno psicocultural. (Machismo as a psychocultural phenomenon). *Revista Latino-Americana de Psicologia*, *4*(3), 292–309.

Griffith, M. S. (1977). The influence of race on the psychotherapeutic relationship. *Psychiatry*, *40*(1), 27–40.

Helms, J. E. (1985). Cultural identity in the treatment process. In P. Pedersen (Ed.), *Handbook of cross-cultural counseling and therapy*. Westport: CT: Greenwood Press.

Howard, C. P. (1984). *Predisposing, enabling and need factors related to patterns of help-seeking among black women*. Unpublished manuscript. University of Michigan.

Hynes, K., & Werbin, J. (1977). Group psychotherapy for Spanish-speaking women. *Psychiatric Annals*, *7*(12), 42–63.

Immigrants issue: The changing face of America. (1985, July 8). *Time*, *126*, 1.

Jackson, A. M. (1983). A theoretical model for the practice of psychotherapy with black populations. *Journal of Black Psychology*, *10*(1), 19–27.

Jackson, G. (1976). The African genesis of the black perspective in helping. *Professional Psychology*, *7*(3), 363–367.

Jones, E. E. (1974). Social class and psychotherapy: A critical review of research. *Psychiatry*, *37*, 307–319.

Kinzer, N. (1973). Women in Latin America: Priests, machos and babies or Latin American women and the Manichea heresy. *Journal of Marriage & the Family*, *35*, 299–312.

Lerman, H. (1985, August). *From Freud to feminist personality theory: Getting from here to there*. Paper presented at the 93rd annual convention of the American Psychological Association, Los Angeles.

Lin, K., Inui, T. S., Kleinman, A. M., & Womack, W. W. (1982). Sociocultural determinants of the help-seeking behavior of patients with mental illness. *Journal of Nervous & Mental Disease*, *170*(2), 78–85.

Lin, T. Y., & Lin, M. C. (1981). Love, denial and rejection: Responses of Chinese families to mental illness. In A. Kleinman & T. Y. Lin (Eds.), *Normal and abnormal behavior in culture*. Dordrecht, Netherlands: D. Reidel.

Lopez–Garriga, M. (1978). Estrategias de autoafirmación en mujeres puertorriqueñas (Strategies of self-affirmation among Puerto Rican women). *Revista de Ciencias Sociales*, *20*, 259–267.

Mays, V. M. (1985). The black American and psychotherapy: The dilemma. *Psychotherapy: Theory, Research, & Practice*, *2*, 379–388.

Mays, V. M. (in press). *Black women, work and stress: The development of a focused support group approach*. Journal of Community Psychology.

Mays, V. M., & Howard, C. S. (1987a). *Symptom and service utilization patterns in a national sample of black women: Implications for psychotherapy research*. Manuscript under review.

Mays, V. M., & Howard, C. S. (1987b). *Selflessness in black women: A therapeutic issue*. Manuscript under review.

Mbiti, J. S. (1969). *African religions and philosophies*. New York: Doubleday.

Neighbors, H. W. (1984). Professional help use among black Americans: Implications for unmet needs. *American Journal of Community Psychology, 12*(5), 551–566.

Neighbors, H. W. & Jackson, J. S. (1984). The use of informal and formal help: Four patterns of illness behavior in the black community. *Journal of Community Psychology, 12*(6), 629–644.

Ossirio, P. G., Aylesworth, L. S., & Lasater, L. (1979). *Mental health related needs among the Indochinese refugees in the Denver metropolitan area.* LRI Report No. 21 for Park East Comprehensive Community Mental Health Center, Inc., Denver.

Padilla, A. M., & Ruiz, R. (1973). *Latino mental health: A review of literature.* Rockville, MD: National Institute of Mental Health.

Pedersen, P. B., & Marsella, A. J. (1982). The ethical crisis for cross-cultural counseling and therapy. *Professional Psychology, 13*(4), 492–500.

Robinson, C. R. (1983). Black women: A tradition of self-reliant strength. In J. H. Robbins & R. J. Siegel (Eds.), *Women changing therapy: New assessment, values, and strategies in feminist therapy.* New York: Haworth Press.

Schlachet, B. L. (1984). Female role socialization: The analyst and the analysis. In C. M. Brody (Ed.), *Women therapists working with women: New theory and process of feminist therapy.* New York: Springer.

Senour, M. N. (1977). Psychology of the Chicana. In J. L. Martinez (Ed.), *Chicano psychology.* New York: Academic Press.

Sluzki, C. E. (1979). Migration and family conflict. *Family Process, 18,* 379–403.

Smith, B. (1985). Some home truths on the contemporary black feminist movement. *Black Scholar,* March/April, 4–13.

Snowden, L. R., Collinge, W. B., & Runkle, M. C. (1982). Help seeking and underservice. In L. R. Snowden (Ed.), *Reaching the underserved: Mental health needs of neglected populations.* Beverly Hills, CA: Sage.

Solomon, B. B. (1982). The delivery of mental health services to Afro-American individuals and families: Translating theory into practice. In B. A. Bass, G. J. Wyatt, & G. J. Powell (Eds.), *The Afro-American family: Assessment, treatment, and research issues.* New York: Grune & Stratton.

Stanley, L., & Wise, S. (1983). *Breaking out: Feminist consciousness and feminist research.* London: Routledge & Kegan Paul.

Steiner, S. (1974). *The islands: The worlds of the Puerto Ricans.* New York: Harper Colophen Books.

Stevens, E. (1973). Machismo and marianismo. *Transaction-Society, 10*(6), 57–63.

Sue, D. W., & Sue, S. (1972). Ethnic minorities: Resistance to being researched. *Professional Psychology, 3,* 11–17.

Sue, S., McKinney, H., Allen, D., & Hall, J. (1974). Delivery of community mental health services to black and white clients. *Journal of Consulting & Clinical Psychology, 42,* 794–801.

Trotman, F. (1984). Psychotherapy of black women and the dual effects of racism and sexism. In C. M. (Ed.), *Women therapists working with women: New theory and process of feminist therapy.* New York: Springer.

Tyler, F. B., & Gatz, M. (1976). Development of individual psychosocial competence in high school settings. *Journal of Consulting & Clinical Psychology, 45,* 441–449.

Vontress, L. E. (1971). *Counseling Negroes.* New York: Houghton-Mifflin.

Ward, N. T. (1981). Counseling from a black perspective. In E. Mizio & A. J. Delaney (Eds.), *Training for service delivery to ethnic minority clients.* New York: Family Service Association of America.

Warren, R., Jackson, A., Nugaris, J., & Farley, G. (1973). Differential attitude of black and white patients toward treatment in child guidance clinic. *American Journal of Orthopsychiatry, 43,* 384–393.

Wong, J. (1983). Appropriate mental health treatment and delivery systems for Southeast Asians. In Special Service for Groups (Ed.), *Bridging cultures: Southeast Asian refugees in America.* Los Angeles, CA: Special Services for Groups.

Yamamoto, J., James, D. C., & Palley, N. (1968). Cultural problems in psychiatric therapy. *Archives of General Psychiatry, 19,* 45–49.

CHAPTER 12

Feminist Therapies with the Elderly

Elizabeth Midlarsky

Some life events and processes appear unfair and unconscionable. To many individuals, the lot of growing old, often bound in relative poverty and loneliness, failing health, limited roles and multiple losses, may comprise one of those occasions. In addition to the physical health problems and depletions associated with advanced age, mental health problems appear to increase in frequency, as well. Elderly people (those born prior to 1920) are highly reluctant to admit to psychological problems, preferring to couch disorder in physical terms, so that it becomes difficult to determine the actual prevalence of psychopathology (Lawton, 1976). However, community surveys yield estimates of 20% to 45% of elderly with psychological disorders (Busse & Pfeifer, 1975; Gruenberg, 1978; Kay, 1977).

In addition to the probability that old age is related to the increased prevalence of psychopathology, there are numerous indications that the elderly are less well served by the mental health establishment than are members of any other age cohort. Indeed, it is estimated that approximately 85% of the elderly are not receiving appropriate attention. Largely for reasons related to the system of reimbursement for the costs of care, the aged have been subject to "all-or-none" treatment. Little preventive or outpatient care exists, and the incontrovertible evidence of emotional problems—particularly in the absence of adequate familial support—frequently results in confinement within a primarily custodial nursing home (Eisdorfer & Cohen, 1982).

Several factors may account for the undeniable inadequacies in provision of mental health services. One source may be the "agism" existing within our society, wherein psychopathology may be viewed as simply part of an inevitable and permanent decline. In the words of Lesnoff-Caravaglia (1984c), if power resides in the hands of the old, and not the young, "we might well find in vogue the trembling hand and shuffling gait . . . the young feigning sensory loss and graying the hair . . . to appear venerable . . . when caution is preferred over imprudence, and deliberate action over trial and error, then youth is a lament and old age a herald." In the field of mental health, Sigmund Freud was the original architect of the position that the elderly are not suitable candidates for psychotherapy, "owing to the accumulation of material [such that] so much time would be required that the end of the cure would be reached . . . [when] importance is no longer attached to nervous health" (Freud, 1959, p. 245). More recent theorists have promoted the view of development as ongoing rather than fixed in early childhood (Erikson, 1963). However, despite the general recognition that old age may be a developmental stage with a nature responsive to the individual's physical and psychosocial conditions, there has been a virtually intractable reluctance to treat the elderly for mental health problems.

In some cases, failure to treat may be attributable to lack of knowledge about the nature and manifestations of psychopathology in the aged, which may hamper accurate diagnosis (Kidd, 1982, reports a 30% rate of misdiagnosis), so that a reversible problem may be assessed as an inescapable concomitant of the aging process. A contributor to the problem is the lack of sufficient training, as is the highly complex nature of the diagnostic process in a group whose emotional problems are complicated and sometimes obscured by interacting biological and social factors, and even the sheer number of problems. Another barrier comes from the fact that the field of clinical gerontology is notably lacking in an empirically grounded knowledge base regarding age-specific psychopathology and treatment (cf. Storandt, Siegler, & Eliase, 1978; Zarit, 1980). Where proper diagnosis is made, there may be few resources available for the provision of treatment. Even among otherwise qualified therapists, there remains a "therapeutic nihilism" (Eisdorfer & Cohen, 1982) associated with the relentless underlying pessimism about the value of mental health care for "helpless, hopeless" older adults who are presumably close to death (Cyrus-Lutz & Gaitz, 1972; Kahana & Coe, 1969). This view, of course, excludes from consideration the boundlessly resilient, competent and long-lived elderly who are all around us (Midlarsky & Kahana, 1983; in pressb). In addition, even where good mental health facilities exist, many elderly persons and their families may roundly deny the existence of emotional difficulties, and view engagement in psychotherapy as an admission of ineradicable weakness. Elderly persons engaging in treatment may depict the rigidity and inflexibility associated with insecurity and diminished sensory capacity. In many of these cases, the sole means for alleviating distress may be active outreach efforts, which employ novel therapeutic approaches—and which omit, where necessary, insistence on the labeling of problems as "psychiatric" (Sargent, 1980).

In this brief summary, we can see that the late adult years are a period in which both women and men are at high risk for adverse emotional responses. In addition, both are victims of the failures in service provision associated with their inescapable membership in a highly visible minority group. However, old age is also a period in which there are far more women than men. In this sense, it can be said that aging, while preferable to its deadly alternative, is largely a woman's problem.

Now, despite the fact that women outnumber men among the elderly, and suffer problems unique to their sex, in most existing publications on the mental health of the aged, women are lumped in with "all elderly." One current theme in the literature of gerontology is that the present for the elderly is continuous, in some senses with the past (Livson, 1978; Lowenthal, Thurnher, & Chiriboga, 1975). This may be true even though somewhat different characteristics and tendencies may come to the forefront in old age, concomitant with personal and environmental realities for the individual. In the present of the aged woman, the younger years are not merely part of the march of years past, but an irrevocable part of them, contributing to their present and their future. Analysis of the life situations and stresses imposed on women and men, and their differing reactions throughout the life span, certainly evokes the possibility that the process of aging may also differ for the two sexes. This may be especially true for today's cohort of elderly persons, who were largely postmeridian when the current women's movement occurred.

In order to partly redress a situation in which little attention is generally given to the problems experienced by older women, and their alleviation, this chapter will focus on mental health concerns and treatment considerations for older women. Of course, older men also experience difficulties within our agist society, and a feminist approach to their problems is potentially quite beneficial. However, the double burden imposed by both agism and sexism on the aged woman appears to warrant a distinct and focused treatment. In order to accomplish the goal of sensitizing the reader to some of the concerns relevant to therapy, it first will treat general factors associated with well-being. This will be followed by a brief review of the literature regarding psychopathology in women, and a summary of feminist considerations in psychotherapy.

PROBLEMS OF THE OLDER WOMAN

In many respects, the aging woman may be free of earlier burdens and stresses; e.g., of rigid sex role expectations, intense demands for nurturance, conflicts between gratification of one's own and others' needs, and the like. On the other hand, she may be faced with decrements in physical characteristics associated with beauty, including cosmetic skin changes, weight changes and the bowed back of osteoporosis; increased risk for uterine and breast cancer; as well as sensory loss, diabetes, arthritis, and organic brain changes (Eisdorfer & Cohen, 1982; Steinhauer & Auslander, 1984). Psychosocial conditions serving as stressors may include exposure to the double jeopardy of sexism and agism, with their associated powerlessness, residence in transitional urban areas, the multiplicity of role changes with the end of active parenting, coping with adult children, retirement from employment and reduction of income, as well as the widowhood that so frequently occurs in the lives of women (Butler & Lewis, 1977; Langer, 1980; Langer & Rodin, 1976; Lopata, 1975). Other psychosocial problems include social isolation and boredom, fear of death and invalidism, relegation to custodial institutions, even of those in relatively good health (de Beauvoir, 1972), and the patronizing attitudes and even death wish by children to whom one has devoted much of one's life.

Review of the literature regarding psychosocial problems of the aged woman reveals five that have received at least a modicum of systematic attention. These are retirement, poverty, widowhood and aloneness, sexuality, and exposure to crime and violence.

Retirement

On an a priori basis, retirement has the potential to be associated with advantages and/or disadvantages, depending on a variety of personal and situational factors. The individual gives up the role associated with her or his employment, and acquires another role, "retired person." She or he may lose income from the employment, but may also earn the right to obtain economic support without the stigma attached to unemployment insurance and welfare payments. The individual acquires a great deal of leisure time, but also the possible pressures associated with responsibility for managing and filling one's own time. There are time and freedom to develop new relationships, but also the loss of friends and associates with whom the person may have related to in both expressive and instrumental ways at work (Atchley, 1975). Numerous cases have been reported in difficulties in adjusting to retirement.

Negative outcomes cited include feelings of uselessness among up to 30% (Streib & Schneider, 1971), income difficulties, and yearning for one's job (Harris, 1975).

Gerontologists have frequently assumed that retirement from paid employment is likely to be a far more serious problem for men than for women. For example, on the basis of responses by 36 women, 20 of whom were unmarried, Cumming and Henry (1961, p. 144) concluded that retirement is not as important an issue for women as it is for men, because work is less important in the lives of women in comparison with other roles. "It is as though they add work to their lives the way they would add a club membership." According to Burgess (1960, p. 20), retirement is a less salient stress for the woman "because a woman as long as she is physically able retains the role and satisfactions of homemaker." As late as 1973, Zena Blau wrote that retirement adversely affects the *man* because it

> deprives a man of the respect accorded the breadwinner in the American family and constrains him to assume a role similar to that of a woman. In this respect, retirement is a more demoralizing experience for men than for women. Women may choose to work, but according to cultural prescription, they are not obliged to do so. (Blau, 1973, p. 29)

Empirical data, however, challenge the assumption that men have more difficulty associated with retirement than do women. For example, Lowenthal and Berkman (1967) found that retired women in the San Francisco area were more likely than retired men to have psychiatric difficulties, and Streib and Schneider (1971) reported that women are more likely to experience a significant increase in feelings of uselessness upon retirement. While it is often assumed that retirement is less disruptive for women because they can always return to full-time involvement in homemaking, employed women, particularly in the group who now are elderly, may be more likely to have given up (or never engaged in) a satisfying family life. At retirement, employed women who had been married are more likely to be single, whether due to widowhood, divorce, or never having married than their male counterparts. Hence, the assumption that they can automatically become absorbed in fulfilling roles within the family context may simply be incorrect. In any event, these results certainly point to the need by mental health professionals to guard against the tendency to assume that retirement is not an issue for the elderly woman—or conversely, that it is. For the relatively young feminist therapist, involvement in career may be of primary importance, and a source of her identity. However, in order to serve the needs of her client best, assumptions about the importance of paid employment should give way to unbiased evaluation of the values or priorities of the particular woman in therapy. Evaluation of the magnitude and nature of the loss for the individual may then be used as a first step in determining therapeutic approaches— if any are needed—to this issue.

Poverty

In recent years, economic conditions have improved to the extent that the average older person no longer inevitably faces financial hardship. Yet, data indicate that certain subgroups of elderly including women, racial and ethnic minorities, and persons living alone are likely to experience poverty. Women in all ethnic and racial groups, especially if not living in a family, are more likely to be poor than are men in those same groups (Atchley, 1980). Indeed, half of all single women over 65, and 80% of women over 80, have incomes below the poverty line, and the poverty rate for older women is 60% higher than for older men. Furthermore, many of the women who are poor when they are old are newly poor; i.e., they did not experience or anticipate poverty during middle age (Nathanson, 1984). For the older woman living alone, poverty is very likely. This poverty unfortunately occurs when she feels most vulnerable in other ways, as well.

A diversity of factors cause the poverty of aged women. One is longevity. Almost any person living many years beyond retirement could potentially become poor, and women far outlive men. Second, many women—particularly among those who are now old—were socialized to be homemakers who were economically dependent on male breadwinners. Among those women, many became displaced homemakers in their forties when they still had children to support. These "newly poor" received little reliable support from their former husbands, or from Social Security, and had great difficulty obtaining jobs. Women who worked often had jobs that were low paying and/or part-time, and moved in and out of the the workforce, usually because of family responsibilities. They are typically ineligible for private pension plans, receive little in the way of Social Security benefits, and have little in the way of savings (Moss, 1970).

In many cases, the existence of insufficient financial resources also constitutes a threat to the independent living that so many older people crave. Consider, for example, the woman who lives alone in a small but comfortable apartment and pays for rent and other necessities out of her Social Security check. At the age of 72, she suffers the acute phase of an illness, requiring her to remain in a health care institution for six weeks. While her medical expenses are covered, her only financial resource is now a reduced Social Security benefit—e.g., $25, designed to serve as pocket money in the institution. Because she has no other income or savings with which to pay the rent, she will probably lose her home. This essentially healthy and competent individual, now over the worst of her illness, may consequently discover that with no other place to live, she will have to remain in the institution (cf. Atchley, 1980).

The outpatient therapist is not very likely to encounter these poor elderly women in her practice. In most cases, even though poverty (not just reduced income) affects mental health, individual sufferers tend to simply not be "therapy minded." Many elderly individuals, both women and men, are highly reticent about revealing their yearly incomes even in an in-depth interview in which they are assured of confidentiality; in most cases, the reported reason for reticence is embarrassment (Midlarsky & Kahana, in press b). However, the skilled therapist working with any elderly client should be aware that perceived financial inadequacy may be a problem for that client even when no direct mention of finances is made. Preservation of dignity is a critical theme in the lives of many elderly persons, and in our society, poverty is associated with loss of the sense of dignity. Furthermore, certain concomitants of poverty, such as extreme social isolation, may be important factors to consider in planning for adequate treatment.

Widowhood and Aloneness

There are several routes to aloneness in old age. These include widowhood, divorce, separation (e.g., from a spouse who may be residing in a health care institution), and the aloneness of the individual who never married. Of these four, widowhood is the one most likely to occur in old age, and thus to require adjustment. For example, while one of every two marriages in the U. S. ends in divorce, only about one-sixth of the divorces occurs after the age of 45, and divorce is highly infrequent during old age. The average age for the onset of widowhood is 56, and over two-thirds of widows live alone from the time of their husband's demise until their own death (Lesnoff–Caravaglia, 1984c). Like poverty, widowhood is a greater problem for women than men, with 51% of women and only 14% of men over 65 being widowed at least once (U.S. Bureau of Census, 1981).

Whatever the source of the aloneness, many more women than men live alone during old age. Because women tend to live longer than men, and also tend to marry men older than themselves, most ultimately outlive their spouses. In our society, younger and newer means more beautiful, whether one is considering cars or people, so that it is not surprising that aged women are at a great disadvantage in regard to remarraige (Butler & Lewis, 1977; Vinick, 1978). By the eighth decade of life, only 6% of women are married, in comparison with 36% of men (Troll, 1984).

For many women, the onset of widowhood is the first event making them feel truly old, and alone. For traditional women, upon the death of their husband they are alone for the first time in their lives. Furthermore, after years of dependency both for finances and decisions about every important aspect of their lives, they may feel helpless, abandoned, and overwhelmed. Also, for these women the loss of status as "the wife of . . ." may be hard to live with, and may be a status impossible to replace. For others, even if the marriage was not ideal, their husband was the one who primarily confirmed their identity, served as a source of their self-esteem, was their only (and perhaps will be their last) sex partner, and was the one peer with whom they could share their present and their past (cf. Lopata, 1979; Silverman, 1972). As one widow in my own therapy practice, a self-sufficient professional, remarked about the loss of her husband of 40 years

> with Ralph's death, above all, the shared memories, the small chuckles about each child at 2 and 10 and 18, the remembered vacations and crises and traumas—the history—are all lost. Never will there be another man who will look at me, at 62, and see also the girl of 23. Now that my parents and he are all gone, there will never be a friend or companion or lover who can share those aspects of life with me again.

According to Helena Lopata (1973), factors significantly contributing to the reaction to widowhood include age, social class, prior relationship with one's husband (those with better relationships adjusted more readily), personality and life-style. Many women in a diversity of groups do report that their social lives are disrupted as a result of widowhood, and report the "fifth wheel syndrome" (Lopata, 1975).

Widowhood has been found to be an important source of distress both for elderly women and men. Investigators have primarily discovered that widowhood is associated with hospitalization for depression (Turner & Sternberg, 1978). However, clinical depression is far from a universal phenomenon, with 33% clinically depressed at one month, and 13% at one year after the death. Also, in most cases the sadness and grief are not sufficient to require hospitalization (Clayton, 1973). In addition to the significant, albeit not overwhelming increase in morbidity, investigators have found that there is an increase in mortality among elderly persons who are widowed (Jacobs & Ostfeld, 1977). In sum, both the frequency of widowhood and the possibility of adverse reactions are factors that the therapist should keep in mind in her work with elderly women.

In approaching the elderly widow, Silverman and Cooperband (1984) point out two analytically separate problems with which the bereaved woman needs to cope. These are the experience of grief and the need to change roles, with their associated behaviors. In regard to grief, they make the important point that grief should be treated not as a form of individual psychopathology but as a normal reaction to the loss of a significant other. What most grieving women need is someone to whom they may speak about their grief, without feeling that it is somehow inappropriate to do so. Several writers (e.g., Gaitz, 1977; Post, 1982; Silverman, 1972) have suggested that there is considerable discomfort with death in our society, and grieving, the visible reminder of death, evokes negative reactions and consequent avoidance of the grief-stricken individual. The ability of the therapist to listen uncritically to the expressions of grief by the widow unable to find support within her own network, may be making a vital therapeutic contribution. The elderly individual may be more "fortunate" than younger women in finding role models of widows in her own age cohort. However, unlike the younger widow, her state of aloneness is more likely to be permanent. Making a smooth transition to this role, especially for the woman with a history of dependency on her husband, may become an important goal for the counseling relationship.

Sexuality

How many times do we read about an elderly couple getting married, perhaps in their nursing home residence, and experience either revulsion or the feeling that it is "cute" of them; such sentiments probably result from socialization within an agist society (Masters & Johnson, 1981). Sex among the elderly—like sexuality in children, particularly before Freud's writings were popularized—seems somehow "unnatural." Yet, in a recent summary of the literature on aging and sexuality, White (1982) found that like so many other characteristics, sexual attitudes, feelings and, where possible, sexual behaviors, are largely a continuation of lifelong patterns. Indeed, in their cross-cultural study of sexuality in older adults, Winn and Newton (1982) found that 84% of elderly women continued to be interested and/or active sexually.

Recent investigations have outlined several reasons for the decline or termination of sexuality, where it does occur among women. White

(1982) notes that one source may be health changes or disabilities. Some of the physical conditions impeding sexual activity, which may have a higher prevalence among the elderly, include limbs that are paralyzed or stiff, pain, heart disorder, or hypertension, and uterine contractions causing pain among a minority of women who have had hysterectomies. Furthermore, the woman's fear that her aged body is unattractive, or diminished sensory capacity, can lead to the suppression or diminution of arousal (Duddle, 1982). Lack of opportunity is another cause of the decline in sexual behavior. The woman may discourage sexual relationships because of her fear that sexual activity will evoke adverse symptoms in her husband. On the other hand, her husband's participation may diminish because he feels unable to perform. The elderly woman may be a widow or divorcee, with little opportunity to meet her preferred type of partner. Even if a suitable partner is available, her upbringing may preclude behavior inviting or accepting sexual advances. If she does, however, the results may sometimes be quite satisfying. From my own case files, we have the following example:

> Seventy-two-year old Martha formed a warm relationship with 68-year-old Ralph, a widower. They were close companions for over a year when her granddaughter mentioned to them both that they seemed rather "hip" for people who hadn't lived through the "sexual revolution." (Actually, they had only held hands up until then.) One thing led to another, and the relationship gradually became more sexual in nature. Everyone around Martha noticed that she was "blooming," and the formerly reticent Ralph became expansive and happy. Martha said that she felt like a young woman again. When she looked in the mirror, she saw a "pretty girl"; she giggled again, and felt warm and loved. While most of their sexuality was expressed through "cuddling," both felt considerable satisfaction.

With no danger of unwanted pregnancy, little danger of sexually transmitted diseases, and few physiological barriers that are insurmountable, sexual activity among the elderly would appear to be a natural, enjoyable and harmless outlet when it does occur. Major barriers within our society appear to be a lack of opportunity, fear of disapproval or ridicule by family or by staff within institutional settings, and discomfort with "illicit relationships."

For the mental health professional working with elderly clients, the following may be useful. First, he or she should attempt to become aware of her or his own manner of dealing with this issue. Discomfort, a patronizing attitude or disapproval by the therapist are not helpful. Second, because sexual difficulties may be due to misinformation about such facets as the effects of physiological changes associated with aging on sexual performance, and how to accommodate, the therapist should either become informed or develop good referral sources. Third, the therapist should be aware that it is likely that most sexual problems are due to problems in the interpersonal relationship, or feelings about one's aging self. Another source of difficulty may be that medications interfere with sexual performance; hence aged persons may be encouraged to be assertive in discussing their sexual needs and preferences with prescribing physicians. Also relevant here are the individual's living arrangements; both therapists and clients should understand that adults are entitled to privacy, and seek input regarding an appropriate arrangement.

Crime and Victimization

A major concern, particularly among elderly women residing in urban areas, is that they will become victims of crime. Stories abound of elderly neighbors defrauded by unscrupulous repairmen, and robberies, rapes, and beatings (Malinchak, 1980). The role of the mental health profession may be to help the elderly woman discern actual risks so that she may best protect herself, while desensitizing her to unrealistic fears that threaten her sense of competence to retain her cherished independence. While diverse crimes may potentially be committed against this or any other social group, three will be briefly considered here: rape, spouse abuse, and geriatric parental abuse.

Rape. Rape is an offense that is reported less by elderly women than by younger women, but which is probably underreported. Whatever the actual frequency of occurrence, the fear of rape may curtail the mobility of many older women, and when a rape does occur, it is far more likely to lead to permanent damage—and even death—than in younger women (Davis & Brody, 1979).

In addition to experiencing the types of consequence experienced by younger women (cf. Midlarsky, 1977, 1980), the older victim has additional bases for viewing the rape as a massive trauma. She was brought up in accordance with strict social mores; her husband was likely to have been her sole sexual partner; since his (probable) death, she has probably wondered about her competence to cope on her own. The sexual nature of this violent crime may lead her to feel intense guilt, shame—and incompetence to protect herself. So great may be her embarrassment that she may be unable to report the rape, or to discuss it even with a confidante or therapist. Failure to discuss it may lead to the incubation of anxiety, and thus to intense upset to the point of terror, as well as depression. The older woman who was assaulted may have been a ready rape victim primarily because she was incapacitated by illness, and in some cases, the shock of the rape may be fatal.

The recent NIMH study by Davis and Brody (1979) does a good job of summarizing initial research about rape victimization and how to prevent it, in groups of elderly women. In addition, a need exists to train rape counselors and physicians to be alert to potential signs that an aged woman has been raped. While therapeutic techniques successfully employed with younger victims may well be applicable to the elderly victim (e.g., Resick, 1983), some additional factors may have to be considered with these older individuals. For example, (a) the reticence to disclose details of this embarrassing event may necessitate a more active role on the part of the counselor, (b) the necessity for assurances of confidentiality may never be greater, (c) it may be advisable to employ elderly counselors, trained to empathize with the plight of their peer victim, and (d) the elderly victim may need more extensive follow-up, to ensure that her needs for health care are met, and that her ability to care for her daily needs is brought as close as possible to the former level of functioning.

Spouse abuse. According to Fields (1976), women of all classes, ethnic/social groups and ages may be subject to abuse by their husbands. While the prevalence of spouse abuse in couples over 65 has not been determined, it seems likely that it occurs to a lesser extent than in those same people at an earlier age. The older woman may be reluctant to leave even a battering relationship because, relative to the younger woman, she may be even more insecure about "making it on her own"—especially "after all these years." Also, violence may feel "normal" after many years of living with it, she may view any marriage to be preferable to the rather certain alternative of loneliness (Resick, 1983; Walker, 1979). On the other hand, by the time a woman reaches her mid- to late-sixties, she is likely to be divorced, separated, or widowed, so that many of the earlier violent relationships may have been terminated.

There are few published works which shed light on the prevalence of spouse abuse among the elderly, or the behavior of elderly spouses in a violent marriage. However, in a study by Pfouts (1978), of 35 violent families served by a welfare department, several elderly women were found to be struggling with the decision to leave. Where the women did indeed disengage from the relationship, an approach in which services were provided promptly and generously were said to appear helpful. According to Rathbone-McCuan (1984), while there are currently no empirically based therapeutic interventions with victims, elderly abusive husbands typically refuse to become involved in treatment so that wives are counseled alone, and the preponderance of services consist of emergency support and crisis intervention.

Geriatric parental abuse. This form of interpersonal violence could also be termed "maternal abuse." In most cases, it appears that mothers—who have the greater longevity—are the victims of abuse or neglect by adult children, overburdened by the care of an older, often impaired parent who may be a drain on the younger family's resources. According to Rathbone-McCuan (1980), examination of a series of case studies suggested that the victim is typically an elderly female who is dependent and vulnerable, and there is a history of disorder either on the part of the victim or the caretaker (e.g., psychiatric disorders, mental retardation, or alcoholism). There is typically a history of interpersonal violence and often of similar previous incidents. Now, the consequences of even a single episode of abuse can readily bring about the death of a frail, older person. Hence persons involved in work with families in which an older adult resides should be alert to signs of extreme strain which could lead to abuse or neglect.

Identification of an abuse situation is the first, and often most problematic step. Unlike younger victims, the older victim may rarely leave the house, and is not likely to attend organized activities in which signs of abuse may become apparent. Even when an opportunity arises to report the situation, the victim may refuse to do so. Turning to others to help protect her from the cruelty of her own child may feel like the admission of her own failure as a parent. In my own case files, conversely, are examples of the acceptance of the abuse as an elderly mother's expiation of her "guilt" as a parent. While reports by the victim are rare, a neighbor or other family member privy to the situation may urge the people involved to seek help.

When identification of an abusive situation is made, Hooyman, Rathbone-McCuan, and Klingbeil (1982) recommend that several steps be taken in assessment and intervention, that may be applied and later evaluated. These include (a) determination of whether there has been a pattern of abusive episodes or whether only a single episode occurred, (b) evaluation for other forms of neglect, (c) determination of the extent of harm or damage, (d) determination of factors precipitating the abuse, and (e) consequences of it; also, (f) as the focus of the intervention may be either to make environmental changes, or to help the abuser learn to control anger, the therapist needs to determine the caretaker's levels of anger and control; (g) evaluation should also be made of the situation, to discover whether there are other problems needing intervention. In an approach which manifests concern both for the abuser and the abused, intervention is suggested in which both parties are helped to work on (1) their *interaction,* (2) *self-management and self control* of their own behaviors and responses (e.g., violence; chronic complaining), and (3) possible *environmental changes,* in the form of respite care to alleviate the burden of the caretaker, or perhaps even alternative living arrangements for the elderly person.

Unfortunately, at present only a very few communities have resources upon which abused older women can rely (Rathbone-McCuan & Voyles, 1982). The raising of community awareness and the development of additional supports to families charged with the burden of caring for impaired elderly, as well as for the elderly victims, are clearly warranted.

MENTAL DISORDERS AND THE AGED WOMAN

At every stage of the life span—with old age comprising no exception— women are more likely to be diagnosed as mentally ill than are men (Hess & Markson, 1980). What is undetermined are the relative proportions of variance attributable to actual differences in prevalence, the greater propensity of women to verbalize their problems, and/or sexist diagnostic practices. Among the elderly, an additional factor is that longevity among women creates the opportunity for disorders of all kinds to become apparent. Of the mental disorders common to old age, the ones more frequently observed among women are prescription drug abuse, depression, and dementia. A brief treatment of these is presented below.

Prescription Drug Abuse

Because of their greater longevity, associated with a slow decline in physiological functions, older women typically suffer from a multiplicity of physical disorders. Each of those disorders may carry with it a host of recommended and prescribed medications. As most elderly persons are not "psychology-minded," and prefer to attribute stress reactions to physical problems (Lawton, 1976), self-administration of medications may become, for some, a substitute for other more productive means of problem solving. Still another source of the overuse of drugs may be forgetfulness. The older person, especially if living alone, may sometimes take a second dose of medication, because the first was forgotten. In any event, while the overuse of prescription drugs is frequently cited as a problem at all ages, and by both sexes, elderly women abuse these drugs more than any other group (Lesnoff-Caravaglia, 1984a).

Depression

Depression has been identified as among the most prevalent psychiatric disorders in the United States, and as one of the most treatable disorders afflicting the elderly (Hanley & Baikie, 1984; Simpson, Woods, & Britton, 1981). Because of wide variations among studies of prevalence among the elderly, in regard to sample characteristics, methods of assessment and diagnostic criteria, highly divergent estimates of prevalence have been made (e.g., Gurland, Dean, Cross, & Golden, 1980). Thus, for example, surveys of older community residents have reported that the majority of elderly respondents are depressed (e.g., Gaitz, 1977). However, the full complement of symptoms necessary to diagnose major depressive episodes in accordance with the DSM–III appear to be present only in 4% to 6% (Blazer & Williams, 1980), with 10–15% of cases serious enough to require intervention (Post, 1982). Studies have also indicated that, as is the case earlier in life, both mild and major depressions are reported to be higher among older women than among older men. Although it is difficult to obtain exact figures for prevalence, Blazer and Williams (1980) have reported a ratio of two women to every man with diagnosable clinical depression.

In regard to probable causation, aging carries with it multiple losses— e.g., in the area of physical functioning, perceived control over one's environment, of loved ones and financial resources. As women are more long-lived than men, they may well experience a greater number of losses. Their greater involvement in social networks, and emotional investment in relationships may also occasion more pain as losses occur. Blazer and Williams (1980) have pointed out that much of the "depression" of the elderly may be grief and decreased morale, rather than a pathological state. In many cases, although it is frequently overlooked, outpatient psychotherapy may be the preferred means to alleviate the distress and enhance the functioning of those experiencing difficulties in adapting to the growing chain of losses as they move up in years.

Neurotic and Personality Disorders

Referrals or self-referrals of the elderly for neurotic-level disorders are very infrequent. This may be the case both because knowledge about normal aging makes it difficult to distinguish relatively mild disorders from age-related personality changes, and partly because very few are referred for treatment. The prevalence of diagnoses among the more therapy-minded younger persons within our society makes it likely, however, that treatment for neurotic problems in future cohorts of elderly women will increasingly be considered by the mental health professions.

Dementia

One of the most dreaded aspects of aging is what is variously termed "senility," chronic brain syndrome, Alzheimers disease, or dementia. Whatever it is called, this group of disorders consists of the impairment in intellectual functioning, memory loss, and disturbances in judgment. If one considers the entire range of dementias from mild through severe, then approximately 15% of persons over 60 are affected, as are 20% over 80 (Jarvik, Ruth, & Matsuyama, 1980). Contrary to the stereotype, not all individuals with organic brain disorder have an irreversible disease. Ten to 20% have disorders that are partly or fully reversible, attributable to factors such as infections, drug effects, social isolation, depression, feelings of incompetence, and finances (Eisdorfer & Cohen, 1978). Even among the irreversible dementias, there is little disagreement that many individuals manifest disabilities more severe than accounted for by the organic illness alone—a phenomenon termed "excess disability" (Brody, Kleban, Lawton, & Silverman, 1971). The existence of both reversible organic disorders and excess disability require careful individualized assessment and treatment of the individual, rather than the assumption, at the first signs of "senility" that the person is one of the "hopeless aged" (Kleban, Lawton, Brody, & Moss, 1975).

Elderly women are particularly likely to be given a diagnosis of dementia, with a ratio of women to men of 2 to 1 (Hess & Markson, 1980). Gruenberg (1977) speculates about some of the psychosocial factors that may impinge on the elderly poor, especially women, including those that may be associated with apparent "organic changes." He notes that an important stress may come from the loss of domestic roles as children leave and husbands die. While approximately 30% of women over 65 were in the workforce, for most, the domestic role was primary. Aged women are also more likely to have been widowed longer, less likely to be actively employed at present, poorer, and hence generally to be less optimally stimulated than are men.

Understimulation of the kind experienced by many older women has indeed been found to be related to apparent organicity. In an experimental situation Heron (1957) found that college students exposed over long periods of time to a very boring environment showed signs of impaired thinking, irritability, depression, and even hallucinations.

For the older woman, with a lesser educational background and less stimulation throughout her life than is true for most college students, isolation may leave few rich images on which to draw. Overstimulation may have adverse effects, as well. However, Patterson and Eberly (1983) have shown that older persons helped to prepare for the high level of arousal which often accompanies environmental change may be more successful at coping with that change. Furthermore, Kahana and Kahana (1983) have suggested that the reduction of excessive environmental demands has the potential to enhance adjustment by promoting person–environment fit.

An important note here for the mental health professions is that even the organically impaired older woman is able to articulate her feelings and preferences (Kahana & Kahana, 1983), and may have the capacity to benefit from therapy (Butler & Lewis, 1977).

FEMINIST CONSIDERATIONS IN THERAPY

All indicators point to a continued increase in the proportion of aged, at least for the next two to three decades. Attendant upon this increase, certain current problems will become even more acute. The current emphasis on custodial versus outpatient treatment will put an inordinate strain on already taxed and often inadequate facilities. The continued absence of a therapeutic orientation, in or outside of institutions, and the paucity of empirically based treatments and qualified personnel will further serve to hamper the delivery of needed services. Future cohorts of elderly women are likely to be less "poor, dumb, and ugly" (Troll, 1984), more therapy-minded and desirous of help to remain independent as long as possible. Hence, the need for qualified therapists sensitive to the needs and realities of the life circumstances of the older woman— whatever their theoretical orientations—may increase with each passing year.

Little empirical evidence exists regarding the relative efficacy of diverse treatments. However, there are preliminary indications that certain approaches hold promise. These include individual therapy, often short-term and problem-centered, and designed to overcome barriers to treatment. Hence, telephone sessions and home visits have been used for individuals with mobility or transportation problems; apparent success increases where emphasis is on the psychoeducational nature of the treatment, in order to counter the stigma of considering oneself a "patient." The mutual interaction of group therapy has been considered useful, as have innovative treatments such as assertiveness training, "friendly visiting," pet therapy, stress management, environmental intervention, mutual help groups, peer counseling, and involvement in meaningful activities on behalf of others (Butler & Lewis, 1977; Cormican, 1977; Gaitz, Popkin, Pino, & VandenBos, 1985; Kahana & Kahana, 1983; Midlarsky & Hannah, 1982; Midlarsky & Kahana, in press b; Sargent, 1980; Silverman, 1980).

In addition to the availability of a wide range of treatment options, the elderly woman in distress both needs and deserves therapists with preparation that goes beyond adequate technical education. Important additional therapist qualifications include genuine comprehension of the older woman's life situation, and willingness to listen to her with unbiased ears. Needed are mental health professionals who view impairment not as an inevitable "biological destiny" associated with aging, but rather as a potentially reversible problem, or at least one with which some individuals may learn to optimally cope. In contrast to the prevailing situation in which only the "unique" older woman—the aging poet, professional, or artist—is recognized as worthwhile, the sensitive therapist may help *each* woman to value the contribution that she has made—and may persist in making—to the well-being of others and ultimately, to her own (Midlarsky & Kahana, 1983). Recognition of one's own true value, as seen through the eyes of a nurturant other, may be a first step toward better adaptation by some older women.

Some general guidelines for the therapist working with elderly women are as follows:

1. *Be aware of ideals, stereotypes and beliefs that get in the way of treatment.* In addition to her awareness of sexism, and its adverse impact, the able therapist should familiarize herself with "agist" stereotypes. She should then become aware that she, herself, as a member of a younger cohort, may harbor unconscious, negative perceptions regarding older women—including the causes of their problems and the locus of responsibility for outcomes. Even the feminist therapist may view the older woman in accordance with a medical model, wherein problems are attributed to biological causes, and therefore deemed irreversible.

2. *Offer to provide training in assertiveness, problem solving, and decision making where it may be useful.* Even if "only" used in deciding that the habits of her roommate in her congregate housing arrangement are the source of much discomfort, and asserting her right to move, the woman's sense of accomplishment may overcome feelings of unmitigated helplessness.

3. *Understand that the current life situation of the elderly woman may be an important source of her problems.* The therapist needs to familiarize herself with the possible physical and environmental factors which help shape her client's responses. In order to be of help she

must understand that, unlike many realities of the younger adult years, many circumstances in the lives of older adults are intractable. In helping her client sort out which problems are due to her "inadequacies" and which are due to the conditions of her life, the therapist is likely to enhance the individual's self-concept and ability to cope.

4. *Gain perspective on the social and cultural conditions shaping the older woman's choices and their current outcomes.* The traditional therapist may start from the premise that the older woman is bitter due to lack of fulfillment if she never married and had children, or if she has been widowed for several years. He may feel that the solution is for her to engage in new heterosexual relations. The young feminist therapist, who has had extensive educational opportunities may mourn the "wasted talent" of a bright, older woman who never had meaningful work. Missing in both are awareness of certain realities—e.g., demographic realities regarding the male–female ratio in old age; the fact that even children of fine mothers may neglect them, and that the bright woman barely survived the war in Europe, had to be satisfied with her sixth-grade education and any job that would help pay her bills. The older woman needs and deserves support in developing interpersonal skills and self-concepts essential for enjoying her life, without having to deal with inappropriate and often inaccurate notions about her past failures and inadequacies.

5. *Develop awareness of the economic realities for the aged woman.* The relatively young and affluent therapist may be unaware that at least some of her client's emotional distress may come from having lived in a society which nurtures expectations of "payoffs" for being a "good woman." Yet many elderly women, who worked hard all of their lives, live now in relative poverty.

Needed above all, perhaps, is recognition that the elderly woman deserves more than simply to "live out her time." The best therapist may well be the one who fully accepts the idea that old age can be an active, productive, and enjoyable period in the life of each individual (Midlarsky & Kahana, in press,a,b). Here, as in younger clients, the role of the therapist may be not only to alleviate suffering, but to help every woman to enhance and enrich each moment of her life.

REFERENCES

Atchley, R. (1975). *The sociology of retirement.* Cambridge, MA: Schenkman.
Atchley, R. (1980). *The social forces in later life.* Belmont, CA: Wadsworth.
Blau, Z. (1973). *Old age in a changing society.* New York: New Viewpoints.

Blazer, D., & Williams, C. D. (1980). Epidemiology of dysphoria and depression in an elderly population. *American Journal of Psychiatry, 137,* 439–444.

Brody, E., Kleban, M., Lawton, M., & Silverman, H. (1971). Excess disabilities of mentally impaired aged. *Gerontologist, 11,* 124–133.

Burgess, E. W. (1960). Aging in western culture. In E. W. Burgess (Ed.), *Aging in western societies.* Chicago: University of Chicago Press.

Busse, E. W., & Pfeiffer, E. (1975). Functional psychiatric disorders in old age. In E. W. Busse & E. Pfeiffer (Eds.), *Behavior and adaptation in late life.* Boston: Little, Brown.

Butler, R. N., & Lewis, M. I. (1977). *Aging and mental health.* St. Louis: C. V. Mosby.

Clayton, P. R. (1973). The clinical morbidity of the first year of bereavement: A review. *Comprehensive Psychiatry, 14,* 151–157.

Cormican, E. J. (1977). Task centered approaches with the elderly. *Social Casework, 58*(8), 490–494.

Cumming, E., & Henry, W. H. (1961). *Growing old: The process of disengagement.* New York: Basic Books.

Cyrus–Lutz, C., & Gaitz, C. M. (1972). Psychiatrists' attitudes toward the aged and aging. *Gerontologist, 12,* 163–167.

Davis, L. J., & Brody, E. M. (1979). *Rape and older women: A guide to prevention and protection.* U. S. Department of Health, Education, and Welfare, National Institute of Mental Health, National Center for the Prevention and Control of Rape, Washington, DC: Superintendent of Documents, U.S. Government Printing Office.

de Beauvoir, S. (1972). *The coming of age.* New York: Putnam.

Duddle, C. M. (1982, February). Sexual problems of the elderly. Some practical solutions. *Geriatric Medicine.*

Eisdorfer, C., & Cohen, D. (1978). The cognitively impaired elderly: Differential diagnosis. In M. Storandt, I. Seigler, & M. F. Eliase (Eds.), *The clinical psychology of aging.* New York: Plenum.

Eisdorfer, C., & Cohen, D. (1982). *Mental health care of the aging.* New York: Springer.

Erikson, E. H. (1963). *Childhood and society.* New York: Norton.

Fields, M. D. (1976). Wife beating: The hidden offense. *New York Law Journal, 175*(83), 1–7.

Freud, S. (1959). On psychotherapy. In S. Freud, *Collected papers* (Vol. 1). London: Hogarth Press.

Gaitz, C. M. (1977). Depression in the elderly. In W. Fann, I. Koracan, A. Pokorny, & R. Williams (Eds.), *Phenomenology and treatment of depression.* New York: Spectrum.

Gaitz, C. M., Popkin, S. J., Pino, C. D., & VandenBos, G. R. (1985). Psychological interventions with older adults. In J. E. Birren & K. W. Schaie (Eds.), *The psychology of aging* (pp. 755–788). New York: Van Nostrand Reinhold.

Gruenberg, D. (1978). Epidemiology of senile dementia. In R. Katzman, R. Terry & K. Bick (Eds.), *Alzheimer's disease, senile dementia and related disorders.* New York: Raven Press.

Gruenberg, E. M. (1977). The failures of success. *Millbank Memorial Quarterly (Health and Society), 55*(1), 3–24.

Gurland, B., Dean, L., Cross, P., & Golden, R. (1980). The epidemiology of depression and dementia in the elderly: The use of multiple indicators of these conditions. In J. O. Cole & J. E. Barrett (Eds.), *Psychopathology in the aged.* New York: Raven Press.

Hanley, I., & Baikie, E. (1984). Understanding and treating depression in the elderly. In I. Hanley & J. Hodge (Eds.), *Psychological approaches to the care of the elderly* (pp. 213–236). New York: Methuen.

Harris, L. (and associates). (1975). *The myth and reality of aging in America.* Washington, DC: National Council on Aging.

Heron, W. (1957). The pathology of boredom. *Scientific American, 196*(1), 52–56.

Hess, B. B., & Markson, E. W. (1980). *Aging and old age.* New York: Macmillan.

Hooyman, N. R., Rathbone-McCuan, E., & Klingbeil, K. (1982). Serving the vulnerable elderly: The detection, intervention and prevention of familial abuse. *Urban & Social Change Review, 15*(2), 9–14.

Jacobs, S., & Ostfeld, A. (1977). An epidemiological review of the mortality of bereavement. *Psychosomatic Medicine, 39,* 344–357.

Jarvik, L. F., Ruth, V., & Matsuyama, S. (1980). Organic brain syndrome and aging. *Archives of General Psychiatry, 37,* 280–286.

Kahana, B., & Kahana, E. (1983). Stress reactions. In P. M. Lewinsohn & L. Teri (Eds.), *Clinical Geropsychology* (pp. 116–138). New York: Pergamon.

Kahana, E., & Coe, R. M. (1969). Self and staff conceptions of institutionalized aged. *Gerontologist, 9,* 164–267.

Kay, D. (1977). The epidemiology of brain deficit in the aged. In C. Eisdorfer & R. O. Freedle (Eds.), *The cognitively and emotionally impaired aged.* Chicago: Yearbook Medical Publications.

Kidd, C. B. (1982). Misplacement of the elderly in hospitals. A study of patients admitted to geriatric and mental hospitals. *British Medical Journal, 5318,* 1491–1495.

Kleban, M. H., Lawton, M. P., Brody, E. M., & Moss, M. (1975). Characteristics of the mentally impaired aged profiting from individualized treatment. *Journal of Gerontology, 30,* 90–96.

Langer, E. J. (1980). *Old age: An artifact?* Washington, DC: National Research Council.

Langer, E. J., & Rodin, J. (1976). The effects of choice and enhanced personal responsibility for the aged. *Journal of Personality & Social Psychology, 34,* 191–198.

Lawton, M. P. (1976). Geropsychological knowledge as a background for psychotherapy with older people. *Journal of Geriatric Psychiatry, 9,* 221–223.

Lesnoff-Caravaglia, G. (Ed.). (1984a). *The world of the older woman: Conflicts and resolutions.* New York: Human Sciences Press.

Lesnoff-Caravaglia, C. (1984b). Double stigmata: Female and old. In G. Lesnoff-Caravaglia, (Ed.), *The world of the older woman* (pp. 11–20). New York: Human Sciences Press.

Lesnoff-Caravaglia, G. (1984c). Widowhood: The last stage in wifedom. In G. Lesnoff-Caravaglia (Ed.), *The world of the older woman (pp. 137–143).* New York: Human Sciences Press.

Livson, F. B. (1978). Problems of personality development in middle-aged women: A longitudinal study. In J. Hendricks (Ed.), *Being and becoming old* (pp. 133–140). Farmingdale, NY: Baywood.

Lopata, H. Z. (1973). *Widowhood in an American city.* Cambridge, MA: Schenkman.

Lopata, H. (1975). Couple-companionate relationships in marriage and widowhood. In N. Glazer–Malbin (Eds.), *Old family/New Family* (Chap. 5). New York: VanNostrand.

Lopata, H. Z. (1979). *Women as widows.* New York: Elsevier.

Lowenthal, M. J., & Berkman, P. (1967). *Aging and mental disorder.* San Francisco: Jossey–Bass.

Lowenthal, M., Thurnher, B., & Chiriboga, D. (1975). *Four stages of life.* San Francisco: Jossey–Bass.

Malinchak, A. (1980). *Crime and gerontology.* Englewood Cliffs, NJ: Prentice–Hall.

Masters, W. H., & Johnson, V. E. (1981). Sex and the aging process. *Journal of the American Geriatric Society, 29*(9), 383–390.

Midlarsky, E. (1977). Women, psychopathology, and psychotherapy. *JSAS: Catalog of Selected Documents in Psychology, 96,* 191–196.

Midlarsky, E. (1980). Research on rape. In R. Green & J. Weiner (Eds.), *Methodology in sex research.* Washington, DC: U.S. Government Printing Office.

Midlarsky, E., & Hannah, M. E. (1982). Innovations in mental health. *Journal of Psychiatric Treatment & Evaluation, 4,* 417–422.

Midlarsky, E., & Kahana, E. (1983). Helping by the elderly: Conceptual and empirical considerations. In M. Kleiman (Ed.), *Interdisciplinary Topics in Gerontology* (Vol. 17, pp. 10–24). Basel, Switzerland: S. Karger.

Midlarsky, E., & Kahana, E. (in press a). Altruistic lifestyles: A contributory model of late life adaptation. *Gerontology Review.*

Midlarsky, E., & Kahana, E. (in press b). *For the sake of others: Altruism and helping by the elderly.* Beverly Hills, CA: Sage.

Moss, Z. (1970). It hurts to be alive and obsolete, or, the aging woman. In P. Morgan (Ed.), *Sisterhood is powerful.* New York: Vintage Books.

Nathanson, P. (1984). Legal issues affecting older women. In G. Lesnoff–Caravaglia (Ed.), *The world of the older woman* (pp. 71–91). New York: Human Sciences Press.

Patterson, R. L., & Eberly, D. A. (1983). Social and daily living skills. In C. M. Lewinsohn & L. Teri (Eds.), *Clinical geropsychology (pp. 116–138).* New York: Pergamon.

Pfouts, J. H. (1978). Violent families: Coping responses of abused wives. *Child Welfare, 27*(2), 32–43.

Post, F. (1982). Functional disorders. In R. Levy & F. Post (Eds.), *The psychiatry of late life* (pp. 197–221). Oxford: Blackwell Scientific Publications.

Rathbone-McCuan, E. (1980). Elderly victims of family violence and neglect. *Social Case Work, 61*(5), 196–304.

Rathbone-McCuan, E. (1984). The abused older woman—A discussion of abuses and rape. In G. Lesnoff-Caravaglia (Ed.), *The world of the older woman* (pp. 49–70). New York: Human Sciences Press.

Rathbone-McCuan, E., & Voyles, B. (1982). Case detection of abused elderly parents. *American Journal of Psychiatry, 139*(2), 189–192.

Resick, P. A. (1983). Sex-role stereotypes and violence against women. In V. Franks & E. D. Rothblum (Eds.), *The stereotyping of women*. New York: Springer.

Santos, J. F., & VandenBos, R. (1982). *Psychology and the older adult.* Washington, DC: American Psychological Association.

Sargent, S. S. (Ed.). (1980). *Nontraditional therapy and counseling with the aged.* New York: Springer.

Silverman, P. R. (1972). Widowhood and preventive intervention. *Family Coordinator, 21,* 95–102.

Silverman, P. R. (1980). *Mutual helpgroups: Organization and development.* Beverly Hills, CA: Sage.

Silverman, P. R., & Cooperband, A. (1984). Widow to widow. The elderly widow and mutual help. In G. Lesnoff-Caravaglia (Ed.), *The world of the older woman* (pp. 144–161). New York: Human Sciences Press.

Simpson, S., Woods, R. T., & Britton, P. G. (1981). Depression and engagement in a residential home for the elderly. *Behavior Research & Therapy, 19,* 435–438.

Steinhauer, M. B., & Auslander, S. S. (1984). Policy directions and program design: Issues and implications in services for older women. In G. Lesnoff-Caravaglia (Ed.), *The world of older women* (pp. 175–186). New York: Human Sciences Press.

Storandt, M., Siegler, I. C., & Eliase, M. F. (Eds.). (1978). *The clinical psychology of aging,* New York: Plenum.

Streib, G. G., & Schneider, C. J. (1971). *Retirement in American society.* Ithaca, NY: Cornell University.

Troll, L. E. (1984). The psychosocial problems of the older woman. In G. Lesnoff–Caravaglia (Ed.), *The world of the older woman* (pp. 21–35). New York: Human Sciences Press.

Turner, R. J., & Sternberg, M. P. (1978). Psychosocial factors in elderly patients admitted to a psychiatric hospital. *Age & Aging, 7,* 171–177.

U. S. Bureau of the Census. (1981). *Statistical Abstract of the United States.* 102nd Ed., Washington, DC.

Vinick, B. (1978). Remarriage in old age. *Family Coordinator, 27*(4), 359–363.

Walker, L. E. (1979). *The battered woman.* New York: Harper & Row.

White, C. B. (1982). Sexual interest, attitudes, knowledge and sexual history in relation to sexual behavior in the institutionalized age. *Archives of Sexual Behavior, 11,* 11–21.

Winn, R. L., & Newton, N. (1982). Sexuality in aging: A study of 106 cultures. *Archives of Sexual Behavior, 11,* 283–298.

Zarit, S. (1980). *Aging and mental disorders.* New York: Free Press.

CHAPTER 13

Future Directions: Development, Application, and Training of Feminist Therapies

Lenore E. A. Walker
Mary Ann Dutton Douglas

INTRODUCTION

Feminist therapy has developed as a response to the deficiencies in mainstream therapies which reflected biases against women. Its development has paralleled the rise of the women's movement in America. Much of the early, first generation development came out of a grassroots support system first revealed in the Consciousness-Raising (C-R) groups of the late 1960's. There, like in the groups set up during the Chinese Revolution from which the C-R group was modelled, women spoke "bitterness" or told the ugly side of how their lives were for them. While their personal stories were each seen as individually important, put together the stories had a major political impact by documenting the harm done to women in the name of therapy.

At first, excuses were made for the stories that trickled out of those groups. The mental health establishment responded by blaming individuals recognizing there are always bad therapists. Individual women's credibility was attacked by presenting accusations or evidence of their other deviant behavior. Women "libbers" were labeled pejoratively, as man-hating, bitter, bra-burning, unnatural women in an attempt to discredit their voices. But, the groundswell would not be quieted, the personal became political and women who had their consciousness raised stopped going to the most blatant sexist therapists. From both inside and outside of the mental health profession, a search began for more women-oriented approaches to therapy, ones which would support women's positive mental health, help reverse the negative effects of living in a sexist society, and overcome personal challenges.

Unfortunately, in those early days only a small portion of women were impacted by the early wave of feminist activity, leaving the mainstream of women unaware of the accusations against traditional psychotherapy's mislabelling, conforming to patriarchal status quo, medication pushing, and androcentric-biased therapy. Phyllis Chesler's book, *Myth of Madness,* published in 1972, documented the terrible abuse of women in the name of therapy. Women who did not conform to the rigid sex-role expectations were labelled mentally ill, ostracized in the community and warehoused in institutions. The Broverman et al. (1970) study documented the dual standard of mental health norms for males and females. Adoption of these norms was thought of as necessary to be considered a healthy person, but they were different than women's norms. This reflects the double-bind for women as the dominant culture's expectation is that women's primary roles are to serve men and children. The American Psychological Association (APA), the largest of the mental health scientist/practitioner organizations, appointed a task force to document sex-bias or sex-role stereotyping which existed in psychotherapeutic practice among psychologists (APA, 1975). Their report cited numerous examples of how traditional psychotherapy fostered adaptation to these double standards in both direct and subtle ways. Although psychoanalysis was singled out as particularly offensive because its theory has so many blatantly sexist assumptions, numerous other techniques were also cited, with examples continuing to be published (APA, 1978).

THE RISE AND FALL OF THE MEDICAL MODEL

This period of naming the biases in psychotherapeutic practice coincides with two other major influences of the times. First, was the anti-psychiatry and anti-medical model of mental diseases and second, was the rise in the number of women, especially feminist identified women, in the psychological profession. The rise of treatment for mental disease took a giant leap forward in the 1950's in America when returning World War II combat soldiers filled the veteran's hospitals for treatment of emotionally based disorders. Congress appropriated training money and psychologists, social workers, and psychiatric nurses joined the medical doctors in providing hospital based and out-patient treatment. The discovery of major tranquilizers at this time revolutionized the delivery of mental health services along the medical profession model.

Soon critics of this system began to appear and doctors such as R.D. Laing (1967) and Thomas Szaz (1961) publicly questioned the usefulness of a disease model to explain responses to difficult environmental conditions. Psychologists such as Rogers (1951) added empirical data to demonstrate that a different kind of intervention might be sufficient to facilitate positive mental health growth. Rogers believed that the observed symptoms may be indicative of a blockage in the person's striving for such growth. Therapy need only help remove the blockage and the person can go on to fully function again. Restructuring personality was not seen as necessary. A whole group of newer therapies constituting what came to be known as the human potential movement and including such therapies as sensitivity training, gestalt, and other existential, body-mind techniques grew as an alternative to the psychodynamic, pathology based model. Although these therapies enjoyed popularity and competed with the more internal psychodynamic systems, all were based on the norms for the healthy adult who had the characteristics of males and not of females. This situation is even further compounded when we realize that more women than men use the mental health system, a trend noted after the initial use by veterans in the 1950's (cf. Russo, 1984). In fact, estimates range that as high as 70% of all mental health consumers are women. Yet, then as now, there was no systematic training required in the psychology of women.

DEVELOPMENT OF FEMINIST THERAPY THEORY

The growth of powerful women leaders with a feminist theoretical orientation occurred in all the psychotherapy professions, although they were most visible in organized psychology. Fresh from experiencing gender bias in their own graduate training programs, this first generation of large numbers of women trying to develop a psychology career with few female role models, began to congregate together at professional meetings for mutual support. They found each other in the way most grassroots organizations begin; usually by talking aloud to their neighbors in the few programs which challenged prevailing sexist assumptions. In 1969, the Association for Women in Psychology (AWP) was founded and in 1972 those AWP members who were also APA members successfully petitioned the APA to form a division to study the psychology of women—Division 35. Here women psychologists with feminist political views could find like-minded women (and men) to share ideas about research, training and application of scientific, psychological information about the human behavior of one-half of the population. A review of APA annual convention programs from that year forward demonstrate the knowledge explosion about the new psychology of women.

The biases pointed out by the earlier feminists became the subject of countless scientific studies. The results confirmed women's stories. Psychological truths based on male standards were simply inadequate at best and harmful at worst to explain and help resolve women's psychological dilemmas (Franks & Burtle, 1976; Rawlings & Carter, 1977; Franks & Rothblum, 1983). Social psychologists studied differences in the way women and men behaved in a variety of situations (Frieze et al, 1978; O'Leary, Unger, & Wallston, 1985), developmental psychologists began to study women's life cycle and found it to be different than the Piagetian or Freudian models (cf. Silverman & Conarton, Chapter 3), and clinical psychologists began to measure the differences in the therapy experience for men and women (cf. Walker, 1984). Much of this early work is reviewed in the theory chapters of this book. But, the side of the story rarely told is how those early women psychology researchers emotionally supported each other when supervisors, department chairs, local faculty, and colleagues were indifferent or even hostile to this new women's scholarship. As new empirical data became available to support the feminist position (cf. McHugh, Koeske, & Frieze, 1986), a quiet but powerful revolution was fueled, not just in professional clinical areas but in all of scientific psychology.

Psychoanalysis was found to be most filled with androcentric bias, not a big surprise since the theory rests on the belief that mental illness is caused by repression into the unconscious of memories (real or imagined) and frequently this includes memories of real, not imagined, sexual assaults which occurred when the woman was a child. Psychoanalysis rests on a verbal cathartic method which facilitates the accessibility of repressed material. The fact that the repressed material for women frequently included memories of real sexual assault which were traumatic for the victim and impacted on her future development still has not yet been adequately addressed by present day psychoanalysts.

FIRST GENERATION FEMINIST THERAPY THEORY

Feminist therapists began to design better therapy systems reflecting the early feminist's political as well as psychological views. Lerman (1976) was one of the earliest authors to write about the need to have a clear feminist philosophy. This meant adopting an active stance toward resolving the inequality between women and men, because of the belief that inequality itself causes mental health problems. Rawlings

& Carter (1977) clarify the difference between a nonsexist and a feminist philosophy holding that a feminist adds the political activism as a treatment component. Although clients are not expected to become political activists, a common misunderstanding in the early days, they are exposed to such possible activism as an empowerment technique. Political activism is offered as simply one more option in a whole array of alternatives from which to pick and chose on the way to becoming a whole, psychologically independent person. Although in the beginning, feminist therapists were unlikely to fully disclose all of the negative consequences of political activism, usually because they too were naive and unaware of the harshness of the punishment meted out by the dominant culture, (as Fodor discusses in Chapter 5) today both the positive and negative consequences are presented and in some cases even modelled.

Feminist therapy techniques are fairly well known and discussed more fully by Cammaert & Larsen, in Chapter 2. The personal is political which means that the woman is encouraged to tell her story and bond together with other women to form collective power. There is an attempt to be egalitarian and deal directly with power relationships. Therapists are encouraged to use self disclosure when necessary or at the very least, to place their values out in the open for scrutiny. The notion that therapists could be value-free or even neutral, no matter how much psychoanalysis they personally experience, was rejected. Science simply reflects the dominant culture's bias in ordering facts to find "truth" and in this case it is an androcentric cultural bias that places an undue reliance in quantitative and experimental methodology (cf. McHugh, et al., 1986).

Although feminist therapists rejected much of the current therapy theories as gender-biased, the therapy techniques were not totally discarded. The verbal cathartic method was still used, although free association was given less importance than a mutually active therapy process. Women's experiences were validated by listening to them and acknowledging their importance. Change was seen as being initiated in either the affective, cognitive, or behavioral domains and then generalized to the other areas. The therapist was viewed as a role model, facilitator or teacher, more than a neutral stimulus on which to transfer unresolved feelings or expected to become a "mother" or "father" surrogate.

While the therapeutic relationship was accorded importance, it was not expected that all therapy work could be accomplished through the spontaneous recreation of old, faulty learnings or experiences using the therapist–client relationship process. Bibliotherapy, body work, dream analysis, political analysis, skill enhancement, and crisis intervention became important techniques beyond the traditional ones. Changing faulty thinking patterns and attitudes is a cornerstone in feminist therapy. Separating women's internal world from overt oppression experienced daily became a major goal of feminist therapy.

Sensitivity to other forms of oppression against women, for example, major responsibility for parenting children and reproductive issues, as well as to oppression of other groups defined by race, ethnic and cultural minority, sexual orientation, age, or physical able bodiness, became hallmarks of the feminist contribution to all therapies. By picking and choosing appropriate techniques from the mainstream theories, first generation feminist therapy developed as a hybrid. Its philosophy came from feminist political analysis and its applied techniques came from the best of those already available in the broader therapy community. The theories upon which feminist therapists relied remained multiple as feminists had not yet addressed the revision of theories to fit compatibly with feminist philosophy.

SECOND GENERATION FEMINIST THERAPY

The second generation of feminist therapy development, which is represented in this volume, came about in the 1980's as feminists attempted to revise mainstream therapy theories in response to first generation feminist criticism. Along with the conservative political climate within the United States, came reprisals and cutting back of openly feminist political activities. Actually, many of the feminist political leaders took the movement and mainstreamed it to all women. This slowed the growth of new ideas but hastened its spread and widened its sphere of influence. Ideas of revolution were replaced by strategies to slowly move into positions of power. Women began moving up the corporation ladders, became entrepreneurs, professionals, and other wage earners, and entered the mainstream political arena. To be sure, backlashes have occurred, and new, strong, feminist identities have had to withstand the strong conservative trend to get women back into the preferred role of serving the patriarchy. Feminist therapy has not only survived this onslaught but has thrived. In 1982, the Feminist Therapy Institute, an international organization, was formed to be a place where theory, techniques, and training could be fostered. Growth of positive applications, rather than continued criticisms of what is wrong with mainstream therapy, characterizes this second phase of development.

Some of the most exciting applications of feminist theory appear in this book. Daugherty and Lees in chapter 3 discuss the movement in psychoanalysis away from Freudian orthodoxy as feminist psychoanalysts began to modify both the theory and techniques used. The work of personality theorists challenged the Freudian concept of personality development where women were seen as unfulfilled until they bore a male child with the coveted penis they supposedly lost. Some suggest such a theoretical construct only served to cover up adult male sexual exploitation of children: both girls and boys. Herman, (1981), Lerman, (1985), Masson, (1984) and Rush (1980) all present different facets of the argument, only made possible, however, with Freud's original contribution acknowledging childhood sexuality. Carmen et al. (1984) findings of the high percentage of those inpatients in mental hospitals who were sexually and physically abused as children make us wonder why so many elaborate diagnostic labels needed to be created simply to explain the various psychological effects of exposure to violence exploitation and powerlessness.

Learning to understand how personal feelings develop and impact on emotional well-being has been an enduring feature of the psychodynamic approach. The work of psychoanalytic revisionists such as Jean Baker Miller (1976, 1986) and her colleagues at the Stone Center (Kaplan and Surrey, 1984; Jordan, 1984) has challenged the analytic establishment to revise its theories of healthy ego development. Originally coming from concepts about healthy separation and individuation leading to a person's autonomy, the revisionists suggest that, at least for women, a relational ego growing out of concepts about attachment and relatedness is more accurate. It is too soon to tell if such integration is possible to justify Daugherty and Lees' optimism that a feminist psychoanalysis is possible.

The addition of systematic analysis of both cognition and behavior has been a major contribution of the behavioral school of therapy. As Fodor describes in Chapter 5, understanding how women learn social messages has been crucial in designing ways to overcome the negative sex role socialization. Behaviorism explains the conditioning process by which we adapt to sex role standards and provides for the analysis of shaping and extinction techniques to adopt new beliefs and behavior patterns. The concept of cognitive restructuring, whereby faulty beliefs are replaced by more women's experience, has been an important technique incorporated into feminist therapy. Like all techniques, it can be used to support any particular ideology. The emphasis on cognition adopted by the cognitive behavior therapists is an area that has been heavily influenced by the feminists as the theory developed. But, as Fodor so aptly points out, other areas in behaviorism have not undergone the same feminist scrutiny. The very techniques of applied behavioral analysis utilize the traditional empirical concepts which are value-laden with dominant patriarchal standards as discussed further on. Cognitive-behavior therapy has contributed the notion that action, not just process, is responsible for the therapeutic changes observed. The integration of emotion, as a domain equal to behavior and cognition, is an area of the theory which is still necessary to make it more compatible with feminist sensitivities.

The recognition that women, like all people, live within a complex system of interrelatedness has been an important contribution of systems theory, usually employed by family therapists. Bograd, in Chapter 6, analyzes the benefits of thinking about women in context but clearly points out the system's therapists intentional and perhaps, unwitting reinforcement of sexism in that context. Failure to utilize a feminist political analysis of the family system perpetuates the patriarchal order and continues women's oppression. Noted family therapists are actually hostile to feminism, recognizing its ideology calls for reform in their theories. For example, Minuchin (1985) in his book *Kaleidoscope* actually analyzes a case of an adolescent daughter who is hostile to her abusive father. He says it is the mother's fault for preventing the father/daughter relationship from developing appropriately. The mother's protection of her child from the father's violence is pathologized while the father's brutality is ignored, exonerating him from having to experience its consequences, one of which might be the current loss of his daughter's love and companionship. This kind of myopia must coninue to be challenged to help family systems theory reach its potential to enhance the quality of life for all family members, not just for men and children to be served by women in the typical patriarchal style.

Even feminists get caught up in the ease of functional system's analysis, as Bograd discusses, and can succumb to the popular codependency theories. For example, much of the recent work in the field of addiction treatment falls into the seductive codependency trap resulting in blaming women for staying in relationships with an alcoholic or other drug dependent partner. Lost is the needed feminist analysis which provides the cultural understanding for why most women desire to stay with partners, even those in addictive and abusive relationship patterns. Certainly, a feminist analysis modifies the techniques needed to help women heal from exposure to nurturing through a drug-induced, or other addictive, fog. Pathologizing women for not changing powerful societal influences which keep them in self-destructive addictive cycles reinforces feelings of helplessness instead of providing the re-empowerment needed to move toward positive mental health growth.

Co-dependency like traditional systems theories still needs a thorough feminist scrutiny by feminist visions. An important feminist principle to include is to address the relationship by first strengthening its individual members as equally viable human beings. Then, when each member has made some critical independent changes, developed some new skills, and feels empowered, they can come together again with a focus on analyzing desired system changes to promote maintenance of individual as well as system growth.

Other therapy theories have also been challenged and in varying degrees have been impacted by feminist critique. Jungian theory, thought by some to be relatively gender neutral because of its emphasis on a balance between the masculine and feminine energies, has benefited from a feminist analysis of what constitutes the feminine. Silverman and Conarton in Chapter 3 present a popular Jungian myth with a new feminist interpretation. The prize of ointments found in the box were originally seen as desirable because they could enhance woman's innate beauty, but in the feminist version their symbolism has been reinterpreted as desirable because they could enhance woman's innate healing ability. The Humanistic School of therapy encompassing Gestalt, Rogerian, and Existential theories have received feminist criticism that its attempt to enhance all human potential is too often translated to mean enhancing only man's potential because when women are subsumed under the generic man, their concerns are frequently unmet. Leaders in this theoretical school frequently insist that a feminist analysis biases the more neutral human emphasis and, thus feminism is unnecessary. As the influence of this group has been more indirect than for other therapy theories, serious feminist challenges have not yet been mounted.

Perhaps the area where the human potential movement has been most impacted is in its openness about sensual touch in group therapy sessions. In recognition of the negative psychological effects of misinterpretation or deliberate crossing of boundaries into a sexual relationship, those therapies advocating freer sensual and sexual expression have had to change their techniques. Large financial awards to clients who have been sexually exploited by a therapist have persuaded even those therapists who did not like or agree with this feminist analysis to modify their behavior. Empirical data documenting the harm and legal penalties (cf. Bouhoustos, 1984) overcame the few resistant self-serving proponents. Thus, second generation feminist therapy theory has made major impacts in virtually all therapy techniques and subsequently, in theory, during this second generation mainstreaming effort.

THIRD GENERATION FEMINIST THERAPY THEORY

As the preceding commentary indicates, second generation feminist therapy theory has developed from the introduction of feminist therapy into traditional therapy theories. The third generation has just begun with the attempts to form a complete feminist psychological theory of women's development integrated together with theories about change and emotional growth. Thus, a reintegration of feminist political analysis blended together with the scientific data about the psychology of women and the knowledge about the psychological impact of various life experiences, including socio-cultural factors on woman's development, forms the basis of feminist psychological theory. The developments of a feminist psychological theory will provide a more complete basis from which to further develop the practice and evaluation of feminist therapy. The feminist theory building thus far has been focused on the women's development. What is yet needed, beyond further elaboration of feminist theory of women's development, is a feminist theory of male behavior. It is when an adequate feminist theory of both female and male behavior exists that we can most effectively derive therapy techniques for helping women and men in their efforts toward change and personal growth.

Some criticize this theory-building process as the reverse of how theories usually develop; usually theory comes before its applications. But, feminist therapy developed out of a dissatisfaction with other therapy theories' techniques. It came out of a grassroots movement which concentrated on an activist not contemplative approach. An already established political philosophy served as its conceptual anchor. The urgency of finding ways to fix women's broken lives had priority. It has taken the newer developments created by second generation feminist therapy theorists to excite others to the need for a theory of our own (Brown, 1986, Lerman, 1976, 1986, Rosewater, 1984). The skeleton of such a theory is presented throughout this book.

The understanding of development of womens' personality, different from the previous male standard, has begun by those feminists trained in several different theoretical schools. Silverman and Conarton outline phases which contribute to female development in this theory. The eight phases are: (1) bonding, (2) orientation toward others, (3) cultural adaptation, (4) awakening and separation, (5) development of the feminine, (6) empowerment, (7) spiritual development and, (8) integration. The energy source is open-ended with a natural propulsion toward curiosity and growth. A primary striving is toward relatedness and connection with others in a meaningful contextual environment. This connectedness needs to be in balance with careful boundaries between self and others—a life-long struggle. Socialization occurs according to the appropriate learning paradigms which encompass all variables in the context, not just those easy to measure or which have special therapeutic approval. Emotional and social growth interact with biological factors to produce unique personalities. Emotional sensitivity propels movement to higher stages of development although movement through the eight phases can be considered a continuous spiral repeating themselves at deeper or more particularized levels, as conceptualized by Silverman and Conarton.

Healthy development includes a pluralistic focus on oneself in relation to family. As Mays and Comas-Dias point out, in Chapter 11, the feminist definition of multicultural family systems includes members who have multiple and flexible roles. Community, again defined as pluralistic, and one's responsibilities to others, as well as to oneself, are also important factors in development. Autonomy is only valued insofar as its contribution to interdependent relationships. That is, women must be empowered and sufficiently skilled to function independently or autonomously at times but also as part of a complex interdependent system at other times. Autonomy for its own sake is not seen as a natural feminine state (Kaplan and Surrey, 1984).

Development under this model is seen to proceed in a somewhat orderly fashion with relatedness and emotional intimacy occurring first and separation and individuation only occurring as it becomes necessary to fit into an androcentric social system. We suggest that women develop dual personality systems, one to function within women's worlds and one to function within the dominant culture. As women impact on the dominant culture changing the androcentric bias, there will be more integration in their own personality development. It is the current lack of integration that frequently gets labelled as personality disorders today. Identity as a woman begins early in this model, as it occurs in the second stage when intimacy becomes differentiated. Her identity continues to unfold as the woman moves in and out of all the developmental phases. Sexuality, which is a form of intimacy, may develop out of sequence causing emotional intimacy and boundary problems should sexual exploitation or abuse occur in childhood. Caretakers need to provide a violence free environment where children gradually obtain power over their lives for optimum emotional growth to occur.

The concept of spirituality is an important phase of development for women. Silverton and Conarton suggest it does not have full meaning until well into the middle adult years. But, the belief in a Greater Being and other spirituality occurs in many young girls, particularly those who chose to be nuns or leaders within organized religions (Hendricks, 1984). The concept of different levels of consciousness which are accessible to the woman using various techniques is a more feminist concept than a single unconscious which is seen as largely inaccessible without a therapist's help. Again, the notion of continuously spiraling through these developmental phases, stopping to develop any one at a particularly relevant time is a part of this integrated theory.

An integrated feminist therapy theory might look at emotional disorders as a disruption of "normal" development within a particular social/environmental system. That is, for example, "normal" development within what kind of social/environmental system? Can we expect to rear girl children in an environment which we would consider "normal" at this point? We think not, since misogynous culture is not "normal" or healthy for women (or men). However, even given these limitations, certain events can be expected to disrupt any development. Therapy techniques, in this system, would be selected according to the disruption. Crisis intervention would be the treatment of choice if a woman is battered or raped. The goal is to help her regain her own sense of power, to keep herself safe and get on with life. Sometimes the best way to empower the woman is to refer her to a battered women's shelter which provides her with physical safety and group support. Other times, it might be to give her voice so her story is heard in a court proceeding through the therapist's expert witness testimony. Anxiety or panic disorders might be treated using a cognitive behavioral therapy approach along with an analysis of earlier developmental disruptions and sociocultural conditioning. Treatment for bipolar affective disorders might use a combination of anti-depressant medication, a feminist analysis of environmental conditions which could cause depression, and cognitive behavioral techniques to change faulty thinking patterns. Basically, the feminist treatment approach would include a holistic analysis of stressors from both inside and outside the person.

Although all persons probably can benefit from integrated feminist treatment approach, it is particularly useful with special populations who may fall outside of mainstream American values. This includes men who wish to integrate their emotional side with their more intellectualized male value system so as to become egalitarian partners as Ganley describes in Chapter 9. Or, it may address the real stressors for women raising children without the help of a loving partner, and in some cases, trying to protect children from abusive fathers as Rawlings presents in Chapter 8. Lesbian and gay affirming therapies have many similarities to feminist therapy. Brown, in Chapter 10, discusses the sensitivity of feminist therapy to lesbian women's issues. The Feminist Therapy Institute has expended much energy to avoid the polarization that characterized earlier political groups between heterosexual and lesbian women (cf. Rosewater & Walker, 1985). Mays and Comas-Dias's Chapter 11, analyzing the usefulness of feminist therapy with women of color is a welcome addition to the literature. Although espousing anti-racist values, feminist therapy is just beginning to address the specific issues of oppression for racial and ethnic minority women. Feminist theory embraces the pluralistic values; the therapy techniques operationalize them. Midlarsky makes it clear in Chapter 12 that feminist therapy has yet to integrate its anti-ageist values into appropriate therapy techniques with the growing elderly population.

EMPIRICAL TESTING OF THE FEMINIST THERAPY THEORY MODEL

The next step after filling in the skeletal model of feminist theory articulated in the previous section is to empirically test it. Here feminist research psychologists have provided useful new guidelines to promote sex-fair research. McHugh, et al. (1986) review and build upon the work of Frieze et al (1978), Grady (1981), O'Leary, Unger & Wallston (1985), Sherman & Denmark (1978), Unger (1979), Wallston (1981) and others, mostly social psychologists and non-therapists who caution against using sex-biased methods to test our theories. There are suggestions for avoiding excessive confidence in traditional methods, care in examining exploratory models and learning to interpret with a clear recognition of areas in which researchers are cautioned so as to conduct non-sexist evaluations.

The questions which need to be addressed include a testing of the feminist therapy theory against older, more well-known therapy theory models to determine if the model can stand alone and if it accounts for elements others have determined belong in a therapy theory. Corey (1977) provides a clear outline for evaluating the key concepts in the psychotherapy systems. He suggests using such key concepts in the personality theory, the philosophical assumptions, and the actual therapeutic approaches used by proponents. Since the feminist therapy theory proposes a spiral development model that is both circular and flows up and down, non-linear measures will need to be used to empirically test variables at the different levels. Some of the more advanced statistical analyses in multivariate analysis and causal modeling might be appropriate. Variables to measure include the comprehensiveness of the feminist mental health theory, efficacy of techniques to enhance positive growth in that system, efficacy of techniques to change the impact of sexist attitudes, thinking patterns, and behaviors, techniques to keep oneself safe from others and from one's own destructive actions, and so on. Eventually, it may be possible to attempt to measure the efficacy of feminist therapy as compared to other treatment alternatives.

Care, of course, must be taken to avoid the pitfalls which have plagued other therapy outcome researchers (cf. Johnson & Auerbach, 1984). Few clear effects have been found when comparing different therapy processes. However, other variables such as age and experience of males doing therapy with females have been found to be a factor. Young, inexperienced male therapists have been found to be the least effective with women clients regardless of their theoretical perspective (Orlinsky & Howard, 1980). Some have suggested these men be prohibited from providing psychotherapy to women until they grow older and gain experience by practicing on other men! Another alternative may be to include specific components geared to redress their deficiencies while they are still in training programs. With newer research suggesting that androgynous sex role attitudes may be more influential in determining therapy outcome than gender alone (Beutler, Crago & Arizmendi, 1986), the importance of directly addressing trainees' stereotype sex role attitudes in psychotherapy training becomes empirically established. This is one example of feminist influence on both the evaluation and training of mainstream psychotherapy.

MAINSTREAMING TRAINING IN FEMINIST THERAPY

There are three major arguments that need to be resolved before feminist therapy training is mainstreamed in traditional graduate programs. The first is the need to demonstrate relevance of such mainstreaming; the second, is the philosophical debate between the segrationists and the integrationists; and the third is the determination of whether any form of psychotherapy is consistent with feminist ideals.

The first argument is an old one whereby keepers of the tradition ask the change agents to demonstrate the expected positive effects of the proposed changes. In this arena, graduate department chairs have been notoriously reluctant to let anything new into an already established curriculum. So, by virtue of being near the end of a long list of "musts" that students must learn, even the most persuasive arguments don't bring results. After all, how much more persuasive data can be obtained than the above-cited therapy outcome studies. Training in the psychology of women should be a core topic and not placed in the elective category. Male students should be exposed to feminist supervisors and feminist theory throughout their training. So should women students. Perhaps any program which fails to demonstrate the presence of feminist faculty, qualified to teach and provide supervision in feminist clinical practice and research, should be considered to be in violation of accreditation standards. Here even the liberal trainers begin to disagree, citing traditional academic freedom arguments as a defense. Currently, the APA is considering a proposal to expand the accreditation process. Perhaps they will be persuaded by feminist scholars and activists to include mandating a portion of the curriculum to mastery of the psychology of women. But, this approval doesn't resolve the lack of attention given to the new feminist scholarship in the other mental health disciplines, especially psychiatry.

Those disciplines requiring a licensing examination prior to independent practice could encourage candidates to learn about feminist theory by testing them on a certain body of required knowledge. In fact, a few such questions are now routinely asked on the national examination for psychology licensure. But, no data are available to support if there is a greater likelihood of proper application of the knowledge base to the women they treat. Another method is to more fully educate consumers, a tactic used by several groups of women professionals. As feminist professionals move into governance positions within their own organizations, regulations may begin to change so as to better protect consumers, hopefully without damaging the therapeutic relationship.

The second major argument concerning the separatists apprehension that women's issues will get such short attention in an integrated setting, so that creativity and professional growth will be reduced, is harder to resolve. As we have seen, until women came together, feminist therapy did not exist. The theoretical development thrives best in all feminist groups concerned with its growth. Others argue that it already has enough proponents and sufficient respectability to flourish in integrated settings also. Our conclusion is to avoid the dichotomous either/or argument and do both: foster creative growth and development of feminist ideology by continuing to meet in feminist networks AND integrate feminist theory and practice into the mainstream.

The third major argument is also difficult to resolve as it raises fundamental questions about the purpose of psychotherapy. Radical feminists have suggested that therapy which encourages adaptation or even personal growth causes complacency with the status quo (Wycoff, 1977). Institutional change and an overthrow of the patriarchy which perpetuates inequality for women are thought to be better means of achieving lasting positive mental health (cf. Dobash & Dobash, 1981; Wardell, Gillespie & Leffler, 1983). The argument is a compelling one for long term political strategies as has been previously presented by these authors (Douglas, 1985; Walker, 1984).

However, the other side of the argument is also compelling. An activist therapy which promotes women's empowerment may be necessary even if only as an interim step to strengthen women. The learning theory concept of shaping applies here. It requires identifying small feasible changes which build toward an end goal. The positive reinforcement received as each step is mastered propels the continued movement toward the long term goal. Such a shaping plan is empowering, rather than discouraging, because goals are within reach. The overthrow of patriarchy is a feminist political goal and one which is controversial, especially as feminism becomes more mainstreamed. The rise of any societies' middle class gives a large group an investment in retaining privilege by making the system work for them. This holds true for American women who have made just enough progress within the last decade to believe that the current system can be modified by them so they too can achieve their personal goals. Only time will tell if the feminist dream of such a pluralistic society can be achieved.

DISSEMINATION OF FEMINIST THERAPY

Much of what has been written here assumes that the reader is interested in feminist therapy systems and may be considering utilizing feminist therapy techniques in her or his own practice. Perhaps it would be relevant to evaluate yourself using a Feminist Self Analysis Task developed by Douglas for students in her graduate training program. This can be found in Table 1.

Goals of Dissemination

Feminist therapy knowledge and practice needs to systematically introduced into the mental health system to meet the following goals:

1. More people need to learn about feminist scholarship about women, as the larger the number who identify with a feminist prospective, the greater the likelihood of changing sexist attitudes, thoughts, and behaviors.
2. There is a need to institutionalize feminist ideology within the existing mental health training systems so it becomes the norm rather than a specialized area.
3. There is a need to change the gender-biased attitudes, thoughts, and behavior of those already engaged in the practice of psychotherapy. It is especially important to reach those in policy making positions to encourage profeminist positions and eliminate those policies which are harmful to women.

Table 1. Feminist Self-Analysis Test for Psychotherapists

A. DESCRIPTION OF SELF
Describe yourself with regard to gender, appearance, age, race or ethnicity, sexual preference, religion, employment history and current status, economic resources, educational history, and physical ablebodiness. The level of self-disclosure is your choice.

B. FAMILY OF ORIGIN ISSUES ABOUT SEX-ROLE
Describe the legacy of a female (male) role handed down by your mother (or other significant adult female). What factors contributed to her particular role as a female in your family. Describe the legacy of a female (male) role handed down by your father (or other significant adult male). What factors contributed to his particular role as a male in your family.

C. SEX-ROLE IDENTIFICATION
Discuss your sex-role identification by describing your current attitudes and beliefs about acceptable behavior, thoughts, and feelings for your gender.

D. SOCIAL SUPPORT SYSTEMS
Describe the family, social, and community networks which provide social and emotional support to you.

E. VICTIM/SURVIVOR EXPERIENCES
In what ways have you experienced yourself as a victim/survivor during your lifetime. In what ways have others either seen you also as a victim/survivor or failed to see you in those roles.

F. SUCCESS/COMPETENCE EXPERIENCES
In what ways have you experienced yourself as a successful and competent individual. In what ways have others seen you as a competent person or failed to see you in that role.

G. ANALYSIS OF SOCIAL POWER
Discuss the personal power which you experience based on all of the information above. Describe how your sense of personal power has changed over time and how you would like to experience change in the future.

H. IMPACT ON ROLE AS PSYCHOTHERAPIST
Describe how each of the above issues impacts upon your effectiveness as a psychotherapist. Specifically address your role as therapist with female and male clients separately, as well as clients with individual differences based on age, sexual preference, sex-role identification, physical ablebodiness, rate or ethnicity, and economic status.

I. IMPACT OF THIS EXERCISE FOR YOU
Describe in what ways this exercise has had a personal and professional impact for you.

4. It is necessary to recruit those willing to provide feminist supervision for both men and women therapists in content and process areas of feminist therapy and to continue to mainstream it into existing therapies. As it becomes more of a norm, the demand for feminist supervisors will predictably increase.

5. Changes are necessary in policy areas which impact on women's lives. A graphic example was the move on the part of policy makers within the American Psychiatric Association to add several new categories to the 1987 revision of the diagnostic manual, the DSM-III, which are pejorative to women and have no empirical data to support them.

The Politics of Dissemination

Strong bonds have been formed between many of those who are leaders in developing feminist therapy theory. The Feminist Therapy Institute provides a gathering place for a limited number. The Association for Women in Psychology has a membership of over a thousand or so scientists and practitioners, many of whom usually attend the annual meeting. Various professional associations, who have Committees on Women and Women's Caucuses at association conferences, maintain networks to encourage these bonds between like-minded feminists. A new organization, The National Coalition for Women's Mental Health, may prove to be a strong organizing force to help set national women's mental health policy.

In the beginning, many formal and informal tests were set up to try to tell the real feminists from those who were just looking for an intriguing ideology. Once the negative social consequences of feminism became clearer, it became apparent that no one who wasn't committed to a feminist vision would want to be considered a feminist. Political correctness rules relaxed and self-identified definitions of feminist became acceptable, provided behavior was congruent with feminist ideals. Thus, there is less concern about being a "real" feminist; there is now room for a pluralistic view of feminism. Incorporating values from various domains (e.g., based on class, racial, ethnic, or other socio-political definition) is important.

Coalition building is another strategy to get the feminist therapy theory on another group's agenda. One strategy, if possible, is to start with a successful joint venture that has created mutually positive feelings. The development of the National Women's Mental Health Agenda, a project funded by a small grant and the American Psychological Association, was able to develop a document on which most everyone attending the interdisciplinary meetings could agree. A strong showing was made during the presentation of the document at a special 1985 Congressional breakfast where key members of the Congressional Caucus on Women's Issues, heads of the various government agencies having relevance to the topics chosen, national policy leaders, and members of the interdisciplinary professional group who created the document attended. A follow-up Congressional breakfast in 1987 was used to keep it a priority on the legislator's own agendas. The Women's Coalition for Legislative Action is a new group of women mental health professionals who raise funds to elect supportive political leaders. Claiming areas where substantiative agreement can be made helps get those ideas into the mainstream.

In addition to the need to carefully chose the task content upon which coalition building occurs, it is also a good political strategy to build coalitions using a feminist process. Movement toward equal sharing of responsibilities and joint ownership of activities helps redistribute the power created by coalition building in a feminist, non-hierarchical manner. Modeling of effective feminist leadership strategies can reduce the traditional competitiveness and feelings of being a lesser person which can destroy women's coalitions. Congruence between affect, ideology, and behavior is needed for effective dissemination of techniques or theories of how to heal in a feminist way.

An interesting experience in coalition building occurred during 1985 and 1986 when the American Psychiatric Association, a 35,000 membership organization with women constituting only 14% of its members and an even smaller percentage who consider themselves feminists, decided to revise the *Diagnostic and Statistical Manual of Mental Disorders—Third Edition* (DSM-III) (APA, 1980). A coalition formed between the feminist psychiatrists, psychologists, social workers, counselors, psychiatric nurses and other groups which included presenting scientific papers, participating in criteria building sessions, engaging in official political negotiations, picketing meetings, granting media interviews, organizing other mental health groups, and persuading the 90,000 member American Psychological Association to look into publishing its own diagnostic manual. The Coalition Against Ms. Diagnosis was created as a means of organizing political action and disseminating information.

A considerable amount of energy was expended during this battle to try to keep five diagnoses from appearing in the DSM-III-R. There was success with two of the controversial ones, Ego Dystonic Homosexuality which when deleted will remove the last vestiges of homosexuality as a mental illness from the Nosology and Paraphiliac Coercive Disorder, originally called Paraphiliac Rapism, a category which classifies sex offenders on the basis of their obsession with sex acts, which then deemphasizes the violence of their sex acts and could have given rapists a legal excuse for their criminal behavior. Three other controversial categories objected to because of their perjoritive bias against women were delegated to a special appendix, ignoring accusations by feminists that there are no empirical data to support their inclusion at all, leaving others to speculate about political or economic motives (cf.

Time, (Leo) November 24, 1985; OMNI, (Guerney) 1986, Psychology Today, (Franklin), January 1987).

Late Luteal Dysphoric Mood Disorder is the title which replaces Premenstrual Dysphoric Mood Disorder, one of these three categories. This one creates a separate mental disorder out of the symptoms of an already recognized gynecological disorder. The proposed Masochistic Personality Disorder was also given a new title, Self Defeating Personality Disorder despite criticisms of the reliability and validity of its accompanying criteria. Feminist critics say 85% of all normally socialized women will fall into such a category which is unable to differentiate them from those who allegedly have such a personality disorder. Sadly, many battered women and rape victims may be denied appropriate feminist crisis intervention and treatment because of the propensity for misdiagnosis. The third newly proposed diagnosis, Sadistic Personality Disorder was originally introduced as a compromise to feminists when their arguments were misconstrued as complaining about the results of the study to develop Self-Defeating Personality Disorders where a three to one bias for women to be so labeled occurred. The offer of a category which was anticipated as being biased in its diagnosis of men was rejected by even those who proposed it, tongue in-cheek, but alas, it was too late to stop the DSM-III Committee from including it in the suggested revisions without any supporting empirical data. Had appropriate research been conducted, it is likely that a diagnosis stressing disorder in use of power would really be the more accurate male counterpart.

These three categories are in the Appendix of the official diagnostic code despite the furor created by women's groups and many men in every mental health discipline, including non-policy makers in psychiatry, too. The process has been widely publicized to alert consumers to the official psychiatric association's attitudes about women. There has been preparation for the filing of civil lawsuits everywhere in the country, should a woman be found to be harmed by the mislabeling and subsequent erroneous treatment. Women are learning the importance of labeling, once again, and see first-hand how traumatic the stigmatization can be. The educational value of this controversy and its impact on dissemination of feminist values has been much greater than ever expected.

Consumer education has been another powerful way to get the feminist message institutionalized. Pamphlets and materials are available from the American Psychological Association's office on Women's Programs. Insistence on therapists meeting the strict *no sexual exploitation* rule has been frequently monitored by women themselves. Clients themselves can learn to monitor boundary violations without disturbing the therapy relationship. And cooperative media who try to bring psychological information to a fascinated public also deliver the feminist message, sometimes in a plain paper wrapper!

ETHICS IN FEMINIST THERAPY

The Feminist Therapy Institute has been struggling with developing an ethical code for feminist therapists which rewards positive behaviors rather than concentrating on punishing rule infractions.

As in other areas of feminist therapy, the ethics code is a proactive rather than a reactive document. "Thou shalt nots" are replaced by their reciprocals so that therapists know what behavior is expected of them. The Feminist Therapy Institute is currently editing a book on feminist ethics (Lerman & Porter, in preparation). Carol Gilligan (1982) has found that women's concept of justice is one that is tempered with compassion and understanding for individual situations. Flexibility in interpretation guides the feminist ethics standards. Perhaps it is this flexibility which will allow feminist therapy theory and practice to meet the challenges of the future.

PREAMBLE

April, 1987

Feminist therapy evolves from feminist philosophy, psychological theory and practice, and political theory. In particular feminists recognize the impact of society in creating and maintaining the problems and issues brought into therapy. Briefly, feminists believe the personal is political. Basic tenets of feminism include a belief in the equal worth of all human beings, a recognition that each individual's personal experiences and situations are reflective of and an influence on society's institutionalized attitudes and values, and a commitment to political and social change that equalizes power among people. Feminism strives to create equal valuing of all people by recognizing and reducing the pervasive influences and insidious effects of patriarchy on people's lives. Thus, a feminist analysis addresses the effects of sexism on the development of females and males and the relationship of sexism to other forms of oppression, including, but not limited to, racism, classism, homophobia, agism and anti-Semitism. Feminists also live in and are subject to those same influences and effects and continually monitor their beliefs and behaviors as a result of these influences.

Feminist therapists adhere to and integrate feminist analysis into all spheres of their work as therapists, educators, consultants, administrators, and/or researchers. Feminist therapists recognize that their values influence the therapeutic process and clarify with clients the nature and effect of those values. Feminist therapists are accountable for the management of the power differential within the therapist/client relationship. Because of the limitations of a purely intrapsychic model of human functioning, feminist therapists facilitate the understanding of interactive effects of the client's internal and external worlds. Feminist therapists possess knowledge about the psychology of women and utilize feminist scholarship to revise theories and practices, incorporating new knowledge as it is generated.

Feminist therapists assume a proactive stance toward the eradication of oppression in their lives and work toward empowering women. They are respectful of individual differences, challenging oppressive aspects of both their own and the clients' value systems. Feminist therapists engage in social change activities, broadly defined, outside of and apart from their work in their professions. Such activities may vary in scope and content but are an essential aspect of a feminist perspective.

Feminist therapists are trained in a variety of disciplines, theoretical orientations, and degrees of structure. They come from different cultural, ethnic and racial backgrounds. They work in many types of settings with a diversity of clients and practice different modalities of therapy, training, and research. Amid this diversity, feminist therapists are joined together by their feminist analyses and perspectives.

Feminist therapy theory integrates feminist principles into other theories of human development and change. As a result, the following ethical guidelines for feminist therapists are additive to, rather than a replacement for, the ethical principles of the profession in which a feminist therapist practices. Feminist therapists also will work toward incorporating feminist principles into existing standards when appropriate.

The code is a series of positive statements which provide guidelines for feminist therapy practice, training, and research. Feminist therapists who are members of other professional organizations adhere to the ethical codes of those organizations. Feminist therapists who are not members of such organizations are guided by the ethical standards of the organization closest to their mode of practice. These statements provide more specific guidelines within the context of and as an extension of most ethical codes. When ethical guidelines are in conflict, the feminist therapist is accountable for how she prioritizes her choices.

These ethical guidelines, then, are focused on the issues feminist therapists, educators, and researchers have found especially important in their professional settings. As with any code of therapy ethics, the well-being of clients is the guiding principle underlying this code. The feminist therapy issues which relate directly to the client's well-being include cultural diversitites and oppressions, power differentials, overlapping relationships, therapist accountability, and social change. Even though the principles are stated separately, each interfaces with the others to form an interdependent whole. In addition, the code is a living document and thus is continually in the process of change.

REFERENCES

American Psychiatric Association. (1980). *Diagnostic and Statistical Manual of Mental Disorders, Third Edition.* Washington, DC: Author.

American Psychological Association. (1974). Report on the task force on sex bias and sex role stereo-typing in Psychotherapeutic practice. *American Psychologist, 30*(1), 1169–1175.

American Psychological Association. (1978). Task force on sex bias and sex role stereotyping in psychotherapeutic practice. *American Psychologist, 33,* 1122–1123.

Beutler, L. E., Crago, M., & Arizmendi, T. G. (1986). Therapist variables in psychotherapy process and outcome. In S. L. Garfield & A. E. Bergin (Eds.), *Handbook of psychotherapy and behavior change* (3rd ed.). New York: Wiley.

Bouhoustos, J. C. (1984). Sexual intimacy between psychotherapists and clients: Policy implications for the future. In L. E. A. Walker (Ed.), *Women and mental health policy* (pp. 207–227). Beverly Hills, CA: Sage.

Broverman, I., Broverman, D. M., Clarkson, F. E., Rosenkrantz, P.S., & Vogel, S. R. (1970). Sex role stereotypes and clinical judgments of mental health. *Journal of Consulting and Clinical Psychology, 34*(1), 1–7.

Brown, L. (1985). Ethical and conceptual issues in theory-building for feminist therapists: Some introductory thoughts. Paper presented at Feminist Therapy Institute, Bal Harbor, FL.

Carmen, E. H., Reiker, P., & Mills, T. (1984). Victims of violence and psychiatric illness. *American Journal of Psychiatry, 141,* 378–383.

Chesler, P. (1971). *The myth of madness.* NY:

Corey, G. (1977). *Theory and practice of counseling and psychotherapy.* Monterey, CA: Brooks/Cole.

Dobash, R. E., & Dobash, R. P. (1981). *Violence against wives.* New York: MacMillian, Free Press.

Douglas, M. A. (1985). The role of power in feminist therapy: A reformulation. In L. B. Rosewater & L. E. A. Walker (Eds.), *Handbook of feminist therapy: Womens issues in psychotherapy,* (pp. 241–249). NY: Springer.

Franklin, D. (1987, January). The politics of masochism. *Psychology Today.*

Franks, V., & Burtle, V. (Eds.). (1974). *Women in therapy.* NY: Brunner/Mazel.

Franks, V., & Rothblum, E. D. (Eds.), (1983). *The stereotyping of women: Its effects on mental health.* NY: Springer.

Frieze, I. H., Parson, J. E., Johnson, P. B., Ruble, D. W., & Zellman, E. L. (1978). *Women and sex roles: A social psychological perspective.* NY: Norton.

Gilligan, C. (1982). *In a different voice: Psychological theory and women's development.* Cambridge, MA: Harvard University Press.

Grady, K. E. (1981). Sex bias in research design. *Psychology of Women Quarterly, 5,* 628–638.

Hendricks, M. C. (1984). Women, spirituality, and mental health. In L. E. A. Walker (Ed.), *Women and mental health policy* (pp. 95–115). Beverly Hills, CA: Sage.

Herman, J. L. (1981). *Father-daughter incest.* Cambridge, MA: Harvard University Press.

Johnson, M., & Auerbach, A. H. (1984). Women and psychotherapy research. In L. E. A. Walker (Ed.), *Women and mental health policy* (pp. 59–77). Beverly Hills, CA: Sage.

Jordan, J. V. (1985). The meaning of mutuality. Stone Center Work in Progress #23. Wellsley, MA.

Kaplan, A. G., & Surrey, J. L. (1984). The relational self in women: Developmental theory and public policy. In L. E. A. Walker (Ed.), *Women and mental health policy* (pp. 79–94). Beverly Hills, CA: Sage.

Laing, R. D. (1967). *The politics of experience.* NY: Pantheon Books.

Leo, J. (1985, December). Battling over masochism: The feminists and the psychiatrists debate "self defeating" behavior. *Time Magazine.*

Lerman, H. (1976). What happens in feminist therapy? In S. Cox (Ed.), *Female psychology: The emerging self* (pp. 378–384). Chicago: SRA.

Lerman, H. (1986). *A mote in Freud's eye.* New York: Springer.

Lerman, H., & Porter, N. (Eds.). (in preparation). *Handbook on feminist ethics in psychotherapy* (working title). NY: Springer.

Masson, J. M. (1984). *The assault on truth: Freud's suppression of the seduction theory.* NY: Farar, Straus & Giroux.

McHugh, M. C., Koeske, R. D., & Frieze, I. H. (1986). Issues to consider in conducting non-sexist psychological research. *American Psychologist, 41*(8), 879–890.

Miller, J. B. (1976). *Toward a new psychology of women.* Boston: Beacon Press.

Minuchin, S. (1985). *Family kaleidoscope: Images of violence and healing.* Cambridge, MA: Harvard University Press.

O'Leary, V., Unger, R. K., & Wallston, B.S. (Eds.). (1985). *Women, gender and social psychology.* Hillsdale, NJ: Erlbaum.

Orlinsky, D. E., & Howard, K. I. (1980). Gender and psychotherapeutic outcome. In A. Brodskey & R. Hare-Mustin (Eds.), *Women and psychotherapy.* NY: Guilford Press.

Rawlings, E. I., & Carter, D. K. (Eds.). (1977). *Psychotherapy for women: Treatment toward equality.* Springfield, IL: Chas. C. Thomas.

Rogers, C. (1951). *Client centered therapy.* Boston: Houghton-Mifflin.

Rosewater, L. B. (1984). Feminist therapy: Implications for practitioners. In L. E. A. Walker (Ed.), *Women and mental health policy* (pp. 267–280). Beverly Hills, CA: Sage.

Russo, N. F. (1984). Women in the mental health delivery system: Implications for research and public policy. In L. E. A. Walker (Ed.), *Women & Mental health policy* (pp. 21–41). Beverly Hills, CA: Sage.

Sherman, E. J., & Denmark, F. (Eds.). (1978). *The psychology of women. New directions of research.* New York: Psychological Dimensions.

Szaz, T. (1961). *The myth of mental illness: Foundations of a theory of personal conduct.* NY: Harper & Row.

Unger, R. K. (1979). *Female and male: Psychological perspectives.* New York: Harper & Row.

Walker, L. E. A. (Ed.). (1984). *Women and mental health policy.* Beverly Hills, CA: Sage.

Wallston, B. S. (1981). What are the questions in psychology of women? A feminist approach to research. *Psychology of Women Quarterly, 5,* 597–617.

Wardell, L., Gillespie, D.C., & Leffler, A. (1983). Science and violence against wives. In D. Finklehor, R. Gelles, G. Hotaling, & M. Straus (Eds.), *The dark side of families* (pp. 69–84). Beverly Hills, CA: Sage.

Williams, G. (1986, November). Mind. *OMNI Magazine.*

Wycoff, H. (1977). Radical psychiatry for women. In E. I. Rawlings & D. K. Carter (Eds.), *Psychotherapy for women* (pp. 370–391). Springfield, IL: Chas C. Thomas.

ADDRESSES OF ORGANIZATIONS

American Psychiatric Association, 1400 "K" St. MW, Washington, DC 20036.

American Psychological Association, 1200 Seventeenth St. NW, Washington, DC 20036

Association for Women in Psychology—C/O Kay Towns, W. 153 Penn State University, Capital Campus, Middletown, PA 17057

Coalition Against Ms . . . Diagnosis, 4527 First Ave, NE, Seattle, WA 98105

Feminist Therapy Institute, 4527 First Ave, NE, Seattle, WA 98105

National Coalition For Women's Mental Health, C/O Nancy Russo, Ph.D., Director, Women's Studies, Arizona State University, Tempe, AZ.

Women's Coalition for Legislative Action, AAP-PLAN, c/o APA, 1200 Seventeenth St. NW, Washington, DC, 20036.

Author Index

A

Abad, J., 246, *247*
Acosta, F.X., 246, *248*
Allen, D., 240, *251*
Alpert, J., 7, *9*
Anzaldua, G., 213, *227*
Arizmendi, T.G., 6, *10*, 289, *286*
Arnkoff, D.B., 107, 110, 112, *114*
Asher, S.J., 157, *182*
Aslin, A.L., 163, *181*
Atchley, R., 255, 257, 258, *270*
Auerbach, A.H., 28, 30, *34, 289, 297*
Ault-Riche, M., 121, *131*
Auslander, S.S., 255, *274*
Austin, N., 167, 173, 180, *184*
Avery, A.W., 177, *184*
Aylesworth, L.S., 241, *250*

B

Bach, 161
Baikie, E., 266, *272*
Bailey, M., 244, *248*
Baird, M., 207, *225*
Baker, L., 120, *133*
Baker, R., 242, 243, 244, *248*
Bandura, A., 95, *114*
Bardwick, J.M., 13, *31*
Bayes, M., 161, *161*
Beach, L.R., *116*
Beavin, J., 120, *133*
Beck, A.K., 110, *114*
Beck, A.T., 97, 103, *114*, 165, *182*
Bell, 188
Belle, D., 23, *32*, 142, *153*
Bem, S., 189, *204*
Benedek, E.P., 162, *182*
Benedek, R.S., 162, *182*
Bergler, E., 208, *225*

Bergman, A., 44, *65, 73, 89*
Berkman, P., 256, *273*
Berl, S., 208, *226*
Berman, J.R.S., 20, 22, *32*
Bernard, J., 142, *153*
Bernardez, T., 7, *10*
Bernay, T., 7, *10*
Beutler, L.E., 6, *10*, 289, *296*
Bieber, I., 208, *225*
Bieber, T., 208, *225*
Billingsley, A., 230, *248*
Birnbaum, H.J., *205*
Blau, Z., 256, *270*
Blazer, D., 266, *271*
Blechman, E., 92, *114*
Block, C.B., 240, 241, 242, 243, 245, *248*
Block, H.L., 7, *10*
Bloom, B.L., 157, *182*
Bograd, M., 8, *10*, 123, 124, *131*
Bolles, R.N., 170, 180, *182*
Boscolo, L., 121, *133*
Bosma, B.J., 24, *32*
Bouhoustos, J.C., 6, *10*, 147, *153*, 284,
    296
Boulette, T.R., 246, *248*
Bourguignon, E., 236, *248*
Bowen, M., 120, *132*
Brannon, R., 217, *226*
Braude, M., 7, *10*
Brehony, K.A., 94, 113, *114*
Brickman, J., 37, *63*, 124, 125, *132*
Britton, P.G., 266, *274*
Brodsky, A.M., 24, *32*, 83, *88*
Brody, C.M., 19, 20, 23, *32*
Brody, E., 262, 263, 267, *271, 272*
Broverman, D.M., 6, *10*, 19, *32*, 74, *88*,
    137, 143, *153*, 187, *204*, 277, *296*

301

Subject Index